Studies in the History of Medieval Religion

VOLUME

PILGRIMAGE TO ROME
IN THE MIDDLE AGES
Continuity and Change

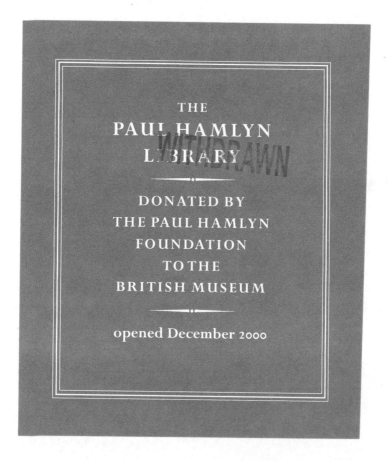

Studies in the History of Medieval Religion

ISSN 0955-2480

General Editor
Christopher Harper-Bill

Previously published volumes in the series
are listed at the back of this volume

PILGRIMAGE TO ROME
IN THE MIDDLE AGES

Continuity and Change

DEBRA J. BIRCH

THE BOYDELL PRESS

First published 1998
The Boydell Press, Woodbridge
Reprinted in paperback 2000

ISBN 0 85115 636 3 hardback
ISBN 0 85115 771 8 paperback

The Boydell Press is an imprint of Boydell & Brewer Ltd
PO Box 9, Woodbridge, Suffolk IP12 3DF, UK
and of Boydell & Brewer Inc.
PO Box 41026, Rochester, NY 14604–4126, USA
website: http://www.boydell.co.uk

A catalogue record for this book is available
from the British Library

Library of Congress Catalog Card Number: 97–52361

This publication is printed on acid-free paper

Printed in Great Britain by
Athenæum Press Ltd, Gateshead, Tyne & Wear

Contents

Maps

For Marion, Bob
and Philip

This book is produced with the assistance of
a grant from Isobel Thornley's Bequest to
the University of London

Preface

This book is based on my Ph.D. thesis, submitted in November 1993, for which I was funded from 1989 to 1992 by the British Academy. I am most grateful to the History Department of Queen Mary and Westfield College, University of London, where I was registered, and especially to my supervisor Miss Brenda Bolton both for encouraging me to pursue this research and for her thorough and patient supervision. I would also like to thank my two examiners, Professor Hugh Lawrence and Professor Malcolm Barber, for their helpful ideas and comments.

There are many other people who have helped me in various ways. I should like to thank in particular Dr Michael Clanchy, Dr Virginia Davis, Dr David D'Avray, Dr Peter Denley, Dr Veronica Ortenberg, Dr Marcus Bull, Mr Geoffrey Harlow, Dr Nicole Bériou, Professor Ludwig Schmugge, Professor R. I. Moore and Dr Frances Andrews. Professor Jonathan Riley-Smith deserves particular thanks.

Essential help has been forthcoming from the libraries available to me. I am grateful to the helpful staff at Queen Mary and Westfield College Library, the University of London Library, the Warburg Institute, the Institute of Classical Studies, the British Library, Dr Williams's Library and the Library of the British School at Rome. I am particularly grateful to my friends and colleagues at the Institute of Historical Research, whose encouragement initially helped me to complete the thesis and subsequently to produce the book.

I am also most grateful to Professor Christopher Harper-Bill for his editorial advice and to the Isobel Thornley Bequest of the University of London for a contribution towards publication costs.

I should also like to thank my mother and step-father, not only for their practical assistance over many years but also for their constant moral support. Finally I should like to thank my husband, Dr Philip de Souza, because without his support and encouragement the thesis and the book would never have been completed.

Abbreviations

AASS   *Acta Sanctorum Bollandiana*, ed. J. Bollandus *et al.*, 61 vols. (Antwerp, 1643–)

ASRSP   *Archivio della R. Società Romana di Storia Patria*

Corpus   R. Krautheimer, S. Corbett, and W. Frankl, *Corpus Basilicarum Christianorum Romae*, 5 vols. (Città del Vaticano, 1937–1977)

EHR   *English Historical Review*

Esplorazioni   B. M. Appollonj-Ghetti, A. Ferrua, E. Josi, E. Kirschbaum, *Esplorazioni sotto la Confessione di San Pietro in Vaticano*, 2 vols. (Città del Vaticano, 1951)

Jaffé   *Regesta Pontificum Romanorum ab Condita Ecclesia ad Annum post Christum Natum MCXCVIII*, ed P. Jaffé, 2 vols. (Leipzig, 1885–1888)

JEH   *Journal of Ecclesiastical History*

JRS   *Journal of Roman Studies*

MEFR   *Mélanges de l'Ecole Française de Rome*

MGH.SS   *Monumenta Germaniae Historica, Scriptores*, 30 vols. (Leipzig, 1826–1934)

MGH Legum *Monumenta Germaniae Historica, Leges* (Hanover, 1883–)

PBSR   *Papers of the British School at Rome*

Peregrinaciones L. Váquez de Parga, J. M. Lacarra and J. U. Ríu, *Las Peregrinaciones a Santiago de Compostela*, 3 vols. (Madrid, 1948–1949)
a Santiago

PL   *Patrologiae cursus completus: Series Latina*, ed. J. P. Migne, 221 vols. (Paris, 1879–1890)

Potthast   *Regesta Pontificum Romanorum inde ab Anno Post Christum natum MCXCVIII ad Anno MCCCIV*, ed. A. Potthast, 2 vols. (Berlin, 1874, reprt. Graz, 1957)

RHGF   *Recueil des Historiens de Gaule et de la France*, 24 vols. (Paris, 1869–1904)

RIS   *Rerum Italicarum Scriptores*, ed. L. A. Muratori, 25 vols. (Milan, 1723–1751)

RS   *Rolls Series*

SCH   *Studies in Church History*

Introduction and Sources

The Nature of Medieval Pilgrimage[1]

For Christians, pilgrimage, the undertaking of a journey to the tomb or shrine of some saint or martyr, or a visit to some other holy place, had its origins in the Bible. This was clearly illustrated in one of two sermons addressed to pilgrims by the great popular preacher of the early thirteenth century, Jacques de Vitry (d.1240).[2] In this sermon he claimed that Abraham was the first pilgrim and all others were his imitators.[3] For just as Abraham had left

---

[1] Pilgrimage is a subject which has continually attracted the interest of historians. See for example, B. J. Kötting, *Peregrinatio Religiosa. Wallfahrten in der Antike und das Pilgerwesen in der alten Kirchen* (Münster, 1950); E. D. Hunt, *Holy Land Pilgrimage in the Later Roman Empire A.D. 312–460* (Oxford, 1982); J. E. Taylor, *Christians and the Holy Places. The Myth of Jewish-Christian Origins* (Oxford, 1993); P. W. L. Walker, *Holy City, Holy Places? Christian Attitudes to Jerusalem and the Holy Land in the Fourth Century* (Oxford, 1990); *Blessings of Pilgrimage*, ed. R. Ousterhout (Urbana and Chicago, 1990); R. Oursel, *Les Pèlerins du Moyen Age* (1963); P. A. Sigal, *Les Marcheurs de Dieu* (Paris, 1974); V. and E. Turner, *Image and Pilgrimage in Christian Culture* (New York, 1978); L. Schmugge, 'Die Anfänge des Organisierten Pilgerverkehrs im Mittelalter', *Quellen und Forschungen aus Italienischen Archiven und Bibliotheken*, 64 (1984), pp. 1–83; J. Sumption, *Pilgrimage. An Image of Mediaeval Religion* (London, 1975); A. Kendall, *Medieval Pilgrims* (London, 1970); E. R. Labande, 'Recherches sur les Pèlerins dans l'Europe des XI et XII Siècles', *Cahiers de Civilisation Médiévale X–XII Siècles*, 1 (1958), pp. 159–169 and 339–347; and by the same author, 'Ad Limina: Le pèlerin médiéval au terme de sa démarche', *Mélanges offerts à René Crozet*, ed. P. Gallais and J.-Y. Riou (Poitiers, 1966), pp. 283–291; A. D'Haenens, 'Aller à Rome au Moyen Age', *Bulletin de l'Institut Historique Belge de Rome*, 50 (1980), pp. 93–129. There are many other more general works concerned with medieval pilgrimage. See for example C. Jenkins, 'Christian Pilgrimages A.D. 500 to 800', *Travel and Travellers in the Middle Ages*, ed. A. P. Newton (London, 1926), pp. 39–69; A. Dupront, 'Pèlerinages et lieux sacrés', *Méthodologie de l'Histoire et des Sciences Humaines, Mélanges en Honneur de Fernand Braudel* (Toulouse, 1973), pp. 189–206; J. Chélini and H. Branthomme, *Les Chemins de Dieu. Histoire des Pèlerinages Chrétiens des Origines à nos Jours* (Paris, 1982); *Cahiers de Fanjeaux*, 15 (Toulouse, 1980); J. Wilkinson, 'Christian Pilgrims in Jerusalem during the Byzantine Period', *Palestine Exploration Quarterly*, 108 (1976), pp. 75–101.

[2] On Jacques de Vitry, see P. Funk, *Jacob von Vitry. Leben und Werke* (Leipzig and Berlin, 1909); A. Forni, 'Giacomo da Vitry, Predicatore e Sociologo', *La Cultura. Rivista di Filosofia Letteratura e Storia*, 18 (1980), pp. 34–89. A small selection of Jacques de Vitry's sermons can be found in *Analecta Novissima Spicilegii Solesmensis Altera*, ed. J. B. Pitra, 2 vols. (Paris, 1885–1888), vol. 2.

[3] For Jacques de Vitry's two sermons addressed to pilgrims, see Paris, Bibliothèque Nationale, Latin MS 3284, fols. 128v–134r. Also on these sermons, see D. J. Birch, 'Medieval Pilgrimage: with particular reference to Rome in the period from Paschal II to Innocent III' (University of London Ph.D. thesis, 1994), pp. 297–319 and 324–362.

behind home, family and friends to go in search of the promised land, so too the pilgrim departed from all that was familiar and set out on a journey as an exile and outcast to some holy place. For this reason in the medieval period the Latin word used to indicate a pilgrim was *peregrinus*, which in Classical Latin had meant a 'foreigner' or 'stranger'.[4]

The belief that certain objects and places were a focus of holiness where pilgrims could come closer to God was one of two related concepts which had a long history in Christian tradition. The second concept was that man's life was itself a pilgrimage: the true Christian was a *peregrinus* on earth and his whole life a pilgrimage, the journey of his soul towards its true home in heaven. So strong were these two concepts in the minds of ordinary men and women, that travelling to the earthly Jerusalem seemed little different to travelling to the heavenly one and pilgrimage came to be popularly regarded as a way of achieving salvation and getting to heaven.[5]

It is this popular belief which perhaps best explains the motivation which lay behind Christian pilgrimage. For the majority of Christians the undertaking of such a journey never developed into a duty or an obligation.[6] Rather, in most cases, the decision to set out on such a journey remained, as indeed it still does, the choice of the individual.[7] Miracle collections, which survive in large numbers, suggest that for some the motivation which lay behind their pilgrimage was the hope of a cure for some illness or injury. Others, perhaps, were motivated by less worthy considerations, such as curiosity, or a desire for a change of routine, or improved opportunities for begging.[8] But, as several historians have argued, for the majority pilgrimage is probably best understood as a manifestation of popular religious enthusiasm.[9] Many pilgrims

---

[4]   See C. T. Lewis and C. Short, *A Latin Dictionary* (Oxford, 1879), s.v. *peregrinus*. On Christian usage of the term, see B. de Gaiffier, 'Pellegrinaggi e Culto dei Santi: Réflexions sur le thème du Congrès', *Pellegrinaggi e Culto dei Santi in Europa fino alla I^A Crociata*, 8–11 Oct. 1961, *Convegni del Centro di Studi sulla Spiritualità Medievale*, IV (Todi, 1963), pp. 11–35, esp. pp. 12–15.

[5]   *Atlas of the Christian Church*, ed. H. Chadwick and G. R. Evans (London, 1987), p. 76.

[6]   Here there is an obvious comparison with Moslems, upon whom the Koran lays the obligation of making a pilgrimage to Mecca at least once during their lifetime. See R. Barber, *Pilgrimages* (Woodbridge, 1991), pp. 30–47; M. Cook, *Muhammad* (Oxford, 1983), pp. 45–47.

[7]   Pilgrimages could only be imposed upon Christians as punishment for some crime or misdemeanour. On penitential pilgrimages, see C. Vogel, 'Le Pèlerinage Pénitential', *Pellegrinaggi e Culto dei Santi in Europa fino alla I^A Crociata*, 8–11 Oct. 1961, *Convegni del Centro di Studi sulla Spiritualità Medievale*, IV (Todi, 1963), pp. 37–94.

[8]   The Council of Chalons-sur-Saône (813) criticised the poor who set out on pilgrimages to obtain improved means of begging. See *Concilia Aevi Karolini*, MGH *Legum* Sectio 3, vol. 2, part 1 (Hanover and Leipzig, 1906), p. 282.

[9]   See for example, R. A. Fletcher, *St James's Catapult. The Life and Times of Diego Gelmírez of Santiago de Compostela* (Oxford, 1984), esp. p. 83. 'It is with the thirsty soul (an unfashionable and uncomfortable concept) that we must start if we are to understand pilgrimages.' M. G. Bull, *Knightly Piety and the Lay Response to the First Crusade: The Limousin and Gascony c.970–c.1130* (Oxford, 1993), p. 206. See also M. Barber,

undertook long and arduous journeys to the shrine of a saint or martyr because they believed that such holy men and women had the ability to intercede with God on their behalf. They believed that prayers offered at their tombs, or at shrines where some associative relic was treasured, would secure the saint's intercession and so ease their road to the heavenly kingdom.

Nowhere is this popular religious enthusiasm amongst pilgrims better illustrated than in an account written by Suger, abbot of St Denis (d.1151), describing the crowds of pilgrims who were accustomed to gather at the abbey on feast days 'to seek the intercession of the saints' and 'to worship and kiss the holy relics, the Nail and the Crown'.[10] The numbers of pilgrims were so great that not all were able to gain access to the church, whilst those inside were so tightly packed that they were unable to move.[11] Suger describes the agony of many women, who were caught in the crush and were so distressed that they cried out in pain as though in labour, whilst more were trampled underfoot.[12] Such was the density of the crowd that often discomfort or impatience seems to have led to anger and rioting, forcing the monks displaying the relics to escape with them through the windows of the church.[13]

Whatever the pilgrim's motivation, however, it was strongly argued, notably by Jacques de Vitry, that the pilgrimage would be of no value if the pilgrim did not conduct himself in a fittingly penitential manner. For just as man during his lifetime must earn salvation by keeping God's commandments, confessing his sins and doing penance for them, then during his pilgrimage to some holy place the individual must make reparation for sins. The penitential nature of pilgrimage meant that the pilgrim must expect to suffer in the course of his travels. This is clearly illustrated in surviving sources such as the early Irish Cambray homily, which refers to pilgrimage as 'white martyrdom'.[14] Red martyrdom was death but white martyrdom was the separation from everything that an individual loved for the sake of God.[15] This theme of suffering was taken up in the sermons of Jacques de Vitry. He outlined the way in which the pilgrim ought to conduct himself on his

The Two Cities. Medieval Europe 1050–1320 (London, 1992), pp. 168–173; C. and R. Brooke, Popular Religion in the Middle Ages. Western Europe 1000–1300 (London, 1984), pp. 14–30.

[10] Suger, De Consecratione, in Abbot Suger on the Abbey Church of St Denis and its Art Treasures, ed. and trans. E. Panofsky, 2nd ed. (Princeton, 1979), pp. 86–89.

[11] Ibid., pp. 86–89.

[12] Ibid., pp. 88–89. Compare the fifty pilgrims trampled underfoot and killed one Lent in the early eleventh century at the church of St Martial of Limoges. See Adémar of Chabannes, Chronique, ed. J. Chavanon (Paris, 1897), p. 173.

[13] Suger, De Consecratione, pp. 88–89.

[14] Thesaurus Palaeohibernicus. A Collection of Old-Irish Glosses Scholia Prose and Verse, ed. W. Stokes and J. Strachan, 3 vols. (Cambridge, 1901–1910), vol. 2, pp. 246–247.

[15] Ibid., vol. 2, pp. 246–247.

journey and the variety of hardships that he must expect to endure.[16] For just as he had sinned with all his limbs, Jacques de Vitry explained, so too must the pilgrim make reparation with all of them.

For the duration of his journey, Jacques de Vitry argued, the pilgrim was to wear only light clothing and was not to be burdened down with worldly goods, particularly money. What money he did carry was to be used only for works of charity. He was to put his trust in Christ for his daily bread. He was to lie at night only on a hard bed, was not to enjoy sleeping late in the morning but was to arise early. Nor was he to dawdle or to spend more than one night in a particular place. Nothing, not wine, women, weddings or brawls, was to distract him from his path. He was to be totally single-minded with his ultimate destination ever fixed in his mind. Tiredness and sore feet were to be his delight.

That there were certainly some pilgrims who failed to conduct themselves in a suitably penitent manner during the course of their journey seems to have been a major reason why throughout the medieval period there were those who were opposed to the undertaking of pilgrimages.[17] What use were such journeys, Maurice of Sully, bishop of Paris (1160–1196), was moved to ask, if those who undertook them left behind their villages but not their vices?[18]

Some pilgrims, even if they set out with good intentions, seem to have been distracted from their road. For this reason St Boniface (d.754) seems to have wanted to prohibit women from undertaking pilgrimages particularly to Rome, claiming that many died on the way and that others fell into prostitution in the towns of France and Italy.[19] Other pilgrims, forgetful of the penitential nature of their journey, seem to have been content to take large amounts of money with them. In the twelfth century Honorius of Autun suggested that money expended on such journeys might instead be used for works of charity.[20] Money was better spent, he believed, upon the poor than upon a visit to Jerusalem. A similar suggestion was made by Lambert le Bègue in an apology addressed to the antipope Calixtus III (1168–1178). In this he reckoned that money spent upon pilgrimages might be used instead for nourishing the hungry and thirsty, clothing the naked, helping strangers and ransoming captives.[21]

As well as those who criticised the way in which many pilgrims conducted their journey, there were also those who challenged the popularly held beliefs

---

[16] Ms. Latin 3284, fols. 129r–129v.

[17] G. Constable, 'Opposition to Pilgrimage in the Middle Ages', *Religious Life and Thought (11th–12th Centuries)* (Variorum Reprint, London, 1979), pp. 125–146.

[18] C. A. Robson, *Maurice of Sully and the Medieval Vernacular Homily* (Oxford, 1952), pp. 108–109.

[19] St Boniface et Lul, *Epistolae*, MGH *Epistolae*, 3 (Berlin 1892), esp. pp. 354–355.

[20] Honorius of Autun, *Elucidarium*, PL 172, col. 1152.

[21] Constable, 'Opposition to Pilgrimage', p. 144.

concerning the value of pilgrimage and expressed doubts as to whether these journeys really were of any spiritual value. Certainly widespread reservations were expressed as to whether monks and nuns should ever be allowed to undertake pilgrimages[22] and there was concern over priests who abandoned their flocks to depart on these journeys. Nor was it unanimously agreed that pilgrimages were of any value to lay men and women. Theodulph of Orléans (d.821) argued that the way to heaven was through good works not pilgrimage,[23] whilst a ninth-century Irish poem proclaimed that a journey to Rome involved much labour and little profit, for the pilgrim would not find the King whom he sought there unless he brought Him with him.[24]

Holy Places

Such criticism, however, did nothing to undermine or to dampen the popular enthusiasm for pilgrimage. Individuals continued to set out on such journeys, choosing for themselves both the time of their departure and, most important of all, their destination. Jerusalem was undoubtedly the most important goal for Christian pilgrims. Not only did the Christian faith have its historical origins there in the Holy Land sites of the crucifixion and the empty tomb, but it was widely believed that Jerusalem would be the scene of the Second Coming of the Messiah.[25] It was here that pilgrims could see for themselves the sites mentioned in the Bible and here most importantly, as Paulinus of Nola explained, that 'they could see and touch the places where Christ was present in the body'.[26] The sites and attractions which pilgrims found in the Holy Land were unique and pilgrimage to these places was, therefore, always popular but most particularly when the sites were in Christian hands making the journey easier and travel safer.

There were, of course, many other places to which the Christian pilgrim might travel. Some, such as Rome, Compostela, Canterbury, Cologne, Tours, Chartres, St Gilles and Milan, attracted pilgrims from the far flung corners of Christendom. Other, more remote sites, such as those associated with St Gilbert of Sempringham, Godric of Finchale, St Thomas Cantilupe and St

---

[22] Ibid., pp. 125–146 and by the same author 'Monachisme et pèlerinage au Moyen Age', Religious Life and Thought (11th–12th Centuries) (Variorum Reprint, London, 1979), pp. 3–27.

[23] Theodulph of Orléans, Carmina, MGH Poetae Latini, 1 (Berlin, 1881), p. 557.

[24] Thesaurus Palaeohibernicus, vol. 2, p. 296.

[25] Belief in the Second Coming was so strong that when reporting the campaigns of the Emperor Septimus Severus, Tertullian (c.160–c.240) could describe how the new Jerusalem was seen hovering in the skies over Judaea for forty days. See Tertullian, Adversus Marcionem, ed. and trans. E. Evans, 2 vols. (Oxford, 1972), vol. 1, pp. 246–249 (bk III, 24.4).

[26] Paulinus of Nola, Epistolae, PL 61, 407.

Gibrien of Reims, never acquired an international reputation, but attracted their pilgrims from amongst the local population.

What these holy places had in common, however, was that their popularity tended to 'fluctuate with fashion'.[27] Since Christian pilgrims could freely choose their destination for themselves, this inevitably led to fierce rivalry and competition amongst these pilgrimage centres, as those who jealously guarded the relics sought to prove that a pilgrimage to their saint or martyr was more effective and rewarding than a visit to that of their neighbour's. The production of miracle collections advertising the power of a particular saint, the acquisition of new relics frequently by theft, church consecrations and the translation of relics were some of the means by which interest might be created or particular holy places promoted and advertised. Nor was such promotional advertising necessary only for the smaller pilgrimage centres. Most, both great and small, were at one time or another forced by competition from other tombs or shrines to advertise and increase their own attractions.

Rome and Medieval Pilgrimage

This book, like the Ph.D. thesis on which it is based, is concerned primarily with pilgrimage to Rome from Late Antiquity to the end of the thirteenth century, concentrating most closely upon the period from Paschal II to Innocent III (1099–1216). Pilgrims had been travelling to this city since at least the second century, drawn in particular by the famous martyrs buried there, the most important of which were two of Christ's apostles, Peter and Paul. So strong were the city's associations with these apostles that pilgrimage to Rome was often referred to in the medieval period as a pilgrimage *ad limina apostolorum*, 'to the threshold of the apostles'. The *limen*, or threshold, was a place which had religious connotations.[28] For early Christian writers it had represented the threshold beyond which the Christian community joined for its celebration and had been a threshold which only the faithful could pass. This idea of the *limen* or threshold in connection with saints and martyrs was developed in Rome, notably by Pope Damasus (366–384). For him the *limen* of a saint was an actual physical place. It was the area around the tomb of a saint or martyr in a cemetery where the faithful gathered for veneration and prayer. In the fourth century Prudentius (348–405), in a hymn addressed to St Lawrence, extended Damasus's idea of the *limen* from its associations with the cemetery tomb to the large basilicas built in Rome and dedicated in honour of the martyrs, especially those built by Constantine in honour of

---

27 Brooke, *Popular Religion*, pp. 21–22.
28 See M. Maccarrone, 'Pellegrinaggio a S. Pietro e il Giubileo del 1300', *Rivista di Storia della Chiesa in Italia*, 34 (1980), pp. 363–429, esp. pp. 404–410.

Saints Peter and Paul.[29] Thereafter the pilgrimage to Rome was frequently referred to as a pilgrimage *ad limina apostolorum*, a pilgrimage to the thresholds, or tombs, of Saints Peter and Paul within their respective basilicas.

Whilst pilgrimage to Rome had this special name, by the middle of the twelfth century the pilgrims who travelled there had also acquired a name of their own. They were commonly known as *Romipetae*, or 'Rome-seekers'.[30] Although this was a term which could be applied to anyone who travelled to the apostolic city, whether bishops or abbots confirming their appointment or appellants to the papal court,[31] it was a term most commonly associated with those whose primary reason for journeying there was pilgrimage. Its first known use was in canon 14 of the First Lateran Council of 1123. This canon was concerned with attempting to ensure safe passage for pilgrims and singled out those travelling to Rome for special mention. Indeed, it stated that anyone who seized or robbed *Romipetae* or *peregrini*, those travelling *ad limina apostolorum* or to other holy places, was to be excommunicated until satisfactory reparations had been made.[32] Whether the term *Romipetae* was in common usage before the twelfth century is uncertain.

This book analyses various aspects of pilgrimage to Rome. Consideration is given to what motivated ordinary men and women to choose Rome as the destination for their pilgrimage, as well as to a variety of different aspects of the journey there: the routes which *Romipetae* used; the places that they might have visited along the way; where they might have stayed *en route*; what such travel might have cost; and the dangers inherent in such a journey. The various hazards that pilgrims faced during the course of their journey led to attempts to try to improve their safety as they travelled. An analysis is made of the special privileges which they were granted and which, by the twelfth century, gave pilgrims a special status in medieval society.

Those pilgrims who arrived safely in Rome would probably have spent much of their time visiting the city's basilicas. An investigation of surviving sources suggests which churches may have been the most popular with these visitors.[33] Consideration is also given to other sites which they may have visited, where they might have done their shopping, purchased their souvenirs and whether the interests and demands of twelfth-century *Romipetae* might have been different from those of their earlier counterparts. As well as analysing how these twelfth-century pilgrims spent their time in Rome, an

---

[29] Prudentius, *Peristephanon*, in *Opera*, trans. H. J. Thomson, 2 vols. Loeb Classical Library (London, 1962–3), vol. 2, pp. 138–139.

[30] Du Cange, *Glossarium Mediae et Infirmae Latinitis*, 10 vols. (1883–1887), vol. 7, p. 212.

[31] See for example, Matthew Paris, *Chronica Maiora*, ed. H. R. Luard, 7 vols. RS 57 (London, 1872–1883), vol. 5, p. 96.

[32] *Conciliorum Oecumenicorum Decreta*, ed. J. Alberigo *et al.*, 3rd ed. (Bologna, 1973), p. 193.

[33] Throughout I refer to the names of Roman churches in the Italian form, e.g. S. Pietro, S. Paolo, S. Sebastiano, but have anglicised saints' names when referring to the person, e.g. St Peter, St Paul, St Sebastian.

investigation is made of the accommodation in which they might have stayed.

An important part of this book is the attempt to assess Rome's popularity with pilgrims in the twelfth century, leading to the conclusion that pilgrimage to the apostolic city may well have been in decline at this time. As well as a discussion of possible reasons for this decline, an analysis is made of the positive initiatives, notably those of Innocent III and his thirteenth-century successors, to reverse this trend by promoting Rome's attractions.

Sources

The study of medieval pilgrimage is a particularly difficult and daunting task because of the nature of the evidence. The information that does survive often consists only of chance references and these are scattered throughout a wide range of medieval sources. As well as the problems caused by the disparate nature of the evidence there are also other difficulties. Firstly, the majority of pilgrims have left no trace of their undertaking at all, causing one historian to refer to them as 'the clouds of witnesses whose names we may never know'.[34] Secondly, the information which has survived tends to provide us with an unbalanced picture. It tells us in large part about the wealthy and socially important members of medieval society who undertook pilgrimages, but reveals little or nothing about the ranks of lesser men and women. Additionally, information about centres of pilgrimage often concerns only the most popular places, notably Jerusalem, Rome and Compostela. Evidence relating to the many smaller pilgrimage shrines which covered the Christian world is rarer. A third problem presented by late eleventh- and twelfth-century sources is the difficulty of distinguishing between pilgrims and crusaders. Frequently sources refer to *peregrini* travelling to the Holy Land but it is often impossible to assess whether they were ordinary pilgrims or those 'armed pilgrims' who had taken the cross.[35] This book draws on a wide variety of medieval sources both narrative and documentary. The range of sources and the problems associated with some of them are detailed below.

Itineraries and Pilgrims' Accounts

As well as containing references to individual pilgrims, narrative sources, such as chronicles and histories, can also occasionally yield up detailed itineraries, which provide important information about the main routes used by those travelling to the apostolic city. One such can be found in the *Chronicle*

---

[34] C. R. Cheney, *Pope Innocent III and England, Papste und Papsttum*, 9 (Stuttgart, 1976), p. 25.
[35] E. R. Labande, 'Pellegrini o Crociati? Mentalità e Comportamenti a Gerusalemme nel secolo XII', *Aevum*, 54 (1980), pp. 217–230.

attributed to Benedict of Peterborough, which is now widely accepted to be the first draft of the *Chronicle* written by Roger of Howden.[36] In this can be found the detailed route taken by Philip Augustus from Otranto in the heel of Italy back to France in 1191, which seems to have included a visit to Rome.[37] Also extant are the itineraries of Wolfger, who first as bishop of Passau (1191–1204) and then as patriarch of Aquileia (1204–1218) made several journeys across the Alps on business.[38] Not only are his itineraries important for detailing the major routes across the eastern Alpine passes and across northern and central Italy but they are also a vital source of information about the expenses of travel. Other itineraries can be found in the *Chronicle* written by Emo (d.1237), abbot of the Premonstratensian house of Verum in Frisia,[39] and in the *Annales* of Albert of Stade.[40] Albert's itinerary takes the form of a fictitious dialogue and may well have been based on his experiences and the knowledge which he acquired during his own journey to Rome in 1236. Other surviving itineraries include those of Odo, bishop of Rouen who travelled to Rome in 1253[41] and of Matthew Paris, monk of St Albans (c.1200–1259). Prefixed to his *Historia Anglorum* in the British Library manuscript collection, Matthew Paris's itinerary takes the form of a strip map, read from the bottom upwards.[42] Where he acquired this detailed, although sometimes confused, information is uncertain since Matthew himself is not known to have made the journey to Rome. It is possible, however, that the inspiration for his maps came from the large mural maps like those of Hereford and Ebstorf.[43] That the Ebstorf map, made c.1230–1250,[44] may have been known to Matthew is suggested by the inclusion in his *Chronica Maiora* of a head of Christ similar to that found on the Ebstorf map.[45]

Another vital source of information about the routes and conditions of travel are accounts written by pilgrims themselves. Several narratives survive

36 See D. M. Stenton, 'Roger of Howden and Benedict', *EHR*, 68 (1953), pp. 574–582. On Roger of Howden, see F. Barlow, 'Roger of Howden', *EHR*, 65 (1950), pp. 352–360.

37 Benedict of Peterborough, *The Chronicle of the Reigns of Henry II and Richard I A.D. 1169–1192*, ed. W. Stubbs, 2 vols. RS 49 (London, 1867), vol. 2, pp. 227–230. It seems likely that Roger of Howden, if indeed he was the author, was amongst those accompanying the French King on this journey. See Stenton, 'Roger of Howden and Benedict', p. 580.

38 I. V. Zingerle, *Reiserechnungen Wolfger's von Ellenberchtskirchen, Bischofs von Passau, Patriarchen von Aquileja* (Heilbronn, 1877).

39 *Emonis Chronicon*, MGH.SS 23, pp. 470–471.

40 Albert of Stade, *Annales Stadenses*, MGH.SS 16, pp. 335–340.

41 F. Ludwig, *Untersuchungen Über die Reise und Marschgesschwindigkeit im XI und XIII Jahrhundert* (Berlin, 1897).

42 British Library MS Royal 14 c vii, fols. 2r–4r. For other copies of these itineraries, see G. B. Parks, *The English Traveller to Italy. The Middle Ages (to 1525)*, Storia e Lettura, 46 (Rome, 1954), pp. 179–182.

43 See S. Lewis, *The Art of Matthew Paris in the Chronica Maiora* (London, 1987), esp. pp. 374–376.

44 On the Ebstorf map itself, see B. Hahn-Woernle, *Die Ebstorfer Weltkarte* (1989).

45 Lewis, *Art of Matthew Paris in the Chronica Maiora*, p. 36.

which were written by pilgrims after visits to Jerusalem and the Holy Land. We have, for example, the account of an anonymous pilgrim from Bordeaux who travelled to the Holy Land in 333[46] and that of Egeria, a pious lady-traveller from north-western Spain, who went there c.381–384.[47] Other Holy Land pilgrims who have left accounts of their pilgrimages include Saewulf who travelled to the Holy Land c.1101–1103,[48] Abbot Daniel from Russia who made the journey in 1106–1108,[49] Theoderic, a German monk, who went there c.1170,[50] and John Phocas who travelled there in 1185.[51] Also extant is a recently discovered guide in the Beinecke Rare Book and Manuscript Library Ms. 481.77, which was written by a pilgrim, probably of Italian origin, who travelled to the Holy Land sometime during the twelfth century.[52]

Unfortunately accounts written by pilgrims who visited Rome are rare. The best known is undoubtedly that of Sigeric, archbishop of Canterbury, who travelled to the apostolic city in 990 to collect his pallium from Pope John XV (985–996).[53] Also extant is the twelfth-century narrative of Nikolas Bergsson (d.c.1159), an Icelandic abbot of the Benedictine house of Munkathvera. Unfortunately, it is unclear when Nikolas set out from Iceland on his pilgrimage which was to take him first to Rome and then on to the Holy Land. It is probable that he reached Rome c.1150, as his arrival in Jerusalem seems to have been prior to the capture of Ascalon in 1153, but probably after the dedication of the church of the Holy Sepulchre in July 1149.[54] This Old Icelandic text, purportedly written at Nikolas's dictation, consists of his itinerary from Iceland to Rome, an account of his pilgrimage in Rome and his itinerary to the Holy Land, together with a description of how he spent his time there.[55]

---

[46] *Itinerarium Burdigalense*, ed. P. Geyer and O. Cuntz, *Corpus Christianorum Series Latina*, 175 (1965), pp. 1–26.

[47] *Egeria's Travels*, ed. J. Wilkinson (London, 1971). See also P. Devos, 'La Date du Voyage d'Egérie', *Analecta Bollandiana*, 85 (1967), pp. 165–194.

[48] *Jerusalem Pilgrimage 1099–1185*, ed. J. Wilkinson, J. Hill and W. F. Ryan (London, 1988), pp. 94–116.

[49] *Ibid.*, pp. 120–171.

[50] *Ibid.*, pp. 244–273.

[51] *Ibid.*, pp. 315–336.

[52] L. F. Davis, 'A Twelfth Century Pilgrim's Guide to the Holy Land', *Yale University Literary Gazette*, 65 (1990), pp. 11–19. I am grateful to Dr Michael Clanchy for this reference.

[53] *Memorials of St Dunstan Archbishop of Canterbury*, ed. W. Stubbs, RS 63 (London, 1874), pp. 391–395.

[54] J. Hill, 'From Rome to Jerusalem: An Icelandic Itinerary of the mid-twelfth century', *Harvard Theological Studies*, 76 (1983), pp. 175–203, esp. pp. 176–177.

[55] For the Old Icelandic text with a Latin translation, see E. C. Werlauff, *Symbolae ad Geographiam Medii Aevi ex Monumentis Islandicis* (Hauniae, 1821). When quoting the text of Nikolas of Munkathvera, references are to Werlauff's edition unless otherwise stated. I would like to thank Mr Geoffrey Harlow for his help with the Old Icelandic. The text is also available in English. For the itinerary from Iceland to Rome, see F. P.

In addition to the accounts of Archbishop Sigeric and Abbot Nikolas we also have that of Gerald of Wales. Gerald was born at Manorbier Castle in Pembroke c.1145 into a noble Norman family.[56] In 1176, after the death of his uncle, who had been bishop of St David's, Gerald was the choice of the chapter there to succeed to the bishopric. Unfortunately for him, Henry II seems to have favoured another candidate, Peter de Leia. Gerald was forced to withdraw his candidacy and went to Paris to study canon law, returning to England in 1176. On the death of Peter de Leia, Gerald was elected to the bishopric of St David's for a second time. His election was again disputed, not this time by King John, but by Hubert Walter, archbishop of Canterbury. Gerald's subsequent appeal to the papacy lasted for four years and involved three journeys to the papal court. After his appeal ended in failure he seems to have made a fourth journey to the apostolic city c.1204, which he records was 'purely for the sake of pilgrimage'. A short description of this pilgrimage survives in his *De Invectionibus*,[57] together with a description in his *Speculum Ecclesiae* of some of the sites which he saw during his four visits to the apostolic city.[58]

In addition to these celebrated accounts, a few descriptions survive written by pilgrims who travelled to Rome in 1300 to attend the Jubilee, notably those of William of Ventura,[59] Giovanni Villani[60] and Giles of Muisis.[61]

Accounts of Other Visitors to Rome

Further important information about Rome as a pilgrimage centre is provided by those who travelled there for reasons other than pilgrimage. One of the most important of these visitors was Master Gregory.[62] Little is known about Gregory himself, although it seems likely that he was an Englishman. The only extant manuscript of his text is in England and Ranulph Higden, the

Magoun Jr., 'The Pilgrim-Diary of Nikulas of Munkathvera: The Road to Rome', *Medieval Studies*, 6 (1944), pp. 314–354. For Nikolas's stay in Rome, see F. P. Magoun Jr., 'The Rome of Two Northern Pilgrims: Archbishop Sigeric of Canterbury and Abbot Nikolas of Munkathvera', *Harvard Theological Review*, 33 (1940), pp. 267–289. For his pilgrimage to Jerusalem, see Hill, 'From Rome to Jerusalem: An Icelandic Itinerary of the mid-twelfth century', pp. 175–203 and *Jerusalem Pilgrimage*, pp. 215–219.

56 On Gerald of Wales, see J. J. Hagen's introduction to his translation of Gerald's *Gemma Ecclesiastica* (Leiden, 1979), pp. ix–xv.

57 Gerald of Wales, *De Invectionibus*, *Opera*, ed. J. F. Dimmock, G. F. Warner and J. S. Brewer, 8 vols. RS 21 (London, 1861–1891), vol. 1, pp. 125–196. See esp. p. 137.

58 Gerald of Wales, *Speculum Ecclesiae*, in *Opera*, ed. J. F. Dimmock, G. F. Warner and J. S. Brewer, 8 vols. RS 21 (London, 1861–1891), vol. 4, esp. pp. 268–290.

59 William of Ventura, *Chronicon Astense*, RIS 11, col. 192.

60 Giovanni Villani, *Historie Fiorentine*, RIS 13, col. 367.

61 A. D'Haenens, 'Gilles li Muisis, Pèlerin de la Première Année Sainte (1300)', *Bulletin de l'Institut Historique Belge de Rome*, 29 (1955), pp. 31–48.

62 Master Gregory, *The Marvels of Rome*, ed. and trans. J. Osborne (Toronto, 1987).

only medieval writer to make use of this, was also English.[63] The date of Gregory's journey to Rome is also uncertain. However, references to the poems of Hildebert of Lavadin (d.1133) suggest that the text must probably have been written after the first quarter of the twelfth century but its use in the *Polychronicon* of Ranulph Higden means that it must pre-date 1340.[64] Osborne, who has produced the most recent translation and commentary upon the text, favours an early thirteenth- rather than a twelfth-century date for Master Gregory's visit.[65] Despite these uncertainties concerning dating, Master Gregory's account is still a valuable source for what it reveals about the practices of pilgrims in medieval Rome.

Another source is provided by Benjamin, a rabbi from Tudela in northern Spain.[66] Setting out from Tudela in 1160 he began a journey that was to last thirteen years and took him to both Rome and the Holy Land. His account of these travels was written in the first person and was a record, according to the preface, of: 'what he saw or what was told to him by men of integrity whose names were known in Spain'.[67] Although Benjamin's main interests were undoubtedly in the activities of the Jews in the major cities through which he passed, his text is useful for some of the beliefs which it suggests may have been current in twelfth-century Rome.

Pilgrim Guides

Also of value are the so-called 'pilgrim guides'. Three such guides appeared in Rome in the seventh century. The earliest of these three was little more than a catalogue of the cemeteries which could be found outside the city walls.[68] The other two, however, were rather more comprehensive. One, entitled *Notitia Ecclesiarum Urbis Romae*,[69] probably dating from the pontificate of Honorius I (625–638),[70] began at the church of SS. Giovanni e Paolo inside the city itself and then guided the reader from the Via Flaminia in a clockwise direction around the cemetery churches which lay outside the walls, finishing with the climax of the tour at S. Pietro. A second guide, entitled *De Locis Sanctis Martyrum*,[71] written a little after the *Notitia Ecclesiarum Urbis*

63 *Ibid.*, p. 10.
64 *Ibid.*, p. 11.
65 *Ibid.*, pp. 11–15.
66 The account of Benjamin's travels can be found in *Early Travels in Palestine*, ed. T. Wright (London, 1848), pp. 63–126.
67 *Ibid.*, p. 63.
68 *Codice Topografico della Città di Roma*, ed. R. Valentini and G. Zuchetti, 4 vols. *Fonti per la Storia d'Italia*, 81, 88, 90 and 91 (Rome, 1940–1953), vol. 2, pp. 49–66.
69 *Ibid.*, vol. 2, pp. 67–99.
70 This guide can be dated to the pontificate of Honorius I because it mentions this pope by name but there is no reference to any building work carried out by his successors.
71 *Codice Topografico*, vol. 2, pp. 101–131.

Romae,[72] directed the reader in the opposite direction, beginning at S. Pietro and following an anti-clockwise path ending on the Via Flaminia at S. Valentino *al Ponte Milvio*. It would seem probable, however, that *Romipetae* themselves would not have used such texts, firstly because there was no means available of mass-producing them and secondly because most pilgrims would not have been able to cope with a Latin text. It seems more likely that these guides were not written with the intention of telling *Romipetae* where they should go and what they should see but that they actually provided a record of what pilgrims were already doing. This hypothesis is given further weight by a list of pilgrim sites visited in the late sixth century by John, chaplain to the Lombard queen Theodolinda. At each catacomb or shrine, John, following a popular custom, removed a small amount of oil from the lamps used as illumination and sealed it in small *ampullae*, labelling each one with the name of the holy place. A surviving copy of a partial list of these labels indicates that John made a clockwise tour of the shrines around Rome, beginning at S. Pietro and following the same sequence as indicated in the later pilgrim guides.[73]

Similar sources survive from the twelfth century. The *Mirabilia Urbis Romae* was written perhaps c.1140 by a certain Benedict, a canon of S. Pietro.[74] It was a description of the city, which contained numerous stories and legends and an account of what could be seen by the visitor as he wandered around Rome. Also extant is the *Guide to Compostela*. This forms the fifth book of the so-called *Codex Calixtinus*, wrongly attributed to Pope Calixtus II (1119–1124) and probably put together in its present form c.1139 by a certain Aymery Picaud of Parthenay-le-Vieux.[75] It has been argued on the basis of the limited manuscript tradition that the *Guide to Compostela* probably only had a very limited circulation,[76] while Hohler has even argued that, although

---

[72] As well as mentioning the building work carried out by Honorius I, this guide also directs the pilgrim to the basilica of S. Valentino erected by Pope Theodore I (642–649).

[73] *Codice Topografico*, vol. 2, pp. 29–47. See also P. Llewellyn, *Rome in the Dark Ages* (London, 1971), p. 177.

[74] *Mirabilia Urbis Romae*, ed. and trans. F. M. Nichols, 2nd ed. (New York, 1986).

[75] Book one of the *Codex* consists of a collection of offices, hymns and sermons in honour of St James; book two contains the miracles performed by this saint; book three consists of collected stories concerning the life of St James and the discovery of his tomb; book four contains the *Historia Karoli Magni et Rotholandi* attributed to Bishop Turpin. See *Liber Sancti Jacobi, Codex Calixtinus*, ed. M. M. Whitehill, 2 vols. (Santiago de Compostela, 1944). See also *The Miracles of Saint James: Translations of the 'Liber Sancti Jacobi'*, ed. T. Coffey, L. Davidson and M. Dunn (New York, 1996). For the pilgrim guide itself I have used throughout the edition of J. Vielliard which contains the Latin text with a French translation. See *Guide du Pèlerin de Saint-Jacques de Compostelle*, ed. J. Vielliard, 3rd ed. (Mâcon, 1963). There is now also an English translation, *The Pilgrim's Guide to Santiago de Compostella*, ed. W. Melczer (New York, 1993).

[76] Professor Jeanne Krochalis of Pennsylvania State University suggested this on the basis

written in the form of a guide, it was not intended for this purpose. He believes that it was more likely the manual of a nomadic grammar master, used to teach boys Latin.[77] Although doubts over the purpose of this *Guide* should be borne in mind, it is still important for the information which it contains.

Libri Indulgentiarum

Other useful narrative sources for the study of pilgrimage include the *Libri Indulgentiarum*.[78] These consist of lists of indulgences which could be gained by pilgrims at particular shrines. De Rossi believed that these *Libri Indulgentiarum* could probably still be found in libraries and archives throughout Europe.[79] No one, however, has attempted such a systematic search and little is known about them, how many there are, for how many pilgrimage centres they survive, or when they were first produced. At the beginning of this century, however, J. R. Hulbert searched through the catalogues of the British Museum and found nine manuscript versions in Latin or a vernacular, dating from the fourteenth and fifteenth centuries and more amongst the earliest printed books.[80] Hulbert also noted that he had found more of these texts relating to Rome than to any other pilgrimage centre, indicating, he suggested, a systematic plan in the city's propagation. Only a thorough search for these indulgence lists in other libraries and archives will reveal whether this is the case and whether the numbers of such texts concerning Rome are considerably greater than for other pilgrimage sites.

Acta Sanctorum

Another valuable narrative source is the *Acta Sanctorum*, which contains references to a large collection of twelfth-century pilgrims.[81] Such a source, however, should be treated with great caution. In many cases the *Vita* of a particular saint was not written until long after his death and, since it is often

that the *Guide* has only a limited manuscript tradition, and that these manuscripts show very little sign of wear, in a paper given at the London University Palaeography Seminar on 28 February 1991.

[77] C. Hohler, 'A Note on *Jacobus*', *Journal of the Warburg and Courtauld Institutes*, 35 (1972), pp. 31–80. I am grateful to Dr Michael Clanchy for this reference.

[78] Indulgences, offered from the late eleventh century onwards, enabled individuals to substitute other devotional acts for traditional penances. See B. Hamilton, *Religion in the Medieval West* (London, 1986), pp. 47 and 129–131.

[79] G. B. de Rossi, *La Roma Sotterranea*, 3 vols. (Rome, 1864–1877), vol. 1, p. 162.

[80] J. R. Hulbert, 'Some Medieval Advertisements of Rome', *Modern Philology*, 20 (1922–23), pp. 403–424.

[81] *Acta Sanctorum Bollandiana*, ed. J. Bollandus *et al.*, 67 vols. (Antwerp, 1643–1883, reprt. Brussels, 1902–1970) [cited as *AASS*].

our only source for this individual, there is no means of verifying its contents. *Vitae* written by contemporaries should also be treated with caution, as it is possible that the undertaking of a pilgrimage may have been a *topos* regularly attributed to holy men and women. Medieval hagiographers, Geary has noted, wrote the *Vitae* of particular saints not to tell their readers anything about the particular saint's personality or individuality but to show how the saint exhibited characteristics of sanctity common to all saints of all times.[82] What can be said, however, is that there seems to be no overall pattern to the majority of the *Vitae*, as far as pilgrimages are concerned. Some holy men and women are attributed with just one journey to a place of pilgriamge. Some biographers make no claims of pilgrimage for their subjects at all, whilst others show that a particular saint or martyr travelled to many holy places.

Liber Pontificalis

As well as saints' lives, there are also the biographies of medieval popes which can be found in the *Liber Pontificalis*.[83] It is likely that the *Liber Pontificalis*, in its earliest form, was put together towards the beginning of the sixth century.[84] The author is unknown but seems to have been reliant upon earlier lists of the holders of the Roman See and upon other information which he searched out and, in some cases, probably made up. This version of the *Liber Pontificalis* contained the lives of the popes down to AD 530 but unfortunately has not survived except in two epitomes. What we do have is a second edition made shortly after the first, no later than the 540s, in which some of the earliest lives were reworked. After this no more additions seem to have been made to the *Liber Pontificalis* until the early seventh century. From then on, until 870, the biographies of the popes all seem to have been written

---

[82] P. Geary, *Furta Sacra. Thefts of Relics in the Central Middle Ages* (Princeton, 1978, rev. ed. 1990), p. 9. See also H. Delahaye, *The Legends of the Saints*, trans. D. Attwater (London, 1962), pp. 68–78.

[83] *Liber Pontificalis*, ed. L. Duchesne, 2 vols., 2nd ed., *Bibliothèque des Ecoles Françaises d'Athènes et de Rome* (Paris, 1955), vol. 3, additions et corrections de Mgr. L. Duchesne publiées par C. Vogel (Paris, 1957). All references to the *Liber Pontificalis* in this book are to Duchesne's edition. A translation of some of the lives found in the *Liber Pontificalis* is now available. See *Book of Pontiffs*, ed. and trans. R. Davis (Liverpool, 1989), which contains the lives of the popes from St Peter to Constantine (708–715), *Lives of the Eighth-Century Popes*, ed. and trans. R. Davis (Liverpool, 1992) and *Lives of the Ninth-Century Popes*, ed. and trans. R. Davis (Liverpool, 1995). On the *Liber Pontificalis*, see also R. Davis, 'The Value of the Liber Pontificalis as Comparative Evidence for Territorial Estates and Church Property from the Fourth to the Sixth Century', unpublished Ph.D. thesis (University of Oxford, 1976); T. F. X. Noble, 'A New Look at the *Liber Pontificalis*', *Archivum Historiae Pontificae*, 23 (1985), pp. 347–358.

[84] On the composition of the *Liber Pontificalis*, see Davis, *Value of the Liber Pontificalis*, esp. pp. 167–184.

by contemporaries. Of the popes of the tenth to the mid-eleventh centuries the *Liber Pontificalis* records little beyond their names and the length of their pontificates.

A product of the Gregorian reform seems to have been a reawakened interest in the venerable *Liber Pontificalis* and in the first half of the twelfth century a continuation was written ending with the *Vita* of Honorius II (1124–1130).[85] Also contained in Duchesne's edition are the series of *Vitae* written by Cardinal Boso, chamberlain to Hadrian IV and later cardinal priest of S. Pudenziana. This series begins with a very brief account of the pontificates of the popes of the late ninth, tenth and early eleventh centuries.[86] It is followed by a rather isolated note on John XII (955–964)[87] and then by a series of *Vitae* of the popes from Leo IX (1049–1054) to Alexander III (1159–1181).[88] Popes Victor III and Urban II are omitted and the *Vita* of Alexander III stops in 1178, three years before the end of his pontificate. Also extant are the *Vitae* written by Martin of Troppau (d.1279). His *Vitae* begin with Innocent II (1130–1143) and end with John XXI (1276–1277).[89] These later *Vitae* are concerned largely with political events. They contain much less information about papal building campaigns and about the welfare provisions which these popes made in Rome, details so usefully provided in the *Vitae* of many of their earlier counterparts.

Gesta Innocentii Papae III

As well as the brief life of Innocent III (1198–1216) entered in the *Liber Pontificalis* by Martin of Troppau (d.1279),[90] also extant is the anonymous *Gesta Innocentii Papae III*.[91] Although its narrative ends in 1208, it is a vital source for Innocent's pontificate and contains information about his provisions for pilgrims. The value of this source lies in the fact that it was composed by someone in close contact with this pope, who had access to the papal registers. It was not an account of day-to-day events but a highly organised work, which dealt with three main themes: the desperate situation

---

85 See *Liber Pontificalis*, vol. 2.
86 *Ibid.*, vol. 2, pp. 353–354.
87 *Ibid.*, vol. 2, p. 354.
88 *Ibid.*, vol. 2, pp. 354–446. An English translation exists of the *Vita* of Alexander III. See Boso, *Life of Alexander III*, trans. G. M. Ellis (Oxford, 1973).
89 *Liber Pontificalis*, vol. 2, pp. 449–458. On the other later continuators of the *Liber Pontificalis*, see *ibid.*, vol. 2, pp. xlv–li.
90 *Ibid.*, vol. 2, pp. 451–453.
91 *Gesta Innocentii Papae III*, PL 214, cols. xvii–ccxxviii. The most recent study of the *Gesta* as a source is that of B. M. Bolton, 'Too Important to Neglect: The *Gesta Innocentii Papae III*', *Church and Chronicle in the Middle Ages: Essays Presented to John Taylor*, ed. G. A. Loud and I. R. Wood (London, 1991), pp. 87–99.

in the papal states following Imperial occupation, the influence of the Roman Church throughout Christendom and the pope's relationship with the city of Rome itself. It has recently been argued, on the basis of this highly organised structure, that the *Gesta*'s author may have finished his account in 1208 not because he died but because his task was complete.[92] The *Gesta* was a work composed for a local audience in the patrimony, intended to present to them Innocent's triumph over his enemies and his success in reclaiming the papal state, its lands and subjects, a task which, it perhaps seemed to Innocent and his biographer, had been completed by 1208.[93]

Miracle Collections

To these narrative sources for the history of pilgrimage should be added miracle collections.[94] These often give detailed accounts of miracles and cures carried out at a particular tomb or shrine. They usually include details about the recipients of the miracle, frequently names and where they were from. Miracle collections, therefore, not only provide a list of miracles and cures but also information about individual pilgrims and about the importance of particular saints and martyrs. They can show whether these holy men and women could draw pilgrims to their tombs and shrines only from a local area or from much further afield. Whilst miracle collections survive for some of Christendom's more popular and well known centres of pilgrimage, such as the shrine of St James at Compostela[95] and that of St Thomas at Canterbury,[96] they are often our chief source of information for many other, often smaller, pilgrimage centres, such as the tombs of St Gilbert at Sempringham,[97] St Godric at Finchale,[98] St Frideswide at Oxford,[99] St William at

92 Bolton, 'Too Important to Neglect: The *Gesta Innocentii Papae III*', pp. 98–99.
93 *Ibid.*, pp. 98–99.
94 On miracles, see the very useful article by P. A. Sigal, 'Reliques, Pèlerinage et Miracles dans l'Eglise Médiévale (XIe–XIIIe Siècles)', *Revue d'Histoire de l'Eglise de France*, 76 (1990), pp. 193–211. See also R. C. Finucane, 'The Use and Abuse of Medieval Miracles', *History*, 60 (1975), pp. 1–10; R. C. Finucane, *Miracles and Pilgrims. Popular Beliefs in Medieval England* (London, 1977); B. Ward, *Miracles and the Medieval Mind. Theory, Record and Event 1000–1215* (London, 1982, rev. 1987); H. Delahaye, 'Les Premiers *Libelli Miraculorum*', *Analecta Bollandiana*, 29 (1910), pp. 427–434.
95 *Liber Sancti Jacobi*, vol. 2, pp. 259–287.
96 *Materials for the History of Thomas Becket, Archbishop of Canterbury*, ed. J. C. Robinson, 7 vols. RS 67 (London, 1875–1895), vols. 1 and 2.
97 *Book of St Gilbert*, ed. R. Foreville and G. Keir, Oxford Medieval Texts (Oxford, 1987), esp. pp. 264–335.
98 Reginald of Durham, *Libellus de Vita et Miraculis S. Godrici heremitae de Finchale*, ed. J. Stevenson, Surtees Society, 20 (1847).
99 Philip, prior of St Frideswide's *Miracula S. Frideswidae*, AASS Oct. VIII, pp. 567–590.

Norwich,[100] St Gilles in Provence[101] and the shrines of the Virgin at Soissons,[102] at Chartres[103] and at Rocamadour.[104]

Documentary Sources

A wide variety of documentary sources, including papal bulls,[105] letters[106] and other ecclesiastical correspondence, often contain valuable information concerning pilgrimage, particularly about the dangers involved in such an undertaking, voicing concerns or complaints about attacks perpetrated upon pilgrims on the roads. Letters of recommendation which survive amongst the Merovingian and Carolingian *formulae* reveal that pilgrims carried such documents in order to prove that they were genuine pilgrims entitled to safe passage.[107] Equally important in this context is the Carolingian legislation[108] and the canons of church councils,[109] which indicate that throughout the medieval period the right of pilgrims to travel in safety had to be constantly restated. These conciliar decrees are also important because they reveal that pilgrims not only had the right to safe passage but also enjoyed other important privileges which gave them a special status in medieval society. Also

---

[100] Thomas of Monmouth, *Life and Miracles of St William of Norwich*, ed. A. Jessopp and M. R. James (Cambridge, 1896).

[101] Peter William, *Miracula S. Aegidii*, MGH.SS 12, pp. 316–323.

[102] Hugh Farsit, *Libellus de Miraculis B. Mariae Virginis in Urbe Suessionensi*, PL 179, cols. 1777–1800.

[103] *Miracles de Notre Dame de Chartres*, ed. A. Thomas, *Bibliothèque de l'Ecole des Chartes*, 42 (1881), pp. 505–550.

[104] *Miracles de Notre Dame de Rocamadour au XIIe siècle*, ed. and trans. E. Albe (Paris, 1907).

[105] *Collectione Bullarum Sacrosancta Basilicae Vaticana*, ed. A. Albani, 3 vols. (Rome, 1747–1752).

[106] Surviving papal letters up to those of Innocent III can be found in PL. Those of Gregory IX onwards have been published by the *Bibliothèque des Ecoles Françaises d'Athènes et de Rome*. For those of Honorius III, see *Registers*, ed. P. Pressutti, 2 vols. (Rome, 1888–1895) and Honorius III, *Opera Omnia*, ed. C. A. Horoy, 2 vols., *Medii Aevi Bibliotheca Patristica* (Paris, 1879). See also *Acta Pontificum Romanorum Inedita*, ed. J. Pflugk-Harttung, 3 vols. (Stuttgart, 1881–1886); *Regesta Pontificum Romanorum ab condita ecclesia ad annum post Christum natum* MCXCVIII , ed. P. Jaffé, 2 vols. (Leipzig, 1885–1888) [cited as Jaffé]; *Regesta Pontificium Romanorum inde ab Anno Post Christum natum* MCXCVIII *ad Anno* MCCCIV , ed. A. Potthast, 2 vols. (Berlin, 1874, reprt. Graz, 1957) [cited as Potthast].

[107] See below pp. 74–75.

[108] See esp. MGH *Legum*, Sectio 2, vols. 1 and 2 (Hanover, 1883).

[109] *Sacrorum Conciliorum Nova et Amplissima Collectio*, ed. J. D. Mansi et al., 55 vols. (Venice and Florence, 1759–1962); *Histoire des Conciles*, ed. H. Leclerq, 11 vols. (Paris, 1907–1952); and also *Conciliorum Oecumenicorum Decreta*. Important too are the decretal collections. See Burchard of Worms, *Decreta*, PL 140, cols. 537–1058; Ivo of Chartres, *Decretum*, PL 161, cols. 9–1036; *Corpus Iuris Canonici*, ed. A. Friedberg, 2 vols. (1879–1881).

useful are the *fueros* which survive amongst Spanish sources.[110] These usually contain a particular town's privileges, the customary law of the area and regulations relating to the practical administration of urban life and occasionally include provisions concerning pilgrims.

Charters

Amongst the most useful documentary sources are charters found in the cartularies of religious houses.[111] Such charters may contain information concerning pious donations made to the religious house and include gifts given by pilgrims. Sometimes such a gift might be made to atone for a pilgrim's past misdemeanours, probably with the intention of securing divine protection for the journey. Alternatively the donation might be made in return for aid from the religious house for financing the pilgrimage itself. Frequently such charters include information about the pilgrim's destination. The nature of the contents of these charters means, however, that they only really give us information about pilgrims who belonged to the wealthier ranks of medieval society, those who had land or money to donate. Furthermore, these charters usually only produce evidence of pilgrimages made to shrines several hundred miles away, for it was these long distance journeys which created problems of finance, or which raised very real fears about potential dangers and hazards which might be encountered *en route*.

The varied nature of surviving monastic cartularies has meant that the majority examined for the purposes of this book are those of religious houses in France. It is only these charters which are sufficiently detailed to contain substantial information about pilgrimages. As so many cartularies have survived it has only been possible for me to examine a small selection. An attempt has been made at selection from a variety of geographical areas in order to take account of any local variations. The areas were chosen on the

---

110 On *fueros*, see A. MacKay, *Spain in the Middle Ages. From Frontier to Empire, 1000–1500* (London, 1977), pp. 55–56; H. Dillard, *Daughters of the Reconquest. Women in Castilian Town Society, 1100–1300* (Cambridge, 1984), pp. 3–9.

111 On charters and their use as a source, see esp. G. Constable, 'Medieval Charters as a Source for the History of the Crusades', *Monks, Hermits and Crusaders in Medieval Europe* (Variorum Reprint, London, 1988) VIII, pp. 73–89; and J. S. C. Riley-Smith, *The First Crusaders, 1095–1131* (Cambridge, 1997). As I have used so many cartularies, I only give very abbreviated references to each of them in the footnotes. The abbreviations together with a full reference to the cartularies are listed in the bibliography. The numbers given refer to the number of the charter and not to pages, except where indicated. I include volume numbers where charters are not numbered continuously from volume to volume or where this makes the references easier to find. Many of the names of people and places in these charters have modern equivalents, which I have used where they are known to me. Otherwise I have cited the original Latin, underlined. I am grateful to Professor Riley-Smith for helping me with the identification of many of these places.

basis of the availability of cartularies and include the region north of the Loire, Orléans, Tours, Le Mans, Angers and Blois and to the south including Poitou, Aunis, Saintonge and a few from Bordeaux and the areas of Limoges, Mâcon and Autun as well as a few from Montpellier and Grenoble.[112] References to pilgrimages in charters found in the cartularies of religious houses of other countries, such as England, Spain, or Italy, and in Imperial sources, are much rarer.

Sermons

Sermons addressed to pilgrims are also a useful source of information. One of the best known is undoubtedly the very long *Veneranda dies* sermon, which is contained in Book I of the *Codex Calixtinus*.[113] Intended to be read to pilgrims on the second feast day of St James, 20 December, it is particularly useful to the historian, containing as it does a wealth of information about pilgrimage, its aims and dangers.

Two sermons were also addressed to pilgrims by the great popular preacher of the early thirteenth century, Jacques de Vitry (d.1240).[114] The first, intended for a general audience of lay people, outlines the Biblical justification for pilgrimage and gives advice on practical matters, particularly the manner in which pilgrims ought to conduct themselves on their pilgrimages. The second is more scholarly, intended perhaps for a clerical audience, and develops the popular medieval theme of the way in which man's life on earth is itself a pilgrimage.

Also extant is the sermon addressed to pilgrims by the thirteenth-century Franciscan preacher, Guibert of Tournai (d. c.1284). His sermon addressed to pilgrims is heavily dependent upon those of Jacques de Vitry, incorporating many passages and *exempla* from the latter's sermons word-for-word.[115]

Archaeological and Architectural Evidence

Archaeological and architectural evidence can also be useful in the study of pilgrimage. The re-designing and re-building of churches with large naves, galleries and annular crypts was a common response to the need to cater for large crowds of pilgrims. Such architectural features, therefore, are often a good indicator of a pilgrimage centre's increasing popularity. Where early medieval churches are still standing, architectural features can sometimes

---

[112] I am grateful to Dr Marcus Bull for his advice on the selection of areas and cartularies.
[113] *Codex Calixtinus*, vol. 1, pp. 141–176.
[114] See above, pp. 1–4.
[115] Guibert of Tournai, *Sermones ad Omnes Status de Novo correcti et emendati* (1510). See also M. Papi, 'Crociati, Pellegrini e Cavalieri nei Sermones di Gilberto di Tournai', *Studi Francescani*, 73 (1976), pp. 373–409.

still be detected despite constant additions and alterations carried out in later centuries. Where the original medieval churches have not survived, archaeological excavations can sometimes reveal useful information. Perhaps the most important example here is the excavation work carried out earlier this century under the basilica of S. Pietro, Rome, which uncovered the remains of the Constantinian church which had stood until the sixteenth century.[116]

Other Non-literary Sources

Some pilgrims have left evidence of their presence at tombs and shrines in the form of *graffiti*. One of the most important discoveries of this kind was made during the excavations beneath the present basilica of S. Pietro which revealed *graffiti* in the form of names and prayers of pilgrims for the spiritual well-being of friends and family.[117] Other *graffiti* in the form of prayers and invocations to Saints Peter and Paul have also been discovered at the cult centre of these two apostles on the Via Appia at S. Sebastiano. Here too the pilgrims frequently included their own names.[118]

Items which used to belong to pilgrims are occasionally uncovered. Most important of these are the badges which they wore on their hat or collar.[119] Purchased at the pilgrimage centre to which they had travelled, badges were an important token, a sign that the pilgrimage had been made. The Musée de Cluny possesses one of the largest collection of pilgrim badges, although many can also be seen in the Museum of London and in the Vatican Museums.

In addition to badges, the bodies of pilgrims have occasionally been uncovered. One of the most recent discoveries of this kind, amongst the most important in this country, was the discovery of a pilgrim burial inside Worcester Cathedral in 1986, made during excavations under the south-east tower. What was uncovered was the skeleton of a man still fully clothed. Beside him lay a long wooden staff, with double pronged iron tip and a cockle shell, reminiscent of the cockle shell associated with pilgrimage to Compostela.[120] Such a discovery, however, does emphasise one of the major problems faced by those studying medieval pilgrimage. Although the body of this pilgrim has been dicovered, we know nothing about him, neither his name, nor where he was from, nor how or when he came to Worcester, nor, with perhaps the

116 See below, pp. 27–33.
117 Toynbee and Ward Perkins, *Shrine of St Peter*, pp. 162–167; M. Guarducci, *Pietro in Vaticano* (Rome, 1984), pp. 68–77; Maccarrone, 'Pellegrinaggio', esp. pp. 370–378.
118 See Toynbee and Ward Perkins, *Shrine of St Peter*, pp. 167–182.
119 On pilgrim badges, see below, pp. 77–79.
120 On this discovery, see H. Lubin, *The Worcester Pilgrim*, Worcester Cathedral Publications, 1 (1990).

exception of Compostela, even the pilgrimage centres which he might have visited. This is unfortunately true of the majority of pilgrims. While the presence of so many pilgrimage centres across medieval Europe is a witness to the widespread popular enthusiasm for pilgrimage, of the individual pilgrims we can rarely if ever know much.

1

The Cult of Saints and Pilgrimage to Rome

Surviving evidence suggests that pilgrims had begun travelling to Rome by at least the end of the second century. We know, for example, of the pilgrimage made there by Abercio, bishop of Phrygia at this time[1] and of that of Origen c.212.[2] It has recently been argued by Maccarrone that a parallel can be drawn between pilgrimages to Rome and to Jerusalem at this early date.[3] A pilgrimage to the Holy Land enabled the pilgrim to see the places so intimately connected with his faith, those sites where the biblical events had actually taken place. The same was also true to a lesser extent of Rome, for here the Church had been founded by two of Christ's apostles, Peter and Paul.[4] In the late fourth century, however, the popularity of Rome as a destination for pilgrims was dramatically increased by the development of the cult of saints. The purpose of this introductory chapter, therefore, is to consider the spread of this cult and its consequences for Rome. Special consideration will also be given to the city's two most important saints, Peter and Paul.

The Cult of Saints

Rome's popularity as a pilgrimage centre undoubtedly grew with the development of the cult of saints in the late fourth and fifth centuries. Some of the most recent and exciting research in this field has been carried out by Peter Brown. Citing the inscription on the tomb of St Martin at Tours

> Here lies Martin the bishop, of holy memory, whose soul is in the hand of God; but he is fully here, present and made plain in miracles of every kind

---

1   M. Guarducci, 'L'Inscrizione di Abercio a Roma', *Ancient Society*, 2 (1971), pp. 174–203, esp. p. 176.
2   Eusebius, *Ecclesiastical History*, trans. K. Lake, 2 vols. Loeb Classical Library (London, 1926), book 6, chpt. 14, vol. 1, pp. 48–51.
3   See Maccarrone, 'Pellegrinaggio', esp. pp. 368–369.
4   As early as the end of the first century the apostolic associations of the Roman Church were already a source of fierce pride. See Clement's *First Epistle to the Corinthians*, in *Early Christian Writings*, trans. M. Staniforth, rev. A. Louth (London, 1987), p. 25.

Brown illustrates the growth in the belief that the saint in heaven was also present in his tomb.[5] Miracles carried out at the tomb, such as the curing of the sick and the exorcism of demons, were all clear evidence of this presence. Here, therefore, is an interesting contrast with motives for visiting the Holy Sepulchre in Jerusalem. For pilgrims went to the Holy Sepulchre precisely because it was empty, 'a testimony to the resurrection of the Saviour',[6] but they travelled to the shrines of martyrs because they believed these holy men to be actually there, ready to respond to their prayers.

In addition to the saints' ability to perform miracles, it was widely believed that they had intercessory powers and would, if requested, intercede with God on man's behalf. This is evident from early Christian and Patristic writings. In his *Liber de Viduis*, St Ambrose (d.397) stated that a person guilty of great sin was not fit to pray for himself and should, therefore, procure others to pray on his behalf. It was the martyrs who should be entreated, he claimed, who, having washed away their sins with their own blood, could obtain blessings for all.[7] Prudentius (348–405), writing of the martyrs of Calahorra in northern Spain, noted that no man who prayed to them sincerely had ever done so in vain,[8] 'for they listen to our prayer and straightway carry it to the ear of the everlasting King'.[9] In turn St Augustine (354–430) maintained that 'although we ourselves might be unworthy to ask for blessings from God, we still might ask for them *per amicos*'.[10]

The cult of saints was viewed by non-Christians with abhorrence. One of the most vivid condemnations was made by the pagan Eunapius of Sardis (c.345–c.420) in his *Lives of the Philosophers and Sophists* written c.396.

For they collected the bones and skulls of criminals who had been put to death for various crimes, men whom the law courts of the city had condemned to punishment, made them out to be gods, haunted their sepulchres and thought that they became better by defiling themselves at their graves. Martyrs the dead men were called and ministers of a sort and ambassadors from the gods to carry men's prayers.[11]

[5]   P. Brown, *The Cult of the Saints. Its Rise and Function in Latin Christianity* (London, 1981), p. 4.

       Hic conditus est sanctae memoriae Martinus episcopus
       Cuius anima in manu Dei est, sed hic totus est
       Prasens manifestus omni gratia virtutum.

[6]   Eusebius, *Life of Constantine the Great*, Select Library of the Nicene and Post-Nicene Fathers of the Christian Church, ed. H. Wace and P. Schaff, New Series, vol. 1 (Oxford, 1890), book 3, chpt. 28, p. 528.

[7]   St Ambrose, *Liber de Viduis*, PL 16, cols. 247–276, col. 264.

[8]   Prudentius, *Peristephanon*, vol. 2, pp. 98–101.

[9]   *Ibid.*, vol. 2, pp. 98–101.

[10] St Augustine, *Sermones*, PL 38, col. 1462.

[11] Eunapius of Sardis, *Lives of the Philosophers and Sophists*, trans. W. C. Wright, Loeb Classical Library (London, 1952), pp. 424–425. See also Brown, *Cult of the Saints*, pp. 6–7.

While such polemic caused men like St Jerome (c.348–420)[12] and St Augustine[13] to attempt to justify the cult of saints, it did little to undermine its popularity. The shrines which sprang up wherever Christianity spread were witness to this. St Augustine himself, in the last book of his *De Civitate Dei*, describes some of the miracles carried out at local shrines of St Stephen, the first martyr, in North Africa, particularly in the colonies of Calama and Hippo. Apologising that he is unable to include all the miracles worked by the saint at these shrines, he writes, 'if I should omit all else and undertake to write only the miracles of healing . . . many books would have to be written'.[14] An anonymous account of the fourth century reveals the rapid spread of the cult of saints in Egypt.[15] Nor had its popularity declined by the sixth century for a Coptic source reveals the activities of three pagans, who, in the guise of pilgrims, travelled from shrine to shrine in Upper Egypt robbing them as they went. Their haul included an altar cloth, gold and silver chalices and even silk garments removed from one saint's body.[16]

The evidence of Paulinus of Nola (c.353–431) suggests that by the end of the fourth century the cult was flourishing in southern Italy. St Felix, he says, 'rejoices that his walls cannot contain the pious multitudes . . . and that dense throngs disperse through numerous doorways'.[17] While many of those who came to St Felix's churches at Nola appear to have been local peasants, intent on enjoying their funeral banquets,[18] it is apparent from Paulinus's account that others may have come from further afield with rather more serious intentions. Indeed, he draws attention to small cells above, yet close to the shrine, built especially for those 'whom the longing to pray, not the desire to drink, has led hither for the rightful veneration of Saintly Felix'.[19] By this time too the cult was well established in northern Italy. In 386 the bodies of two martyrs, Protase and Gervase, were opportunely discovered by Ambrose, bishop of Milan (d.397), 'their bones intact and with much blood'.[20] They were translated to his new basilica,[21] where they immediately began to perform miracles, curing the blind and casting out demons.[22] The

12 See for example St Jerome, *Liber Contra Vigilantium*, PL 23, cols. 353–368.
13 See for example St Augustine, *De Civitate Dei*, trans. W. M. Green, 7 vols. Loeb Classical Library (London, 1972), vol. 3, book 8, chpt. 27, pp. 138–145.
14 *Ibid.*, vol. 7, book 22, chpt. 8, pp. 238–239.
15 L. Th. Lefort, 'La Chasse aux Reliques des martyrs en Egypte au IV Siècle', *La Nouvelle Clio*, 6 (1954), pp. 225–230.
16 J. Drescher, 'Apa Claudius and the Thieves', *Bulletin de la Société d'Archéologie Copte*, 8 (1942), pp. 63–86.
17 *Paulinus' Churches at Nola*, ed. R. Goldschimdt (Amsterdam, 1940), pp. 52–55.
18 *Ibid.*, pp. 62–65.
19 *Ibid.*, pp. 54–55.
20 St Ambrose, *Epistolae*, PL 16, Ep. 22.2, col. 1063. See also F. H. Dudden, *The Life and Times of St Ambrose*, 2 vols. (Oxford, 1935), esp. vol. 1, pp. 298–320.
21 St Ambrose, *Epistolae*, Ep. 22.2, col. 1063. See also Paulinus, *Vita Sancti Ambrosii*, PL, 14, esp. col. 34.
22 Severus, a blind man, had his sight restored during the translation of the relics. See

evidence of Prudentius indicates that by the end of the fourth century the cult was also popular in Spain. In his *Peristephanon*, for example, he mentions the prayers offered by those who sought aid from the martyrs of Calahorra,[23] as well as the cult of St Eulalia in Merida.[24]

Even north of the Alps, where Christianity spread, the cult flourished. One of the most famous tombs there was that of St Martin of Tours (d. 397). Not only did this Bishop carry out miracles during his own lifetime but also, as we have seen, posthumously. Such were the wonders wrought at St Martin's tomb, that in his *History of the Franks*, Gregory of Tours (573–594) recounts how, in 478, Perpetuus, then bishop of the city, decided to have a large, new basilica built over the tomb of St Martin, judging the small chapel then in existence to be unworthy.[25] Indeed, as Brown has argued, wherever Christianity spread in the early Middle Ages it brought with it the 'presence' of the saints, covering the Christian world with a grid of shrines.[26]

Rome was the richest of all the cities of the West in relics and shrines and thus the development of the cult of saints undoubtedly enhanced this city's importance as a pilgrimage centre. Whilst some of the earliest pilgrims had visited the city because of the apostolic associations of the church which had been founded there, the numerous Christian saints and martyrs buried in the cemeteries outside its walls provided an even greater attraction.[27] Prudentius in his *Peristephanon* describes the crowds who flocked to the tomb of Hippolytus on the Via Tiburtina.[28] 'Scarcely', he writes, 'can the broad plains hold the joyous multitudes.'[29] At the church itself, Prudentius describes the 'struggling waves of people' at the door way trying to gain admittance.[30] The large crowds which began to gather in Rome around the tombs of the martyrs are also recorded by St Jerome, who praised the 'enthusiasm and the throngs'.[31]

Rome's importance as a pilgrimage centre is most fully explained, however, by its possession of the bodies of the apostles, Peter and Paul. Not only had they been fundamental in the foundation of the Christian Church in

Paulinus, *Vita Sancti Ambrosii*, col. 34, and St Ambrose, *Epistolae*, Ep. 22.2, col. 1063 and Ep. 22.9, cols. 1064–1065 for other miracles.

23 Prudentius, *Peristephanon*, vol. 2, pp. 98–101.

24 *Ibid.*, vol. 2, pp. 143–157. See also R. Collins, 'Merida and Toledo: 550–585', *Visigothic Spain: New Approaches*, ed. E. James (Oxford, 1980), pp. 189–219.

25 Gregory of Tours, *History of the Franks*, ed. and trans. O. M. Dalton (Oxford, 1927), pp. 58–59. On Martin of Tours, see C. Stancliffe, *St Martin and His Hagiographer. History and Miracle in Sulpicius Severus* (Oxford, 1983).

26 Brown, *Cult of the Saints*, p. 12.

27 G. Bardy, 'Pèlerinages à Rome vers la fin du IV Siècle', *Analecta Bollandiana*, 67 (1949), pp. 224–235.

28 Prudentius, *Peristephanon*, vol. 2, pp. 318–319. See also G. Bertonière, *The Cult Centre of the Martyr Hippolytus on the Via Tiburtina*, BAR International Series, 260 (1985).

29 Prudentius, *Peristephanon*, vol. 2, pp. 318–319.

30 *Ibid.*, vol. 2, pp. 320–321.

31 Hunt, *Holy Land Pilgrimage*, p. 24.

Rome but most importantly from the viewpoint of later pilgrims, there too
both had been martyred and buried, St Peter supposedly on the Vatican Hill
and St Paul on the Ostian Way.

St Peter

As Prince of the apostles and keeper of the keys to heaven, St Peter was
active in building up the organisation of the Christian Church in Palestine as
well as in preaching the Gospel. To this end he visited Antioch in Syria,
where he became bishop,[32] and possibly also Corinth.[33] His visit to Rome is
not explicitly affirmed in the New Testament, although the reference to
'Babylon' in his First Epistle is usually identified with this city.[34] Early Christian writings confirm the tradition of St Peter's visit to Rome, of his institution of the episcopal succession and of his martyrdom by crucifixion during
the reign of the Emperor Nero (54–68), probably c.64 AD.[35]

By the end of the second century, surviving evidence suggests that one site
on the Vatican Hill was particularly associated with St Peter. In his *Ecclesiastical History*, Eusebius preserved the observations of Gaius, a Roman priest
who, during the pontificate of Zephyrinus (198/9–217), in a dispute with the
Montanist Proclus, reported that on the Vatican Hill and Ostian Way there
could be found the *trophies* of those who had founded the Church in Rome.[36]
It is uncertain, however, what Gaius meant by the term *trophy*. Did it indicate
the actual sites at which St Peter, and indeed St Paul, had been buried, or did
it refer only to sites where each were commemorated? Unfortunately the
answer to this puzzle does not seem to have been made any clearer by the
excavations carried out earlier this century below the present Vatican Basilica, during which the *trophy* seen by Gaius at the end of the second century
was rediscovered.[37]

---

[32] Galatians 2.11. The feast of St Peter's Chair in Antioch is 22 February.
[33] 1 Corinthians 1.12. Eusebius (*Ecclesiastical History*, book 2, chpt. 25, vol. 1, pp. 182–
183) reports the contents of a letter of the late second century written by Dionysius,
bishop of Corinth, to the Romans: '. . . for both of them [Saints Peter and Paul] taught
together in our Corinth and were our founders . . .'.
[34] 1 Peter 5.13.
[35] For these traditions in Early Christian literature, see J. T. Shotwell and L. R. Loomis,
The See of Peter (New York, 1927), pp. 56–96.
[36] Eusebius, *Ecclesiastical History*, book 2, chpt. 25, vol. 1, pp. 180–183: 'But I can point
out the trophies of the Apostles, for if you want to set out for the Vatican or along the
Ostian Way you will find the trophies of those who founded this Church.' The word
used by Eusebius is τὸ τρόπαιον meaning a trophy or monument.
[37] On these excavations, see B. M. Apollonj-Ghetti, A. Ferrua, E. Josi and E.
Kirschbaum, *Esplorazioni sotto la Confessione di San Pietro in Vaticano*, 2 vols. (Città del
Vaticano, 1951) [cited as *Esplorazioni*]; E. Kirschbaum, *The Tombs of St Peter and St
Paul*, trans. J. Murray (London, 1959); Guarducci, *Pietro in Vaticano*. The following
pages on the excavations depend heavily on J. Toynbee and J. Ward Perkins, *The Shrine
of St Peter and the Vatican Excavations* (London, 1956).

These excavations were the result of accident rather than design, stemming from the desire of Pope Pius XI (1922–1939) to be buried next to Pope Pius X (1903–1914) in the grottoes immediately below the present basilica. Only thirty-six hours before the funeral workmen preparing space for the crypt came across a small vaulted chamber not marked on Renaissance plans. It was this discovery in 1939 which prompted the new pope, Pius XII (1939–1958), to sanction full-scale excavations beneath the basilica.

These excavations revealed that the area of the Vatican Hill on which the trophy had been built had long been used for burials, certainly by pagans and possibly also by Christians. The trophy itself, dated by archaeological evidence to c.150–170,[38] was set into the eastern side of a so-called 'Red Wall'[39] and faced onto an open courtyard. It consisted of three niches, one of which was below ground level and certainly of a later date than the foundations of the Red Wall into which it was cut. The other two were above ground level, contemporary with the wall and recessed into it. The lower of these two niches was narrower and separated from the one above it by a travertine slab, which projected about one metre forward from the wall. This slab was supported by a pair of marble colonettes, which themselves rested upon a second travertine slab, which projected from the Red Wall on a level with the floor of the courtyard. A further discovery was made below ground level, beneath this second travertine slab, corresponding approximately with the centre of the trophy. A small, empty, rectangular space was uncovered and below this an accumulation of earth containing a wide variety of coins, some dating from as late as the fourteenth century. Thus although the building of the trophy had covered over this space, some kind of grating must have been in place to enable such votive offerings to be made. Nor was this the end of the excavators' finds. A narrow recess was discovered at the base of the foundations of the Red Wall. At the back of this recess a number of reburied bones were found, which were certainly human.

Were these the bones of St Peter himself and did the trophy mark the actual place of his burial? Unfortunately, these are questions to which there can be no conclusive answers. It might be asked whether the body of St Peter, or even that of St Paul, would ever have been recovered after execution or whether the preservation of bodily relics would have been important as early

---

[38] The Liber Pontificalis (vol. 1, p. 125) attributes the construction of a memorial to St Peter to Pope Aneclitus at the end of the first century. The excavations, however, produced no evidence of a memorial as early as this. It is perhaps possible, therefore, that there is a confusion in the Liber Pontificalis between Pope Aneclitus and the later Pope Anicetus, whose pontificate is traditionally dated to c.155–65, which would accord well with the archaeological evidence. See Toynbee and Ward Perkins, Shrine of St Peter, p. 155. On the trophy, see Esplorazioni, vol. 1, pp. 119–144; Toynbee and Ward Perkins, Shrine of St Peter, pp. 135–167.

[39] It was called the 'Red Wall' because it had been covered in plaster which had then been painted bright red.

as the first century AD.[40] A further puzzle is provided by several layers of graffiti.[41] These had been cut into the north face of a buttressing wall, built to support the Red Wall, which had developed a serious crack not long after its construction. The graffiti, probably dating from the late third century, take the form of prayers and invocations and are all in Latin with the exception of one in Greek. This had been cut into the plaster of the Red Wall itself and was probably earlier than the rest. It is also the only one to mention the apostle by name. This is in striking contrast to the graffiti below the church of San Sebastiano on the Via Appia, where both Saints Peter and Paul were thought to have received temporary burial, possibly immediately after their martyrdom,[42] and where both apostles are persistently invoked by name. Again there can be no satisfactory explanation of this problem but the existence of the graffiti on the buttressing wall does indicate that the trophy was considered an important object of veneration.

What is more important than whether or not this particular site on the Vatican Hill was actually the burial place of St Peter is that by the early fourth century this is precisely what was believed. Eusebius's own interpretation of Gaius's observations concerning the trophies of the two apostles makes this clear. Indeed for him there seems to have been no doubt that Gaius was referring to the very places 'where the sacred relics of the apostles are deposited'.[43]

That the trophy on the Vatican Hill was widely believed to mark the place where St Peter's relics had been buried is also indicated by the decision of the Emperor Constantine (306–337) to build a large basilica dedicated to the saint, over 85 metres long complete with nave and double aisles, on the site of the Vatican Hill.[44] Most significant of all was the fact that the basilica was designed and built in such a way as to ensure that the trophy itself stood up above floor level and was positioned in the very chord of the apse. The construction of this basilica around the trophy was certainly a massive undertaking, which involved the cutting back of the south-eastern slope of the hill and the creation of an enormous platform to provide a flat surface for the floor of the church. The creation of this platform alone involved the dump-

---

40 Toynbee and Ward Perkins, Shrine of St Peter, pp. 155–56.
41 On the graffiti, see Esplorazioni, vol. 1, pp. 129–132; Toynbee and Ward Perkins, Shrine of St Peter, pp. 162–182; Maccarrone, 'Pellegrinaggio', pp. 370–378; Guarducci, Pietro in Vaticano, pp. 68–77.
42 This belief was certainly current in the sixth century. See Gregory the Great's letter of 594 to the Empress Constantina. Gregory the Great, Regestri Epistolarum, PL 77, col. 703. For a discussion of the cult centre on the Via Appia, see Toynbee and Ward Perkins, Shrine of St Peter, pp. 167–182; H. Chadwick, 'St Peter and St Paul in Rome: the Problem of the Memoria Apostolorum ad Catacumbas', Journal of Theological Studies, 8 (1957), pp. 31–52.
43 Eusebius, Ecclesiastical History, vol. 1, pp. 182–183.
44 On the Constantinian basilica, see Esplorazioni, vol. 1, pp. 147–172; Toynbee and Ward Perkins, Shrine of St Peter, pp. 195–239.

ing of more than a million cubic feet of earth, which completely engulfed much of the Vatican cemetery.[45] Only the desire to venerate a very special site could have led to the undertaking of such a highly complex building project.

The significance of this building work at S. Pietro becomes all the more apparent if it is compared with some of the other building campaigns carried out during the reign of Constantine. The tombs of St Agnes and St Lawrence were both buried deep within catacombs. Instead of trying to dig out the catacombs to incorporate the tombs within their own churches,[46] Constantine's architects simply built *martyria*, free-standing halls, close to the site of each catacomb.[47] That these early fourth-century builders were prepared to undertake a project on the Vatican Hill which incorporated the *trophy* of St Peter within the basilica itself, must surely be an indication of the importance placed upon this particular site.

The appearance of the *trophy* in its new setting can be pieced together from various sources, including surviving remains,[48] a fifth-century ivory reliquary discovered early this century at Samagher near Pola in Istria,[49] the *Liber Pontificalis*[50] and the description of Gregory of Tours.[51] A platform, about 9 metres square, raised slightly above the level of the rest of the church, was constructed around the *trophy*. This projected into the transept and was enclosed by a low railing. The *trophy* and platform were covered by a canopy which was supported by four marble columns. These were arranged in such a way that to the right and left of the rear columns, two more were placed, thus forming a continuous screen between the apse and transept. The *Liber Pontificalis* states that these columns were brought from Greece.[52] Not only are they clearly visible on the Pola casket, they are still extant in the present S. Pietro, reused by Bernini (1598–1680) to embellish the galleries of Saints Helena, Veronica and Andrew. Twisted like sticks of barley sugar, they stand nearly five metres high, decorated with finely carved foliage in which little *putti* play. The Pola casket also shows clearly that a lamp hung directly from the centre of the canopy and was perhaps that described in the *Liber*

---

[45] *Ibid.*, p. 197.

[46] Such projects were undertaken in the following centuries. See chapter four.

[47] *Liber Pontificalis*, vol. 1, pp. 180–182.

[48] *Esplorazioni*, vol. 1, pp. 161–172; Toynbee and Ward Perkins, *Shrine of St Peter*, pp. 195–211.

[49] T. Buddenseig, 'Le Coffret en ivorie de Pola. Saint Pierre et le Lateran', *Cahiers Archéologique*, 19 (1959), pp. 157–195; A. Angliolini, *La Capsella Eburnea di Pola* (Bologna, 1970); M. Guarducci, *La Capsella Eburnea di Samagher, Atti e Memorie della Società Istriana di Archeologia e Storia Patria*, n.s. vol. 26 (Trieste, 1978).

[50] *Liber Pontificalis*, vol. 1, pp. 176–178.

[51] Gregory of Tours, *Miraculorum Libri Duo*, PL 71, cols. 705–828, esp. cols. 728–729.

[52] *Liber Pontificalis*, vol. 1, p. 176. J. B. Ward Perkins, 'The Shrine of St Peter and its Twelve Spiral Columns', *JRS*, 42 (1952), pp. 21–33.

Pontificalis, which was made of gold and set with fifty dolphins (lights).[53] The design on the casket also reveals that both niches of the *trophy* which had been recessed into the Red Wall were above floor level in the fourth-century basilica and that a crucifix was placed on the travertine slab which divided them. The casket also suggests that doors were placed across the lower of these two niches. This accords well with the evidence of Gregory of Tours. He describes the shrine as seen by his deacon, Agiulf, probably in 590 before the death of Pelagius II.[54]

> Whosoever wishes to pray, for him the doors that give access to the place are unbolted and he enters the precinct over the tomb and a small window is opened and placing his head within he asks for whatever he requires'[55]

Gregory of Tours's description reveals another practice of those pilgrims who were sufficiently privileged to be given access to the central precinct. They would lower, he writes, strips of cloth, or *brandea*, down onto the tomb itself. These would be noticeably heavier when removed, having absorbed some of the goodness of the Saint.[56]

Gregory of Tours's account is, however, not without its problems. In particular it notes that the tomb was beneath the altar.[57] There is some dispute about what this actually means, as it is specifically stated in the *Liber Pontificalis* that it was Gregory the Great (590–604) who enabled mass to be celebrated directly over St Peter's body.[58] Ruysschaert has suggested that the travertine slab between the two niches may have served as the altar of the Constantinian shrine.[59] Toynbee and Ward Perkins favour a less literal interpretation of the description of Gregory of Tours, suggesting that a moveable altar stood somewhere in the central precinct beneath the canopy.[60] A third explanation, perhaps the least likely, may be that the sixth-century alterations to the tomb had already been carried out by the time that Agiulf left

---

[53] *Liber Pontificalis*, vol. 1, p. 176. See *Book of Pontiffs*, p. 115.

[54] On the date of Agiulf's visit to Rome, see J. Ruysschaert, 'Réflexions sur les Fouilles Vaticanes', *Revue d'Histoire Ecclésiastique*, 48 (1953), pp. 573–631 and 49 (1954), pp. 5–58, esp. p. 41.

[55] This text is translated in Toynbee and Ward Perkins, *Shrine of St Peter*, pp. 212–213. For the Latin text *PL* 71, cols. 728–729: 'Sed qui orare desiderat, reseratis cancellis quibus locus ille ambitur, accedit super sepulchrum; et sic fenestella parvula patefacta, immisso introsum capite, quae necessitas prout efflagitat.'

[56] *Ibid.*, col. 729.

[57] Gregory of Tours, *Miraculorum Libri Duo*, col. 728: 'Hoc enim sepulchrum sub altari collocatum valde rarum habetur.'

[58] *Liber Pontificalis*, vol. 1, p. 312.

[59] Ruysschaert, 'Réflexions sur les Fouilles Vaticanes', pp. 46–47. If this explanation is accepted then it must be noted that the *Liber Pontificalis* ignores the fact that mass could already be celebrated directly over St Peter's body.

[60] Toynbee and Ward Perkins, *Shrine of St Peter*, p. 213.

Rome in 590 and were thus anterior to the pontificate of Gregory the Great. This argument is examined in the *Corpus Basilicarum Christianorum Romae*.[61] Here it is noted that whilst it is impossible to date the alterations conclusively, the absence of any mention of an annular crypt in the description of Gregory of Tours must be significant. Indeed, it is surely unlikely that Agiulf would have failed to notice such a feature had it already existed and there seems no reason why Gregory of Tours should omit to mention it in such a detailed description of the tomb area. Moreover, Gregory of Tours's description accords with other evidence for the appearance of the Constantinian shrine and nothing in his account suggests that major changes had already been carried out before Gregory the Great was elected pope in September 590.

The remodelling of the shrine area, which probably took place during the pontificate of Gregory the Great, was certainly so extensive that it destroyed almost all trace of the Constantinian shrine. The purpose seems to have been two-fold: the placing of the altar directly over the tomb, thus satisfying the growing emphasis upon the close association of altar and relic which had developed during the fifth and sixth centuries and the installation of an annular crypt.[62] Initially the floor of the Constantinian apse was raised about 1.5 metres above that of the nave forming a new presbytery. To allow for two flights of steps which would give access to this presbytery, the platform had to be extended six metres forward into the transept, which destroyed almost all trace of the Constantinian shrine. This new platform also completely covered over the *trophy* itself, apart from the lower half of its eastern face which was left exposed. The upper half of the *trophy* was incorporated into the altar which was now set directly over the tomb in the chord of the apse. The columns which had supported the Constantinian canopy and those which had formed the screen between apse and transept were dismantled and reused to form a screen dividing the shrine area from the rest of the church. At the same time, a semi-circular passage was hollowed out below ground around the back of the shrine, following the curve of the apse. From the apex of this passage another was dug out which led to the *trophy* itself. To allow for head-room, the floor of the crypt was sunk over half a metre below the floor of the original Constantinian church. Steps were then placed at each end of the semi-circular passage to allow access to the crypt.

The installation of the annular crypt was a vital step in the development of Rome as a pilgrimage centre. Gregory of Tours's account suggests that only a very few privileged visitors would have been allowed into the inner precinct to pray at the Constantinian shrine. The creation of an annular crypt

---

[61] R. Krautheimer, S. Corbett and W. Frankl, *Corpus Basilicarum Christianarum Romae*, 5 vols. (Città del Vaticano, 1937–1977) [cited as *Corpus*], vol. 5, p. 278.

[62] *Esplorazioni*, vol. 1, pp. 173–188; Toynbee and Ward Perkins, *Shrine of St Peter*, pp. 211–221; Krautheimer, *Rome*, pp. 85–87.

meant that for the first time large numbers of pilgrims could gain access.[63] Its design ensured that they approached the shrine in an orderly fashion and prevented the build-up of unruly crowds which might cause damage. The pilgrim would enter the crypt via the steps at one end. He would proceed around the passage until he was level with the corridor which led to the *trophy* itself. He would probably pause at the head of this corridor to offer his prayers, before moving on to leave the crypt via the steps at the other side.

St Paul

Like St Peter, the Apostle Paul was also martyred in Rome during the reign of the Emperor Nero. As apostle to the Gentiles, he had undertaken several missionary journeys, the first to Cyprus and Asia Minor in c.47–49,[64] the second to Macedonia in c.50–52[65] and the third to Ephesus, Macedonia and Achaia in c.53–58.[66] On his return to Jerusalem after this third journey, the Jews of the city stirred up a riot against him and, as a Roman citizen, he was taken into custody for his own protection. As Jewish hostility increased, Paul was moved to Caesarea, where he was held for two years, probably 58–60. The Jews sought to have him tried in Jerusalem but Paul exercised his rights as a Roman citizen and appealed to Caesar. He was sent to Rome but was shipwrecked on Malta, where he remained for three months.[67] Eventually arriving in Rome, he was held there for two years but seems to have been able to rent his own house, receive visitors and to preach the Gospel. The tradition of the Early Church supposes that Paul was tried in Rome but set free, continuing thereafter with his missionary work perhaps in Spain and possibly also in the East.[68] Once again, however, he was arrested, imprisoned in Rome and finally beheaded c.67, probably somewhere on the Ostian Way.

While we do not know whether or not the *trophy* on the Ostian Way, as seen by Gaius, was the true place of burial of St Paul, the interpretation of Gaius's words in Eusebius's *Ecclesiastical History* indicates that this belief was current by the early fourth century. For this reason too, as in the case of the building work on the Vatican Hill, a church dedicated to St Paul was built over the *trophy* at this time. The *Liber Pontificalis* records that, in the early

63 Annular crypts modelled on that at S. Pietro were soon built in other churches. See chapter four.
64 Acts 13.1 – 14.28.
65 Acts 15.36 – 18.22.
66 Acts 18.23; 19.1–40. For maps showing St Paul's journeys, see *Oxford Illustrated History of Christianity*, ed. J. McManners (Oxford, 1990), pp. 24–25, and also *Atlas of the Christian Church*, pp. 16–17.
67 Acts 27.
68 See for example Clement's *First Epistle to the Corinthians*, in *Early Christian Writings*, p. 25, where it is suggested that St Paul taught at 'the furthest limits of the West', probably a reference to Spain.

fourth century, the Emperor Constantine, on the advice of Pope Silvester (314–335), built a church on the Ostian Way dedicated to St Paul.[69] According to the Liber Pontificalis, Constantine placed there sacred vessels of gold, silver and bronze and endowed the new basilica with many properties.[70] The authenticity of this entry in the Liber Pontificalis, however, has been questioned. Raymond Davis suggests that it may well have been a later interpolation,[71] an argument also favoured by Krautheimer, who suggests that Constantine's construction on the Ostian Way was not a grand basilica at all but merely a small church.[72]

While both Davis and Krautheimer are suspicious about problems and inconsistencies in the text of the Liber Pontificalis which relate to Constantine's patronage at S. Paolo, there are also other reasons for their doubts. The site where St Paul was thought to have been buried seems to have lain on the edge of the main road to Ostia but also close to a side road which led to the Tiber. Such was the position of these two roads that only a small space between them would have been free for the building of a church. That Constantine did not order the moving of the side road to enable the construction of a large basilica is apparent from other evidence. The first is a rescript dating from c.384, from the ruling emperors, Valentinian II, Theodosius I and Arcadius to the prefect of the city, Sallustius.[73] In this the emperors declared their intention to enlarge the existing church of S. Paolo in view of the long-standing veneration attached to the site and because of the growing crowds, an indication perhaps that the existing church was already too small.[74] The rescript also stated that if the church was to be rebuilt on a large scale, the old road at the back of the existing church would have to be relocated.[75] The contents of this fourth-century rescript are confirmed by archaeological evidence. Excavations carried out after the great fire at S. Paolo in 1823 managed to locate the old road behind the Constantinian apse.[76] On this evidence, it seems likely that Constantine only had a small church built on the Ostian Way, certainly not on the scale of the large basilica constructed on the Vatican Hill and that it was not until the end of the fourth century that a sizeable church dedicated to St Paul was

---

69 Liber Pontificalis, vol. 1, pp. 178–179.
70 Ibid., vol. 1, pp. 178–179.
71 Davis, Value of the Liber Pontificalis, pp. 229–232, and also Book of Pontiffs, p. xxii.
72 Corpus, vol. 5, p. 97.
73 Epistulae Imperatorum Pontificum Aliorum Inde ab Anno CCCLXVII usque ad Annum DLIII Datae, ed. O. Guenther, Corpus Scriptorum Ecclesiasticorum Latinorum, 35 (Vienna, 1895), Ep. 3, pp. 46–47. For a dispute concerning the excessive cost of rebuilding this basilica, see Prefect and Emperor. The Relationes of Symmachus A.D. 384, ed. and trans. R. H. Barrow (Oxford, 1973), esp. pp. 140–141.
74 Ibid., Ep. 3, p. 46. Krautheimer (Rome, p. 42) suggests that the initiative for the rebuilding probably came from Pope Damasus (366–384).
75 Ibid., Ep. 3, p. 47.
76 Kirschbaum, Tombs of St Peter and St Paul, pp. 165–194.

constructed. It is also likely, therefore, that the entry in the *Liber Pontificalis* concerning Constantine's building work at S. Paolo, was added at a later date in an attempt to show that the large basilica there, like the Lateran,[77] S. Pietro,[78] S. Lorenzo *fuori le mura*,[79] SS. Marcellino e Pietro,[80] S. Agnese[81] and S. Croce,[82] also owed its venerable construction and subsequent embellishment to the patronage of Constantine.

While both Saints Paul and Peter had been honoured with similar *trophies* before the end of the second century, in the early fourth century, although Constantine commissioned a large basilica dedicated to St Peter, his building work on the Ostian Way was almost certainly on a much less lavish scale. To Constantine, St Peter, keeper of the keys to heaven and fountainhead of the Apostolic Succession, seems to have been rather more important than his fellow apostle Paul. It was not until the end of the fourth century that St Paul's popularity had grown sufficiently for the building of a large church dedicated to him. Krautheimer attributes this to the fact that by this time the Christian Church was led by intellectuals. They recognised St Paul as apostle to the Gentiles, as philosopher, as teacher of the heathen and thus as the champion in their fight against the pagans who still remained in the ranks of the Roman aristocracy.[83]

The continuing importance of St Paul is further reflected by the building campaigns and the gifts which continued to be given to this basilica on the Ostian Way during the fifth and sixth centuries. During the pontificate of Sixtus III (432–440), the Emperor Valentinian III (425–455) decorated the *confessio* with silver weighing 200lb.[84] Repair work was carried out during the pontificate of Leo I (440–461) after the basilica had been partially destroyed by 'divine fire'.[85] Gifts were made during the pontificate of Hilarus (461–468),[86] while Pope Symmachus (498–514) had the apse renewed when it was in danger of collapse.[87] Here too he had a *matroneum* built[88] and an apse-vault and provided a picture to decorate the area behind the *confessio*, while over it he had placed a silver image of the Saviour and the twelve apostles

---

77 *Liber Pontificalis*, vol. 1, pp. 172–175.
78 *Ibid.*, vol. 1, pp. 176–178.
79 *Ibid.*, vol. 1, pp. 181–182.
80 *Ibid.*, vol. 1, pp. 182–183.
81 *Ibid.*, vol. 1, pp. 180–181.
82 *Ibid.*, vol. 1, pp. 179–180.
83 Krautheimer, *Rome*, p. 42.
84 *Liber Pontificalis*, vol. 1, p. 233. The *confessio* was the name given to the area in front of an altar above a martyr's tomb. Also on Sixtus III, see R. Krautheimer, 'The Architecture of Sixtus III: A Fifth-Century Renascence', *De Artibus Opuscula XL. Essays in Honor of Erwin Panofsky*, ed. M. Meiss, 2 vols. (New York, 1961), vol. 1, pp. 291–302.
85 *Liber Pontificalis*, vol. 1. p. 239.
86 *Ibid.*, vol. 1, p. 244.
87 *Ibid.*, vol. 1, p. 262.
88 This was a part of the church constructed for the use of women.

weighing 120 pounds.[89] According to the *Liber Pontificalis* other rich gifts to the basilica were made during the pontificates of Hormisdas (514–523)[90] and John I (523–526).[91]

Archaeological investigations carried out at S. Paolo found traces of the extensive repairs carried out during the pontificate of Leo I but work carried out on the instructions of Pope Symmachus could no longer be identified. In fact the next major remodelling after that of Leo I which could be clearly detected had involved the transept, shrine and altar. During an extensive building campaign the floor of the transept had been raised 90 centimetres above that of both nave and aisles. Five steps then had to be installed to give access to the newly raised transept. With this rise in floor level, the *trophy* of St Paul was now buried with only 10 centimetres emerging above the new floor, over which the High Altar was placed. A crypt was then also constructed adjoining the back of the buried *trophy*.[92]

But when had the building campaign taken place? It seems likely that work at S. Pietro, which had involved the remodelling of the Constantinian shrine, had been carried out during the pontificate of Gregory the Great.[93] Surviving evidence suggests that it is probably also to his pontificate that this very similar campaign at S. Paolo should be ascribed. In the *Liber Pontificalis* it is stated that it was Gregory the Great who enabled mass to be said over the body of St Peter. Here too it is recorded that this Pope also enabled mass to be said directly over the body of St Paul.[94] Furthermore, in a letter of 594 addressed to Constantina, wife of the Byzantine Emperor Maurice (582–602), Gregory expressed his desire to make improvements to the shrine of St Paul and indicated that to this end some excavation work had already been carried out.[95]

At both S. Pietro and S. Paolo, therefore, Gregory I seems to have carried out similar building campaigns. These enabled the celebration of mass directly over what were believed to be the graves of the two apostles and, most importantly, allowed improved access for the crowds of pilgrims to their shrines. These projects may have been undertaken in response to the large crowds already being drawn to Rome as the cult of saints grew in popularity. They may also have been prompted in part, however, by anticipation and expectation of the even greater numbers of pilgrims, who could be expected to begin making the journey *ad limina apostolorum*, as a result of the initiation

---

[89] *Liber Pontificalis*, vol. 1, p. 262.

[90] *Ibid.*, vol. 1, pp. 271–272.

[91] *Ibid.*, vol. 1, p. 276.

[92] *Corpus*, vol. 5, pp. 162–63.

[93] See above.

[94] *Liber Pontificalis*, vol. 1, p. 312: 'Hic fecit ut super corpus beati Petri missas celebrarentur; item et in ecclesiam beati Pauli apostoli eadem fecit.'

[95] Gregory the Great, *Regestri Epistolarum*, col. 701.

of one of Gregory I's most important policies, that which has been termed his 'missionary strategy'.[96] It was surely fitting that Gregory the Great in particular should have been anxious to carry out similar building campaigns at both S. Pietro and S. Paolo, honouring the two apostles equally. St Peter may have been the first bishop of Rome and the keeper of the keys to heaven but it was St Paul, the apostle to the Gentiles, who had been the missionary, the preacher of the Christian faith, the apostle upon whose work in particular Gregory the Great saw himself building, as he set about converting northern Europe to Christianity.

[96] R. A. Markus, 'Gregory the Great and Missionary Strategy', SCH, 6 (1970), pp. 29–38.

2

The Journey to Rome

The building work of Gregory the Great at both S. Pietro and S. Paolo, whilst undoubtedly intended to provide better access to the tombs of these saints for the many pilgrims already travelling there, may also have been carried out in anticipation of the even larger crowds which might be expected as a result of his 'missionary strategy'.[1] Gregory's judgment was certainly correct, for as Christianity spread through the successor states of northern Europe, so pilgrims began travelling to Rome in ever-increasing numbers. This flow of pilgrims was also fuelled by the rapidity of the Muslim advance through the Near East in the seventh century, which made pilgrimage to the Holy Land increasingly difficult.[2] If pilgrims were unable to follow in the footsteps of Christ himself, then at least in Rome they would find two of his apostles.

The purpose of this chapter is to consider the journey to Rome.[3] Beginning with an analysis of what motivated pilgrims to set out on such a journey, this chapter then presents an account of the main routes used by these *Romipetae*, mainly through close examination of surviving itineraries. Focusing in particular upon the twelfth century, consideration will also be given to the places that they may have visited *en route* and to more practical matters,

---

[1] On the conversion of Northern Europe to Christianity, see R. E. Sullivan, 'The Papacy and Missionary Activity in the Early Middle Ages', *Medieval Studies*, 17 (1955), pp. 46–106; Markus, 'Gregory the Great and Missionary Strategy', pp. 29–38; J. Richards, *Consul of God. The Life and Times of Gregory the Great* (London and Boston, 1980), pp. 228–250; E. Demougeot, 'Grégoire le Grand et la Conversion du Roi Germain au VIe Siècle', *Grégoire le Grand, Colloques Internationaux du Centre de la Recherche Scientifique, Chantilly 15–19 Sept. 1982* (Paris, 1986), pp. 191–203.

[2] R. Collins, *Early Medieval Europe* (London, 1991), pp. 127–143.

[3] There is a wide range of literature on medieval travel. See for example, N. Ohler, *The Medieval Traveller*, trans. C. Hillier (Woodbridge, 1989); M. Rowling, *Everyday Life of Medieval Travellers* (New York, 1971); J. J. Jusserand, *English Wayfaring Life in the Middle Ages*, trans. L. T. Smith, 4th ed. (London, 1950); Parks, *English Traveller to Italy*; E. Cohen, 'Roads and Pilgrimage: A Study in Economic Interaction', *Studi Medievali*, 3rd Series, 21 (1980), pp. 321–341; A. A. Settia, 'Strade e Pellegrini nell'Oltrepo pavese: Una Via *Romea* dimenticata', *Annali di Storia Pavese*, 16–17 (1988), pp. 79–89. I would like to thank Dr Frances Andrews for this reference.

such as the best time of year to set out on pilgrimage to Rome and the length of the journey. Other issues discussed in this chapter include the types of accommodation which the pilgrim might have found along the way, the expense which a pilgrimage to Rome might have entailed and the dangers involved in undertaking such a journey.

Motivation

Before considering the actual journey itself, an analysis should be made of the motivation which led pilgrims to set out on a journey to Rome in the first place. Some pilgrims may have travelled to the apostolic city for the same reason that they travelled to many other holy places, in the hope of a cure for some disease or ailment. A charter of 1063 in the cartulary of St Trinité de Rouen records the pilgrimage that Germund and his wife, Bersenta, were intending to make to Rome. They were undertaking the journey, the charter notes, because they were unable to have children.[4] Some places in Rome were certainly associated with healing. There were riots in the city in the ninth century, when it was rumoured that Bishop Hatto of Freising intended to remove the body of Pope Alexander I, for his tomb was a place where people were accustomed to seek healing.[5] The church of SS. Cosma e Damiano was another *locus* which had long attracted the sick and suffering, for this church had been built on the site of a temple of Castor and Pollux which had been a pagan healing place.[6]

There is no evidence, however, that the majority of pilgrims who travelled to Rome did so in the hope of miracle cures for diseases or ailments. There are no miracle books associated with either the tomb of St Peter or with that of St Paul, nor is there any evidence that their tombs were places where cures were granted. Indeed, according to the *Chronicle* of Monte Cassino, an Englishman, both deaf and dumb, who travelled *ad limina apostolorum* c.787 in the hope of a cure, was eventually healed by St Benedict at Monte Cassino.[7] Rather Benedicta Ward has suggested that pilgrims undertaking the journey to Rome probably did so because they would have known through the *Acts of the Apostles* of the miracles which St Peter had already performed and which were evidence of his divinely given powers, in particular his power, as the door-keeper of heaven, to absolve from sin.[8] They travelled to Rome, she has argued, because there, at the tombs of the apostles, pilgrims believed that they would receive absolution from their sins and the assurance of safe

---

4 Rouen, p. 452. I would like to thank Professor Jonathan Riley-Smith for this reference.
5 *Translatio Sanctorum Alexandri Papae et Iustini Presbyteri*, MGH.SS 15, pp. 286–288.
6 See Ward, *Miracles and the Medieval Mind*, p. 118.
7 *Chronicon Monasterii Casinensis*, MGH.SS 7, p. 590. This may of course have just been good propaganda for Monte Cassino.
8 Ward, *Miracles and the Medieval Mind*, pp. 117–120.

conduct into heaven. These were certainly the very sentiments expressed in Alcuin's *Life of St Willibald*:

> The city of Rome, the head of the world, rejoices especially in the very glorious triumphs of the apostles, Peter and Paul. Daily the races and people flock to this place with devoted heart so that each by compunction of faith might either weep for their crimes or ask in the hope of a more abundant life in heaven, that entry be granted to them.[9]

Exactly the same sentiments were expressed by Richard, abbot of St Vannes, in a sermon written after his return from Rome in 1026.[10] Cnut, who travelled to Rome in 1027, also justified his pilgrimage in similar terms:

> Wise men have told me that the Apostle Peter has received from God the power of binding and loosing and carries the keys of paradise. I therefore deemed it useful in no ordinary way to seek his patronage before God.[11]

This religious conviction and motivation which lay behind the undertaking of some pilgrimages to Rome is also apparent from a small amount of charter evidence. This demonstrates that some pilgrims knew even before setting out that their journey could be so arduous and dangerous that they might possibly die. As a result we know that a few *Romipetae* made arrangements for the distribution of their property should they fail to return home. In 951, Ralph and his wife, Adalaide, agreed that should one or other of them die in the course of their journey to Rome, their property would then belong to the survivor. If both died, the land was to be left to the monastery of Uzerche.[12] Before setting out for Rome c.1060 Ketel and his step-daughter, Ælfgifu, made similar arrangements. They agreed that whoever lived the longer would inherit the whole of their estate at Onehouse. If both died on their pilgrimage, however, their estate was to pass to the monks of Bury St Edmunds.[13]

---

9   Alcuin, *Vita Willibrordi Archiepiscopi Traiectensis*, MGH *Rerum Merovingicarum*, 7 (1920), p. 139; Parks, *English Traveller to Italy*, p. 77.

10   H. Dauphin, *Le Bienheureux Richard Abbé de Saint-Vanne de Verdun*, *Bibliothèque de la Revue d'Histoire Ecclésiastique*, Fasc. 24 (Louvain and Paris, 1946), p. 379.

11   Florence of Worcester, *Chronicon*, ed. B. Thorpe, 2 vols. (London, 1848–1849), vol. 1, p. 186; William of Malmesbury, *De Gestis Regum Anglorum*, ed. W. Stubbs, 2 vols. RS 90 (London, 1887–1889), vol. 1, pp. 221–222; Ward, *Miracles and the Medieval Mind*, p. 124.

12   Uzerche, no. 120.

13   *Anglo-Saxon Wills*, ed. and trans. D. Whitelock (Cambridge, 1930), no. xxxiv. Fears for their safety were not only limited to pilgrims travelling to Rome. For similar arrangements made by those travelling to Jerusalem, see for example Saint Cugat del Vallés, vol. 3, no. 821; Montpellier, no. 103; Tulle et Rocamadour, no. 28; Cluny, vol. 5, no. 4145. Similar arrangements were also made by William Stephani before his departure to Spain. See Aniane, no. 138. See also *Codice Diplomatico Bares. Le Carte di Molfetta*, ed. F. Carabellese (Bari, 1912), no. 17, for a prospective pilgrim to Compostela who made a will at Molfetta in March 1148 before setting out. I am grateful to Professor Donald Matthew for this reference.

These pilgrims seem to have believed, therefore, that the reward to be gained from a pilgrimage to Rome was worth the risk of hardship and even death.[14]

Itineraries

Having determined to undertake the journey to Rome, the pilgrim had to get there. In the Middle Ages those individuals who had made the journey to Rome and returned, must have been a vital source of information about the routes, roads and conditions to be expected along the way. Such information might be passed on by them verbally. A considerable oral tradition is possible in many places – monasteries, royal courts, ports and major cities – but evidence for it is extremely hard to discover. That there was also a written tradition is suggested by the itineraries which survive. Indeed, the writing of such itineraries may well have had a serious intention. Whilst they served as a record of the achievements of a particular individual, it is likely that they were not written primarily with this purpose in mind but as a vital source of information for others who intended to make a similar journey.

Several itineraries survive from the medieval period which detail the various routes to Rome. The earliest and perhaps the best known is that of Sigeric, archbishop of Canterbury, who set out for the city c.990 to collect his pallium from Pope John XV. A list survives of the seventy-nine stages of his return journey as far as the English Channel.[15] Three itineraries date from the twelfth century. Nikolas, who in 1155 became first abbot of the Benedictine house of Munkathvera in Iceland, travelled to Rome c.1150 and then on to the Holy Land. A detailed account of the stages of his journey are extant, all taken down at his own dictation.[16] We also have the itinerary of Benjamin, a rabbi from Tudela in Spain, who arrived in Rome c.1160.[17] His account is particularly useful for the information which it gives of the route from Spain to Rome. Also of interest is the itinerary of Philip Augustus as recorded in a draft of the *Chronicle* of Roger of Howden, wrongly attributed to Benedict of Peterborough.[18] Returning from the Holy Land, Philip arrived at Otranto in October 1191 and whilst making his way back to his own kingdom, stopped at Rome where Pope Celestine III showed him some of the city's most prized relics.[19]

---

[14] There is perhaps a parallel here with many crusaders, who willingly departed on a journey on which they knew they would face hardships and dangers. See J. S. C. Riley-Smith, *What were the Crusades?* (London, 1977), esp. pp. 63–65.

[15] *Memorials of Saint Dunstan*, pp. 392–395.

[16] Werlauff, *Symbolae ad Geographiam Medii Aevi*, pp. 15–22; Magoun, 'Pilgrim Diary', pp 314–354; O. Springer, 'Mediaeval Pilgrim Routes from Scandinavia to Rome', *Medieval Studies*, 12 (1950), pp. 92–122.

[17] *Early Travels in Palestine*, pp. 63–126.

[18] See above pp. 8–9.

[19] Benedict of Peterborough, *Chronicle*, vol. 2, pp. 227–230.

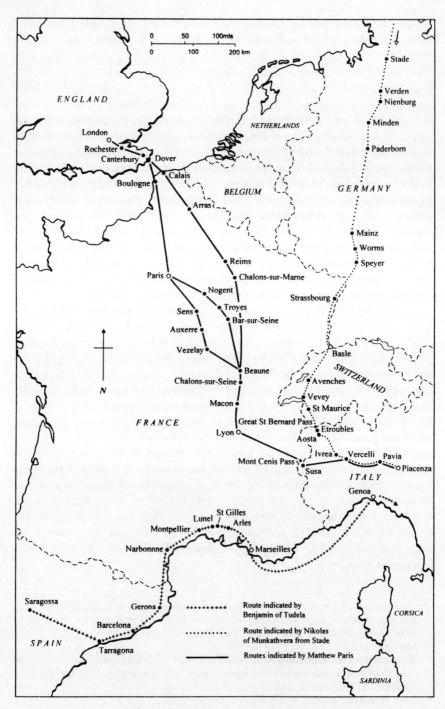

Pilgrimage routes to northern Italy

A number of thirteenth-century itineraries survive. We have those written by Wolfger, bishop of Passau and patriarch of Aquilea, a frequent traveller across the Alps, who went to Rome in 1204 and again in 1208[20] and that of Emo, abbot of the Premonstratensian Monastery of Verum, who made the journey from Frisia to Rome in 1211.[21] Also extant is the itinerary incorporated into the *Annales* of Albert of Stade, which takes the form of a fictitious dialogue in which Firri, a traveller, asks his friend Tirri to tell him the best way to get to Rome.[22] We also have the itinerary of Odo, bishop of Rouen, who set out for Rome on 30 December 1253, beginning the return journey in the following July[23] and the detailed itinerary of Matthew Paris. Taking the form of a strip map, to be read from the bottom upwards, Matthew's itinerary shows various routes from London to Rome and beyond to Apulia.[24] Each place name is accompanied by a drawing, usually a building. Whilst these are representational, some variations do occur such as the drawing accompanying Sutri, where a pelican sits astride a roof top,[25] while the Alps are drawn as a swirling mass.[26] In addition we have the itinerary of Giles of Muisis, abbot of the monastery of St Martin of Tournai, who in 1300 went to Rome to be present at the first Jubilee.[27]

The Routes to Rome

These itineraries suggest that there were several major routes to Rome, which did not change greatly from the ninth to the thirteenth centuries.[28] Of these itineraries, one of the latest, that of Matthew Paris, is the most comprehensive guide to the main routes across France. Setting out from London, Matthew Paris's map suggests that the main route passed through Rochester and Canterbury to Dover.[29] Here the pilgrim would have boarded a ship to take him across the Channel. A few references to pilgrims undertaking such voyages survive in our sources. Huneberc of Heidenheim recorded the

---

[20] Zingerle, *Reiserechnungen*, esp. pp. 64–75 for all his journeys over the Alps.

[21] *Emonis Chronicon*, pp. 470–471.

[22] Albert of Stade, *Annales*, pp. 335–340.

[23] Ludwig, *Untersuchungen*, pp. 107–109.

[24] British Library MS Royal 14 c vii, fols. 2r–4r. On these itineraries see Parks, *English Traveller to Italy*, pp. 79–182. See also Lewis, *Art of Matthew Paris in the Chronica Maiora*, pp. 321–376.

[25] *Ibid.*, fol. 4r.

[26] *Ibid.*, fol. 3r.

[27] D'Haenens, 'Gilles li Muisis', pp. 31–48.

[28] In this section I only propose to give a rough outline of the general routes. For itineraries which give a very different route to those of the ninth to thirteenth centuries outlined below, see British Library MS Harley 2321, fols. 118v–121v, of the fifteenth century.

[29] British Library MS Royal 14 c vii, fol. 2r.

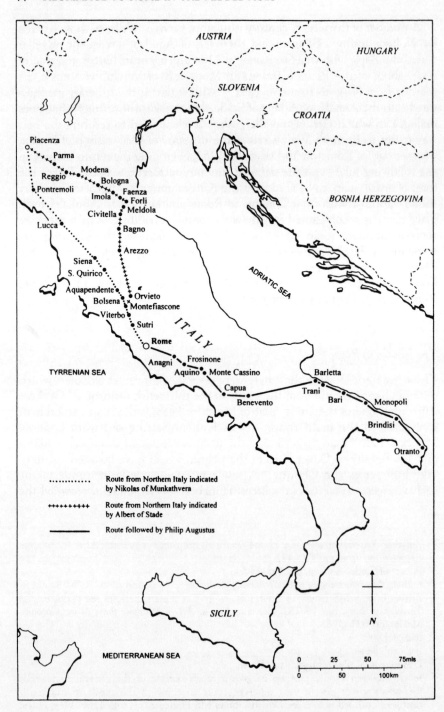

Pilgrimage routes to Rome

pilgrimage of St Willibald, begun probably c.720, in the company of his father and brother. Having paid their fares, they set sail to the noise of shouting sailors and creaking oars.[30] Eadmer, the biographer of St Anselm, archbishop of Canterbury (1093–1109), records the near capsize of their ship whilst sailing from Dover to Wissant,[31] while a reference in the *Pipe Rolls* for the reign of Henry II notes that in 1185 the Master of the Templars crossed the Channel on a boat laden with 'poor pilgrims'.[32]

On the other side of the Channel, Matthew Paris's map indicates three routes, all of which came together at Beaune.[33] One, starting from Boulogne, passed through Paris itself and then took a course via Nogent, Troyes and Bar-sur-Seine. The second, beginning at Calais, took a more easterly passage through Arras, Reims and Châlons-sur-Marne, almost identical to the route which Sigeric had followed in the tenth century. A third route, also starting at Boulogne, passed east of Paris and then turned south via Sens, Auxerre and Vézelay. From Beaune only one route is indicated. This passed through Châlons-sur-Seine, Mâcon and Lyon and over the Alps by the Mont Cenis Pass.[34]

There were other westerly passes over the mountains not mentioned by Matthew. These included the Simplon Pass, which was used by Odo of Rouen in February 1254 on his outward journey to Rome.[35] This Pass, however, does not appear to have been greatly used for much of the medieval period, largely because the approach to it seems to have been both difficult and dangerous.[36] Of much greater importance than the Simplon was the Great St Bernard.[37] Instead of continuing south towards Lyon as Matthew Paris's map indicated, those wishing to cross by the Great St Bernard continued at first a little further east towards Besançon. From here they turned southwards towards Pontarlier and Vevey on the bank of Lake Geneva, from where the road led them directly over this Pass. This route seems to have been popular throughout the medieval period. Sigeric had used it in the tenth century,[38] whilst Giles of Muisis travelled that way at the end of the

---

[30] Huneberc of Heidenheim, *The Hodoeporicon of St Willibald*, in *Anglo-Saxon Missionaries in Germany*, trans. and ed. C. H. Talbot (London, 1954), p. 157. The Latin text can be found in *MGH.SS*, 15, part 1, pp. 80–117.

[31] Eadmer, *The Life of St Anselm Archbishop of Canterbury*, ed. and trans. R. W. Southern (London, 1962), pp. 98–99.

[32] *Pipe Roll 31 Hen. II*, p. 233.

[33] All these routes can be found in British Library MS Royal 14 c vii, fols. 2r–2v. Also see map, p. 42.

[34] See *ibid.*, fol. 3r.

[35] Ludwig, *Untersuchungen*, pp. 107–109.

[36] J. E. Tyler, *The Alpine Passes. The Middle Ages (962–1250)* (Oxford, 1930), pp. 72–73.

[37] *Ibid.*, pp. 68–72.

[38] Sigeric's return route from Rome (*Memorials of St Dunstan*, p. 394) reads Ivrea, Poley, Aosta, S. Rémy, St Peter's Castle, Orsieres, St Maurice, Vervey (?), Vevay, Lausanne, Orbe, Yverdun (?), Pontarlier, Nodz, Besançon.

thirteenth.[39] Its main importance lies in the fact that it was easily accessible from many areas of northern Europe. The international nature of the traffic using this Pass was indicated by Nikolas of Munkathvera. At Vevey, he noted, the roads of the Franks, Flemings, Southern French, English, Saxons and Scandinavians all converge.[40]

Nikolas's itinerary shows that the Great St Bernard Pass was particularly convenient for those travelling to Italy not only from France but also from the Western Empire. The first stage of Nikolas's journey was by sea from Iceland to Norway.[41] From here he travelled across Denmark, although he noted that other Icelanders opted for a route from Norway via Deventer or Utrecht.[42] Leaving Denmark, he travelled to Stade and thence to Verden, Nienburg, Minden, 'where the dialects change', Paderborn and Mainz, also noting another commonly used route to this city, which passed slightly further east through Hildesheim.[43] From Mainz only one road is indicated, that through Worms, Speyer, Strassbourg, Basle, Soleure, Avenches and Vevey.[44]

A less conventional route from Stade to the Alps was recorded in the conversation between Tirri and Firri. In reply to Firri's request that Tirri tell him about the route to Rome, Tirri immediately asked which way he wished to go. To this Firri replied that he wanted to proceed via the Valley of Maurienne, which led the traveller over the Mont Cenis Pass.[45] The route which Tirri then explained went much further west than the way by which Nikolas had travelled. From Stade, Firri was to travel to Bremen and then through Thecklenburg, Münster, Neuss, Maastricht to St Trond. From here he was to journey to Beaufort and then on to Vervins, Neufchâtel, Reims and Châlons-sur-Marne, from where the route was very similar to that proposed by Matthew Paris.[46] Those who chose to follow this route, however, must have done so with a specific reason in mind, for it was longer and further than the route over the Great St Bernard. Tyler has noted that Emo, travelling from Verum in Frisia in 1211, followed a route similar to that suggested by Tirri.[47] It seems, however, that Emo had to travel this way to Rome because he had first to go to the Premonstratensian house of Premontré, where he was given letters for the pope by the abbot Gervase.[48] His return

[39] Giles's more detailed return route from Rome (D'Haenens, 'Gilles li Muisis', pp. 47–48) reads Ivrea, Carema, Châtillon, Nus, Aosta, St Rhémy, Great St Bernard, St Peter's Castle, Martigny, St Maurice, Villeneuve, Lausanne, Cossonay, La Sarraz, Les Clées, Jougné, Pontarlier.
[40] Werlauff, *Symbolae ad Geographiam Medii Aevi*, p. 18.
[41] *Ibid.*, p. 15.
[42] *Ibid.*, p. 17.
[43] *Ibid.*, p. 16. See map, p. 42.
[44] *Ibid.*, pp. 17–18.
[45] Albert of Stade, *Annales*, p. 335.
[46] *Ibid.*, pp. 335–336.
[47] Tyler, *The Alpine Passes*, p. 13.
[48] *Emonis Chronicon*, p. 470.

journey seems to have been more conventional, taking him over the Great St Bernard and home by way of Basle.[49]

As well as the westerly passes over the Alps, there were central and easterly ones, about which, however, there is much less information. The St Gotthard Pass, mentioned in surviving itineraries for the first time by Albert of Stade,[50] is certainly not known to have been regularly used before the thirteenth century. Tyler has argued that it is likely that it had not been opened up before this date. He cites a number of twelfth-century travellers, including Nikolas of Munkathvera, who made detours to cross the Alps by other passes, which the existence of the St Gotthard would have rendered unnecessary.[51] Another route, also briefly mentioned by Albert of Stade, was that over the Septimer Pass, probably one of the most important central passes over the Alps before the opening up of the St Gotthard.[52] Of the easterly passes, that over the Brenner was probably the most important. It was certainly considered by Firri as a viable homeward route and it was also used by Wolfger, bishop of Passau.[53] Lower than many of the other passes across the Alps, the Brenner was free from snow for much of the year. It could be approached along three main roads from the north. The main route, as described by both Albert and Wolfger, started at Augsburg and passed through Schongau, Partenkirchen and Innsbruck.

Once across the Alps, there were several routes which could be followed. Those crossing via the Mont Cenis travelled to Susa and then on to Vercelli.[54] It was at Vercelli that they would probably have met up with their counterparts, who had travelled over the Great St Bernard and thence to this city through Aosta and Ivrea.[55] From Vercelli the general route seems to have been by way of Pavia and Piacenza to Parma.[56] It was in this area that those travelling over the more westerly passes might have encountered those

[49] Ibid., pp. 471–472.

[50] Albert of Stade, Annales, p. 338.

[51] Tyler, The Alpine Passes, pp. 89–97. One of the itineraries from England to Rome contained in British Library MS Harley 2321, fols. 119v–121v, suggests that the use of the St Gotthard Pass may have opened up a new route to Rome, which completely by-passed France. The main route indicated is as follows: Dover, Calais, Gravelines, Dunkirk, Bruges, Ghent, Dendermonde, Malines, Diest, Bilsen, Maastricht, Aix-la-Chapelle, Cologne, Bonn, Rheinbach, Andernach, Coblenz, Bingen, Worms, Spires, Lauterberg, Hagenau, Strassburg, Basle, Luzern, an unnamed hospital, Chapel of St Gotthard, Bellinzona, Lugano, Como, Milan. See also Hulbert, 'Some Medieval Advertisements of Ancient Rome', pp. 403–424.

[52] Albert of Stade, Annales, p. 340. See also Tyler, The Alpine Passes, pp. 105–110.

[53] Albert of Stade, Annales, p. 339. See also Zingerle, Reiserechnungen, pp. 64–75.

[54] British Library MS Royal 14 c vii, fol. 3v; Emonis Chronicon, p. 471; Albert of Stade, Annales, p. 337.

[55] For example, Memorials of Saint Dunstan, p. 394; D'Haenens,'Gilles li Muisis', p. 47.

[56] British Library MS Royal 14 c vii, fol. 3v. Compare, for example, with Albert of Stade, Annales, p. 337; D'Haenens, 'Gilles li Muisis', p. 47.

who had journeyed over the more central ones. Indeed, the route proposed by Albert of Stade from the Septimer or St Gotthard Passes guided the traveller to Milan and thence to Piacenza.[57] From here he had to decide whether to take the easterly or westerly route across the Appenines. The former, as indicated by Matthew Paris, passed from Parma to Reggio and then on to Modena and Bologna, where those who had travelled over the more easterly Alpine passes joined the main routes through the Italian peninsula.[58] From Bologna the easterly route traversed Imola, Faenza, Forli and Rieti.[59] The westerly route in Matthew Paris's map is much confused. Nikolas of Munkathvera, however, used this route, making his way from Piacenza to Borgo San Donnino and thence to Pontremoli, Luni, Lucca, Siena, S. Quirico, Aquapendente, Bolsena, Viterbo and Sutri.[60] A second westerly route seems to have been that from Arezzo to Perugia, Assisi, Foligno and Spoleto.[61]

It was also along this western route that those who had come from Spain frequently travelled. In 1160, Rabbi Benjamin of Tudela set out from Saragossa on a journey that was to last thirteen years.[62] While his main interest was in the activities of the Jews in the major cities through which he passed, his account provides an indication of the general route from Spain to Rome. From Saragossa, Benjamin travelled to Tarragona and then on to Barcelona, Gerona, Narbonne and Montpellier.[63] From Montpellier, he travelled to Lunel and thence to Bourg de St Gilles, 'a place of pilgrimage,' he noted, 'visited by the inhabitants of distant countries and islands'.[64] From St Gilles, Benjamin travelled to Arles and thence to Marseilles whence a four day sea voyage brought him to Genoa. From here he travelled to Pisa and Lucca, from where, after a journey lasting six days, he arrived in Rome.[65]

Finally in this consideration of the main routes to Rome, there are also the

---

57 Albert of Stade, *Annales*, p. 340.
58 British Library MS Royal 14 c vii, fols. 3v–4r.
59 Much of Matthew's map is confused beyond Pavia. A clearer indication of the easterly route can be found in the itinerary of Albert of Stade (*Annales*, pp. 337–338) which gives a general route from Parma as follows: Reggio, Modena, Bologna, Imola, Faenza, Forli, Meldola, Civitella, Bagno, Arezzo, Orvieto, Montefiascone, Viterbo, Sutri. See map, p. 44.
60 Werlauff, *Symbolae ad Geographiam Medii Aevi*, p. 20. For clarification of the general route, we might compare the major stopping places of Sigeric (*Memorials of St Dunstan*, pp. 392–394) which read Sutri, Viterbo, Aquapendente, S Quirico, Siena, Lucca, Luni, Pontremoli, Piacenza; or those of Philip Augustus (Magoun, 'Italian Itinerary', p. 369), Sutri, Viterbo, Aquapendente, Radicofani, Siena, Castelfiorentino, Galleno, Lucca, Luni, Sarzana, Pontremoli. See map, p. 44.
61 British Library MS Royal 14 c vii, fol. 4r. This route is found on the extreme right hand edge of the folio, towards the bottom. It consists merely of the place names and no illustrations.
62 *Early Travels in Palestine*, pp. 63–126. See map, p. 42.
63 *Ibid.*, p. 64.
64 *Ibid.*, p. 65.
65 *Ibid.*, p. 66.

roads to and from southern Italy. This route seems to have been utilised by those interested in seeing the pilgrimage sites of the south.[66] It was also from the ports of southern Italy that pilgrims could set sail for the Holy Land. The variety of places where ships could be boarded by those wishing to undertake this journey was indicated by Saewulf, who made a pilgrimage to the Holy Land c.1102. 'Some pilgrims', he remarked, 'embark at Bari, others at Barletta, some at Siponto, or at Trani; while others take ship at Otranto . . . we set sail from Monopoli.'[67]

After his pilgrimage in Rome, Nikolas of Munkathvera himself wished to set out for the Holy Land. Leaving Rome, he first travelled south to Tusculum and then made his way to Aquino, Monte Cassino and Benevento.[68] From there he probably went to Salerno and to Siponto[69] and thence to Barletta, Trani, Melfi and Bari.[70] Nikolas also noted a rather more easterly route which seems to have been regularly used. This passed from Rome in the direction of Capua along Trajan's way. This route then led to Terracina, 'now a small town because the Romans destroyed it',[71] Fondi, Capua and then to Benevento, not far from Monopoli and Brindisi.[72] Philip Augustus, returning home from Jerusalem in 1191, travelled first to Rome, following a route not dissimilar to that followed by Nikolas of Munkathvera, although in reverse. Landing at Otranto, his route led him through Brindisi, Monopoli, Bari, Trani and Barletta.[73] From there he travelled on to Salpi, Benevento, Capua, San Germano and thence to Monte Cassino.[74] His route then led him to Aquino, Frosinone and then out of Sicilian territory where he had to seek permission from the Emperor Henry VI to cross imperial lands.[75] The last stage of the journey to Rome took the French king through Anagni and Montefortino.[76]

A slightly different route through southern Italy is indicated by Rabbi Benjamin of Tudela. On leaving Rome, it was a journey of four days to Capua.[77] From there he went to Pozzuoli, where he noted that, in the sum-

---

[66] See for example Bernard the Monk, *Itinerarium*, PL 121, cols. 569–574. See also F. Avril and J.-R. Gaborit, 'L'*Itinerarium Bernardi Monachi* et les Pèlerinages d'Italie du Sud pendant le Haut-Moyen-Age', MEFR, 79 (1967), pp. 269–298.

[67] *Jerusalem Pilgrimage*, p. 94.

[68] Werlauff, *Symbolae ad Geographiam Medii Aevi*, p. 25. For this stage of Nikolas's pilgrimage see also *Jerusalem Pilgrimage*, pp. 215–218.

[69] *Ibid.*, p. 26.

[70] *Ibid.*, p. 26.

[71] *Ibid.*, p. 26.

[72] *Ibid.*, p. 26. A similar route was followed initially by St Willibald, travelling first to Fondi, a little east of Terracina, and thence to Gaeta, where he boarded a ship for Naples. (*Anglo-Saxon Missionaries in Germany*, pp. 159–160.)

[73] Benedict of Peterborough, *Chronicle*, vol. 2, p. 227.

[74] *Ibid.*, vol. 2, pp. 227–228.

[75] *Ibid.*, vol. 2, p. 228.

[76] *Ibid.*, vol. 2, p. 228.

[77] *Early Travels in Palestine*, p. 68.

mer, people from Lombardy, afflicted with diseases, gathered to take advantage of the hot springs, which could bring not only relief from pain but frequently a permanent cure as well.[78] From Pozzuoli, Benjamin went to Naples, Salerno, Amalfi, Bavento, Melfi, Ascoli and then to Trani, where he noted that pilgrims, who wanted to travel to Jerusalem, assembled because of the convenience of its port.[79] Benjamin himself continued further south through Bari, Taranto, Brindisi to Otranto, where he himself set sail for the Holy Land.[80]

While these itineraries suggest that the main routes to Rome had changed little between the ninth and thirteenth centuries, some surviving sources suggest that for parts of the twelfth century some of these routes may have been very dangerous. Leaving Rome c.1150, Henry of Blois, bishop of Winchester, travelled by sea to Spain and visited Compostela before returning home. John of Salisbury recorded that the Bishop took this route in order to avoid the hostility of the Tuscans, Lombards and Burgundians.[81]

It is likely that travel through the Italian peninsula continued to prove both difficult and dangerous for much of the second half of the twelfth century, as the Italian communes fought first each other and then the Emperor, Frederick Barbarossa, who in 1167 in support of his antipope, Paschal III, sacked Rome itself. Jocelin of Brakelond, recounting the adventures of Abbot Samson in Italy in 1161 as he travelled back from the Curia, noted that 'all clerks carrying letters from the Lord Pope Alexander were seized and some imprisoned, some hanged and others sent to the Pope with their lips and noses lopped off'.[82] Although Samson was travelling disguised as a Scot, even 'uttering threatening words after the fashion of the Scots', he was seized and searched.[83] It seems possible that genuine *Romipetae* may have suffered a similar fate. Surviving evidence suggests that some travellers were certainly reluctant to travel across the Italian peninsula on account of the dangers. Richard, archbishop-elect of Canterbury, travelling to Rome in 1174, spent Christmas at Piacenza.[84] On setting out again for Rome he decided that the

---

[78] *Ibid.*, p. 68. In the first century Mary of Cleophas seems to have found a cure here for a disease referred to as *elephantia*. See *De Sancta Maria Cleophae*, AASS Apr. I, esp. pp. 813–814.

[79] *Ibid.*, pp. 69–70.

[80] *Ibid.*, p. 70.

[81] John of Salisbury, *Historia Pontificalis*, ed. M. Chibnall, Oxford Medieval Texts (Oxford, 1986), p. 80. Also on the difficulties of the journey to Rome, see charter no. 3 dated 1129 in the cartulary of Vignory.

[82] Jocelin of Brakelond, *Chronicles concerning the Acts of Samson Abbot of the Monastery of St Edmund*, trans. H. E. Butler (London, 1949), p. 48.

[83] *Ibid.*, p. 49. For the characteristics of other nations see Jacques de Vitry, *Historia Occidentalis*, ed. J. F. Hinnesbusch (Fribourg, 1972), p. 92 and the article by L. Schmugge, 'Über nationale Vorurteile im Mittelalter', *Deutsches Archiv für Erforschung des Mittelalters*, 38 (1982), pp. 439–459.

[84] Ralph de Diceto, *Ymagines Historiarum*, ed. W. Stubbs, 2 vols. RS 68 (London, 1876), vol. 1, p. 388.

journey through Tuscany was too dangerous and thus decided to travel to Genoa instead.[85] There he boarded a ship bound for Cività Vecchia and for nine days endured 'the ferocity of the sea . . . and the assaults of pirates'.[86] Travelling to Sicily in 1176, John, bishop of Norwich, chose not to travel along the route which would have taken him first to Rome, because of the threat posed by the Lombards. He preferred instead to travel by sea from Genoa.[87] Nor does the journey seem to have been any safer when Folmarus, archbishop of Treves, made his return journey from Rome c.1186, disguised as a *servilius* from Verona.[88] He managed, he related, to survive the dangers of the mountains and the narrow footpaths but a graver peril still, he noted, were the guards who watched the roads giving exit from and entrance to the Italian peninsula.[89] Indeed, the situation had still not improved by 1198, when the chapter of Canterbury complained that they were unable to send original documents to Rome because of the wars and bloodshed on the continent.[90]

Travel in the Italian peninsula seems to have remained difficult in the early thirteenth century. In 1210, William the Breton could report that the Emperor, Otto IV, was deliberately hindering the journey of pilgrims trying to make their way to Rome, placing robbers in his camps who attacked them as they passed.[91] We know too that on his way to Genoa in 1216 for embarkation to the Holy Land, Jacques de Vitry avoided travelling through Italy, preferring the sea route instead.[92] A letter of Innocent IV dated 1246, complaining that the Emperor Frederick II was hindering pilgrims who were trying to make the journey to Rome, shows that travel there was still hazardous in the middle of the thirteenth century.[93]

The dispute over King John's accession to the English throne in 1199 and the war with Philip Augustus which broke out in 1202 were further sources of difficulty for those wishing to travel to Rome.[94] Gerald of Wales, who set out on his first journey to Rome in 1199, reported that he was unable to follow a direct route to Rome across France.[95] Instead, he recorded how he had to

85 *Ibid.*, vol. 1, p. 388.
86 *Ibid.*, vol. 1, p. 388.
87 *Ibid.*, vol. 1, p. 416.
88 *Ex Gestis Trevirensium Archiepiscoporum*, RHGF vol. 18 (Paris, 1879), pp. 672–673.
89 *Ibid.*, pp. 672–673.
90 *Epistolae Cantuarienses*, in *Chronicles and Memorials of the Reign of Richard I*, ed. W. Stubbs, 2 vols. RS 38 (London, 1864–1865), vol. 2, p. 276.
91 William the Breton, *De Gestis Phillippi Augusti*, RHGF 17 (Paris, 1878), p. 85.
92 Jacques de Vitry, *Lettres*, ed. R. B. C. Huygens (Leiden, 1960), pp. 76–77.
93 Innocent IV, *Registers*, ed. E. Berger, 4 vols. *Bibliothèque des Ecoles Françaises d'Athènes et de Rome*, 2nd series (Paris, 1884–1921), vol. 1, no. 1896.
94 See B. M. Bolton, 'Philip Augustus and John: Two Sons in Innocent III's Vineyard?', *The Church and Sovereignty c.590–1918: Essays in Honour of Michael Wilks*, SCH, Subsidia 9 (Oxford, 1991), pp. 113–134.
95 Gerald of Wales, *De Rebus a se Gestis*, in *Opera*, ed. J. F. Dimmock, G. F. Warner and J. S. Brewer, 8 vols. RS 21 (London, 1861–1891), vol. 1, esp. p. 118: 'Cum itaque propter

travel through Flanders and Hainault and, much to his discomfort, through the forest of the Ardennes, which was full of thieves and robbers.[96] Gerald's third journey to Rome was made in 1203. By this time sailing across the Channel was very difficult because, as a result of the war between John and Philip Augustus, English shipping could not land on the coast of Boulogne and so there was no longer any direct crossing from Dover.[97] Once across the Channel the situation was little better. Gerald was informed by pilgrims and others whom he met on the road that at St Omer all Englishmen were being seized, robbed and imprisoned.[98] Hoping to travel in safety, Gerald decided to set out for Douai and Cambrai 'where the roads were safer for travel . . . and to avoid Artois where Englishmen were arrested'.[99] Unfortunately Gerald nearly suffered this fate and was obliged to pay a heavy ransom.[100] Nor was Gerald's return journey any safer. 'For no one coming from the lands of the king of England', Gerald reported, 'be he pilgrim or cleric or monk . . . was safe in the realm of the Franks because of the war between the kings.'[101]

Stops on the Way

The route that a pilgrim chose to follow may have depended not only upon the information to which he had access but in some cases also on the places that he might have wanted to visit along the way. Seeing the shrines and holy places that were passed *en route* certainly seems to have been an essential part of the pilgrimage.[102] Indeed, incorporated within the twelfth-century pilgrims' *Guide to Compostela* was a large chapter on the shrines which pilgrims could visit in the course of their journey. At Arles, they could see the shrine of St Trophimus, first bishop of the city.[103] Worth visiting, depending on the route taken, was the shrine of St Gilles,[104] or that

---

weram grandem, quae inter regem Franciae Philippum et comitem Flandriae Baldewinum qui regi Angliae Johanni tunc adhaeserat, orta fuit, recta via per Franciam ire non poterat'. [When therefore because of the great war which broke out between Philip king of France and Baldwin count of Flanders, at that time an ally of King John, a direct route was not open through France.]

96 *Ibid.*, vol. 1, p. 118.
97 Gerald of Wales, *De Jure et Statu Menevensis Ecclesiae* in *Opera*, ed. J. F. Dimmock, G. F. Warner and J. S. Brewer, 8 vols. RS 21 (London 1861–1891), vol. 3, p. 238.
98 *Ibid.*, vol. 3, p. 239.
99 *Ibid.*, vol. 3, p. 239.
100 *Ibid.*, vol. 3, p. 239.
101 *Ibid.*, vol. 3, p. 292.
102 Cohen, 'Roads and Pilgrimage', shows how many of the shrines which grew up along the main pilgrimage roads to Compostela declined in popularity at the same time as the pilgrimage to St James. She shows that the shrines which remained popular throughout the Middle Ages were usually those which were also located on trade routes.
103 *Guide du Pèlerin*, pp. 34–35.
104 *Ibid.*, pp. 36–47.

of William of Aquitaine at Toulouse.[105] Not to be missed were the relics of St Foy at Conques[106] and those of St Mary Magdalene at Vézelay.[107] Those travelling through Orléans might stop to see the wood of the True Cross,[108] or the relics of St Evortius, bishop of Orléans.[109] At Poitiers pilgrims could see both the relics of St Hilary[110] and the head of St John the Baptist.[111] At Saintes they could visit the relics of St Eutrope,[112] or those of Blessed Sevin at Bordeaux.[113] Those pilgrims making their way to Rome from Spain or south-western France must have frequented many of these shrines as well. We know from the itinerary of Benjamin of Tudela that the route to Rome from Spain passed through St Gilles and from the itinerary of Matthew Paris that Vézelay certainly lay on one of the main routes to Rome.

For *Romipetae* travelling across France, perhaps following one of the routes suggested in Matthew Paris's map, there was an equally bewildering number of holy places that could be visited. Some pilgrims perhaps might have chosen to visit the tomb of St Martin at Tours,[114] or the abbey of St Denis near Paris, whose claim to possess the body of this saint was rigorously disputed during the eleventh and twelfth centuries.[115] Other pilgrims undoubtedly took the opportunity of visiting the tomb of St Geneviève in Paris itself.[116] At Chartres they could see the tunic of the Virgin,[117] at Reims the

---

[105] *Ibid.*, pp. 46–49.

[106] *Ibid.*, pp. 48–51. On Conques's acquisition of these relics, see Geary, *Furta Sacra*, pp. 58–63.

[107] *Guide du Pèlerin*, pp. 50–53. Vézelay's claim to possess the relics of this saint was laid in the eleventh century. For the story of how St Mary Magdalene came to be buried in France, see Sumption, *Pilgrimage*, p. 37.

[108] *Guide du Pèlerin*, pp. 58–59. On these relics see A. Frolow, *La Relique de la Vraie Croix. Recherches sur le Développement d'un Culte*, Archives de l'Orient Chrétien, 7 (Paris, 1961), no. 46, p. 187, and no. 257, p. 286. Also on Orléans, see T. Head, *Hagiography and the Cult of Saints. The Diocese of Orléans, 800–1200* (Cambridge, 1990).

[109] *Guide du Pèlerin*, pp. 58–59.

[110] *Ibid.*, pp. 60–63.

[111] *Ibid.*, pp. 62–63. After the Wood of the True Cross and Holy Blood, this must have been one of the most popular and most claimed relics. As well as Orléans, after the Sack of Constantinople in 1204, Amiens, Paris and Venice also all laid claim to this saint's head. For the claims of the first two see J. Ebersolt, *Orient et Occident* (Paris, 1954), pp. 83–84. For Venice's possession, see P. E. D. Riant, *Exuviae Sacrae Constantinopolitanae*, 3 vols. (Geneva, 1878), vol. 2, p. 262.

[112] *Guide du Pèlerin*, pp. 64–79.

[113] *Ibid.*, pp. 80–81.

[114] On pilgrimage churches, esp. St Martin at Tours, see K. J. Conant, *Carolingian and Romanesque Architecture [800–1200]* (Harmondsworth, 1959), pp. 91–103.

[115] Sumption, *Pilgrimage*, pp. 38–39. Hugh, bishop of Lincoln, visited St Denis whilst on pilgrimage in 1200. See *Life of St Hugh of Lincoln*, ed. D. L. Douie and H. Farmer, 2 vols. (London, 1961–1962), vol. 2, pp. 153–154.

[116] J. Dubois, and L. Beaumont-Maillet, *Sainte Geneviève de Paris* (Paris, 1982).

[117] Sumption, *Pilgrimage*, p. 49. Pilgrims seem to have participated in the rebuilding of the cathedral here c.1144. See Ward, *Miracles and the Medieval Mind*, p. 150.

shrine of St Remigius,[118] or a relic of the True Cross in the cathedral at Sens, supposedly given by Charlemagne.[119] Some of these pilgrims perhaps also stopped at Cluny to pray at the altar dedicated to saints Peter and Paul. In 1080 William of Warenne and his wife Gundrada, unable to complete their pilgrimage to Rome because of the war between Pope Gregory VII and Henry IV, managed to travel as far as Cluny, where they were able to venerate the two apostles instead.[120] At Maurienne pilgrims could see a finger of John the Baptist, which, according to the itinerary of Albert of Stade, had been brought to that place by a certain virgin.[121]

In his itinerary, Nikolas of Munkathvera listed all the places that pilgrims following his route could see. At Hildesheim they could visit the church of St Mary where the relics of St Godehard were preserved,[122] while at Paderborn they could visit the shrine of St Liborius, bishop of Le Mans (d.390), whose relics were translated to Paderborn in 836.[123] Nikolas had little to say about Cologne, except that pilgrims would find the archbishop's throne in the church of St Peter. Had Nikolas travelled this way just a few years later he would certainly have mentioned the relics of the Magi, translated to Cologne from Milan in 1164 by Rainald of Dassel and which transformed Cologne into one of the principal pilgrimage centres of Western Europe.[124]

Surviving evidence suggests that pilgrims were prepared to visit shrines that did not lie directly on their route, even if this meant making substantial detours. It is recorded in the *Life of St Hugh of Lincoln* that, whilst on pilgrimage in 1200, he visited famous shrines and monasteries, 'including not only those on or near his route but many a good distance from it'.[125] Nikolas of Munkathvera's itinerary noted too that detours from the main route were to be considered. Whilst the direct route from Vercelli to Rome lay through Pavia, many, he noted, might prefer to go first to Milan.[126] Another place which Nikolas considered worth visiting was Lucca and especially the cathedral dedicated to St Martin. Here the pilgrim could see the famous *Volto*

118 The body of St Remigius was translated to St Remi by Pope Leo IX in 1049. See Anselm the Monk, *Dedicatio Ecclesiae et Translatio S. Remigii*, AASS Oct. I, pp. 176–185.

119 Frolow, *Relique de La Vraie Croix*, no. 75, p. 206.

120 Cluny, vol. 4, no. 3561, pp. 689–696. Also see N. Hunt, 'Cluniac Monasticism', *Cluniac Monasticism in the Central Middle Ages*, ed. N. Hunt (London, 1971), pp. 1–10, esp. p. 8.

121 Albert of Stade, *Annales*, p. 337.

122 Werlauff, *Symbolae ad Geographiam Medii Aevi*, p. 16.

123 *Ibid.*, p. 16. P. Simon, *Sankt Liborius Sein Dom und Sein Bistum* (Paderborn, 1936).

124 On the Three Kings of Cologne, see B. Hamilton, 'Prester John and the Three Kings of Cologne', *Studies in Medieval History Presented to R. H. C. Davis*, ed. H. Mayr-Harting and R. I. Moore (London and Ronceverte, 1985), pp. 177–191. One of the itineraries in British Library MS Harley 2321, fols. 119v–121v, of the fifteenth century, mentions that at Cologne 'the relics of the Magi, the eleven thousand virgins and other saints' can be seen.

125 *Life of St Hugh of Lincoln*, vol. 2, p. 153.

126 Welauff, *Symbolae ad Geographiam Medii Aevi*, p. 19.

Santo, a crucifix, supposedly made by Nicodemus 'in the image of God Himself'.[127] It has spoken twice, Nikolas recorded, once giving its shoe to a poor man and a second in favour of a man who had been much slandered.[128]

There were other sites to the south of Rome which *Romipetae* traditionally visited.[129] These included Monte Cassino, 'where the body of St Benedict lay'[130] and the finger of the Apostle Matthew and an arm of a certain Bishop Martin which were preserved nearby in the church of St Andrew.[131] Other popular sites included St Angelus de Monte Aureo,[132] the shrines of St Bartholomew at Benevento,[133] St Nicholas at Bari[134] and also Monte Gargano, where St Michael's cave was located, wherein was kept a silken cloth that the saint himself gave to the place.[135]

When Should the Pilgrim Set Out for Rome?

According to the itinerary of Albert of Stade the best time to set out on pilgrimage to Rome was around the middle of August. He gave several reasons for this. At this time of year the air was warm, the roads were dry and there was little danger from flooding. The long days provided plenty of time for walking, the nights for resting. At this time of year it was also easy to find food.[136]

It was certainly much safer to cross the Alps in summer than at any other time of year. Yet even then, Nikolas of Munkathvera commented, there was snow on the Great St Bernard Pass.[137] Conditions were obviously much

---

127 *Ibid.*, p. 20. See also, Magoun, 'Pilgrim Diary', p. 341; A. Guerra, *Notizie Storiche del Volto Santo di Lucca* (Lucca, 1881).

128 Werlauff, *Symbolae ad Geographiam Medii Aevi*, p. 20.

129 On these pilgrimage sites, see Avril and Gaborit, 'L'*Itinerarium Bernardi Monachi*, pp. 269–298.

130 Benedict of Peterborough, *Chronicle*, p. 228. On the supposed theft of St Benedict's body by monks of Fleury in the early seventh century, see Adrevaldus Monachus Floriacensi, *Historia Translationis S. Benedicti*, in *Les Miracules de Saint Benoit*, Société de l'*Histoire de France* (Paris, 1858), pp. 1–13.

131 Werlauff, *Symbolae ad Geographiam Medii Aevi*, p. 25.

132 Visited by Bernard the Monk (*Itinerarium*, PL 121, col. 574) c.870.

133 Benedict of Peterborough, *Chronicle*, vol. 2, pp. 227–228.

134 *Ibid.*, vol. 2, p. 227; Werlauff, *Symbolae ad Geographiam Medii Aevi*, p. 26.

135 Werlauff, *Symbolae ad Geographiam Medii Aevi*, p. 26.

136 Albert of Stade, *Annales*, p. 340. Although food may have been easier to find during the summer months, shortages at this time of year were not unknown. John, bishop of Norwich, travelling to Sicily in 1176, was troubled by a shortage of food and tormented in the Auvergne by the moans of those who lay starving in the streets. See Ralph de Diceto, *Ymagines Historiarum*, vol. 1, p. 416. Another chronicler even reports that during 1196 the situation was so bad that starving wolves took to devouring men. See *Ex Annalibus Aquicinctensis Monasterii*, RHGF vol. 18 (Paris, 1879), p. 549.

137 Werlauff, *Symbolae ad Geographiam Medii Aevi*, p. 18.

worse in winter. According to Florence of Worcester, in 959 Aelfsige, arch-bishop of Canterbury, was frozen to death in the Alps, whilst on his way to Rome to collect his pallium.[138] Such a death was probably not uncommon and we know that c.1215, John de Liro, travelling from Liège to Rome, suffered the same fate.[139] Other examples further illustrate the dangers and difficulties of Alpine travel during the winter months. Lampert of Hersfeld, in describing the return journey of Henry IV over the Mont Cenis Pass at the beginning of 1077, mentioned the precipitous mountains and the sheets of ice on which the travellers slipped and fell.[140] A second account records the close brush with death experienced by Rudolph, abbot of St Trond, and Alexander, archdeacon of Liège, in December 1128, when they were caught in an avalanche on the Great St Bernard Pass.[141] Late in 1151, whilst crossing the Alps, Peter the Venerable, abbot of Cluny, wrote a letter to Basil, prior of La Grande Chartreuse. In this he complained of the hazards of mountain travel during the winter months.[142] A letter written by John, a monk of Canterbury, in 1188 recorded his experiences of travel over the Great St Bernard Pass. He described it as a place of torment, where the ground was so slippery that he was unable to stand.[143]

Yet if the crossing of the Alps was safest in the summer months, the well-informed pilgrim would not wish to arrive in Rome at the height of summer. For at this time of year in the extreme heat, the incidence of malaria was at its height.[144] Peter the Venerable, in a letter addressed to Pope Lucius II, commented on the unhealthiness of the Roman air and the way in which it was accustomed to bring death.[145] Gervase of Canterbury recorded what seems to have been a particularly bad outbreak of the disease in 1188, which killed many people, especially pilgrims.[146] The Annales Marbacenses recorded that in this same year, the pilgrims who returned to Alsace from Rome were almost all starving and infected with disease.[147]

Surviving evidence suggests, however, that there was some awareness of the problem of malaria amongst pilgrims. In a letter to the prior, Ernulf, and monks of Canterbury, St Anselm recorded his arrival in Chartres on his way to Rome. He was received there with great joy but with much wonder that he

---

138 Florence of Worcester, Chronicon, vol. 1, p. 138.
139 De S. Lutgarde Virgine, AASS June III, p. 245.
140 Lampert of Hersfeld, Opera, ed. O. Holder-Egger (Hanover, 1852), p. 286.
141 Gesta Abbatum Trudonensium, MGH.SS 10, p. 307.
142 Peter the Venerable, Letters, ed. G. Constable, 2 vols. Harvard Historical Studies, 78 (Massachusetts, 1967), vol. 1, pp. 434–435.
143 Epistolae Cantuarienses, vol. 2, p. 181.
144 For a twelfth-century case history, see U. T. Holmes and F. R. Weedon, 'Peter of Blois as a Physician', Speculum, 37 (1962), pp. 252–256.
145 Peter the Venerable, Letters, vol. 1, pp. 311–312.
146 Gervase the Monk, The Chronicles of the Reigns of Stephen, Henry II and Richard I, in The Historical Works of Gervase of Canterbury, ed. W. Stubbs, 2 vols. RS 73 (London, 1879–1880), vol. 1, p. 429.
147 Annales Marbacenses, MGH.SS 17, p. 165.

had undertaken the journey because of the great heat. No pilgrim hurried on his way in such conditions, he was told, and he was persuaded to wait before resuming his journey to Rome until the time arrived when the pilgrims again began to set out.[148]

In spite of this awareness of malaria among some pilgrims, the number of deaths recorded in surviving sources, which were almost certainly the result of malaria, are a clear indication of just how many did succumb to this disease.[149] Perhaps one of the most poignant stories concerned a group of monks from Christ Church, Canterbury, who had set out for Rome in 1188. A letter addressed to the house by the prior, Honorius, who had also gone there, confirmed the deaths of five of the monks, Ralph, Haymo, Edmund, Simon and Humphrey.[150] At the same time the prior complained of his own sickness and that of the bishop of Ostia. Further brethren despatched from the house at the end of 1188 were to discover that both had since died.[151] The gloom and despondency which these deaths had caused at Christchurch seems to have manifested itself again ten years later, in a letter of 1198 addressed to Pope Innocent III. 'Be kind', they entreated the Pope, 'to the brethren last sent out, if they are still alive.'[152] A letter from the Pope,

---

[148] St Anselm, Epistolae, PL 159, esp. col. 113 and cols. 216–217.

[149] A. Celli-Fraentzel, 'Contemporary Reports on the Medieval Roman Climate', Speculum, 7 (1932), pp. 96–106. Surviving sources contain many examples of those who died in or around Rome in the twelfth century. On the death of Abbot Theoderic of Petrihusensis and his companions in 1116, see Casus Monasterii Petrihusensis, MGH.SS 20, p. 659. Imar O'Hagan died in Rome in 1134 (Annals of the Kingdom of Ireland by the Four Masters, ed. J. O'Donovan, 7 vols. (Dublin, 1857), vol. 2, p. 1047) as did William of Trehinac, fifth prior of Grandmont c.1187 (Chronicon B. Iterii Armarii Monasterii S. Marcialis, ed. H. Duplès, Société de l'Histoire de France (Paris, 1874), p. 62). Hugh, bishop of St Andrews died in Rome in 1188 (Benedict of Peterborough, Chronicle, vol. 2, pp. 43–44) as did Henry, bishop elect of Dol (ibid., vol. 2, p. 44). Hugh, bishop of Auxerre died there in 1206 (Ex Historia Episcoporum Autissiodorensium, RHGF 18, p. 730), whilst a boy in the retinue of William of Andres died in the city in 1207 (William of Andres, Chronicon, MGH.SS 24, p. 743), as did Nevelus, bishop of Soissons (Alberic of Tre Fontaneis, Chronica, MGH.SS 23, p. 886). A certain Ademarus deu Perrier died a peregrinus in Rome in 1215 (ibid., p. 779), and Eugenius, archbishop of Armagh died there in the following year (Dublin, vol. 1, p. 279). Another Rome pilgrim was Rahere, a canon of St Paul's Cathedral in London. Taken seriously ill whilst in Rome on pilgrimage in the early twelfth century, he promised that if he survived he would return to London and found a hospital. He did survive and duly returned to found St Bartholomew's. See Book of the Foundation of St Bartholomew's Church in London, ed. N. Moore, Early English Text Society (London, 1923); E. J. Kealey, Medieval Medicus. A Social History of Anglo-Norman Medicine (Baltimore, 1981).

[150] Epistolae Cantuariensis, vol. 2, p. 254.

[151] Ibid., vol. 2, pp. 269–270. Gervase the Monk (Chronicles of the Reigns of Stephen, Henry II and Richard I, vol. 1, p. 429) records that the prior, Honorius, was buried in the Lateran cloister and the monks in various of the city's churches.

[152] Epistolae Cantuariensis, vol. 2, p. 445.

however, which seems to have crossed with that of the monks, informed them of the death of their two representatives at the Holy See.[153]

Ideally, therefore, the pilgrim should set out from home early enough to cross the Alps before winter had set in but late enough so that he arrived in Rome after the heat of the summer had subsided. These dangers may perhaps have persuaded some pilgrims to spend the winter in Rome and to set out on their homeward journey so that they crossed the Alps in the spring, thus avoiding again both the hazards of Alpine travel during the winter months and the heat of Rome in summer.

To Walk or to Ride?

The traditional image of the pilgrim tends to be that of a lone individual travelling on foot, bearing little more than his scrip and staff. The reality, however, long before the twelfth century, was, for many, rather different. Surviving evidence shows that it was not considered unusual for those who could afford it, to take a horse or a mule on such a journey, either to carry the baggage or to ride upon. In 793 King Offa, whilst travelling to Rome, purchased certain meadows in the region of Flanders, which were to be given over to the use of pilgrims, specifically so that they might always have access to hay and straw with which to feed their animals.[154] We also know that in 1075, Hugh, son and successor of Eudes Doubleau, gave to the monastery of Vendôme the tithe from the seigneurie of Mondoubleau. In return, on his departure on pilgrimage to Rome he received money and a horse.[155] In 1089 Hugh Langesinus made a donation of land to the monastery of Cormery and received money and a mule before beginning his journey to Rome.[156] Sometime during the reign of William Rufus (1087–1100), Hugh of Insula gave to the abbey of Marmoutier, with the consent of his brothers Roger and Gervase, the mill of Torlavilla, which he held from the duke of Normandy. In return, the prior, Ralph, gave him a mule, which Hugh passed on to Roger, who was about to go to Rome.[157] In 1126 on their outward journey to Rome, Rudolph, abbot of St Trond, and Alexander, archdeacon of Liège, had just crossed the Alps when they were attacked by robbers. Everything that they had was taken but after 'much labour and much fear', they recovered their horses.[158] The author of the Guide to Compostela certainly expected the pilgrim to have a horse, exhorting him not to let it drink from the River

---

153 Ibid., vol. 2, p. 443.
154 Matthew Paris, Chronica Maiora, vol. 1, pp. 358–359.
155 Vendôme, vol. 1, no. 250.
156 Cormery, no. 42.
157 Calendar of Documents Preserved in France AD 918–1206, ed. J. H. Round (London, 1899), no. 1178, p. 426.
158 Gesta Abbatum Trudonensium, p. 306.

Salatus, in the region of *Lorchus*, because it was 'a river of death'.[159] He also advised the pilgrim about the best method of getting himself and his horse aboard the small narrow ferry boat at St Jean-de-Sorde, without falling into the water.[160] There are also charters which refer to pilgrims walking to their destination but whether these pilgrims really made their journeys on foot, or whether this is simply a standard charter formula, is uncertain.[161]

There were many pilgrims, however, who would not have been able to afford a horse or a mule and would have had no choice but to travel on foot. If we accept the evidence of the *Acta Sanctorum* then there were also those who positively delighted in the hardships of walking. On his frequent pilgrimages to Rome, St Bobone (d.c.986) always took a mule with him but he scarcely ever rode upon it, preferring instead to wear himself out with the effort of walking.[162] St Aderald, who became archdeacon of Troyes c.990, set out for Rome sometimes travelling on horseback but more often making his way on foot. Having come to a river too deep even for his horse, he undressed and swam across. On reaching the other side, he dressed, putting on all but his shoes. He then travelled safely across the Alps and Appenines, still with *nudis pedibus*. He did this 'not twice, not thrice', commented his biographer, 'but twelve times'.[163] St Adelelmus (d.c.1100) set out on his pilgrimage to Rome in bare feet, taking nothing with him and denying that material things were necessary for those seeking the kingdom of heaven.[164] St Aibert (d.1140) and his companions made their pilgrimage to Rome on foot, using the mule which they had with them only to help weak and infirm pilgrims whom they met on the road,[165] while St Gerlac (d.c.1170) also walked to Rome, wearing nothing on his feet, and then spent seven years in the city tending the sick and practising great austerities.[166]

The blessing to be obtained by the hardship of pilgrimage is noted in a sermon addressed to pilgrims by that great popular preacher of the early thirteenth century, Jacques de Vitry. There was 'nothing more efficacious and satisfying than the labour of the pilgrimage'.[167] 'For just as a man sins with all his limbs', Jacques de Vitry wrote, 'so too must he make reparation with them all.'[168] While there were undoubtedly many pilgrims for whom the journey would have involved great toil, labour and reparation with their limbs, there seem to have been many others for whom Jacques de Vitry's model remained only an ideal.

---

159 *Guide du Pèlerin*, pp. 12–13.
160 *Ibid.*, pp. 20–21.
161 See for example, Lezat, no. 189 and Chateaudun, no. 37.
162 *De S. Bobone seu Bovo*, AASS May V, pp. 186–7.
163 *De S. Aderaldo Archidiacono*, AASS Oct. VIII, p. 992.
164 *De S. Adelelmo sive Elesme*, AASS Jan. II, p. 1057.
165 *De S. Ayberto Presbytero*, AASS April I, p. 675.
166 *De S. Gerlaco eremita in Belgio*, AASS Jan. I, p. 307.
167 Bibliothèque Nationale Latin Ms. 3284, fol. 129v.
168 *Ibid.*

The Length of the Journey

Whether the pilgrim travelled by horse or on foot obviously affected the length of time the journey would take him. The number of shrines and holy places that he visited along the way was also an important factor. While it is difficult, therefore, to say how long the pilgrim would spend on his journey, some very rough calculations are possible. The itinerary of Matthew Paris, by its longest route, listed about forty-five stages for the journey between Rome and the Channel, a journey time of just over six weeks, if we accept that each place mentioned represents an over-night stop. A working figure of about 1,150 miles has been suggested for the distance.[169] This means that Matthew's itinerary assumed an average of about twenty-five miles a day, probably only possible on horse-back. Many travellers, however, would not have been able to guarantee making the journey with quite such speed. Indeed, as Poole has argued, Matthew Paris's map only allows for two stages for the journey across the Alps, which might not be possible in winter, nor does it allow for breaks in the journey, whether forced or planned.[170] Sigeric's itinerary lists seventy-nine stages between Rome and the Channel, accomplished in a little over eleven weeks.[171] Again taking the figure of 1,150 miles, these calculations suggest that Sigeric was travelling on average about fourteen and a half miles a day. Here we might compare the journey made by Odo of Rouen, who took seventy-two days to reach Rome.[172] As he took a little less time than Sigeric but was starting from Rouen and not the Channel, it is probable that their speed of travel was similar. Both were undoubtedly travelling much more slowly than the pace indicated by Matthew Paris's itinerary, which may suggest that they were walking, or, if on horseback, that they stopped off regularly along the way.

Nikolas of Munkathvera's itinerary also gives some indication of the length of the journey to Rome from Iceland. He frequently gives the number of days required to travel between two places. The number of days needed to complete this journey was certainly in excess of fifty-nine but we cannot be more accurate as Nikolas does not always remember to include the figures, nor is it entirely clear from his itinerary whether he himself was walking or riding. Yet what is certain from these very rough calculations is that the pilgrim coming from England, France, the Western Empire or beyond was likely to be on the road for several months before he reached Rome. Having spent some time in the city itself and having made the return journey, many would probably have been away from home for the best part of a year.

---

[169] Parks, *English Traveller to Italy*, p. 183.
[170] R. L. Poole, 'The Early Correspondence of John of Salisbury', *Studies in Chronology and History*, ed. A. L. Poole (Oxford, 1934), pp. 259–286, esp. p. 263.
[171] *Memorials of Saint Dunstan*, pp. 392–395.
[172] Ludwig, *Untersuchungen*, pp. 107–109.

Accommodation

For those spending such long periods on the road, there must have been places for them to stay along the way. Unfortunately the itineraries which we have contain surprisingly little information about the accommodation that was available. In the dialogue between Tirri and Firri, there is only a single reference to this subject. One route home through the Brenner mentioned by Tirri would have taken Firri through the Pusterthal. Here, however, Tirri warned that everything was very expensive and the *hospitia* very bad.[173] What Tirri meant by *hospitia*, however, is uncertain but it is possible that he was referring to the inns of this region. Indeed, for those with money to spend, inns must have been an important source of hospitality. The information which survives about the frequent journeys of Wolfger, bishop of Passau and patriarch of Aquilea, suggests that such establishments were able to provide rather more than just meals, a bed for the night and stabling for horses. At many, medicines could also be obtained[174] and some even seem to have provided a laundry service.[175]

Those with less money to spend would have had to survive as best they could and, for the most part, would probably have been reliant on charity. Some would perhaps have found food and a bed for the night at a hospice. Nikolas of Munkathvera mentions three hospices that he saw and perhaps stayed at during the course of his journey. The first of these was located on the Great St Bernard Pass.[176] This was supposedly built by one St Bernard of Menthon but most of what we know about this man was not written until the fifteenth century and is thus unreliable.[177] The only concrete facts seem to be that he was of noble birth, was an archdeacon of Aosta and died in 1081. The actual date of the foundation of the hospice is also uncertain since the foundation charter has not survived. The second hospice mentioned in Nikolas's itinerary was located in the vicinity of Piacenza. Nikolas called it the hospice of Eric,[178] probably Eric I, king of Denmark (1095–1103).[179] The third hospice mentioned was that built by Matilda, countess of Tuscany (d.1115).[180] Its location is uncertain but it seems to have lain somewhere between Lucca and Siena.[181] This, Nikolas claimed, Matilda had built in

---

173 Albert of Stade, *Annales*, p. 339.
174 Zingerle, *Reiserechnungen*, p. 55.
175 *Ibid.*, p. 54.
176 Werlauff, *Symbolae ad Geographiam Medii Aevi*, p. 18.
177 On this hospice and its foundation, see A. Donnet, *Saint Bernard et les Origines de l'Hospice du Mont-Joux* (St Maurice, 1942) and by the same author, *Le Grand Saint-Bernard*, *Trésors de Mon Pays*, 45 (Neufchâtel, 1950), esp. pp. 10–13.
178 Werlauff, *Symbolae ad Geographiam Medii Aevi*, p. 19.
179 Magoun, 'Pilgrim Diary', p. 337.
180 Werlauff, *Symbolae ad Geographiam Medii Aevi*, p. 21.
181 Magoun, 'Pilgrim Diary', p. 342.

redemption of a pledge made to Monte Cassino and the hospice was duty bound to accommodate all travellers overnight.[182]

That accommodation was insufficient particularly in the Alpine regions, however, is noted in the Life of Peter, archbishop of Tarentaise (1141–1171).[183] There was such a shortage of accommodation that this archbishop took it upon himself to set up shelters not only in his own archbishopric but even in areas outside his jurisdiction. These establishments were supplemented by others, such as the thirteen Alpine outposts opened up in the twelfth century by the Benedictine abbey of Chalais.[184]

The number of hospices seems to have increased dramatically in the course of the twelfth and thirteenth centuries. Many of these were founded by the Hospitallers, who by 1113 already had hospices functioning at St Gilles, Asti and Pisa, as well as at Bari, Otranto, Taranto and Messina.[185] Some of these establishments catered specifically for pilgrims and crusaders about to set sail for the Holy Land but those particularly at Asti and Pisa may well also have been used by those on their way to Rome.

There must have been many other places along the roads to Rome where pilgrims would have found shelter.[186] We know, for example, that in c.1110 Gandulf, a nobleman of Piacenza, and his wife Gisla provided funds for the building of a 'hospital'.[187] This was built not far from Piacenza, at a place known as Fontana Fredda on one of the main routes used by pilgrims on their way to Rome, and was dedicated in honour of St Peter. That it was indeed used by pilgrims is clear from a privilege granted to this 'hospital' by Nicholas IV in 1292, which refers to it as place where both pilgrims and the 'poor of Christ' were cared for.[188]

Whilst there must also have been accommodation for pilgrims situated in the vicinity of Rome itself, in places like Viterbo and Sutri, little is known about it. There was, however, a 'hospital' located at Cantaro close to Albano.

182 Werlauff, Symbolae ad Geographiam Medii Aevi, p. 21.
183 De Sancto Petro, AASS May II, p. 327. Walter Map had to look after Peter during his stay at the court of King Henry II at Limoges in 1173. For Map's comments on his character and miracles, see Walter Map, De Nugis Curialium, ed. and trans. M. R. James, rev. C. N. L. Brooke and R. A. B. Mynors (Oxford, 1983), pp. 131–141.
184 M. Mollat, The Poor in the Middle Ages. An Essay in Social History, trans. A. Goldhammer (London, 1986), p. 92. Also on the increase in hospices, Settia, 'Strade e Pellegrini', pp. 83–86.
185 Hospital of St John in Jerusalem, vol. 1, no. 30. See also J. S. C. Riley-Smith, The Knights of St John in Jerusalem and Cyprus c.1050–1310 (London, 1967), p. 40.
186 A number of 'hospitals' are listed by Kehr (Italia Pontificia, 8 vols. (Rome, 1906)) as possibly used by pilgrims, but little information survives.
187 Ibid., vol. 5, pp. 518–519. The term used to describe the foundation is hospitalis. Whether it was a true hospital intended primarily for the sick, or rather an inn perhaps providing some casual care for those who fell ill, is uncertain. For further discussion of 'hospitals', see chapter six.
188 Nicholas IV, Registers, ed. E. Langlois, 2 vols. Bibliothèque des Ecoles Françaises d'Athènes et de Rome (Paris, 1886–1893), vol. 2, p. 917, no. 6862.

Most of what we know about this 'hospital' is found in a Bull of September 1154 of Anastasius IV, addressed to 'John Crassus, prior of the *hospitalis*, to John the priest, to Ade and Nicholas, clerics of the *hospitalis*, and to the other brothers'.[189] This Bull indicates that the 'hospital' had been constructed with money provided by John Crassus, probably sometime c.1143–1144 during the pontificate of Celestine II.[190] It also indicates that the purpose of this 'hospital' was 'for the reception of the poor and the comfort of pilgrims'.[191] This 'hospital' had been placed under the protection of the papacy by Lucius II, a privilege confirmed by Eugenius III and again by Anastasius IV in his Bull of 1154.[192] That this 'hospital' was still functioning in the late twelfth century is indicated by its inclusion in the *Liber Censuum*.[193]

Another 'hospital' was erected not far from Rome during the early thirteenth century. During Innocent III's perambulation through the southern part of the papal state in 1208 accompanied by his cardinals, a 'hospital' was founded at Anagni next to the church of S. Ascenzo, just outside the city walls.[194] Dedicated to the memory of the Virgin and the Blessed Antony, this 'hospital' catered for the needs of the poor and pilgrims.[195] Hugolino, cardinal bishop of Ostia, the future Gregory IX, was directly responsible for its construction and seems to have paid for this himself.[196] John, bishop of Anagni, assisted in this project by granting the church of S. Ascenzo with all its property. In this way its canons could serve the 'hospital' and income from its land could finance some of the charitable works. The 'hospital's' property seems to have been gradually increased and the list of its possessions in a Bull of Gregory IX dated 1234 suggests that this pope was determined to ensure that the canons of his foundation had the means to carry out their tasks properly.[197]

In addition to these establishments, the pilgrim might receive food and shelter in the monasteries which lay on his route. The obligation to provide hospitality was set out in chapter 53 of the *Rule of St Benedict* (c.480–550).[198]

---

189 *Acta Pontificum Romanorum Inedita*, vol. 3, pp. 157–158. Also on this 'hospital', see Kehr, *Italia Pontificia*, vol. 2, pp. 32–33.

190 *Acta Pontificum Romanorum Inedita*, vol. 3, p. 157.

191 *Ibid.*, vol. 3, p. 157.

192 *Ibid.*, vol. 3, p. 157. Anastasius IV refers to privileges granted by two of his predecessors.

193 *Liber Censuum de l'Eglise Romain*, ed. P. Fabre and L. Duchesne, 3 vols. (Paris, 1905–1910), vol. 1, p. 10.

194 R. A. De Magistris, 'Il Viaggio D'Innocenzo III nel Lazio e il Primo Ospedale in Anagni', *Storia e Diritto*, 19 (1898), pp. 365–78.

195 *Ibid.*, p. 372.

196 On Hugolino, see W. Malaeczek, *Papst und Kardinalskolleg von 1191 bis 1216* (Vienna, 1984), pp. 126–133.

197 De Magistris, 'Il Viaggio D'Innocenzo III', pp. 372–375.

198 St Benedict, *Regula cum Commentariis, PL* 66, cols. 749–752. On St Benedict and the *Rule*, see C. H. Lawrence, *Medieval Monasticism* (London, 1984), pp. 17–35.

The poor and pilgrims received special mention, 'for in them', St Benedict wrote, 'is Christ most truly welcomed'.[199] The reception and care of guests at monasteries, however, was a potential disruption to the daily routine of the house. The famous plan of the monastery of St Gall, dating from c.820, the model for monastic settlements, shows clearly how this problem was to be overcome. Special accommodation was provided for guests and even a special kitchen but all located away from the main monastic buildings so that those staying there would not interfere with daily monastic routine.[200] The same features can be seen again in the plans of Cluny, drawn up after extensive archaeological surveys. There too was a hospice to accommodate guests but once more located at a distance from the main monastic buildings. This hospice seems to have been substantially increased in size as part of the building programme instituted by St Hugh (1049–1109) and enlarged again in the twelfth century during the abbacy of Peter the Venerable (1122–1156) with the addition of a new wing and probably also a chapel.[201]

Yet, the descent of pilgrims upon monasteries in search of hospitality or charity could become a source of irritation. The hordes who were accustomed to arrive at Evesham, particularly around Christmas and Easter, certainly seem to have annoyed the abbey's chronicler.[202] Evidence also exists to show that towards the end of the twelfth and the beginning of the thirteenth centuries, it may not always have been easy for pilgrims to find hospitality at some monasteries.[203] In 1208 Innocent III visited the great Benedictine abbey of Monte Cassino and found that Abbot Roffredo (1190–1209) was failing miserably in his obligation to give alms and hospitality.[204] His successor Atenolfo also neglected these important charitable duties and had to be deposed in 1215.[205] Just how dire the situation had become by then is indicated by a letter addressed to the new abbot, Stephen, by Innocent III in the same year in which he was forced to remind the community how guests ought to be received and treated.[206]

---

[199] St Benedict, Regula cum Commentariis, col. 749.

[200] On St Gall, see W. Horn and E. Born, The Plan of St Gall, 3 vols. (Berkeley 1979); L. Price, The Plan of St Gall in Brief (Berkeley, 1982).

[201] K. J. Conant, 'Medieval Academy Excavations at Cluny', Speculum, 29 (1954), pp. 1–43. See also K. J. Conant, 'Cluniac Building during the Abbacy of Peter the Venerable', Petrus Venerabilis 1156–1956, ed. G. Constable and J. Kritzeck (Rome, 1956), pp. 121–127. On the reception of guests and pilgrims at Cluny, see Udalrico, Antiquiores Consuetudines Cluniacensis Monasterii, PL 149, esp. cols. 764–765.

[202] Chronicon Abbatiae de Evesham ad Annum 1418, ed. W. D. Macray, RS 29 (London, 1863), p. 93.

[203] See B. M. Bolton, ' "Hearts not Purses": Innocent III's Approach to Social Welfare', Through the Eye of a Needle. Judaeo-Christian Roots of Social Welfare, ed. E. A. Hanawalt and C. Lindberg (Missouri, 1994), pp. 123–145.

[204] Innocent III, Registers, PL 215, cols. 1593–1594.

[205] Ibid., PL 217, cols. 249–253.

[206] D. L. Tosti, Storia della Badia di Monte Cassino, 3 vols. (Naples, 1842–1843), vol. 2, pp. 289–292.

The monasteries were not alone in being obliged to provide hospitality for pilgrims.[207] Bishops and priests faced similar responsibilities. As in the case of monasteries, however, evidence exists to show that towards the end of the twelfth century these obligations were sometimes overlooked. Here we are once more indebted to the *Registers* of Innocent III. The many letters addressed by this pope to Berengar II, archbishop of Narbonne (1190–1212), whose province lay astride a great pilgrim route, reveal that amongst this archbishop's many sins was his complete failure to provide hospitality. In 1206 Innocent reminded Berengar that he ought to be concerned not with financial profit but rather with acts of charity and hospitality to the poor and pilgrims alike.[208] Berengar's disregard of all papal warnings resulted in his replacement in 1212 by Arnald Amaury.[209]

The Cost of the Pilgrimage

The foundation of hospices and the provision of food and shelter by monasteries must certainly have reduced the cost of undertaking a pilgrimage. It seems, however, that many pilgrims still found themselves with insufficient funds for their journey. Ralph of Hatfeld and his wife longed to travel to the tomb of St Thomas at Canterbury but had insufficient means. Ingeniously, therefore, they began brewing beer and hoped to fund their pilgrimage from the proceeds.[210] Other sources suggest that pilgrims often ran out of money in the course of their pilgrimage. The *Roman de Mont Saint Michel*, written in the second half of the twelfth century, mentioned tents where vendors displayed all kinds of foodstuffs; wines, breads, fish, venison, fruits and cakes. There was plenty on sale, the author commented, for those who had the means to pay.[211] We also know that Wolfger, bishop of Passau and patriarch of Aquilea, on his frequent journeys across the Alps distributed alms, not only to singing girls at Sutri,[212] minstrels and musicians[213] and others wandering the roads but also to pilgrims.[214]

Unfortunately surviving evidence is such that it is almost impossible to assess how much an individual might have expected to spend on a journey to Rome in the twelfth or early thirteenth centuries. Richard de Anesty, engaged in a law suit to recover land which he claimed was his by right,

---

[207] See below pp. 79–80.
[208] Innocent III, *Registers*, PL 215, col. 884.
[209] Bolton, ' "Hearts not purses" ', pp. 130–132.
[210] *Materials for the History of Thomas Becket*, vol. 2, pp. 253–254.
[211] J. Evans, *Life in Medieval France*, 3rd ed. (New York, 1969), pp. 76–77.
[212] Zingerle, *Reiserechnungen*, p. 26.
[213] *Ibid.*, p. 20.
[214] *Ibid.*, pp. 24 and 74.

recorded that in 1161 he sent two clerks to Rome.[215] He also seems to have engaged a driver to take them, on whose clothing and horses he spent five marks of silver.[216] The two clerks in that journey to Rome, Richard noted, spent twenty-five silver marks and another forty shillings in excess of what he had given them, which they had managed to borrow from a clerk of the bishop of Lincoln.[217] Unfortunately, there is no attempt to account for how the money was spent and as well as the usual travelling expenses, Richard's clerks undoubtedly had to pay a considerable sum at the papal court to have the case heard. In 1162 they returned to Rome, where they stayed for sixty-two days, spending eleven silver marks whilst there.[218] Again there is no indication of what proportion was spent at the papal court or how much the clerks had to spend on food and accommodation.

Important information, however, does survive in the early thirteenth-century itineraries of Wolfger, bishop of Passau and patriarch of Aquilea. At Viterbo, for example, the bishop's itinerary records a payment of thirty *solidi* to a cook and an expenditure of twenty-three *solidi* for bread and another twenty for wine. A further sixteen *denarii* seems to have been paid for a bath.[219] Similar payments made at Aquapendente included twenty-six *solidi* to a cook, another twenty-three for bread and twenty-one for wine.[220] Fodder and grass also seem to have been regularly purchased, on which thirty-five *solidi* was spent at Viterbo and a further twenty-nine *solidi* at Aquapendente.[221] These bills, however, probably covered not only the bishop's meals and accommodation but also an unknown number who travelled in his retinue, so once more we are unable to assess the likely cost for a single individual.

Most of the evidence concerning how much money pilgrims might have taken with them to spend is drawn from charters. A few scattered entries in the cartularies of religious houses record sums of money given to individuals, usually in return for a donation of some kind, suggesting that pilgrims, travelling in particular to Rome and Compostela, often needed to fund their pilgrimages in the same way as crusaders.[222] In 1070 a certain Mathias received five *sous* from the monastery of Vendôme, before he set off on his pilgrimage to Rome. This he deposited as oblations on church altars in the

---

[215] F. Palgrave, *Collected Historical Works*, ed. R. H. I. Palgrave, 7 vols. (Cambridge, 1921), vol. 7, Part 2, p. 21. See also P. Barnes, 'The Anesty Case', *Publications of the Pipe Roll Society*, n.s. vol. 36 (1960), pp. 1–23.

[216] *Ibid.*, p. 21.

[217] *Ibid.*, pp. 21–22.

[218] *Ibid.*, p. 24.

[219] Zingerle, *Reiserechnungen*, p. 42. On medieval currency, P. Spufford, *Handbook of Medieval Exchange* (London, 1986).

[220] *Ibid.*, p. 42.

[221] *Ibid.*, p. 42.

[222] J. S. C. Riley-Smith, *The Crusades. A Short History* (London, 1987), esp. pp. 10–17.

course of his journey.[223] In 1075, Hugh Doubleau, in return for the tithe of the seigneurie of Mondoubleau, received forty *solidi* from Vendôme,[224] while in 1078, Hugh Langesinus received six pounds from the monks of Cormery.[225] An interesting case was perhaps that of Guicher, seigneur of Chateaurenaud, who in 1075, wanting to go on pilgrimage to Rome, approached the monks of Vendôme for a subsidy for his journey. Yet Guicher had long been imposing unjust dues on Prunay and was forced by the monks to recognise the injustice of his actions. This he did and offered to lift the dues if the monks gave him twenty *solidi* for his pilgrimage.[226] How much these individuals spent on their own needs in the course of their pilgrimage and how much they may have distributed in alms, or used as oblations, we shall probably never know.

Whilst the amount of money spent by individuals in the course of a pilgrimage is almost impossible to determine, that many individuals frequently expended large sums on such journeys is suggested by complaints about this aspect of pilgrimage. These complaints became increasingly common, particularly in the twelfth century. Honorius of Autun argued that the relief of the poor was more worthy than a pilgrimage to Jerusalem,[227] while Lambert le Bègue in c.1175 denied that he wanted to abolish overseas pilgrimages but reckoned that the money could be better spent on other things, particularly the redemption of captives, the nourishment of the hungry and thirsty, the consolation of widows and the defence of orphans.[228]

These criticisms of the cost of pilgrimage came at a time of 'religious crisis'.[229] Indeed, from the middle of the eleventh century onwards there was increasing dissatisfaction with the wealth and worldliness of the Church. As a result of this dissatisfaction, there was an attempt at 'a new lifestyle',[230] a return to the *vita apostolica*, based on the lives of Christ and his disciples. In particular, stress was laid upon two aspects: the way in which the disciples had been sent into the world in complete poverty and the communal life which they had enjoyed.[231] It was the ideal of poverty in particular which the author of the *Veneranda dies* sermon hoped to impress upon pilgrims. As the disciples had been sent into the world bearing nothing, 'neither bag nor staff,

223 Vendôme, vol. 1, no. 210.
224 *Ibid.*, vol. 1, no. 250.
225 Cormery, pp. 85–87.
226 Vendôme, vol. 1, no. 251. Professor Riley-Smith tells me that such 'renunciations for cash' were not uncommon.
227 Honorius of Autun, *Elucidarium*, col. 1152. See also Constable, 'Opposition to Pilgrimage', p. 144.
228 Constable, 'Opposition to Pilgrimage', p. 144.
229 B. Bolton, *The Medieval Reformation* (London, 1983), pp. 17–32. Also, C. Morris, *The Papal Monarchy. The Western Church from 1050–1250* (Oxford, 1989), esp. pp. 29–33.
230 Bolton, *Medieval Reformation*, p. 19.
231 *Ibid.*, pp. 19–20.

neither bread nor money',[232] the pilgrim should carry no money, beyond what he intended to distribute to the poor.[233] The author asked his audience to consider what would become of those who carried gold and silver, spent their time eating and drinking and gave nothing in alms.[234] The same message was repeated several times, in particular contrasting the wealth of pilgrims with the poverty of the apostles. If the Blessed Peter had departed from Rome without shoes and, following his crucifixion, went straight to heaven, why was it that so many pilgrims travelled with large sums of money, two sets of clothing and ate rich food and drank strong wine?[235] 'The pilgrim who dies with money in his pocket', he warned, 'will be forever excluded from the kingdom of heaven.'[236] Similarly Jacques de Vitry, in a sermon addressed to pilgrims, stressed the ideal of poverty, emphasising that the pilgrim was not to be burdened with worldly goods, especially money.[237]

The Dangers Involved in Medieval Pilgrimage

It is clear from frequent references in medieval sources that the undertaking of a pilgrimage could be extremely dangerous. Indeed, it was perhaps the sheer number of dangers facing the medieval pilgrim that had led the anonymous biographer of St Fursey (d.653) wryly to comment that this holy man had reached Rome in safety, although in the course of his journey he had travelled through 'the hindrances of Burgundy, the dangers of Italy, the assaults of Passerella, the tricks of Pavia, the treachery of Sutri and the deceits of Carbonella'.[238] The pilgrim had to face not only the perils of natural disaster, disease and warfare but also the very serious problem of robbers and murderers who preyed on them, attracted perhaps by the money which many carried.

The very real fear harboured by those who set out on long journeys is well illustrated by the anonymous author of the Book of St Gilbert. Relating the journey made to Rome in 1202 by those seeking the canonization of St Gilbert, he noted that throughout their journey 'they were extremely anxious and afflicted by many doubts, because they had no experience of such a long journey and such great perils'.[239] The dangers of travel to Rome were also recognised by Pope Innocent III in his letter Vineam Sabaoth of April 1213, addressed to the archbishop, bishops, abbots and priors of the province of

---

232 Luke 9.3.
233 *Liber Sancti Jacobi*, vol. 1, p. 155.
234 *Ibid.*, vol. 1, pp. 155–156.
235 *Ibid.*, vol. 1, p. 156.
236 *Ibid.*, vol. 1, p. 157.
237 Bibliothèque Nationale Latin MS 3284, fol. 129v.
238 *De Furseo Confessore*, AASS Jan. II, p. 50.
239 *Book of St Gilbert*, pp. 180–183.

Canterbury.[240] Yet no one was to claim these difficulties as an excuse for not attending the Fourth Lateran Council.

There are certainly many examples in surviving sources of attacks perpetrated upon pilgrims, of which a few will serve for illustration. In 1126 Rudolph, abbot of St Trond and Alexander, archdeacon of Liège had set out for Rome. Having crossed the Alps they were set upon by robbers, who took all that they had.[241] Henry Zdik, bishop of Olomuc (1126–1150), having set out on a journey to Rome, was attacked and only just escaped with his life.[242] William of Verceil (d.1142), founder of Montevergine, was deterred from undertaking his pilgrimage to Jerusalem after he was set upon by thieves near Orea in southern Italy.[243] Nor was it only those travelling to Rome who faced such dangers. The *Chronicle* attributed to Benedict of Peterborough noted that 'it was the custom at Sorges and Lesperum to attack those on their way to St James'.[244] The biographer of St John, hermit and priest (d.1143), related the activities of thieves who lurked in the woods surrounding Urtica, near the road to Compostela. At night, they ambushed those who passed by, robbing and then killing many of their victims.[245] In 1168, Patrick, earl of Salisbury, was murdered by Guy *de Leszinna*, as he was returning from his pilgrimage to the shrine of St James of Compostela.[246] Nor were women spared. St Bona of Pisa (d.1207), having made a pilgrimage to the Holy Land, was attacked by Muslims on her way home. Henceforth, she lived as a recluse in Pisa, except for her pilgrimages to Compostela and to Rome.[247] The *Chanson de la Croisade Albigeoise* records the fate of those seized by heretics in the Languedoc c.1209. No 'pilgrim' or *Romieu* escaped maltreatment or assault on his journey and many lost eyes or feet, fists or fingers.[248]

Apart from accounts of attacks upon individuals, more general complaints concerning the harassment of pilgrims also survive. In the eleventh century, one Gerald of Galaria preyed upon pilgrims on the roads north of Rome.[249] Gerald had his counterparts in the twelfth century too. Thomas of Marle operated along the roads of northern France, holding pilgrims to ransom and

[240] *Selected Letters of Pope Innocent III Concerning England (1198–1216)*, ed. C. R. Cheney and W. H. Semple (London, 1953), pp. 144–147.
[241] *Gesta Abbatum Trudonensium*, p. 306.
[242] *De Beato Henrico Zdiko, Episcopo in Olomucensi in Moravia*, AASS June V, pp. 140–143. Also *Butler's Lives of the Saints*, ed. and rev. H. Thurstan and D. Attwater, 4 vols. (London, 1956), vol. 2, pp. 643–644.
[243] *De S. Guilielmo Abbate*, AASS June V, pp. 116–117.
[244] Benedict of Peterborough, *Chronicle*, vol. 1, p.132.
[245] *De S. Iohanne Eremita Presb.*, AASS June I, p. 261.
[246] Roger of Howden, *Chronica*, ed. W. Stubbs, 4 vols. RS 51 (London, 1868–1871), vol. 1, pp. 273–274.
[247] *De S. Bona Virgine*, AASS May VII, p. 149.
[248] *Chanson de la Croisade Albigeoise*, trans. E. Martin-Chabot, 3 vols. *Les Classiques de l'Histoire de France au Moyen Age* (Paris, 1931–1961), vol. 2, p. 53.
[249] William of Malmesbury, *Vita Wulfstani*, ed. R. R. Darlington, Camden Society, 40, 3rd Series (London, 1928), pp. 16–17; Sumption, *Pilgrimage*, p. 180.

inflicting terrible tortures upon them if his extortions were not paid.[250] A certain Burdinus was notorious for his attacks upon pilgrims carried out to the north of Rome. During the pontificate of Calixtus II, however, Burdinus was besieged at Sutri, captured, and then humiliated by being paraded on a camel, on which he was forced to ride backwards, using the tail as a rein.[251] Towards the end of the twelfth century, the roads to north the of Rome were once more the haunt of bandits. Guy and Nicholas, both of noble birth, operated in the area of Rispampani, 'wounding, seizing and robbing' those making their way both to and from Rome. [252]

Other complaints concerning individuals also survive. A letter of 1097 from Lambert, bishop of Arras, to the countess of Flanders, complained about attacks perpetrated upon pilgrims on their way to Rome. Pilgrims, he noted, who had crossed many foreign lands unmolested, on reaching the territory under her control, were robbed at Bapaume by G., an otherwise unnamed praepositus. After this praepositus had refused to return what he had taken, the bishop excommunicated him. The bishop's letter, therefore, was an appeal to the countess to use her authority to force the return of the pilgrims' property. If the property was not returned, he threatened to place the whole area, in which the robberies had been committed, under a ban.[253] Another letter which survives, which complained about attacks perpetrated upon pilgrims, was written by Gilbert Foliot, bishop of London (1163–1188) to the suffragan bishops of Canterbury. The attention of the bishop had been drawn to those wishing to travel to Rome, either on pilgrimage or as appellants to the papal court. These travellers were being hampered, robbed, atrociously treated and otherwise impeded on their journey through the realm. Those responsible for such acts were to be excommunicated.[254]

Surviving sources reveal, therefore, that there were a large number of dangers facing the pilgrim. In fact so numerous were the hazards that the fears harboured by many of them that they might never return home, and which led them to make arrangements for the distribution of their property in the event of their death, were probably wholly justified.

While Jacques de Vitry believed that the labour of the journey was an essential part of the pilgrim's reparation for past sins and misdemeanours, some pilgrims certainly sought to ease their toil. Horses to ride upon or to carry the baggage and money to spend along the way were for many pilgrims commonplace. Yet while some pilgrims could lessen the labour of the journey,

---

[250] Self and Society in Medieval France. The Memoirs of Abbot Guibert of Nogent, ed. J. F. Benton (New York, 1970), pp. 184–185; Sumption, Pilgrimage, p.180.

[251] Liber Pontificalis, vol. 2, p. 323; Andreae Danduli, Chronicon, RIS 12, col. 269.

[252] Gesta, col. xxix.

[253] Lambert, bishop of Arras, Epistolae, RHGF vol. 15, p. 183.

[254] Materials for the History of Thomas Becket, vol. 5, pp. 258–259.

there were many hazards which were faced by all. Natural disasters, disease, the activities of thieves and murderers and continual warfare, which made travel along many of the major routes to Rome perilous for much of the twelfth and early thirteenth centuries, were a constant threat to all pilgrims. That many pilgrims were aware of these dangers even before setting out, suggests that the majority of them were motivated by religious considerations and strengthened by the strong conviction that the undertaking of a pilgrimage *ad limina apostolorum* would secure their place in the heavenly kingdom.

3

Obligations and Privileges

By the twelfth century the pilgrim had acquired a special status in medieval society.[1] Certain obligations in particular pertained to his departure on pilgrimage but he also enjoyed commensurate privileges. The right to hospitality, safe passage and exemption from the payment of tolls can all be traced back to at least the Carolingian period. Other privileges such as the pilgrim's right to deal with excommunicants and the guaranteed protection of property during his absence seem to have been acquired later. The purpose of this chapter, therefore, is to examine some of the obligations incumbent upon pilgrims by the twelfth century together with the range of privileges which by then they also enjoyed.

Permission

Whilst all pilgrims were expected to put their affairs in order prior to their departure on pilgrimage, to settle quarrels and to return any property which they held unjustly,[2] one of the pilgrim's other main obligations seems to have been the requirement to obtain permission for the journey before setting out. The need for such permission seems to have applied equally to laymen as well as to monks and clerics. As early as 341, the Council of Antioch had decreed that no *peregrinus* might set out without letters of recommendation,[3] while the Council of Chalcedon of 451 forbade *peregrini clerici* to minister without such letters.[4] It is uncertain, however, what the term *peregrinus* meant in

---

1   On the special status of the pilgrim, see F. Garrisson, 'A Propos des Pèlerins et de leur Condition Juridique', *Etudes d'Histoire du Droit Canonique Dediées à Gabriel le Bras*, 2 (Paris, 1965), pp. 1165–1189; H. Gilles, 'Lex Peregrinorum', *Cahiers de Fanjeaux*, 15 (1980), pp. 161–189; L. Váquez de Parga, J. M. Lacarra and J. U. Ríu, *Las Peregrinaciones a Santiago de Compostela*, 3 vols. (Madrid, 1948–1949) [cited as *Peregrinaciones a Santiago*], vol. 1, pp. 255–279; F. L. Ganshof, 'L'Etranger dans la Monarchie Franque', *Recueils de la Société Jean Bodin*, 10 (Brussels, 1958), pp. 5–36; J. A. Brundage, *Medieval Canon Law and the Crusader* (Madison, Milwaukee and London, 1969).
2   *Liber Sancti Jacobi*, vol. 1, p. 157.
3   *Sacrorum Conciliorum*, vol. 2, col. 1323.
4   *Conciliorum Oecumenicorum Decreta*, p. 93.

these early canons. It is likely that in the case of the Council of Antioch it referred to any traveller outside his parish, and in the case of the canon of the Council of Chalcedon, to wandering clerics.

In the eighth and ninth centuries, as pilgrimage, especially to Rome, became increasingly popular, the Carolingians reissued these canons, often taking them over word for word, and occasionally even referring back to these earlier councils. By this time, however, as pilgrimage was an integral part of medieval life, there seems little doubt that the term *peregrinus* included those whose journey was of a religious nature. This is suggested both by the *formulae* which survive from Merovingian and Carolingian Gaul[5] and by the decrees of various councils. In 755 the Council of Ver forbade monks, who lived according to a rule, to make pilgrimages to Rome or to travel without the permission of their abbot.[6] The *Admonitio Generalis* of 789 decreed that no wandering clerics or *peregrini* were to be received without letters of recommendation and the licence of their bishop or abbot.[7] In 802 a capitulary of Charlemagne repeated the decree of the *Admonitio Generalis*.[8] The Council of Aix-la-Chapelle of 816 reissued canon 7 of the Council of Antioch of 341, stating that no *peregrinus* was to be received without the appropriate letters,[9] whilst a capitulary of Haito, bishop of Basle (c.807–823), decreed that no priest should leave his parish or go on pilgrimage *ad limina apostolorum* without permission from his bishop.[10]

The growth of such legislation in the Carolingian period may have reflected the increasing popularity of pilgrimage as well as growing concern over the rising number of individuals roaming the roads who were not genuine pilgrims at all. Canon 45 of the Council of Chalons-sur-Saône of 813 complained about the number of such travellers.[11] There were those who travelled to Tours, Rome and other holy places purely in the hope of material gain.[12] In addition, the canon complained about the numerous paupers who undertook pilgrimages in the hope of obtaining improved opportunities for begging[13] and those who believed that they were freed from their sins simply by seeing the holy places, forgetful, the canon noted, of the words of St Jerome (c.342–420), that it was praiseworthy not to have been to Jerusalem

5   On these *formulae*, see below pp. 74–75.
6   *Pippini Capitularia, Capitularia Regum Francorum*, ed. A. Boretius, MGH *Legum*, Sectio 2, vol. 1 (Hanover, 1883), p. 35.
7   *Karoli Magni Capitularia*, ed. A. Boretius, MGH *Legum*, Sectio 2, vol. 1 (Hanover, 1883), p. 54.
8   *Ibid.*, p. 102.
9   *Concilia Aevi Karolini*, p. 362.
10 Haito, bishop of Basle, *Capitula Ecclesiastica 807–823*, MGH *Legum*, Sectio 2, vol. 1 (Hanover, 1883), pp. 364–365.
11 *Concilia Aevi Karolini*, pp. 282–283
12 *Ibid.*, p. 282.
13 *Ibid.*, p. 282.

but to have lived well for Jerusalem.[14] These decrees demanding that pilgrims seek permission for their undertaking, therefore, were in part prompted by fears about public order. They may also, as both Constable and Garrisson argue, have been the result of Carolingian concerns for the general welfare of genuine pilgrims.[15] Letters from a bishop or abbot proved that the bearer was a real pilgrim and were presumably only granted once the person approving the pilgrimage had satisfied himself that the journey was being undertaken out of worthy and serious motives and that the would-be pilgrim was truly penitent and confessed.[16]

The content of these letters is suggested by *formulae* which survive from Merovingian Gaul and the Carolingian kingdoms. One such comes from the *Formulae Salzburgensis*.[17] The opening address of this *formula* was directed to bishops, abbots, abbesses, dukes, counts, vicars, gastalds and to all god-fearing men.[18] The writer of the letter then explained who he was, either bishop, abbot or other officer and the purpose of the letter. This indicated that the bearer of the letter had sought licence from him to go to Rome *causa orationis* and that this had been duly given.[19] The writer then requested that all who read it ensured this pilgrim safe passage and gave him hospitality, reminding them by quoting the text of St Matthew that it was their Christian duty so to do.[20] A similar formula is found in the *Formulae Salicae Bignonianae*.[21] This was addressed to 'the kings, counts, bishops, abbots, priests, clerics and all Christian people, who serve God in the provinces of Rome and Lombardy, whether in monasteries or cities, in towns or villages'.[22] The letter then informed the recipient that the pilgrim, whose name was to appear in the document, had sought permission to go to the basilica of St Peter.[23] The recipient was then asked, for love of God and St Peter, to receive the pilgrim as a guest and to grant safe passage to him so that he might return in safety.[24] A similar document in the *Marculfi Formulae* informed the reader that the pilgrim bearing the letter was not, as was the case with many, undertaking a pilgrimage for the sake of idleness.[25] Rather he was enduring a hard and long

---

[14] *Ibid.*, p. 282. St Jerome had written 'non Hierosolymis fuisse, sed Hierosolymis bene vixisse laudandum est'. See St Jerome, *Epistolae, PL* 22, col. 580.

[15] Garrisson, 'A Propos des Pèlerins', p. 1175; Constable, 'Opposition to Pilgrimage', p. 129.

[16] Haito, bishop of Basle noted that all laymen should confess at home, before setting out on their pilgrimage. See his *Capitula Ecclesiastica 807–823*, p. 365.

[17] *Formulae Merowingici et Karoli Aevi*, ed. K. Zeumer, MGH *Legum*, Sectio 5, (Hanover, 1886), p. 440.

[18] *Ibid.*, p. 440.

[19] *Ibid.*, p. 440.

[20] *Ibid.*, p. 440. See Matthew 25.35 and 40.

[21] *Formulae Merowingici et Karoli Aevi*, p. 234.

[22] *Ibid.*, p. 234.

[23] *Ibid.*, p. 234.

[24] *Ibid.*, p. 234.

[25] *Ibid.*, pp. 104–105.

road 'in the name of the Lord', and the reader was urged to share with him whatever he might need to sustain him either on his outward or homeward journey.[26]

The obligation incumbent upon pilgrims to obtain permission for their journey continued beyond the Carolingian period. In the *Decreta* of Burchard, bishop of Worms (d.1025), it was noted that *peregrini* were to have the appropriate letters of recommendation.[27] This obligation was also found in a canon of the Council of Setigenstadt c.1022[28] and in the *Decretum* of Ivo of Chartres (d.1115),[29] both of which recorded that no-one was to go to Rome without licence from a bishop or vicar. The *Veneranda dies* sermon, contained in the twelfth-century *Codex Calixtinus*, reminded pilgrims of their obligation to obtain permission for their pilgrimage,[30] while the *Coutumiers de Normandie*, dating from the thirteenth century, also indicate that pilgrims were expected to obtain permission for their journey. Having received a licence for the pilgrimage in his parish, the *Coutumiers de Normandie* explained that the pilgrim would then be conducted in a procession to the parish boundaries.[31]

An indication that pilgrims did, indeed, seek such permission before their departure is found in a few cartularies. In the cartulary of Chamalières-sur-Loire, an eleventh-century charter records that a certain Arimand was unable to set out on pilgrimage without licence from the prior,[32] while a twelfth-century charter in the cartulary of Sauxillanges recorded that Bernard of Rippa was unable to go on pilgrimage to Jerusalem without permission.[33]

One letter of safe-conduct, surviving from the twelfth century, indicates that such items, by this time at least, could even be obtained from the pope himself. Calixtus II wrote a letter dated 5 July 1121, addressed to Diego Gelmírez, archbishop of Compostela, on behalf of a certain *miles* by the name of Guy.[34] This explained that the said Guy had resolved to go to Compostela, with the intention of visiting the church of Blessed James the Apostle. Calixtus commended Guy to Diego and requested that he be looked after throughout his stay at Compostela.

---

[26] *Ibid.*, p. 105.
[27] Burchard of Worms, *Decreta*, col. 648.
[28] *Histoire des Conciles*, ed. H. Leclerq, 11 vols. (Paris, 1907–1952), vol. 4, pt 2, p. 923.
[29] Ivo of Chartres, *Decretum*, col. 896.
[30] *Liber Sancti Jacobi*, vol. 1, p. 157.
[31] *Coutumiers de Normandie*, ed. J. Tardif, 3 vols. (Rouen 1881, reprt. Geneva, 1977), vol. 3, pp. 215–216.
[32] Chamalières-sur-Loire, no. 211.
[33] Sauxillanges, no. 905.
[34] *Bullaire du Pape Calixte II 1119–1124. Essai de Restitution*, ed. U. Robert, 2 vols. (Paris, 1891), vol. 1, p. 361, no. 247.

The Pilgrim's Equipment

If pilgrims were supposed to carry with them letters of recommendation so that they could be identified as genuine, then the equipment which they bore, further marked them out as individuals whose journey was of a religious nature. The scrip and staff became the traditional *signa peregrinationis*. One of the most valuable sources for this is the *Veneranda dies* sermon. This sermon relates that the pilgrim carried his money in his scrip. This, however, the sermon-writer notes, should be made of leather and ought to be only of a small size.[35] Furthermore, it was always to be open and not bound with chains.[36] The small size of the scrip, the sermon continued, indicated that the pilgrim carried only a very modest sum with him, placing his trust in the Lord for his daily bread.[37] The fact that the pouch was made from the hide of a dead animal was also of significance. This, according to the *Veneranda dies* sermon, was a sign that the pilgrim ought to mortify his own flesh with cold, hunger, thirst and many other labours.[38] That the pilgrim's scrip was always open was a sign that he should spend his own money on the needy and ought then to receive and to give when need arose.[39] The other traditional piece of equipment carried by pilgrims was the staff. The staff was intended to sustain the pilgrim.[40] It acted as his third leg, symbolising the protection of the Holy Trinity enjoyed by the truly penitent and confessed pilgrim against the snares of the devil.

That the scrip and staff came to be recognised by the Church as the *signa peregrinationis* is apparent from the rituals which developed for the ceremonial blessing of these items, usually before the pilgrim set out on his journey. Eadmer described how c.1097 St Anselm, archbishop of Canterbury, received his scrip and staff before setting out for Rome.[41] There is some evidence, however, that this ceremony, at least in the twelfth century, may not always have taken place before the pilgrim departed. In his account of the main routes to Rome from Iceland, Nikolas of Munkathvera noted that those Icelanders who travelled via Utrecht, received there, their 'staff, scrip and a blessing for their pilgrimage to Rome'.[42] Perhaps this is an indication that there were certain places along the main pilgrimage routes where such items could be collected by pilgrims who did not already have them.

The texts for the services at which the scrip and staff were blessed began to appear in the eleventh century, although, as Garrisson argues, it is possible that this ceremony pre-dated the appearance of these texts.[43] In their sim-

---

35 *Liber Sancti Jacobi*, vol. 1, p. 152.
36 *Ibid.*, vol. 1, p. 152.
37 *Ibid.*, vol. 1, p. 152.
38 *Ibid.*, vol. 1, pp. 152–153.
39 *Ibid.*, vol. 1, p. 153.
40 *Ibid.*, vol. 1, p. 153.
41 Eadmer, *Life of St Anselm*, p. 97.
42 Magoun, 'Pilgrim Diary', p. 349.

plest form, such as the Worcester Pontifical, dating from the late eleventh century, the texts indicate that the ceremony was a short one, consisting of prayers, the bestowal of the scrip and staff, followed by further prayers.[44] Later texts suggest that by the twelfth century services had become longer and rather more elaborate. The Ely Pontifical indicated that the ceremony began with the reading of three Psalms, followed by a *Kyrie Eleison*, a *Pater Noster*, a set of verses and responses, a prayer of invocation and a blessing. There then followed three alternative *formulae* for the blessing and bestowal of scrip and staff.[45] It was out of these services for the blessing of the *signa peregrinationis* that a liturgy was developed, probably around the middle of the twelfth century, for the ceremonial blessing and bestowal of the crusader's cross.[46]

The Pilgrim's Badge

By the twelfth century another item, the badge, had become part of the pilgrim's equipment.[47] Whereas the scrip and staff, however, were normally bestowed at the beginning of the pilgrim's journey, his badge, usually sported on hat or collar, could not be purchased until he had reached his destination. Once more, the *Veneranda dies* sermon explained the significance of these tokens. They bore witness to the pilgrim's great labour and were a sign that he had mortified his flesh and overcome his vices.[48] Drunkards, fornicators, usurers and other such people, the sermon added, were not entitled to wear such signs.[49] To William of Tyre, writing c.1180, these tokens were a symbol of a pilgrimage fulfilled.[50] The palm leaf became the traditional symbol associated with pilgrimage to the Holy Land and by the twelfth century,

---

[43] Garrisson, 'A Propos des Pèlerins', pp. 1172–1177. Also on these ceremonies, see J. A. Brundage, 'Cruce Signari: The Rite for Taking the Cross in England', *Traditio*, 22 (1966), pp. 289–310; A. Franz, *Die kirchlichen Benediktionen des Mittelalters*, 2 vols. (Graz, 1960), esp. vol. 2, pp. 271–289.

[44] For the text of the Worcester Pontifical, see Brundage, 'Cruce Signari', p. 298.

[45] *Ibid.*, pp. 303–306.

[46] The work of Garrisson ('A Propos des Pèlerins', pp. 1172–1177), with which Brundage agrees, indicates that the ceremony for the blessing of the crusader's cross developed from the ceremony for the blessing of the scrip and staff, and not the other way around (Brundage, 'Cruce Signari', p. 296).

[47] On pilgrimage badges, see M. Mitchener, *Medieval Pilgrim and Secular Badges* (London, 1986); B. W. Spencer, 'Medieval Pilgrim Badges', *Rotterdam Papers: A Contribution to Medieval Archaeology* (Rotterdam, 1968), pp. 137–153; E. Cohen, 'In Haec Signa: Pilgrim Badge Trade in Southern France', *Journal of Medieval History*, 2 (1976), pp. 193–214.

[48] *Liber Sancti Jacobi*, vol. 1, p. 153.

[49] *Ibid.*, vol. 1, p. 153.

[50] William of Tyre, *Historia Rerum in Partibus Transmarinsi Gestarum*, PL 201, col. 831.

pilgrims could purchase these from stalls in Jerusalem itself.[51] The scallop shell was the symbol which became associated with pilgrimage to Santiago de Compostela. The *Guide to Compostela* indicates that by the middle of the twelfth century, pilgrims could purchase these tokens, probably lead badges rather than real shells, from stalls near the cathedral.[52]

Rome seems to have been the last of the great pilgrimage centres to develop its own badge. In 1199, however, Innocent III granted as a special privilege to the canons of S. Pietro the monopoly of production and sale of these badges for Rome.[53] Produced in two grades, tin and lead, they bore the double image of St Peter with a key and St Paul a sword and the inscription *Signa Apostolorum Petri et Pauli.* The canons were given permission to cast these badges themselves, or to allow others to do so on their behalf, providing that these nominees remained answerable to them.[54] By the fourteenth century, however, if not earlier, pilgrims could also purchase badges bearing a reproduction of the *Veronica,* the cloth on which Christ's suffering face had been imprinted. This was a witness perhaps to the popularity of this relic amongst the *Romipetae.*[55] Other pilgrimage centres, too, developed their own special badges. At Canterbury, pilgrims could purchase badges which bore representations of St Thomas, at St Albans, badges depicting the martyrdom of Alban himself and from Cologne, badges which bore the image of the Magi.[56]

While these badges were undoubtedly a good means by which pilgrimage centres advertised themselves, they did, as the *Veneranda dies* sermon stressed, have a serious purpose as well. They were a sign of the pilgrim's devotion and a witness that his journey had been made. They also marked him out as someone entitled to safe passage and to aid from all Christians. While desire for the profits, therefore, which could be made from this lucrative trade may have been one reason why, by the early thirteenth century, the Church was seeking to control the production of badges, there may have been another more serious purpose. Indeed, it was perhaps because of the spiritual associations which badges sold at the shrines developed, that there was a growing concern to prevent pilgrims being duped by false and worthless badges purchased from elsewhere. One of the most notable cases of this type concerned false badges being sold all along the route to Compostela. In a letter of 1207 addressed to the archbishops of Spain and Gascony, Innocent III instructed them to prohibit the sale in their territory of these *adulterina*

---

[51] See for example, *Chronique d'Ernoul et de Bernard le Trésorier,* ed. M. L. de Mas Latrie, *Société de l'Histoire de France,* 157 (Paris, 1871), p. 193.

[52] *Guide du Pèlerin,* pp. 96–97.

[53] Innocent III, *Registers, PL* 214, cols. 490–491.

[54] *Ibid.,* col. 491.

[55] On the *Veronica,* see below, pp. 114–116.

[56] For the badges produced by the main pilgrimage centres, see Mitchener, *Medieval Pilgrim and Secular Badges.*

insignia, which were known as *conchae*.[57] Those who continued to make and to sell them were to be excommunicated. That the makers of these false badges continued in business, however, is suggested by the reissuing of Innocent III's prohibition by Gregory IX in 1228, by Alexander IV in 1259, by Clement IV in 1266 and by Gregory X in 1272.[58]

The letters of recommendation, the scrip, staff and the badge all distinguished the pilgrim from other travellers who roamed the roads. This was important because it marked them out as individuals who enjoyed special privileges. Notable amongst these were the rights to hospitality, safe conduct and exemption from the payment of tolls.

Hospitality

The Merovingian and Carolingian *formulae*, considered above, emphasised the duty of all Christian people to aid the pilgrim in his undertaking by offering him hospitality. Garrisson argues that in the Carolingian period there was a tendency to transform the ideal of Christian charity into a legal obligation.[59] For although these *formulae* urged those who read them to give hospitality to the pilgrim, legislation was also issued making this compulsory![60] Charlemagne's *Admonitio Generalis* of 789 reminded everyone of their obligation to entertain both the poor and pilgrims.[61] A capitulary of c.802, however, went further.[62] No-one, in any of the Carolingian kingdoms, was to dare to deny hospitality either to rich or to poor pilgrims.[63] Those, this capitulary stated, who were pilgrims, travelling *propter Deum* and *propter salutem animae*, were not to be denied either shelter, warmth or water.[64] Those who were willing to give further aid to the pilgrim were encouraged to do so and reminded of the text of Matthew, '. . . whoever receives one such child in my name receives me'.[65] The responsibilities of the bishops in this respect were given particular emphasis. The Council of Tours of 813 decreed that pilgrims and the poor were to be the guests of bishops and were to be refreshed by them not only in body but in spirit as well.[66]

---

[57] Innocent III, *Registers*, PL 215, col. 1176.
[58] Cohen, 'In Haec Signa', p. 212, note 14.
[59] Garrisson, 'A Propos des Pèlerins', pp. 1185–1188.
[60] Whereas the *Rule* written by St Benedict (c.480–550), for example, had obliged monks to receive travellers as though they were Christ Himself, the legislation of the Carolingian period seems to have made this obligation incumbent upon all Christians, both clergy and laity alike.
[61] *Karolini Magni Capitularia*, p. 60.
[62] *Ibid.*, p. 96.
[63] *Ibid.*, p. 96.
[64] *Ibid.*, p. 96.
[65] Matthew, 18.5.
[66] *Concilia Aevi Karolini*, p. 287.

Attempts were also made to ensure that the means were available to provide for pilgrims. The Council of Riesbach of c.798 decreed that oblations left by the Christian faithful were to be divided into four parts.[67] One portion was to be retained by the bishop himself and to be used for his own work. A second portion was to be distributed among the deacons and priests, a third to the clerics, while the fourth part was to be spent solely on the care of guests and pilgrims. A capitulary of 802, which contained instructions for priests, incorporated similar provisions.[68] This allowed for a three-way division of oblations, one part for the upkeep and decoration of the church, a second part to be retained by the priests themselves and the third to be spent on the care of the poor and pilgrims.

The church's continuing obligation to provide hospitality for pilgrims was further emphasised in the eleventh, twelfth and thirteenth centuries.[69] Burchard of Worms noted that priests ought to labour so that they might be better able to give hospitality to travellers,[70] an obligation also found in the *Decretum* of Gratian, compiled c.1139,[71] and in the *Decretals* of Gregory IX.[72] The canonistic collections of Burchard of Worms, Ivo of Chartres and that of Gratian noted too that priests could, if necessary, entertain their guests in the church.[73] The *Decretum* of Ivo of Chartres recorded that priests could also alienate goods of the Church to minister to the needs of pilgrims, clerics or the needy.[74]

Safe Conduct and Exemption from Tolls

A second privilege to which pilgrims were entitled was the right to safe passage. As we have seen, however, surviving sources show that all too often pilgrims were not able to travel in safety and that they frequently fell victim to the robbers and murderers who preyed on unwary travellers.[75] From the seventh century onwards, in an attempt to combat this growing menace to pilgrims' safety, an increasing number of laws and decrees were issued, which

---

67 *Ibid.*, p. 200.
68 *Karoli Magni Capitularia*, p. 106.
69 Despite this obligation there is evidence that by the late twelfth century there were bishops who were negligent in their duties relating to hospitality and the care of pilgrims. See above, p. 65.
70 Burchard of Worms, *Decreta*, col. 644.
71 The *Decretum* of Gratian can be found in volume 1 of *Corpus Iuris Canonici*. See esp. D.91, c.2.
72 Gregory IX, *Decretalium*, in volume 2 of *Corpus Iuris Canonici*, 3, 41, 1.
73 Burchard of Worms, *Decreta*, col. 690; Ivo of Chartres, *Decretum*, col. 214; Gratian (*Corpus Iuris Canonici*, vol. 1, D.42, c.5) attributes this canon to the Third Council of Carthage of 397.
74 Ivo of Chartres, *Decretum*, col. 236, quoting the Third Council of Toledo of 589.
75 See above, pp. 68–70.

demanded safe passage for pilgrims and which imposed harsh penalties upon all those who continued to attack them. The large number of such laws and decrees which survive reflects, not only the very real dangers which all pilgrims faced but also the continued efforts of both secular rulers and ecclesiastical authorities, particularly from the late tenth century onwards, to provide safe passage for pilgrims.

One of the earliest laws of this type to single out pilgrims is the *Lex Baiwariorum*, dating from the first half of the seventh century.[76] This decreed that no-one was to disturb or to harm anyone on the road, whether he was travelling *propter Deum* or *propter necessitatem*. Anyone who injured, wounded, despoiled, bound, killed or sold such a traveller as a slave was compelled to pay a fine of 160 sous to the royal fisc and to restore twice-over anything which he had taken from the pilgrim. A capitulary of 782–786, the work of Pepin of Italy, imposed harsh penalties upon anyone who murdered a pilgrim. Not only was the perpetrator to suffer the penalty for murder, a fine of sixty *solidi* was also to be paid.[77] A capitulary of 802 grouped pilgrims with widows and orphans. It was decreed that no one was to presume to perpetrate any kind of fraud or injury against them.[78] Pilgrims, like widows and orphans, were clearly recognised as a vulnerable group of society. Travelling unarmed they were unable to defend either themselves or their property and were particularly prone to attack.

Another group with whom pilgrims were frequently connected were merchants. Like pilgrims they spent much of their time on the roads and were also attractive prey because of the goods which they carried. In 850, the East Frankish Emperor, Louis II (d.875), noted that it had come to his attention that those travelling through his realm, both *causa orationis* and *causa negotiandi*, frequently fell victim to robbers, who either wounded or killed them and stole their goods.[79] As a result he issued a capitulary to his counts in which he ordered them to investigate any tales of this kind that they might hear. They were instructed to detain any such perpetrators and to see that they were punished in accordance with the law.[80] In this way Louis hoped that 'his kingdom might be purged of such evil-doers, so that those who travelled for the sake of prayer or business, might do so in safety'.[81] A stern warning accompanied this capitulary of 850. Any count or official who

---

[76] *Lex Baiwariorum*, ed. E. L. B. de Schwind, *MGH.Legum*, Sectio 1, vol. 5 (Hanover, 1888), esp. pp. 335–336.

[77] *Karoli Magni et Pippini Filii Capitularia Italica*, ed. A. Boretius, *MGH Legum*, Sectio 2, Part 1 (Hanover, 1883), esp. p. 193. Also Garrisson, 'A Propos des Pèlerins', pp. 1178–1179.

[78] *Karolini Magni Capitularia*, p. 93.

[79] *Capitularia Hludowici II*, ed. A. Boretius and V. Krause, *MGH Legum*, Sectio 2, vol. 2 (Hanover, 1897), p. 86.

[80] *Ibid.*, p. 86.

[81] *Ibid.*, p. 86.

approved the action of these bandits or was negligent in bringing them to justice would forfeit his office.[82]

Other legislation of the eighth and ninth centuries sought to ensure not only that pilgrims should be safe from attack but, connected with this, that they should also be exempted from the payment of tolls. In 753, the Synod of Metz decreed that pilgrims travelling to Rome or some other shrine were not to be detained at bridges, gates or on boats.[83] No evil was to be perpetrated against them, nor was any toll to be demanded from them.[84] Anyone who sought such payment from a pilgrim was to pay sixty *solidi* as a fine, half to the injured party and the other half to the royal fisc.[85] Canon 22 of the Council of Ver of 755 confirmed this decree of the Synod of Metz, by exempting pilgrims from the payment of tolls, even in those places where they could be demanded legally.[86] This exemption was confirmed again at the end of the eighth century in a letter addressed to King Offa by Charlemagne.[87] In this Charlemagne confirmed that those travelling *ad limina apostolorum* 'for the love of God and the salvation of their souls' were able to go in safety and without disturbance.[88] He added that although merchants who tried to pass themselves off as pilgrims would have to pay tolls, the rest could go in peace.[89]

That these early attempts may have failed to guarantee exemption from the payment of tolls and safe passage for pilgrims is suggested by the fact that laws and decrees of this type continued to be passed. The laws of King Alfred of Wessex (d.899) decreed that strangers and pilgrims were not to be harmed,[90] while the *Leges Ecclesiastici* of King Edgar of England (d.975) stated that pilgrims were to be helped just like poor widows and orphans.[91] In 1027, Cnut went to Rome and described how he had managed to secure an agreement between the pope, emperor and others who were present, that all people of his kingdom, both English and Danes alike, should be able to travel both to and from Rome in safety and free from the payment of tolls.[92] The Norman *Consuetudines et Iusticie* of William the Conqueror also make reference to the safety of pilgrims.[93] These *Consuetudines* were not set down in William the Conqueror's reign but were rather the result of an inquest made

82 *Ibid.*, p. 86.
83 *Sacrorum Conciliorum*, vol. 12, col. 572.
84 *Ibid.*, vol. 12, col. 572.
85 *Ibid.*, vol. 12, col. 572.
86 *Ibid.*, vol. 12, col. 583.
87 Alcuin, *Epistolae*, ed. E. Duemmler, MGH *Epistolae* 4 (Berlin, 1895), pp. 144–146.
88 *Ibid.*, p. 145.
89 *Ibid.*, p. 145.
90 F. Liebermann, *Die Gesetze der Angelsachsen*, 3 vols. (Halle, 1903–1916), vol. 1, p. 43.
91 *Sacrorum Conciliorum*, vol. 18A, col. 524.
92 Liebermann, *Die Gesetze der Angelsachsen*, vol. 1, p. 276.
93 C. H. Haskins, 'The Norman *Consuetudines et Iusticie* of William the Conqueror', EHR, 23 (1908), pp. 502–508.

by Robert and William Rufus after his death, probably c.1091.[94] Item 12 in these customs laid down that no-one was to harm a pilgrim and anyone so doing was to be placed at the Duke's mercy.[95]

From the end of the tenth and particularly during the eleventh centuries, as part of the larger peace movement of the period, the Church itself seems to have taken an increasing interest in the safety and welfare of pilgrims. The Synod of Charroux, held c.989, demanded the cessation of warfare at certain times of the year and the exemption from attack of certain groups, such as travellers and pilgrims.[96] The Council of Enham in 1009 enacted that pilgrims and strangers were not to be harassed or oppressed.[97] The Council of Rouen of 1096 decreed that all churches and churchyards, monks, clerics, nuns, women, pilgrims, merchants and their households, oxen and horses at plough, men leading the plough, men harrowing and the horses with which they harrow, men who flee to the plough, as well as the land of religious houses and the money of the clergy, were to enjoy 'perpetual peace', so that no one 'shall dare to attack, seize, rob or molest them in any way'.[98] In 1099 the Council of St Omer laid down that pilgrims and merchants were not to be robbed.[99]

Measures which sought to protect pilgrims and to ensure them safe passage continued to be promoted during the twelfth century. In the treaty of Devol of 1108 between Alexius Comnenus and Bohemund of Antioch, the Emperor promised protection for pilgrims passing through his lands.[100] The Council of Etampes of 1130 decreed that priests, clerics, monks, pilgrims and merchants were to be safe at all times,[101] while a similar decree was issued in the same year by the Council of Clermont.[102] Canon 10 of the Council of Reims of 1131 decreed that priests, clerics, monks, pilgrims, merchants, serfs and their animals used for ploughing, as well as sheep, should be left in peace at all times.[103] This canon was reissued by the Council of Reims of 1148.[104] It was also decreed, however, that if a breach of this canon occurred, the offender was to be punished in accordance with canon law and that this was the

---

94 Ibid., pp. 502–503.
95 Ibid., p. 508.
96 Brundage, Medieval Canon Law and the Crusader, pp. 12–13.
97 Sacrorum Conciliorum, vol. 19, col. 303.
98 Ibid., vol. 20, col. 923. Compare Orderic Vitalis, The Ecclesiastical History, ed. and trans. M. Chibnall, 6 vols. (Oxford, 1969–1978), vol. 5, pp. 20–21. Chibnall points out that the idea of protection of men at the plough was a piece of old Scandinavian custom, and that the Council of Rouen seems to have further extended this protection to men seeking some kind of sanctuary at the plough.
99 Sacrorum Conciliorum, vol. 20, cols. 971–972.
100 Fulcher of Chartres, Historia Hierosolymitana (1095–1127), ed. H. Hagenmeyer (Heidelberg, 1913), p. 524.
101 Sacrorum Conciliorum, vol. 21, col. 439.
102 Ibid., vol. 21, col. 439.
103 Ibid., vol. 21, col. 460.
104 Ibid., vol. 21, col. 716.

responsibility of the bishop in whose diocese the offence had taken place.[105] The Council of Tours of 1163 issued a similar decree, in which pilgrims were named as just one of a number of groups of society who were not to be harmed.[106] The inviolability of pilgrims was also stressed in the *Decretum* of Gratian[107] and in other collections of the twelfth century, such as the *Penitentiale* of Bartholomew of Exeter.[108]

With the growth in popularity of pilgrimage to Compostela, laws intended to protect pilgrims began to be issued in the Spanish kingdoms, both by the secular rulers as well as the Church.[109] In 1072 Alfonso VI of Leon and Castile (1072–1109), wishing to help pilgrims on their way to Compostela, abolished tolls at the gate of Valcárcel, where it had been the custom to rob and cheat all those passing through, especially the poor and pilgrims on their way to St James.[110] In addition to the abolition of these tolls, Alfonso VI also forbade anyone to harm or disturb any such traveller.[111] Sancho V Ramírez of Aragon and Navarre (1076–1094) enacted similar laws in his own kingdoms. Whilst fixing tolls that travellers could be charged in Jaca and Pamplona, both of which were gateways onto the pilgrimage route to Compostela, he ordered that no such charge might be demanded from pilgrims.[112] Similar laws concerned with the safety of pilgrims on the road followed in the early years of the twelfth century, largely the inspiration of Diego Gelmírez. The decrees of the Council of Leon of 1114, ratified by the Synod of Compostela in the same year, included a declaration that pilgrims, merchants and those at work were to be left in peace.[113] In 1124 pilgrims were included amongst those protected by the Peace of God,[114] while the Council of Palencia of 1129 ordered that anyone who attacked a cleric, monk, traveller, merchant, pilgrim or woman was to be imprisoned in a monastery or sent into exile.[115]

The number of decrees which were issued in an attempt to protect pilgrims as they travelled may well reflect not only the continual dangers which pilgrims faced and the efforts made by both secular rulers and the Church to protect them but the increasing popularity of pilgrimage itself. Indeed, by 1059 pilgrims seem to have been considered such an important group of

---

105 *Ibid.*, vol. 21, col. 716.

106 *Ibid.*, vol. 21, cols. 1183–1184.

107 Gratian, *Decretum* in *Corpus Iuris Canonici*, vol. 1, esp. c. 24, q. 3, c. 23–25.

108 See A. Morey, *Bartholomew of Exeter, Bishop and Canonist. A Study in the Twelfth Century* (Cambridge, 1937), p. 286.

109 On the laws of the Spanish kingdoms concerning pilgrimage, see *Peregrinaciones a Santiago*, vol. 1, pp. 255–279, which deals particularly with the legislation of the thirteenth and fourteenth centuries.

110 *Instrumenta Insigniora ad Historiam Legionensem*, ed M. Risco, *España Sagrada*, 36 (Madrid, 1787), pp. liii–liv.

111 *Ibid.*, p. liv.

112 *Peregrinaciones a Santiago*, vol. 1, p. 260.

113 *Historia Compostellana*, ed. E. Flórez, *España Sagrada*, vol. 20 (Madrid, 1765), p. 192.

114 *Ibid.*, p. 418.

115 *Ibid.*, p. 485.

society that they were included among those deserving of protection in canon 15 of the Council of Rome, presided over by Pope Nicholas II (1059–1061). This canon decreed that anyone found robbing or causing harm to pilgrims, clerics, monks, women, or undefended paupers would be excommunicated until amends had been made.[116] In a Council held at Rome c.1074–1075 by Pope Gregory VII (1073–1085), excommunication was reiterated as the punishment for anyone who dared to seize a priest, monk or pilgrim, or his property.[117]

Papal enactments of the twelfth century, as Brundage has argued, confirmed the protection of pilgrims as a papal obligation.[118] Canon 14 of the First Lateran Council, held in 1123 during the pontificate of Calixtus II, stated that anyone who seized or robbed *Romipetae* or pilgrims, those travelling *ad limina apostolorum* or to other holy places, or who raised new tolls on merchants, was to be excommunicated until satisfactory reparations had been made.[119] Pilgrims again appear in the canons of the Second and Third Lateran Councils. Canon 11 of the Second Lateran Council of 1139 included pilgrims among those who were to be left in peace at all times,[120] while canon 22 of the Third Lateran Council of 1179 also included pilgrims among those who were not to be harmed.[121] According to this canon, anyone who attacked a pilgrim was to be excommunicated until reparations had been made.

Protection from Innkeepers

Other decrees were issued with the specific intention of providing protection for pilgrims staying at inns or hostelries, for innkeepers seem to have enjoyed a particularly notorious reputation. It was probably the owners of such establishments that the author of the *Veneranda dies* sermon had in mind, in his tirade against 'evil hosts'. Some, he complained, promise pilgrims his best beds and then place them in the most uncomfortable ones.[122] Others give pilgrims the best wine but only in order to make them drunk, so that they can rob them more easily while they sleep.[123] Others seem to have been less subtle and patient, slipping a sleeping draught into the pilgrim's cup.[124]

Prompted by the increase in popularity of pilgrimage to Spain in the

---

116 *Sacrorum Conciliorum*, vol. 19, col. 916. This was incorporated in the *Decretum* of Gratian. See *Corpus Iuris Canonici*, vol. 1, c. 24, q. 3, c. 25.
117 *Acta Pontificum Romanorum Inedita*, vol. 2, p. 126.
118 Brundage, *Medieval Canon Law and the Crusader*, p. 13.
119 *Conciliorum Oecumenicorum Decreta*, p. 193. This was incorporated into the *Decretum* of Gratian. See *Corpus Iuris Canonici*, vol. 1, c. 24, q. 3, c. 23.
120 *Conciliorum Oecumenicorum Decreta*, p. 199.
121 *Ibid.*, p. 222.
122 *Liber Sancti Jacobi*, vol. 1, p. 161.
123 *Ibid.*, p. 161.
124 *Ibid.*, p. 161.

twelfth century, the *Fuero de Estella* of 1164 decreed that if any pilgrim or merchant staying at inn noticed that some of his property was missing and accused the innkeeper, his wife or children, then a trial by combat had to ensue.[125] If the innkeeper and his family were beaten this was a sign of their guilt and they then had to give the pilgrim or merchant three times what they had taken from him. They also had to pay the king a fine of sixty *solidi* for their crime and another sixty for the combat. This law, however, also attempted to provide some protection for the innkeeper against cheating pilgrims or merchants. If the innkeeper won the combat, thereby proving his innocence, the pilgrim or merchant was obliged to pay him sixty *solidi*. If the guilty party did not have enough money to pay the reparations, he was to surrender himself with all his goods, both moveable and immoveable, and to swear an oath that he had nothing else. This law was reproduced word-for-word in the *Fuero General* of Navarre.[126]

Other attempts were also made to protect pilgrims from the customs and habits of innkeepers. A law of Toulouse of 1205 decreed that pilgrims who entered the city were not to be harassed by innkeepers.[127] In particular this law stated that innkeepers were neither to seize pilgrims by their lapels, nor by the bridle of their horses or mules, and drag them to their own establishment in the hope of forcing them to stay there.[128] Similar laws were enacted in Rome in the thirteenth century. In April 1235, legislation initiated by the Senator, Angelo Malabranca, placed pilgrims under the direct protection of the Senate[129] and in the September of that year, the Senate legislated to prevent pilgrims being harassed by innkeepers. As in the case of the Toulouse law of 1205, innkeepers were forbidden to kidnap pilgrims off the streets, forcing them to stay in their hostelries, and neither were they to lure them away from rival establishments.[130]

Other Privileges

Pilgrims, therefore, were entitled to hospitality, safe conduct and exemption from the payment of tolls. By the twelfth century they also seem to have had the right to appoint someone to look after their affairs during their absence. The *Leges* of Henry I of England, dating from c.1115, allowed pilgrims going

---

[125] *Fuero del Estella*, ed. G. Holmér, *Leges Hispanicae Medii Aevi*, 10 (Karlsham, 1963), p. 37.

[126] *Peregrinaciones a Santiago*, vol. 1, p. 271.

[127] *Histoire Générale de Languedoc*, ed. C. Devic and J. Vaissète, and later by E. Roschach and A. Molimier *et al.* (Toulouse, 1872–1904, reprt. 1973), vol. 8, cols. 513–516.

[128] *Ibid.*, vol. 8, col. 513.

[129] *Codice Diplomatico del Senato Romano dal 1147 al 1347*, ed. F. Bartoloni, *Fonti per la Storia d'Italia*, 87 (Rome, 1948), pp. 131–134.

[130] *Ibid.*, pp. 143–145.

to 'Rome, Jerusalem or other distant places' to nominate a relative or friend to look after their belongings while they were away.[131]

Another important privilege which pilgrims may have been granted during the twelfth century was the protection of their property during their absence, a privilege also enjoyed by crusaders. In 1145 Eugenius III issued the Bull, *Quantum praedecessores*, which placed under the protection of the Holy See the wife, children and property of the crusader and forbade anyone to disturb them until the crusader's return or death.[132] Brundage has argued that the protection of family and property was probably a privilege which was first given to crusaders and then extended to other pilgrims.[133] There is certainly evidence that protection of property by the Holy See was being extended towards the end of the twelfth century. In a letter of 1195 addressed to the bishop of Amiens, Celestine III placed the property of clerics travelling to Rome under the protection of the Holy See.[134] It is possible, as Garrisson argues, although there is no direct evidence, that this privilege may have been extended to all pilgrims making the same journey to the apostolic city.[135]

By the twelfth century pilgrims also seem to have been entitled to a suspension of legal proceedings during their absence.[136] This privilege seems to have made its first appearance in ecclesiastical law during the pontificate of Alexander III and originally may have been a privilege intended for crusaders. In the decretal *Consultationibus* issued between 1173 and 1176, it was laid down that judgment was not to be given against those who were absent either for reasons of study or pilgrimage.[137] This privilege can also be found in the *Treatise of Laws and Customs* composed by Glanville c.1187. In this it was recorded that the delay in proceedings was dependent upon whether the pilgrimage had been made to Jerusalem or to some other place. If to Jerusalem, then the pilgrim was to be granted at least a year's delay and if

131 Liebermann, *Die Gesetze der Angelsachsen*, vol. 1, p. 582.
132 Otto of Freising, *Gesta Friderici I Imperatoris*, ed. R. G. Waitz, *Scriptores Rerum Germanicarum in Usum Scholarum*, 3rd ed. (Hanover, 1912), pp. 55–57. This Bull is translated in L. and J. S. C. Riley-Smith, *The Crusades, Ideal and Reality, 1095–1274* (1981), pp. 57–59: 'And we decree that their wives and children, goods and possessions should remain under the protection of the holy church, under our protection and that of the archbishops, bishops and other prelates of the church of God. And by apostolic authority we forbid any legal suit to be brought thereafter concerning all the possessions they hold peacefully when they take the cross until there is absolutely certain knowledge of their return or death.'
133 Brundage, *Medieval Canon Law and the Crusader*, p. 168.
134 This was included in the *Decretalium* of Pope Gregory IX. See *Corpus Iuris Canonici*, vol. 2, 2, 29, 1.
135 Garrisson, 'A Propos des Pèlerins', p. 1183.
136 See *ibid.*, esp. pp. 1183–1184; Brundage, *Medieval Canon Law and the Crusader*, pp. 172–174.
137 Alexander III, *Epistolae et Privilegia*, PL 200, cols. 1053–1054.

to elsewhere the delay was to be decided by the king or his justices.[138] A similar privilege can also be found in the *Coutumiers de Normandie* dating from the early thirteenth century.[139]

By the twelfth century pilgrims seem to have been granted several other privileges. According to the *Fuero General* of Navarre they enjoyed protection from their creditors.[140] They were in effect given an extension on the repayment of their loans. This amounted to five days for those travelling to Rocamadour, one month for those travelling to Compostela, three months for those travelling *ad limina apostolorum*, and one year and a day for those journeying to the Holy Land.[141] A decision by Gregory VII at a council held in Rome at an unknown date seems to have given pilgrims the right to deal with excommunicants. This privilege can be found in both the *Decretum* of Gratian[142] and in the *Penitentiale* of Bartholomew of Exeter.[143] Pilgrims also enjoyed the protection of church courts[144] and by the early thirteenth century were also released from the consequences of an interdict.[145]

As pilgrimage grew in popularity during the Carolingian period, it became increasingly necessary to distinguish genuine pilgrims from others roaming the roads. Pilgrims, therefore, had to carry letters of recommendation, issued to them perhaps by the local bishop, abbot or their parish priest. By the twelfth century pilgrims were also marked out by more visible tokens, their scrip, staff and badge. It was necessary for pilgrims to be easily distinguishable for they were entitled to special privileges. They could claim hospitality, and safe conduct as well as exemption from the payment of tolls. Whilst these privileges can be traced back to at least the seventh century, during the late eleventh and twelfth centuries the number of privileges which pilgrims enjoyed began to increase. This may well have been a result of the crusading movement. For while the privileges enjoyed by pilgrims were extended to crusaders, new privileges granted to the crusaders to encourage participation in the crusades seem to have been gradually extended to pilgrims as well.

---

[138] *Tractatus de legibus et consuetudinibus regni Anglie qui Glanvilla vocatur*, ed. D. G. D. Hall (London, 1965), pp. 16–17.
[139] *Coutumiers de Normandie*, vol. 1, p. 36.
[140] *Peregrinaciones a Santiago*, vol. 1, p. 264.
[141] *Ibid.*, vol. 1, p. 264.
[142] Gratian, *Decretum* in *Corpus Iuris Canonici*, vol. 1, c. 11, q. 3, c. 103.
[143] Morey, *Bartholomew of Exeter*, p. 287.
[144] Brundage, *Medieval Canon Law and the Crusader*, p. 170.
[145] Gregory IX, *Decretalium* in *Corpus Iuris Canonici*, vol. 2, 5, 38, 11.

4

Rome of the Pilgrim: Part One

The following two chapters are concerned with how pilgrims spent their time in Rome itself. Where did they go and what did they see? As we have seen, Rome had become established as an important and popular centre of Christian pilgrimage long before the twelfth century. Many of the churches which the twelfth-century *Romipetae* would have visited, and the architectural arrangements which provided them with access to the tombs of the city's saints and martyrs, had been installed many centuries before. This first chapter, therefore, is intended to give a brief outline of some of these crucial building campaigns. It will also show that between the seventh and tenth centuries there were significant changes in the churches that these early *Romipetae* chose to visit. The second of these two chapters will concentrate upon the twelfth-century *Romipetae*, considering how these pilgrims spent their time in the apostolic city and whether there were any significant differences between their interests and those of their earlier counterparts.

The Catacombs

The bodies of the Roman saints and martyrs lay in cemeteries outside the city walls, burial within the city having been banned by Roman law.[1] The gradual change from cremation to inhumation around the second century AD[2] greatly increased the demand for burial space. In time, therefore, old cemeteries were extended below ground forming miles of subterranean passages now known as catacombs.[3] What these were like may be judged from the evidence of St Jerome (c. 348–420), who, when a small boy, used to play in them with his friends. The walls were encrusted with the tombs of the dead and all was in darkness. The descent into the catacombs was like a descent by the living into hell.[4]

[1] J. M. C. Toynbee, *Death and Burial in the Roman World* (London, 1971), pp. 48–50.
[2] *Ibid.*, pp. 39–42.
[3] L. Hertling and E. Kirschbaum, *The Roman Catacombs and their Martyrs* (London, 1960).
[4] St Jerome, *Commentariorum in Ezechielem*, PL 25, col. 375. See also Sumption, *Pilgrimage*, p. 218.

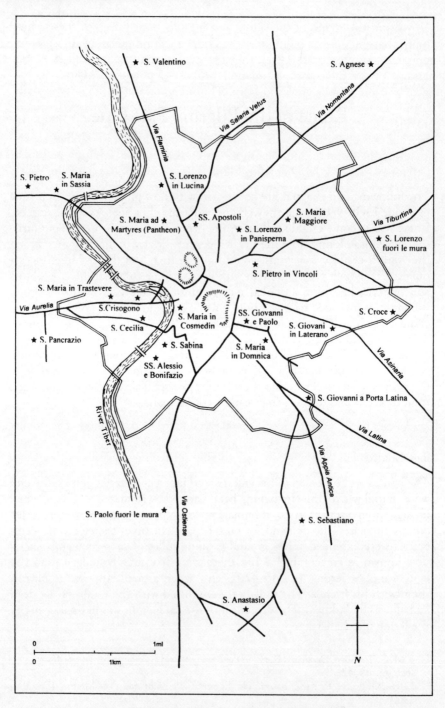

★ S. Valentino

S. Agnese ★

Via Salaria Vetus

Via Nomentana

Via Flaminia

S. Pietro ★

S. Maria in Sassia

S. Lorenzo in Lucina ★

S. Maria ad ★ Martyres (Pantheon)

SS. Apostoli ★

S. Maria ★ Maggiore

★ S. Lorenzo in Panisperna

Via Tiburtina

★ S. Lorenzo fuori le mura

S. Pietro in Vincoli ★

S. Maria in Trastevere ★

Via Aurelia

S. Crisogono ★

S. Cecilia

★ S. Pancrazio

S. Maria in Cosmedin ★

SS. Giovanni e Paolo ★

S. Giovani in Laterano ★

S. Croce ★

Via Asinaria

★ S. Sabina

S. Maria in Domnica

SS. Alessio e Bonifazio

★ S. Giovanni a Porta Latina

Via Latina

River Tiber

Via Appia Antica

Via Ostiense

S. Paolo fuori le mura ★

★ S. Sebastiano

S. Anastasio ★

0 ————— 1ml

0 ————— 1km

N

Roman churches listed in pilgrims' itineraries

It was at the tombs of the saints and martyrs buried deep in these catacombs that pilgrims travelling to Rome hoped to find salvation. In order to
approach these tombs, however, they had to descend into the dark winding
passages of the catacombs, a situation which was potentially dangerous especially if the crowds grew too large. The incorporation of a martyr's tomb
within its own church, therefore, would have numerous benefits. It would
provide pilgrims with open and safe access to the relics of the saint and satisfy
the emphasis upon the close association of altar and relic, which had grown
up during the fifth and sixth centuries. From the late sixth century onwards,
therefore, extensive building campaigns were carried out around the catacombs, some of the most significant of which are described below.

S. Lorenzo fuori le mura

The relics of St Lawrence, a Roman deacon martyred in 258 during the
Valerian persecution, lay buried in a catacomb on the Via Tiburtina. A
fourth-century funerary hall, ascribed by the Liber Pontificalis to Constantine,[5] stood alongside the catacomb and provided a place where pilgrims
might gather for worship. In the sixth century, during the pontificate of
Pelagius II (579–590), a building campaign was initiated which was intended
to provide pilgrims with access to the actual tomb of St Lawrence.[6] Alongside the funerary hall another basilica was built, which was cut into the side
of the Verano cemetery. The tombs around that of St Lawrence were destroyed. The floor of the new basilica was now laid out on the same level as St
Lawrence's tomb, which became the central focus of the church. This tomb
was then decorated by Pelagius II with silver panels.[7] This pope's achieve-
ment in building this church and thereby providing pilgrims with easier
access to the tomb of St Lawrence was considerable. He was acknowledged in
a mosaic inscription set up inside, which praised his transformation of the
'narrow approaches' into a 'large hall'.[8]

This new basilica was less than a third of the size of the earlier funerary
hall. The small size was particularly characteristic of those churches built in
Rome between the sixth and ninth centuries. Yet since Rome was developing
as a popular centre of pilgrimage at this time, we should expect to find
churches built on a grand scale, designed to accommodate the growing numbers of pilgrims. Bryan Ward-Perkins has advanced the most satisfactory
solution yet to this problem. He argues that patrons simply did not have the

5   Liber Pontificalis, vol. 1, pp. 181–182.
6   Ibid., vol. 1, p. 309. Corpus, vol. 2, pp. 1–146.
7   Liber Pontificalis, vol. 1, p. 309.
8   B. Ward-Perkins, From Classical Antiquity to the Middle Ages. Urban Public Building in
    Northern and Central Italy A.D. 300–850 (Oxford, 1984), p. 61.

necessary funds for building on a scale such as that witnessed in Late Antiquity.[9] We might also surmise that the building of a church which necessitated cutting into a hill side and the clearance of a catacomb would have been rather more costly than the building of a free-standing hall. That the builders of S. Lorenzo were certainly aware of the need to provide as much space as possible is, however, clearly demonstrated by the large size of the nave and also by the provision of galleries,[10] placed on three sides of the nave. This was almost certainly the first time that such galleries had featured in Roman church architecture, serving to increase further the basilica's capacity.

S. Agnese

A similar building campaign was undertaken only a few years later by Pope Honorius I (625–638). Like the relics of St Lawrence, those of St Agnes lay buried deep in a catacomb on the Via Nomentana. A church had been built here by Constantine at the request of his daughter, Constantina.[11] We know that Pope Boniface I (418–422) had celebrated the Easter baptism here at least once during his pontificate,[12] yet by the end of the fifth century, the apse was already in a ruinous condition and liable to collapse. It was repaired by Pope Symmachus (498–514), who also renewed the whole church.[13]

The church of S. Agnese was entirely rebuilt in the seventh century by Honorius I, incorporating the tomb of the virgin martyr within it.[14] As at S. Lorenzo on the Via Tiburtina, the building work here necessitated cutting back into the hill-side and the destruction of the other tombs around that of St Agnes. The nave and aisles were then laid out level with the tomb and the galleries, another feature which this church had in common with S. Lorenzo, were placed on three sides of the nave and were accessible from the Via Nomentana.[15] This new building was then most lavishly decorated. Honorius I had the tomb of the saint decorated with silver weighing 252 pounds and over this a large gilded-bronze canopy was placed.[16] The apse was decorated with a fine mosaic, which can still be seen today. Heavily influenced by Byzantine style with its background of gold *tesserae*, St Agnes was portrayed

---

9   *Ibid.*, pp. 58–62.
10 Krautheimer, *Rome*, pp. 85–86.
11 *Liber Pontificalis*, vol. 1, p. 180. The *Liber Pontificalis* calls her Constantia, which was the name of Constantine's sister.
12 *Ibid.*, vol. 1, p. 227.
13 *Ibid.*, vol. 1, p. 263.
14 *Ibid.*, vol. 1, p. 323. Also on this church, *Corpus*, vol. 1, pp. 14–38.
15 On the galleries, see *Corpus*, vol. 1, pp. 35–36.
16 *Liber Pontificalis*, vol. 1, p. 323.

in the centre, flanked by Honorius I himself, as donor, holding a model of the church and by Pope Symmachus (498–514), an acknowledgement of his building work here.[17]

SS. Nereo e Achilleo

Another project of this kind also seems to have been undertaken at the catacomb in which Saints Nereus and Achilleus were buried on the Via Ardeatina. Little is now left of this church and it is consequently difficult to judge when the building work took place. In the *Liber Pontificalis* it was recorded that Pope John I (523–526) 'rebuilt the cemetery of the blessed martyrs Nereus and Achilleus'.[18] Krautheimer's investigations of the remains of this church, however, have revealed that the masonry technique used here was similar to that at S. Agnese, dating from the pontificate of Honorius I.[19] He has also noted that the layout of this church was similar to that of S. Agnese and to the eastern end of S. Lorenzo *fuori le mura*.[20] Krautheimer has argued, therefore, that the evidence of the *Liber Pontificalis* is inconclusive and, whilst John I evidently undertook some work in this cemetery, it may not have been the erection of a basilica. Indeed, the similarities of this church with those of S. Agnese and S. Lorenzo might rather suggest a date in the seventh century.

S. Pancrazio

The laying out of the nave of the church on the same level as a martyr's tomb was not the only method used in Rome to make particular relics more accessible. The annular crypt at S. Pietro, almost certainly installed during the pontificate of Gregory the Great (590–604), was designed to allow large numbers of pilgrims access to what was widely believed to be the apostle's tomb.[21] A crypt modelled on the one installed in this basilica was placed in the church of S. Pancrazio on the Gianicolo, when the original church erected by Pope Symmachus (498–514)[22] was rebuilt during the pontificate of Honorius I c.630.[23] Like the crypt at S. Pietro, that at S. Pancrazio

---

17 W. Oakeshott, *The Mosaics of Rome from the Third to the Fourteenth Centuries* (London, 1967), p. 148; G. Matthiae, *Mosaici Medioevali delle Chiese di Roma*, 2 vols. (Rome, 1967), vol. 1, pp. 169–177; G. B. Ladner, *I Ritratti dei Papi nel Antichità e nel Medievo*, 3 vols. (Città del Vaticano, 1941), vol. 1, pp. 78–79.
18 *Liber Pontificalis*, vol. 1, p. 276.
19 *Corpus*, vol. 3, pp. 131 and 133.
20 *Ibid.*, vol. 3, p. 133.
21 On the annular crypt at S. Pietro, see above, pp. 32–33.
22 *Liber Pontificalis*, vol. 1, p. 262.
23 *Ibid.*, vol. 1, p. 324. Also on this church, see *Corpus*, vol. 3, pp. 153–174.

consisted of two flights of steps which gave access to a semi-circular passage cut out beneath the floor of the apse. Here too a further corridor was installed, which led to the relic chamber, situated directly beneath the high altar. It is unclear, however, whether this church was built over the tomb of St Pancras, incorporating it within the crypt, or whether his relics were translated to their new setting.[24] What is more certain is that by the seventh century, St Pancras must have been considered a particularly important martyr. Not only was the crypt installed in his church a conscious imitation of the one which sheltered the relics of St Peter, one of the city's most important martyrs, but this church was also much larger than others erected in the seventh century. Unlike the churches of S. Agnese and S. Lorenzo, which were comparatively small, measuring only about thirty metres, S. Pancrazio was over fifty metres in length.[25]

S. Valentino

The Liber Pontificalis records that Pope Theodore (642–649) built a basilica on the Via Flaminia dedicated to St Valentine.[26] On the basis of extensive archaeological investigations, however, Krautheimer has argued that it is probably to Pope Julius I (337–352) that the original basilica should be attributed and that the building campaign of Pope Theodore, recorded in the Liber Pontificalis, consisted merely of the installation of a corridor crypt.[27] To allow space for this crypt, the level of the nave had to be raised by 56 centimetres.[28] The aisles of the basilica seem to have retained their old level, so that they remained 56 centimetres below the level of the new nave. This seems to be confirmed by the fact that it was necessary for the builders to construct only four steps to provide access to the crypt from the aisles. The crypt seems to have been focused upon an object placed in, or perhaps found in, a square exedra, which was located a little to the east of the centre of this corridor. Krautheimer has argued that this corridor crypt was installed here so that pilgrims could have subterranean access to a venerated site, perhaps a sarcophagus, but that the laying out of a traditional annular crypt like those found at S. Pietro and S. Pancrazio was impossible.[29] While this crypt is the only one of its kind which has been discovered in Rome, it may have been the inspiration for the ninth-century crypts at S. Quentin and S. Médard at Soissons.[30]

---

[24] See the discussion in Corpus, vol. 3, pp. 172–173.
[25] Ibid., vol. 3, p. 173.
[26] Liber Pontificalis, vol. 1, pp. 332–333.
[27] Corpus, vol. 4, pp. 289–312.
[28] On this corridor crypt, see ibid., vol. 4, p. 308.
[29] Ibid., vol. 4, p. 312.
[30] Ibid., vol. 4, p. 312.

Church Building Inside and Outside the Walls

The building campaigns considered above resulted from the influx of pilgrims seeking salvation through proximity to the relics of the saints and martyrs. The evidence of the Liber Pontificalis suggests in fact that much of the building work carried out to churches during the sixth, seventh and early eighth centuries was concentrated largely, although not exclusively, on those churches which were situated around the catacombs, rather than upon churches located within the city walls.

As well as his building work at S. Agnese and S. Pancrazio, Honorius I's other foundations included S. Apollinarius in the portico of S. Pietro, S. Cyriaco on the Via Ostiensis seven miles from Rome and a church dedicated to St Severinus twenty miles from the city.[31] Additionally, the Liber Pontificalis attributes to his patronage the foundation of three churches within the city walls, S. Lucia in Selcis, SS. Quattro Coronati and S. Adriano.[32] S. Adriano was in fact the old Curia Senatus which Honorius I dedicated as a church.[33] Krautheimer does not rule out the possibility that this was also true of his other two foundations within the walls, suggesting that they were not purpose-built basilicas but rather secular buildings which Honorius took over, furnished and then dedicated as churches.[34] Other new foundations seem to have included an oratory built by Theodore I (642–649) just outside St Paul's gate, which was dedicated to a certain St Euplas,[35] and a church dedicated to St Paul by Leo II (682–683) within the walls close to S. Bibiana.[36]

Just as important as new foundations was the repair work which had to be continually carried out to the fabric of existing churches. The Liber Pontificalis suggests that papal patronage in the second half of the seventh century was concentrated largely upon the work of restoration. Pope Donus (676–678) repaired and dedicated the church of the Apostles on the Via Ostiensis, presumably S. Paolo.[37] During the pontificate of Benedict II (684–685) repair work was required at S. Lorenzo in Lucina situated within the walls as well as at S. Pietro.[38] This repair work at S. Pietro was continued by Pope Sergius I (687–701), who saw to the repair of broken windows and to the renewal of the mosaic which decorated the front of the atrium and which had been partly destroyed.[39] This same pope also rebuilt the oratory of St Andrew

---

[31] Liber Pontificalis, vol. 1, pp. 323–324.

[32] Ibid., vol. 1, p. 324.

[33] Ibid., vol. 1, p. 324. A. Mancini, 'La Chiesa Medioevale di San Adriano nel Foro Romano', Pontificia Accademia Romana d'Archeologia, 40 (1967–1968), pp. 191–245.

[34] Corpus, vol. 4, p. 34.

[35] Liber Pontificalis, vol. 1, p. 333.

[36] Ibid., vol. 1, p. 360.

[37] Ibid., vol. 1, p. 348.

[38] Ibid., vol. 1, p. 363.

[39] Ibid., vol. 1, pp. 374–375.

on the Via Labicana[40] and within the city walls had the damaged roof of the church of S. Euphemia repaired.[41] Collapsing roofs seem to have been a very common problem, probably because the wooden beams and lead from which they were constructed were highly flammable. Similar roof repairs were undertaken by Pope Sergius I at S. Aurea at Ostia, while he also replaced some of the oldest beams at the church of S. Paolo on the Via Ostiensis.[42]

Repairs to the fabric of churches remained a priority for the popes of the early eighth century. During the pontificate of John VII (705–707) the restoration took place of the basilica of S. Eugenia on the Via Latina, 'which for a long time had been roofless and damaged'.[43] Already by the pontificate of Gregory II (715–731) repairs to the roof were again required at S. Paolo, at S. Lorenzo fuori le mura and S. Croce.[44] His successor Gregory III (731–741) had an oratory built at S. Pietro in honour of Christ and the Virgin.[45] At the church of S. Andrea near S. Pietro he renewed the apse vault and roof.[46] On the Via Aurelia he entirely rebuilt the church dedicated to St Calixtus[47] and repaired the roof of the basilica dedicated to Saints Processus and Martinian.[48] On the Via Tiburtina he restored the roof of the basilica of S. Genesio,[49] on the Via Appia he had the roof of the basilica dedicated to St Mark rebuilt[50] and on the Ostian Way he restored five roof beams at S. Paolo and had general repairs carried out to the whole roof.[51] Gregory III's *Vita* in the *Liber Pontificalis* also indicates that he was responsible for repairs carried out to some of the cemeteries.[52] Within the city walls this same pope renewed the roof at S. Maria ad Martyres, enlarged the church of S. Maria in Aquiro,[53] renewed the roof, apse vault and murals at the church of S. Crisogono,[54] replaced five roof beams at S. Maria Maggiore and rebuilt the church of SS. Marcellino and Pietro close to the Lateran.[55] During the pontificate of

[40] *Ibid.*, vol. 1, p. 376.
[41] *Ibid.*, vol. 1, p. 375.
[42] *Ibid.*, vol. 1, pp. 375 and 376.
[43] *Ibid.*, vol. 1, p. 385.
[44] *Ibid.*, vol. 1, p. 397 on S. Paolo and S. Lorenzo, p. 401 on S. Croce.
[45] *Ibid.*, vol. 1, p. 417.
[46] *Ibid.*, vol. 1, p. 419.
[47] *Ibid.*, vol. 1, p. 419.
[48] *Ibid.*, vol. 1, p. 419.
[49] *Ibid.*, vol. 1, p. 419.
[50] *Ibid.*, vol. 1, p. 420.
[51] *Ibid.*, vol. 1, p. 420.
[52] See for example *ibid.*, vol. 1, p. 420.
[53] For these repairs, *ibid.*, vol. 1, p. 419. See also M. D'Onfrio and C. M. Strinati, *S. Maria in Aquiro* (Rome, 1972); V. Bartoccetti, *Santa Maria ad Martyres* (Rome, undated).
[54] *Liber Pontificalis*, vol. 1, p. 418. Also on S. Crisogono, see B. M. Apollonj-Ghetti, *S. Crisogono* (Rome, 1966).
[55] On this repair work see *Liber Pontificalis*, vol. 1, p. 420.

Zacharias (741–752) the church of S. Eusebio collapsed and was repaired,[56] whilst during the pontificate of Stephen II (752–757) the basilica of St Lawrence 'above St Clement's in the third region' was restored,[57] as was the cemetery of St Soteris,[58] whilst repairs were carried out to some of the columns in the atrium of S. Pietro.[59]

Pilgrims in Rome in the Seventh and Early Eighth Centuries

That these churches outside the walls upon which the popes of the sixth, seventh and early eighth centuries lavished so much of their patronage were those at which contemporary pilgrims would have spent most of their time is suggested by the so-called 'pilgrim guides'. These began to appear in Rome in the second half of the seventh century. It seems unlikely that these guides were written for the use of pilgrims themselves but were instead a record of the churches and sites that pilgrims were already visiting.[60] One guide, the *Notitia Ecclesiarum Urbis Romae*,[61] began at the church of SS. Giovanni e Paolo inside the city itself. It then described a pilgrim route which led directly to the Via Flaminia and thence in a clockwise direction around the cemetery churches which lay outside the walls, finishing with the climax of the tour at S. Pietro. A second guide, the *De Locis Sanctis Martyrum*,[62] suggested a route which began at S. Pietro and then followed an anti-clockwise path around the cemeteries and churches which ended on the Via Flaminia at S. Valentino al Ponte Milvio.

During the seventh century, at the time when these 'guides' appeared, it seems that the churches located within the city itself were not significant as pilgrimage churches. Whilst some obviously possessed important relics such as Christ's manger acquired by S. Maria Maggiore c.642, most possessed few, if any, bodily relics.[63] It was at the tombs of the martyrs outside the walls that the actual physical presence of a particular saint was guaranteed. Here he was ready and waiting to listen and indeed to respond to the prayers of individual pilgrims.[64] For pilgrims visiting Rome in the period up to the early eighth century, the churches inside the city walls were important less for their relics than for the liturgical stations held there when they could hear the pope say

56 *Ibid.*, vol. 1, p. 435.
57 *Ibid.*, vol. 1, p. 443. The location of this church is unknown.
58 *Ibid.*, vol. 1, p. 444.
59 *Ibid.*, vol. 1, p. 455.
60 See above pp. 12–13.
61 *Codice Topografico*, vol. 2, pp. 67–99.
62 *Ibid.*, vol. 2, pp. 101–131.
63 Krautheimer, *Rome*, p. 90.
64 See above pp. 23–24.

mass.[65] Indeed it is as stational churches that twenty-one basilicas were entered at the very end of the *De Locis Sanctis Martyrum*, under the title *Istae vero ecclesiae intus Romae habentur*.[66]

Sigeric, a Tenth-century Pilgrim

If the evidence of the building campaigns and the 'pilgrim guides' suggests that the *Romipetae* of the sixth, seventh and early eighth centuries probably spent most of their time outside the city walls, then in later years, certainly by the tenth century, the situation seems to have been very different. In 990, Sigeric, archbishop of Canterbury, travelled to Rome to collect the pallium from Pope John XV (985–996). Not only does an account of the stages of his return journey survive but also a list of the twenty-three churches that he seems to have visited in just two days.[67] This list shows that the route which Sigeric followed around the City was well organised and that fourteen out of these twenty-three churches which he visited lay inside the city walls.

Beginning at S. Pietro, Sigeric's tour led him to S. Maria in Sassia and thence to S. Lorenzo in Craticula, identified as S. Lorenzo in Lucina.[68] Sigeric then proceeded in a clockwise direction outside the walls, visiting the six basilicas of S. Valentino, S. Agnese, S. Lorenzo fuori le mura, S. Sebastiano, S. Anastasio and S. Paolo fuori le mura. Re-entering the city, probably at the Porta Ostiensis, he then went to SS. Alessio e Bonifazio, S. Sabina and S. Maria in Cosmedin, before crossing the Tiber to Trastevere. Here he visited S. Cecilia, S. Crisogono and S. Maria in Trastevere, with the first day's tour ending at S. Pancrazio on the Via Aurelia outside the walls. The second day's tour was spent entirely within the city, beginning at S. Maria ad Martyres. The archbishop then went to SS. Apostoli before proceeding to the Lateran and his meeting with John XV. The afternoon was then spent in visiting four more churches in the centre of Rome, S. Croce, S. Maria Maggiore, S. Pietro in Vincoli and S. Lorenzo in Panisperna.

---

[65] See G. G. Willis, *Essays in Early Roman Liturgy* (London, 1964) and by the same author, *Further Essays in Early Roman Liturgy* (London, 1968).

[66] *Codice Topographico*, vol. 2, pp. 118–131.

[67] This text has been published in *Memorials of St Dunstan*, pp. 391–395. See also V. Ortenberg, 'Archbishop Sigeric's journey to Rome in 990', *Anglo-Saxon England*, 19 (1990), pp. 197–246; G. Caselli, *La Via Romea. Cammino di Dio* (Florence, 1990); B. Peschi, 'L'Itinerario Romano de Sigerico Archievescovo di Canterbury e la lista dei Papa da lui portata in Inghilterra', *Rivista di Archeologia Cristiana*, 13 (1936), pp. 43–60; Magoun, 'Rome of Two Northern Pilgrims', esp. pp. 267–277. See map p. 90.

[68] An inscription on the episcopal throne in S. Lorenzo in Lucina dated 1112 mentioned a relic of the *craticula* amongst the relics of the main altar. See Ortenberg, 'Archbishop Sigeric's journey', pp. 212–213.

Churches within the Walls: their growth in importance for pilgrims

It was from the second half of the eighth century onwards that the churches located within the city walls seem to have gradually grown in importance for pilgrims. The key factor seems to have been the translation of the bodies of the saints and martyrs from the catacombs to the city's churches, which began on a large scale during the pontificate of Paul I (757–767).

The movement of bones from cemeteries, prohibited in a law of AD 386,[69] had been further condemned by Pope Gregory the Great. In a letter of 594, he explained to the Empress Constantina, wife of the Byzantine Emperor Maurice, that it was not the custom in Rome, as in the East, to give or even to touch bodily relics and so was unable to fulfil her request for the head of St Paul.[70] To indulge in the touching or moving of such relics, even if accidentally, Gregory warned, was to invite certain death. Such a fate apparently befell a group of ten monks and masons, who during the pontificate of Pelagius II accidentally broke open the tomb of St Lawrence.[71]

A slackening in the papacy's rigid attitude towards the movement of relics, however, is noticeable as early as the middle of the seventh century. Honorius I may possibly have translated the body of St Pancras into a newly built church, whilst Pope John IV (640–642) had relics brought from Dalmatia and Histria depositing them in the Lateran Baptistery,[72] Theodore I (642–649) had the bodies of Saints Primus and Felician translated from the Via Nomentana to the church of S. Stephano Rotundo[73] and Leo II (682–683) built a church in Rome, close to S. Bibiana, where he deposited the relics of Saints Simplicius, Faustinus, Beatrice and those of many others.[74] That these were not the only translations is suggested by the installation of an annular crypt in the church of S. Crisogono during the pontificate of Gregory III (731–741).[75] This noticeable relaxation of policy may well have been a result, as Osborne has argued, of the growing Greek influence on the Roman Church, particularly as a result of the extensive migration of Greek clergy during the seventh century.[76] Here it is perhaps significant to note that both John IV and Theodore I were themselves of eastern, as opposed to Roman, origin. McCulloh has advanced a further interesting argument concerning the papacy's gradual relaxation of its hitherto stringent attitude towards the

---

69 J. Osborne, 'The Roman Catacombs in the Middle Ages', *PBSR*, 53 (1985), pp. 278–328, esp. p. 287.

70 Gregory the Great, *Epistolae*, PL 71, cols. 700–705. We may suppose that even had Gregory the Great approved the translation of holy relics, he would certainly not have been prepared to part with one so precious.

71 This story is recounted by Llewellyn, *Rome in the Dark Ages*, p. 174.

72 *Liber Pontificalis*, vol. 1, p. 330.

73 *Ibid.*, vol. 1, p. 332.

74 *Ibid.*, vol. 1, p. 360.

75 *Corpus*, vol. 1, pp. 144–164; Apollonj-Ghetti, *S. Crisogono*, pp. 39–58.

76 Osborne, 'Roman Catacombs', pp. 288–289.

movement of bone relics, suggesting that there was a growing dissatisfaction with associative relics in the West and that the popes were coming under increasing pressure to sanction the translation of bodily relics.[77]

The dramatic and large scale translations of relics from the cemeteries to the churches within the city walls which took place in the eighth century during the pontificate of Paul I (757–767), however, must surely have had a specific cause or have been triggered by a particular incident. The *Liber Pontificalis* attributes this pope's policy to the ruined and neglected state of the catacombs.[78] Osborne argues, however, that the main reason was probably because the suburban shrines were no longer considered safe and secure resting places for the martyrs.[79] Rome itself had been besieged by the Lombards from January to April 756 and although there is no evidence that they had damaged the catacombs, it seems that they may have plundered them removing many holy relics for themselves. The *Vita* of Stephen II in the *Liber Pontificalis* certainly condemned the actions of Aistulf, king of the Lombards, who, it was recorded, dug up the sacred cemeteries, stealing many of the saints' bodies.[80] This plundering of the cemeteries and catacombs is also hinted at in the foundation charter of S. Silvestro in Capite as an explanation for Paul I's translation of numerous relics to this church.[81] The obvious means by which to protect the catacombs and cemeteries from further plunder was to translate the relics into churches located within the city walls.

It is surely no coincidence that the removal of the relics for the catacombs coincided with extensive building campaigns within the city walls.[82] In rebuilding S. Maria in Cosmedin, Hadrian I (772–795) provided for the translation of many relics from the cemeteries into the city. In a hall crypt underneath the church, he provided a unique and accessible setting for them. Beneath the chancel of the main church, he had laid out a small underground basilica, supported by columns. Niches, divided by shelves, were cut into the walls and upon these the relics were placed.[83]

Yet an arrangement such as that at S. Maria in Cosmedin meant that the relics still remained rather vulnerable, easy for over-zealous *Romipetae* to touch or remove. Only a more secure and protective shelter would provide

---

[77] J. McCulloh, 'From Antiquity to the Middle Ages: Continuity and Change in papal relic policy from the 6th to 8th century', *Pietas. Festschrift für Bernhard Kotting*, ed. E. Dassmann and S. Frank, *Jahrbuch für Antike und Christentum*, Ergänzungsband 8 (1980), pp. 313–324.

[78] *Liber Pontificalis*, vol. 1, p. 464.

[79] Osborne, 'Roman Catacombs', p. 290.

[80] *Liber Pontificalis*, vol. 1, pp. 451–452. See Geary, *Furta Sacra*.

[81] 'Regesto del monastero di S. Silvestro di Capite', ed. V. Federici, *ASRSP*, 22 (1899), pp. 213–300, p. 257.

[82] On church building in Rome at this time, see R. Krautheimer, 'The Carolingian Revival of Early Christian Art', *Art Bulletin*, 24 (1942), pp. 1–38; Krautheimer, *Rome*, pp. 109–142.

[83] *Corpus*, vol. 2, pp. 300–302; Krautheimer, *Rome*, p. 113.

greater security for the holy relics. This was clearly the reason for the installation of annular crypts in a number of churches located within the city walls
in the course of the second half of the eighth and ninth centuries.[84] For in
this way a safe resting place could be provided for the relics, while still
leaving them accessible to large crowds of pilgrims. Such a crypt seems to
have been installed at S. Susanna during the pontificate of Leo III (795–
816)[85] and another at S. Prassede built during the pontificate of Paschal I
(817–824). Still largely preserved today, the crypt at S. Prassede consisted of
two flights of steps which gave access to two curved passages, which lay over
one and a half metres below the floor level of the nave. These passages
followed the line of the apse wall and from their meeting place a straight
corridor led to a relic chamber, which was presumably directly beneath the
high altar.[86] Recesses found in the walls of the crypt seem to have been
intended to hold lamps. A similar crypt was installed in S. Cecilia in Trastevere, when the fifth-century church was remodelled, also during the pontificate of Paschal I.[87] Krautheimer considers it likely too that a third such crypt
was placed in the church of S. Maria in Domnica at this time.[88] Similar
crypts were installed in the church of S. Marco during the pontificate of
Gregory IV (827–844),[89] at SS. Quattro Coronati during the pontificate of
Leo IV (847–855)[90] and at S. Stefano degli Abissini, located outside the city
walls close to S. Pietro, probably during the pontificate of Leo IV.[91] Annular
crypts were also placed in the churches of S. Martino ai Monti[92] and S. Maria
Nova[93] in the ninth century and at S. Saba in the tenth.[94]

Before the middle of the eighth century pilgrims visiting Rome would probably have spent most of their time at the basilicas and cemeteries outside the
city walls. Visits which these *Romipetae* may have made to basilicas within
the city itself were perhaps prompted not so much by the relics which could
be found there as by their important role as stational churches. The trans-

---

84 On these annular crypts, see B. M. Apollonj-Ghetti, 'La Chiesa di S. Maria di
Vescovio', *Rivista di Archeolgia Cristiana*, 23–24 (1947–1948), pp. 253–303, esp. pp.
271–283.
85 B. M. Apollonj-Ghetti, S. *Susanna* (Rome, 1965), pp. 52–54.
86 Remodelling in the eighteenth century resulted in the extension of this corridor
southwards to form a third entrance to the crypt, necessitating the movement of the
altar and relics to the meeting point of the three passages. See *Corpus*, vol. 3, p. 252.
Also on this crypt see B. M. Apollonj-Ghetti, *Santa Prassede* (Rome, 1961).
87 *Corpus*, vol. 1, p. 110.
88 *Ibid.*, vol. 2, p. 322.
89 *Ibid.*, vol. 2, pp. 218–249.
90 *Ibid.*, vol. 4, esp. p. 30; B. M. Apollonj-Ghetti, *I SS. Quattro Coronati* (Rome, 1964),
pp. 30–35.
91 *Corpus*, vol. 4, p. 19.
92 Krautheimer, *Rome*, p. 136.
93 *Corpus*, vol. 1, p. 239.
94 P. Testini, *San Saba* (Rome, 1961), pp. 33–34.

lation of many precious relics from the catacombs to churches within the city walls on a large scale from the middle of the eighth century certainly affected this pattern, as is clearly demonstrated by the itinerary of Sigeric, archbishop of Canterbury. Yet, as Ward-Perkins has observed, these translations did not lead to the eclipse of many of the old established cemetery churches.[95] Indeed, we know both from the extensive building campaigns which continued to be carried out at the cemeteries and basilicas outside the walls beyond the middle of the eighth century, and from the itinerary of Sigeric, that not only S. Pietro and S. Paolo but also basilicas like S. Sebastiano, S. Pancrazio, S. Agnese and S. Valentino seem to have enjoyed continuing popularity with the Romipetae.

---

[95] Ward-Perkins, From Classical Antiquity to the Middle Ages, p. 56.

5

Rome of the Pilgrim: Part Two

The itinerary of Sigeric, archbishop of Canterbury, suggests that, although by
the end of the tenth century many churches within the walls of Rome had
become popular with pilgrims, many of the old established basilicas outside
the city continued to attract large numbers of visitors. This chapter considers
whether this was still the case in the twelfth century. How did pilgrims
travelling to Rome two hundred years after Sigeric spend their time in the
apostolic city? Where did they go and what did they see? Although we know
of many individuals who travelled to Rome in the twelfth century,[1] few
provide us with any information about the city of the pilgrim at this time.
Indeed most twelfth-century sources have little or nothing to say about how
Romipetae spent their time or what interested them. The main exception to
this is the account written by Nikolas of Munkathvera, an inhabitant of the
'last island',[2] who himself travelled to the city on pilgrimage c.1150. We are
fortunate that this unique description of his stay in the apostolic city has
survived and this chapter, therefore, will consider this text in some detail.
Consideration will also be given to the fierce struggle which developed
during the twelfth century between the canons of the Lateran and Vatican to
attract *Romipetae* to their respective basilicas and also to other matters. Were
there any sites other than the churches which interested these pilgrims and
where might they have done their shopping and purchased their souvenirs?

Some Twelfth-Century Romipetae

A search through a wide variety of primary sources has revealed the names of
a number of twelfth-century pilgrims. Most of these sources, however, have
little or nothing to say about what these *Romipetae* did or saw in the apostolic

---

[1] G. Tellenbach, 'La Città di Roma dal IX al XII Secolo vista dai Contemporanei d'Oltre
Frontiera', *Studi Storici in Onore di Ottorino Bertolini*, 2 vols. (Pisa, 1972), vol. 2, pp.
679–734.

[2] This is the title given to Iceland by Adam of Bremen, *Hamburgische Kirchengeschichte*,
ed. B. Schmeidler, *Scriptores Rerum Germanicarum in Usum Scholarum* (Hanover and
Leipzig, 1917), p. 218. See also p. 286 for his brief description of Iceland.

city. Most only record that a pilgrimage had been or was about to be under-taken. Even those sources which do provide some information about a pil-grim's stay in Rome usually contain only very sketchy details. St Bernard's *Life* of St Malachy, recording the latter's pilgrimage to the apostolic city in 1140, is typical. St Bernard recorded that St Malachy spent a month in the city, 'making visits to the holy places and coming back often to them in prayer'.[3] But which holy places did St Malachy and other twelfth-century pilgrims like him, choose to visit?

Similar sketchy outlines of visits to Rome are often found in the *Vitae* contained in the *Acta Sanctorum*. St Famianus seems to have made a pilgrim-age to Rome from Cologne c.1108 and on arriving there went to the basilicas of the apostles and the Blessed Virgin and 'even to other holy places in the city'.[4] St Chelidonia, who was in Rome c.1111, went, according to her biographer, to the basilicas of Saints Peter and Paul and to the churches of 'other saints',[5] while St Atto, elected bishop of Pistoia in 1133, visited the 'thresholds of the apostles', as well as 'the sacred monuments of Rome'.[6] B. Albert of Sens (d.1181) is said to have gone to the 'basilicas of the apostles',[7] while the biographer of St Raymond of Piacenza (d.1200) noted that this holy man spent some days in Rome, during which he visited the 'principal apostle' and the 'very holy saints and virgins'.[8] While this information seems rather vague and uninformative, we should expect little else. Indeed, even if we accept that all these pilgrimages were actually carried out, it is unlikely that those who wrote these *Lives* would have known the details of all the churches visited by these holy men and women, particularly where the biog-rapher was writing many years after the saint's death. That the writers of these *Lives* seem to assume, however, that their subjects went to the basilicas of Saints Peter and Paul, is an indication of their continuing and central importance as places of pilgrimage.

The only way to produce a more complete picture of the popular pilgrim-age sites in twelfth-century Rome, is to turn to accounts written by visitors themselves. Among the travellers who made their way to Rome in the course

---

[3]   St Bernard of Clairvaux, *The Life and Death of Saint Malachy the Irishman*, trans. R. T. Meyer (Kalamazoo, 1978), pp. 52–53.

[4]   *De Famiano Confessore Ordinis Cisterciensis Anachoreta*, AASS Aug II, p. 391.

[5]   *De S. Chelidonia Virgine apud Sublacum in Latio*, AASS Oct. VI, p. 366.

[6]   *De S. Atto seu Atthone*, AASS May V, p. 195.

[7]   *De B. Alberto Eremita in Territorio Senensi*, AASS Jan. I, p. 402.

[8]   *Vita S. Raymundi Palmarii*, AASS July VI, p. 650. Other saints who are reported to have made a pilgrimage to Rome in the twelfth century include Stephen Harding c.1100 (*De S. Stephano. Tertio Abbate Cisterciensi in Gallia*, AASS April II, esp. pp. 496–497); St Oldegar, bishop of Barcelona (d.1137) (*De B. Oldegario Archiepiscopo Tarraconensi et Episcopi Barcinonensi*, AASS March I, esp. p. 488); St Albert Agricola (d.c.1190) (*De S. Alberto Agricola*, AASS May II, p. 281); St Ludanus (d.1202) (*De S. Ludano Peregrino*, AASS Feb. II, pp. 638–639) and possibly also B. Irmgarde (*De B. Irmgarde Virgine*, AASS Sept. II, esp. p. 274).

of the twelfth century, a small number wrote, or dictated, an account of what they had seen and the places that they had visited in the course of their sojourn in the apostolic city.

Benjamin of Tudela

One of these visitors was Benjamin, a rabbi from Tudela in northern Spain, who arrived in Rome c.1160.[9] Benjamin's main interest was undoubtedly in the activities of the Jews in the major cities through which he passed and this also seems to have been a central part of his visit to Rome. He recorded, for example, that there were two hundred Jews living in Rome at that time.[10] They were 'very much respected', he noted, and a number of them were said by him to be 'officers in the service of Pope Alexander [III]'.[11] The most important of these, Benjamin reckoned to be one R. Jechiel, whom he named as 'steward' of the Pope's household and 'minister of his private property'.[12]

Benjamin's interest seems also to have extended to Rome and its history and particularly to its classical past. His account records that he saw the palace of Vespasian, the Porta Latina and 'numerous buildings and structures entirely different from all other buildings upon the face of the earth'.[13] Benjamin, unfortunately, was naturally less interested in the city's churches and Rome's role as an important centre of Christian pilgrimage. S. Giovanni in Laterano, for example, is mentioned only to help fix the location of a statue of 'Samson'.[14] Benjamin's travels do, however, seem to have taken him to S. Pietro, which he claimed had been built upon the extensive palace of Julius Caesar.[15] While archaeological investigations carried out this century have shown that this was certainly not the case,[16] Benjamin's account is useful, if only for what it reveals about contemporary beliefs concerning one of Rome's most important churches.

Master Gregory

If Benjamin's description of what he saw in Rome tells us little about the city of the twelfth-century pilgrim, some more might perhaps be learnt from the text of another visitor to the city, Master Gregory. We know little about Gregory himself beyond the fact that he was probably English and visited

9   *Early Travels in Palestine*, pp. 63–126.
10 *Ibid.*, p. 66.
11 *Ibid.*, pp. 66–67.
12 *Ibid.*, p. 67.
13 *Ibid.*, pp. 67–68.
14 *Ibid.*, p. 68.
15 *Ibid.*, p. 67.
16 See above, pp. 27–33.

Rome sometime during the twelfth or early thirteenth centuries.[17] Despite the uncertainty surrounding the date of Gregory's visit to the apostolic city, his text is still worth considering for the information which it contains.

Gregory was primarily interested in the monuments of Rome's pagan past. The palaces of Augustus[18] and Diocletian,[19] the Pantheon,[20] the temple of Pallas,[21] triumphal arches,[22] statues[23] and pyramids[24] are just a selection of the sites which he appears to have seen. His itinerary also included a visit to the baths of Apollo Bianeus, where, he recorded, he paid his entrance fee but declined to bathe, put off by the stench of the sulphur.[25]

Gregory himself was certainly not a pilgrim, nor did he regard himself as such. Consciously disassociating himself from these visitors to the apostolic city, he condemned the stories and beliefs which circulated amongst them. In so doing, however, he has provided us with some valuable information about pilgrimage. One of these beliefs, which he condemned, concerned the 'tomb of Romulus' which stood near S. Pietro.[26] Pilgrims, Gregory noted, believed it to be the grain heap of the apostle which was turned to stone when Nero confiscated it. Gregory dismissed this story as 'an utterly worthless tale, typical of those told by pilgrims'.[27] In Gregory's text we discover another practice which seems to have been common amongst pilgrims at this time. Throughout the medieval period, situated in the Vatican Circus, there stood an Egyptian obelisk, which had been brought to Rome by the Emperor Gaius in AD 37.[28] In his text Gregory relates how pilgrims strove to crawl into the narrow space between the obelisk and its base, in the belief that those who managed the feat would be cleansed from their sins.[29] Osborne has speculated that such beliefs were the result of the identification of the obelisk with the site of St Peter's martyrdom, which also resulted in references to the obelisk as 'St Peter's needle'.[30]

---

[17] See above, pp. 11–12.
[18] Master Gregory, Marvels of Rome, p. 28.
[19] Ibid., p. 27.
[20] Ibid., pp. 29–30.
[21] Ibid., pp. 27–28.
[22] Ibid., pp. 30–33.
[23] Ibid., pp. 19–24.
[24] Ibid., pp. 33–35.
[25] Ibid., p. 25.
[26] Ibid., p. 33. This pyramid which stood near S. Pietro was widely believed to contain the remains of Romulus. It was destroyed in 1499, when, in preparation for the Jubilee of 1500, Pope Alexander VI ordered the opening up of a new street from the Tiber to the Vatican.
[27] Ibid., p. 33.
[28] On this obelisk, see A. Barrett, Caligula: The Corruption of Power (London, 1989), pp. 196–201.
[29] Master Gregory, Marvels of Rome, pp. 34–35.
[30] Ibid., p. 91. Nikolas of Munkathvera also refers to 'Petrs Nal'. See Magoun, 'Rome of Two Northern Pilgrims', pp. 286–287.

Gerald of Wales

Gerald of Wales is known to have made at least four visits to Rome. Three of these were certainly concerned with business at the papal court as he sought to prove his claim to be recognised as bishop of St David's. After the failure of his case, he returned to Rome c.1204 'purely for the sake of pilgrimage'.[31] His pilgrimage lasted from Epiphany to Easter and contained in his *De Invectionibus* is a brief account of how he spent his time.[32] Gerald tells us that during his stay in Rome he attended stational masses every day and visited many churches. In this way he seems to have built up ninety-two years worth of indulgences, which he made up to a round one hundred by enrolling himself in the confraternity of the hospital of Santo Spirito.[33]

Gerald was certainly very familiar with Rome and was able to compile a list of the churches which lay both inside and outside the walls.[34] Unfortunately, what we do not know is which or how many of these he himself had managed to visit. Like most *Romipetae* he must have visited S. Pietro and S. Paolo. That he was also familiar with S. Giovanni in Laterano is suggested by the inclusion in his *Speculum Ecclesiae* of a long list of the relics which could be found there.[35] While we can suppose that he had been to other important basilicas like S. Maria Maggiore and S. Lorenzo fuori le mura, it is impossible to know which of the city's other smaller churches he also visited.

Nikolas of Munkathvera

While Benjamin of Tudela, Master Gregory and Gerald of Wales supply us with a small amount of information concerning the beliefs and activities of pilgrims who were in Rome in the twelfth and early thirteenth centuries, our most important source is undoubtedly Nikolas of Munkathvera. Setting out from Iceland on pilgrimage, probably c.1150, Nikolas's journey took him first to Rome and then on to Jerusalem and the Holy Land. An account of his experiences survives in Old Icelandic, allegedly dictated by Nikolas himself.

While Nikolas's account of his tour of the Holy Land in the twelfth century is one of several such accounts which survive, that of his visit to Rome is unique. Indeed, it is the only description which we have written by a twelfth-century pilgrim to Rome. Written in the form of a guide, Nikolas's description of Rome was perhaps intended for use by other pilgrims, providing them with information and even his own personal comments about some

---

31 Gerald of Wales, *De Invectionibus*, p. 137.
32 *Ibid.*, pp. 137–138.
33 *Ibid.*, pp. 137–138. On Santo Spirito, see below, pp. 141–143.
34 Gerald of Wales, *Speculum Ecclesiae*, p. 281.
35 *Ibid.*, pp. 272–276. Professor Riley-Smith has also pointed out that his involvement in a case at the curia would certainly have taken him to the Lateran.

of the major sites. Unfortunately, therefore, as it was written in this form, it omits many of the details which it would have been useful to know concerning Nikolas's own pilgrimage; how long he spent in the city and where he stayed. Nor is there any indication whether the guide represents the full extent of Nikolas's own itinerary. It is certainly possible that he chose to include in his guide only the edited 'high-lights'. Veronica Ortenberg has argued, in relation to the tenth-century itinerary of Sigeric, that the twenty-three churches which he mentioned may not be the only ones which he visited but simply those which had made the greatest impression upon him.[36] Nikolas may have selected the contents of his guide to Rome according to similar criteria.

The evidence of Nikolas's guide suggests that the pattern of pilgrimage had changed little between the tenth and twelfth centuries. Indeed, like Sigeric, two hundred years before, Nikolas visited a variety of churches, both inside and outside the walls.[37] SS. Giovanni e Paolo,[38] S. Maria in Domnica,[39] S. Giovanni a Porta Latina[40] and S. Agnese[41] were certainly among them. This latter church on the Via Nomentana seems to have particularly impressed Nikolas, who described it as the 'most outstanding in the whole city'.[42] Another church was singled out by Nikolas for special mention. This one he referred to as 'All Saints' and is described by him as 'large and splendid'.[43] As Nikolas was also careful to note that this church had a hole in its roof like the Holy Sepulchre at Jerusalem, he must have been referring to the Pantheon, dedicated to S. Maria ad Martyres by Pope Boniface IV (608–615).[44]

The sheer number of churches which Nikolas found in Rome seems almost to have overwhelmed him. 'No-one', he wrote 'is so wise as to know all the churches in the city of Rome.'[45] As the number of churches here was well in excess of 350 by the time of Nikolas's pilgrimage,[46] we might ask how a

---

[36] Ortenberg, 'Archbishop Sigeric's journey', esp. pp. 225–228.

[37] See map p. 90.

[38] On this church, see C. Huelsen, Le Chiese di Roma nel Medio Evo (Florence, 1927), p. 277; M. Armellini, Le Chiese di Roma dal Secolo IV al XIX, 2 vols. (Rome, 1942), vol. 1, pp. 617–627; Corpus, vol. 1, pp. 265–300.

[39] Huelsen, Chiese, pp. 331–332; Armellini, Chiese di Roma, vol. 1, pp. 611–613; Corpus, vol. 2, pp. 311–324.

[40] Huelsen, Chiese, p. 274; Armellini, Chiese di Roma, vol. 1, pp. 635–636; Corpus, vol. 1, pp. 301–316.

[41] Huelsen, Chiese, p. 170; Armellini, Chiese di Roma, vol. 2, pp. 1063–1067; Corpus, vol. 1, pp. 14–38.

[42] Werlauff, Symbolae ad Geographiam Medii Aevi, p. 23.

[43] Ibid., p. 23.

[44] For the dedication, see Liber Pontificalis, vol. 1, p. 317. Also on this church, see Huelsen, Chiese, p. 363; Armellini, Chiese di Roma, vol. 1, pp. 589–592.

[45] Werlauff, Symbolae ad Geographiam Medii Aevi, p. 24.

[46] The city's churches at the time of Leo III (795–816) would appear to number around 117 (Liber Pontificalis, vol. 2, pp. 18–25). See also Huelsen, Chiese, pp. 6–10. By the end of the twelfth century, Gerald of Wales was able to list over 380 (Gerald of Wales, Speculum Ecclesiae, p. 281). Also Huelsen, Chiese, pp. 18–19.

pilgrim selected those which he would visit. Lack of evidence makes this an impossible question to answer. In the case of Sigeric, it has been suggested that his choices may have been influenced by the cults of particular saints which were popular in England in the tenth century.[47] Similar considerations may well have influenced the choice of other pilgrims. Many, however, would perhaps also have visited the churches which others recommended to them in much the same way as a modern-day tourist selects the sites he will go to. The churches which individual pilgrims chose to visit, therefore, were likely to vary considerably.

Some churches, of course, would have been found on the list of virtually all *Romipetae*. The *Lives* in the *Acta Sanctorum*, considered above, suggest the continued popularity of the basilicas of Saints Peter and Paul amongst twelfth-century pilgrims. These were churches which most would surely have wanted to see, and not surprisingly, they are both found in Nikolas's guide.[48] Nikolas also tells us that beneath the high altar at S. Pietro could be found this Saint's sarcophagus, as well as the prison in which he was held.[49] While the archaeological investigations carried out beneath the basilica suggest that the location of a prison there is highly unlikely, Nikolas's comments reveal what were perhaps popular twelfth-century beliefs.[50] Nikolas also states that at S. Pietro only half the bones of St Peter were buried along with half of those of St Paul, whilst the rest of their bones were located at S. Paolo.[51] Again this seems highly unlikely but may well have represented a twelfth-century confusion concerning the temporary burial of both apostles at S. Sebastiano.[52] As well as S. Pietro and S. Paolo, most twelfth-century *Romipetae* would probably also have visited the city's three other patriarchal basilicas, S. Lorenzo fuori le mura,[53] S. Maria Maggiore[54] and S. Giovanni in Laterano.[55] These are again all mentioned in Nikolas's itinerary.[56]

---

[47] For some thoughts on how a pilgrim might have decided what churches to visit, see Ortenberg, 'Archbishop Sigeric's journey', pp. 225–228.

[48] Werlauff, *Symbolae ad Geographiam Medii Aevi*, pp. 23–24.

[49] *Ibid.*, p. 24.

[50] The more traditional site of St Peter and St Paul's imprisonment is the Mamertine Prison near the *Forum Romanum*, now S. Pietro in Carcere.

[51] Werlauff, *Symbolae ad Geographiam Medii Aevi*, p. 24.

[52] See Magoun, 'Rome of Two Northern Pilgrims', p. 284.

[53] Huelsen, *Chiese*, pp. 285–286; Armellini, *Chiese di Roma*, vol. 2, pp. 1075–1086; *Corpus*, vol. 2, pp. 1–146.

[54] Huelsen, *Chiese*, p. 342; Armellini, *Chiese di Roma*, vol. 1, pp. 281–294; *Corpus*, vol. 3, pp. 1–60.

[55] Huelsen, *Chiese*, p. 272; Armellini, *Chiese di Roma*, vol. 1, pp. 121–136; *Corpus*, vol. 5, pp. 1–92.

[56] Werlauff, *Symbolae ad Geographiam Medii Aevi*, pp. 22–23.

New Demands

Pilgrims seem to have been keen to visit churches located both outside and inside the walls of Rome from the late eighth to twelfth centuries but there does, however, seem to have been an important development in popular religious devotion during this time. By the twelfth century pilgrims seem to have wanted more than simply to pray at the tomb of a saint or martyr. For the relics were hidden and invisible, leading some heretics to question whether they were really there at all.[57] By the twelfth century what pilgrims seem to have desired most was a closer contact with the relics. They wanted to be able to see and even to touch them. Significant here, perhaps, is what we know of Philip Augustus' visit to Rome in 1191 on his way home from the Holy Land. Pope Celestine is said not to have conducted Philip Augustus and his retinue to pray at the tomb of a saint or martyr. Rather, we are told, the pope took them to see the heads of Saints Peter and Paul at the Lateran and the *Veronica*, the cloth which bore the imprint of Christ's suffering face, at the Vatican.[58]

This demand for closer and more immediate contact with relics seems to have led to the development of numerous abuses, which Canon 62 of the Fourth Lateran Council of November 1215 appears to have been intended to stamp out.[59] No relic was to be sold, nor was any item to be venerated whose authenticity had not been proved, lest the faithful be deceived by 'worthless fabrications'. Above all this Canon forbade the display of all relics outside reliquaries. That this Canon was not universally obeyed by some pilgrimage centres is suggested by the issuing of local legislation. Canon 9 of the Council of Bordeaux of 1255 decreed not only that relics ought not to be sold but that they should never be removed from their reliquaries.[60] Canon 27 of the Council of Budapest of 1279 repeated the legislation of the Council of Bordeaux, also laying down a series of penalties to be imposed on all clerics and laymen who disobeyed.[61]

---

[57] M. Maccarrone ('La Cathedra Sancti Petri nel Medioevo: Da Simbolo a Reliquia', *Rivista di Storia della Chiesa in Italia*, 39 (1985), pp. 349–447, p. 421) cites the work of the Dominican Moneta da Cremona, in which he attacked the heretical beliefs of Cathars and Waldensians, who had questioned the existence of the bones of St Peter himself.

[58] Benedict of Peterborough, *Chronicle*, p. 228.

[59] *Conciliorum Oecumenicorum Decreta*, pp. 263–264.

[60] *Sacrorum Conciliorum*, vol. 23, col. 859.

[61] *Ibid.*, vol. 24, col. 283.

Lateran/Vatican Rivalry

One result of this growing dissatisfaction with merely praying at a martyr's tomb may have been an increase in the popularity of the Lateran amongst *Romipetae*. Indeed, whilst the Lateran had been founded by Constantine as the Cathedral of Rome and as the Bishop's residence, it had never enjoyed the popularity with *Romipetae* that S. Pietro had. In the twelfth century, however, this may have begun to change with the differing demands and interests of pilgrims. While this basilica did not possess the relics of a saint or martyr beneath its high altar but an Old Testament relic, supposedly the Ark of the Covenant, an unrivalled collection of relics was gathered together in the pope's private chapel of St Lawrence, the *Sancta Sanctorum*. The extent and richness of the relic collection found there is clearly illustrated in the description of the Lateran composed by John the Deacon, a canon of the basilica, sometime during the pontificate of Alexander III (1159–1181).[62] There were not merely the relics of one or two saints but a veritable hoard of them, including relics of the Virgin and even some of Christ himself. In particular, this basilica even claimed to possess bodily relics of Christ, although their very existence was in direct contradiction to the Church's teaching on the Resurrection.[63]

Twelfth-century *Romipetae* certainly seem to have been pleased and excited by what they found at the Lateran. This is clearly suggested by Nikolas of Munkathvera's guide in which he chose to include a list of some of these relics. The blood of Christ, vestments of the Virgin and milk from her breast, a portion of the crown of thorns and many bones of St John the Baptist are a selection from his description.[64]

Nor was Nikolas the only visitor whom we know about who showed a keen interest in, and knowledge of, the Lateran's extensive relic collection. In his *Speculum Ecclesiae*, Gerald of Wales chose to include a long list of the relics kept at the Lateran. Whether he had seen these during his pilgrimage in 1204, or earlier whilst engaged in litigation at the papal court, we do not know. In his list of these relics, however, we find a number of the items mentioned by Nikolas, as well as numerous others, including the rod of Aaron, fragments of the five loaves and two fishes, a vestment of St John the Evangelist and the heads of Saints Peter and Paul, placed there, according to Gerald, by Pope Leo III (795–816).[65] The heads of the two apostles were certainly amongst the most highly prized of the Lateran's collection. From the point of view of the twelfth-century *Romipetae* they may also have

---

62 John the Deacon's description can be found in *Codice Topografico*, vol. 3, pp. 319–373. On the relic collection, see esp. pp. 336–339.
63 Innocent III was acutely embarrassed by their existence. See his treatise *De Sacro Altaris Mysterio*, PL 217, cols. 876–877.
64 Werlauff, *Symbolae ad Geographiam Medii Aevi*, p. 22.
65 Gerald of Wales, *Speculum Ecclesiae*, esp. pp. 272–276.

provided a greater attraction than the body of St Peter, believed to be buried in the basilica dedicated to him on the Vatican Hill.[66] For the body was hidden but the heads could be seen and were even carried through the streets of Rome, together with a relic of the True Cross, in an annual procession on 14 September.[67]

Evidence of the popularity of the Lateran's relics and the increased expectations of the *Romipetae* may be deduced from the appearance of new relics at S. Pietro in the twelfth century. By the end of this century *Romipetae* could find there not only St Peter's body, supposedly buried beneath the high altar, but the very chair used for his enthronement as bishop of Rome, which they could see for themselves.[68] Preserved in the apse of the basilica in a reliquary designed by Bernini c.1666, the chair was first made available for study in 1968. Investigations suggest, however, that the chair has no connections with St Peter. Rather scholars, who have studied this wooden chair with its ivory carvings, suggest that its provenance was north-east Francia, probably in the third quarter of the ninth century. A portrait in the horizontal crossbar at the base of the chair is believed to be that of Charles the Bald.[69] It has also been suggested that it was Charles who transported the chair to Rome for his coronation on Christmas Day 875.[70] Whatever the origins of the chair and however it came to find its way to S. Pietro, by the twelfth century it was believed in Rome that this was the chair which the apostle had used for his enthronement in the episcopal cathedral there.

Maccarrone has argued that at the beginning of the twelfth century this belief probably only existed at a popular level.[71] Avilus, abbot of Tegernsee, who went to Rome at this time reported that he had been able to take home with him relics of St Peter's body, his cross and his chair.[72] If the belief in the chair as a relic existed only at a popular level at this time, as Maccarrone has argued, this may suggest how the abbot managed to acquire a fragment of it without much difficulty.[73] Perhaps more convincing, however, is his argument concerning the silence of Peter Mallius on the subject.[74] Mallius, a canon of S. Pietro, composed a description of the basilica probably during the pontificate of Alexander III.[75] In this he wrote an account of the relics to be

66 See Maccarrone, 'La Cathedra Sancti Petri', esp. p. 421.
67 *Liber Censuum*, vol. 1, pp. 310–311.
68 See *La Cattedra Lignea di S Pietro in Vaticano, Atti della Pontificia Accademia Romana di Archeologia, Memorie*, 10 (1971); Maccarrone, 'La Cathedra Sancti Petri'; L. Nees, 'Charles the Bald and the Cathedra Petri', *Charles the Bald. Court and Kingdom*, ed. M. T. Gibson and J. L. Nelson, 2nd ed. (Aldershot 1990), pp. 340–347.
69 Nees, 'Charles the Bald', p. 341.
70 *Ibid.*, p. 341; Maccarrone, 'La Cathedra Sancti Petri', pp. 384–388.
71 Maccarrone, 'La Cathedra Sancti Petri', pp. 424–425.
72 *Notae Tegernseenses*, MGH.SS 15, part 2, p. 1068.
73 Maccarrone, 'La Cathedra Sancti Petri', p. 425.
74 *Ibid.*, p. 425.
75 Peter Mallius's description of S. Pietro can be found in *Codice Topografico*, vol. 3, pp. 375–442.

found there. Significantly, no mention of the chair occurs in this list of relics.[76] Rather at this time, the canons seem to have still believed that the chair of St Peter was the marble seat in the apse of the basilica which had purely liturgical functions and no status as a relic.[77] Surviving evidence suggests, however, that by the end of the twelfth century the wooden chair from the Frankish kingdom had come to be recognised even amongst the canons of S. Pietro as the real *Cathedra Petri*, used by the apostle. Indeed, the anonymous *Gesta* of Innocent III records that at his episcopal consecration this pope was placed *eiusdem apostoli cathedra* and tells of his delight at the association.[78] There is no doubt, Maccarrone has argued, that for this anonymous author the chair used on that day was the same one as had been used by St Peter himself.[79]

The appearance of the relic of St Peter's chair at the Vatican, therefore, seems to have owed its origins to popular religious belief. The acceptance of this belief by the canons may in part suggest that they realised that something more than the body of an apostle hidden in a tomb was necessary if they were to continue to attract large numbers of *Romipetae* and to rival the relics preserved at the Lateran. They may also have been willing to accept and to cultivate this belief because it provided them with a convenient opportunity to assert their claims to superiority over the Lateran. For much of the twelfth century there had been great rivalry between the two basilicas, each competing for recognition as the official focus of Christian Rome and as the seat of the papacy.[80] Two polemical poems written by Romano, a canon of S. Pietro, probably a contemporary of Pope Innocent III, outlined the case for the Vatican through its possession of the Apostle's chair.[81] Pilgrims visited S. Pietro specifically to venerate the chair. As it was this basilica which possessed the relic, it was, therefore, the right of S. Pietro to title itself *Cattedrale*, an appellation which had been, hitherto, reserved for the Lateran.

---

[76] Maccarrone, 'La Cathedra Sancti Petri', p. 425.

[77] *Ibid.*, pp. 409–419.

[78] *Gesta*, col. xx.

[79] Maccarrone, 'La Cathedra Sancti Petri', pp. 427–429.

[80] R. Krautheimer, *Three Christian Capitals. Topography and Politics* (London, 1983), pp. 94–121; Maccarrone, 'La Cathedra Sancti Petri', esp. pp. 395–432; P. Jounel, *Le Culte des Saints dans les Basiliques du Lateran et du Vatican au Douzième Siècle, Collection de l'Ecole Française de Rome*, 26 (Rome, 1977).

[81] *Codice Topografico*, vol. 3, pp. 379–380.

> Hic cathedram Petri populi venerentur, honorent,
> Principis ecclesiam, caput orbis et urbis adorent.
> Tunc ego prima parens, mater caput ecclesiarum
> Constituta fui; socios cum Petrus in omnes
> Primatum tenuit, Deus et mihi contulit illum,
> Ut clarus populus cathedrales Principis aedes
> Me solam dominam teneat orbisque magistram . . .

Uronica/Veronica

The promotion of an important image, already in the possession of the canons of the Vatican at this time, further suggests that this basilica was trying to attract pilgrims by providing more visible attractions. During Gerald of Wales's visits to Rome he had the opportunity to see the *Uronica* at the Lateran and the *Veronica* at the Vatican.[82] The former was an image of Christ, painted by St Luke and the angels.[83] As it was 'not made with human hand', it was also known as the *Acheropita*.[84] Gervase of Tilbury noted that because of its fearsome effect upon the viewer it had to be kept covered,[85] while Gerald of Wales had heard how a pope, who had presumed to peer too closely at it, had been struck blind.[86]

This remarkable image was not always kept covered in the *Sancta Sanctorum* but was sometimes processed through the streets of Rome. The first reference to the *Acheropita* being carried in procession seems to be that which occurs in the *Liber Pontificalis* in the *Vita* of Sergius I (687–701), on the occasions of the Annunciation, Dormition and Nativity of the Virgin.[87] By the time of the pontificate of Stephen II (752–757) the procession seems to have been 'customary' and the Pope is described as carrying the *Acheropita* through the streets on his shoulders.[88] By the pontificate of Leo IV (847–855) the procession was held annually on 14–15 August, the Feast of the Assumption.[89] Beginning at midnight on 14 August, the *Acheropita* was carried from the Lateran, past SS. Quattro Coronati and the Colosseum, to

---

[82] Gerald of Wales, *Speculum Ecclesiae*, p. 278. 'De duabus igitur iconiis Salvatoris, Uronica scilicet Veronica, quarum una apud Lateranum, altera vero apud Sanctum Petrum.'

[83] On the *Uronica*, see G. Wilpert, 'L'Acheropita ossia L'Immagine del Salvatore nella Cappella del Sancta Sanctorum', *L'Arte. Rivista di Storia dell'Arte Medioevale e Moderna e d'Arte Decorativa*, 10 (1907), pp. 161–177 and 246–262; B. M. Bolton, 'Advertise the Message: Images in Rome at the turn of the Twelfth Century', SCH, 28 (1992), pp. 117–130; E. Kitzinger, 'A Virgin's Face: Antiquarianism in Twelfth Century Art', *Art Bulletin*, 62 (1980), pp. 6–19; I. Wilson, *Holy Faces, Secret Places. The Quest for Jesus's True Likeness* (London, 1991), pp. 40–45 and 162–164; Jounel, *Culte des Saints*, pp. 120–122. On the cult of the *Acheropita* in Lazio, see W. F. Wolbach, 'Il Christo di Sutri e la Venerazione del SS Salvatore nel Lazio', *Atti della Pontificia Accademia de Archeologia, Rendiconti*, 3rd series, 17 (1940–1941), pp. 97–126; C. D. Harding, 'Façade Mosaics of the Dugento and Trecento in Tuscany, Umbria and Lazio', unpublished Ph.D. thesis (University of London, 1983). This image can be seen in the *Sancta Sanctorum*.

[84] Wilpert ('L'Acheropita', p. 166) suggests that it was in fact made by a Roman artist sometime in the late fifth or early sixth century.

[85] Gervase of Tilbury, *Otia Imperialia*, ed. G. G. Leibnitz, *Scriptores Rerum Brunsuicensium* (Hanover, 1707), p. 967.

[86] Gerald of Wales, *Speculum Ecclesiae*, p. 278.

[87] *Liber Pontificalis*, vol. 1, p. 376; Bolton, 'Advertise the Message', p. 126.

[88] *Liber Pontificalis*, vol. 1, p. 443.

[89] Details of the procession were given by Benedict Canonicus in his *Liber Politicus*. See *Liber Censuum*, vol. 2, pp. 158–159.

the steps of the Temple of Venus and Rome, in front of S. Maria Nova. There
the feet of the *Acheropita* were washed and the image of the Virgin of S.
Maria Nova was brought out to meet her son. After this, the procession
continued to S. Adriano where the foot-washing was repeated, arriving
finally at S. Maria Maggiore as dawn broke on 15 August. Innocent III had
this image encased in a silver cover to increase the dramatic impact of this
liturgical drama and also to concentrate attention upon Christ's suffering
face.[90]

During the twelfth century interest seems to have increased in a similar
image at the Vatican, the *sudarium* or *Veronica*.[91] This cloth, used by Veronica to mop Christ's brow as he made his way to Calvary, bore an imprint of
his suffering face. Kept at S. Pietro, Gerald of Wales recorded that it was
usually hidden behind a curtain.[92] This image seems to have become popular
towards the end of the twelfth century and it has been suggested by Wilpert
that at this time a painted image was added to it.[93] It is possible that this
increased interest was a result of the need to provide pilgrims with images or
relics which they could actually see. It is also probable that, at a time of fierce
competition between the Vatican and Lateran, this relic was regarded as a
rival to the *Uronica*. In an attempt to break this rivalry by creating two equal
seats for the papacy, in 1208 Innocent III chose to have the *Veronica* processed through the streets as part of a new liturgical station at his hospital of
Santo Spirito.[94] On the first Sunday after the Octave of Epiphany, the relic
was to be carried in a reliquary of gold, silver and precious gems by the
canons, from its home at S. Pietro to the hospital. His institution of the
procession of the *Veronica* meant that both basilicas had representations of
Christ which enjoyed an equally high profile.

The emphasis placed upon these images of Christ may also have had
another important effect. Rome was now no longer a city associated only
with the two apostles Peter and Paul but now also had associations with
Christ himself. This may have been a particularly important factor in early
thirteenth-century attempts to renew Rome's popularity with pilgrims against
competition from other rival pilgrimage centres which had grown in popularity in the twelfth century.[95]

[90] Bolton, 'Advertise the Message', pp. 119–120.
[91] On this relic, see F. Lewis, 'The Veronica: Image, Legend and the Viewer', *England in the Thirteenth Century. Proceedings of the Harlaxton Conference* (Woodbridge, 1985), pp. 100–106; Bolton, 'Advertise the Message', pp. 117–130; Wilson, *Holy Faces, Secret Places*, esp. pp. 25–129. This relic is believed to be kept at S. Pietro, somewhere in the south-western pier which is one of the main supports of the basilica.
[92] Gerald of Wales, *Speculum Ecclesiae*, pp. 278–279.
[93] J. Wilpert, *Die Römischen Malereien und Mosaiken der Kirchlichen Bauten vom IV bis XIII Jahrhundert*, 4 vols. (Freiburg, 1917), vol. 2, p. 1123.
[94] On Innocent III's introduction of this liturgical station, see *Gesta*, cols. cc–cciii. See also below pp. 142–143.
[95] See chapters seven and eight.

Sight-Seeing

Romipetae undoubtedly spent a large proportion of their time visiting the city's important pilgrimage sites. There is a small amount of evidence, however, which suggests that in some respects the pilgrim was not unlike his modern counterpart, the tourist, in that some of his time was also spent in sight-seeing. Here we might cite the case of the more entrepreneurial of the Roman nobility who seem to have found it lucrative to let out their towers so that pilgrims could climb up them to take in views of the city.[96]

We might also ask how far *Romipetae* were interested in visiting and looking round the monuments of Rome's classical past. Unfortunately we know very little about this. The account of Sigeric's pilgrimage only provides a list of churches which he visited and gives almost no other information concerning what he did. The same is true of Gerald of Wales, who is content to explain that c.1204 he managed to amass one hundred years worth of indulgences.[97] Again we must turn to the description written by Abbot Nikolas. This account is unique because it is the only one written by a pilgrim which concerns itself in any way with the buildings of Rome's pagan past. Nikolas seems to have been particularly impressed by the fortifications of the Crescentii, nowadays the Castel Sant Angelo. This, according to him, was the 'tallest' and 'strongest' structure on that side of the river.[98] In the course of his pilgrimage he also saw the Porta Latina[99] and, probably, the baths of Caracalla.[100] Nikolas was surely not unusual amongst pilgrims in admiring these monuments.[101] What distinguishes Nikolas from other pilgrims, like Sigeric and Gerald of Wales, is that he chose to mention these Classical monuments, whereas they did not. This is, of course, interesting in itself and why this should have been the case we do not know. A possible explanation may be that, coming from outside the Romanised world, from a place where buildings of any size were uncommon, he may have found them more unusual and worthy of note than other pilgrims. Indeed, throughout Nikolas's text it is the size and scale of many of the buildings which frequently gives him cause for comment.

---

[96]   Sumption, *Pilgrimage*, p. 223.
[97]   Gerald of Wales, *De Invectionibus*, vol. 1, pp. 137–138.
[98]   Werlauff, *Symbolae ad Geographiam Medii Aevi*, p. 23.
[99]   *Ibid.*, p. 23.
[100] Nikolas writes that he saw 'that hall that King Diocletian owned'. Magoun ('Rome of Two Northern Pilgrims', p. 283) has argued that the position of the reference to this building in the text (between S. Giovanni *a Porta Latina* and S. Maria *in Domnica*) makes it likely that Nikolas is referring here to the baths of Caracalla. He may also have visited the baths of Diocletian (beside the Via Nomentana) and later confused the two.
[101] Ortenberg, 'Archbishop Sigeric's journey', pp. 201–202, argues that there is no reason to suppose that Sigeric missed such sites, even if they are not recorded in his text.

Mirabilia Urbis Romae

When assessing how the twelfth-century *Romipetae* spent their time in the apostolic city, we may ask how far they were influenced in what they went to see by the so-called *Mirabilia Urbis Romae*.[102] This was a description of Rome perhaps composed by one Benedict, a canon of S. Pietro, c.1140. Beginning with a description of the founding of the city, it then proceeded to list such things as its walls, gates, triumphal arches, hills, baths, palaces, theatres and places of martyrdom.[103] Next followed a list of some of the stories and legends associated with various sites, like the Pantheon, the Colosseum and the Lateran, S. Pietro and S. Paolo.[104] Finally there was a section which described various sites which could be seen as the reader walked around the city. There was information about such places as S. Pietro and its golden pine cone, the Castel Sant Angelo, the Mausoleum of Augustus, the Capitoline, the Forum, the Palatine and the Circus Maximus.[105]

The *Mirabilia* has been described by Brentano as a 'sort of palimpsest with one civilisation written over the other'.[106] Indeed, the Christian city appears superimposed upon the world of Ancient Rome. Where the Temple of Carmentis once stood, we are told, the church of S. Basilo now stands.[107] The church of S. Urso was once Nero's chancery,[108] while S. Maria in Aquiro now occupies the site of what had once been the Temple of Hadrian.[109]

It has been argued by Bloch that the *Mirabilia* 'was meant to be used by pilgrims'.[110] He cites no evidence for this, however, and indeed goes on to note that it is 'therefore all the more remarkable that he [Benedict] dwells at such length on ancient monuments'.[111] Yet the very contents of the *Mirabilia* would seem to suggest that it was certainly not written with pilgrims in mind. Although twelfth-century *Romipetae* may well have had some interest in the city's antiquities, their main concern was undoubtedly with the city's churches, the relics which they possessed and any indulgences that could be gained there. A guide which 'was meant to be used by pilgrims' would surely

---

102 On the *Mirabilia Urbis Romae*, see Brentano, *Rome Before Avignon*, pp. 75–81; R. L. Benson, 'Political *Renovatio*: Two Models from Roman Antiquity', *Renaissance and Renewal in the Twelfth Century*, ed. R. L. Benson and G. Constable (Oxford, 1982), pp. 339–386, esp. pp. 351–355; H. Bloch, 'The New Fascination with Ancient Rome', ibid., pp. 615–636, esp. pp. 630–634.

103 *Mirabilia Urbis Romae*, pp. 3–14.

104 *Ibid.*, pp. 17–30.

105 *Ibid.*, pp. 33–46.

106 R. Brentano, *Rome Before Avignon. A Social History of Thirteenth Century Rome* (London, 1974), p. 80.

107 *Mirabilia Urbis Romae*, p. 40.

108 *Ibid.*, p. 37.

109 *Ibid.*, pp. 37–38.

110 Bloch, 'New Fascination with Ancient Rome', p. 632.

111 *Ibid.*, p. 632.

have been made up principally of this sort of information. It also seems doubtful that large numbers of copies of such a guide could have been produced in the twelfth century and one wonders how many *Romipetae* would actually have been able to read what was, after all, quite a complex Latin text.

Benedict's work seems, therefore, to have been inspired not by the pilgrims who travelled *ad limina apostolorum* but instead by the revival of interest in the classical world, which was a feature of the twelfth century.[112] The author was not concerned with the splendour of the city's churches. Rather his real interest, as he himself says, was in the 'temples and palaces of emperors, consuls, senators and prefects . . . to bring back to human memory how great was their beauty in gold, silver, brass, ivory and precious stones'.[113] The *Mirabilia* reflected the new fascination with and pride in the city's origins and history. It seems to belong not to the category of pilgrim literature but rather to the genre concerned with the description of cities.[114] Descriptions were written of Bergamo by Moses de Brolo c.1112, of London by William Fitzstephen c.1173 and of Chester c.1195. A description of Lodi dates from c.1253, while others of Milan, Padua, Paris and Senlis followed in the early years of the fourteenth century.[115] The increasing popularity of this genre from the twelfth century onwards was the result of the new civic consciousness which spread through the towns of western Europe,[116] sparking a renewed interest in their 'ancient traditions, monuments and topography'.[117]

Shopping

As well as visiting the sites, pilgrims, like their modern counterparts the tourists, would probably also have spent some time shopping and souvenir hunting. The twelfth-century *Guide to Compostela* not only shows that this was indeed the case but even offers some evidence about the goods on sale there. 'After the fountain', the guide tells us, 'there is paradise, with its stone floor, where the pilgrim badges are sold.'[118] Here too wine, shoes, scrips,

112 C. H. Haskins, *The Renaissance of the Twelfth Century* (1927); C. Brooke, *The Twelfth Century Renaissance* (London, 1969); J. B. Ross, 'A Study of Twelfth Century Interest in the Antiquities of Rome', *Medieval and Historiographical Essays in Honour of James Westfall Thompson*, ed. J. L. Cate and E.N. Anderson (Chicago, 1938), pp. 302–321.

113 *Mirabilia Urbis Romae*, p. 46.

114 I would like to thank Dr Michael Clanchy for this suggestion.

115 See J. K. Hyde, 'Medieval Descriptions of Cities', *Bulletin of the John Rylands Library*, 48 (1965–1966), pp. 308–340.

116 *Ibid.*, p. 337.

117 *Mirabilia Urbis Romae*, p. xxvii.

118 *Guide du Pelèrin*, pp. 96–97.

straps, belts, as well as a large variety of medicines and other goods, could also be purchased.[119]

Further evidence of the thriving market at Compostela in the twelfth century is offered by the *Veneranda dies* sermon, in a section which reveals that some of the traders were far from honest.[120] Food seems to have been one of the most important items on sale. Bread, grains, fruit, cheese and meat were all available, although frequently, the author of the sermon complains, pilgrims were overcharged.[121] This sermon provides more evidence about the variety of medicines that were available. Herbs seem to have been particularly important, although the purchaser had to beware that he was not sold rotten goods, or spurious herbs in place of precious ones.[122] The pilgrim was to take care that poultices and other medicines were not fraudulently doctored with foreign substances.[123] As well as necessities such as food and medicines, the sermon confirms the evidence found in the *Guide*, that there were also 'luxury goods' on offer.[124] Yet again, however, the author of the sermon warns against dishonest tradesmen selling belts and other leather goods, who pretend that they are made of deer hide, when in fact they are really made of horse, sheep or pig skin.[125] Cloth was another luxury item on sale, although the pilgrim was often sold a short-measure and charged much more than a native of Compostela.[126] Other goods on sale included candles.[127] The women who sold these wares at the very threshold of the basilica of St James, however, came in for particular criticism in this sermon, for the short wicks which they put in their candles.[128] For the pilgrim with more money to spend, there was a wide range of items which could be bought as gifts for the cathedral. Rings, chalices and candelabra were just a few of these goods.[129] The pilgrim, however, was to avoid those merchants who sold second-rate items made from alloys, instead of pure metal, and with coloured stones, instead of precious gems.[130] Finally there were the money changers, who were also severely criticised by the author of the sermon for their short-changing and cheating of pilgrims.[131]

Such traders, providing for the wants and needs of pilgrims, must have been a feature of many holy places. This is certainly suggested by the *Roman*

---

119 *Ibid.*, pp. 96–97.
120 *Liber Sancti Jacobi*, vol. 1, pp. 141–176.
121 *Ibid.*, vol. 1, p. 165.
122 *Ibid.*, vol. 1, pp. 166–167.
123 *Ibid.*, vol. 1, p.167.
124 *Ibid.*, vol. 1, p. 167.
125 *Ibid.*, vol. 1, p.167.
126 *Ibid.*, vol. 1, p. 167.
127 *Ibid.*, vol. 1, p. 165.
128 *Ibid.*, vol. 1, p. 165.
129 *Ibid.*, vol. 1, p. 166.
130 *Ibid.*, vol. 1, p. 166.
131 *Ibid.*, vol. 1, pp. 165–166.

de Mont Saint Michel, written in the second half of the twelfth century. For in this the author wrote about victuallers setting up tents from where they sold their wares, which included bread, wines, venison, fruit and fish.[132] We also know from fourteenth- and fifteenth-century evidence, that by this time there were a variety of stalls in Rome itself.[133] These were situated in particularly large numbers on the steps leading up to S. Pietro and in the atrium of the church itself. Lists of the names of some of these traders survive, together with a record of what they sold and the rent that they paid for their stall. This evidence suggests that goods available in fourteenth-century Rome were very similar to those which had regularly been on sale in Compostela two centuries before. Ohartir de Francia, John de Tolosa and Johanna de Viterbio were just a few of the stall-holders selling vegetables, bread, fruit and fish.[134] Others like Robert of Aspera and Nardo de Callelongo specialised in oil,[135] while Ceccho de Cassia was just one of the many fig-sellers who operated throughout the city.[136]

These fourteenth- and fifteenth-century lists also suggest that, as at Compostela, there were a large number of apothecaries who plied their wares in Rome.[137] We also know about Robert de Tagliacotio, who was just one of the tooth-pullers with a thriving business on the steps leading up to S. Pietro.[138] In Rome pilgrims would also find cloth sellers, although their absence from the lists after 1384 suggest that they may not have been a commercial success.[139] Those faring rather better were undoubtedly the cobblers, for after travelling such long distances there were probably very few pilgrims who did not require their services.[140] Many other goods were on offer by the fifteenth century to tempt the *Romipetae* to part with whatever money they had left. As well as the vendors of pilgrim badges,[141] there were those like Mele and Benedict who sold books at S. Maria in Turri,[142] where the wares of numerous goldsmiths could also be purchased.[143]

There seems no reason to suppose that such a variety of stalls had not existed in Rome prior to the fourteenth century. The evidence, however, is very scanty. We know that money-changers were well established in Rome by

---

[132] Quoted by Evans, *Life in Medieval France*, pp. 76–77.

[133] P. Pecchai, 'Banchi e Botteghe Dinanzi alla Basilica Vaticana nel Secoli XIV, XV e XVI', *Archivi*, 2nd series, 18 (1951), pp. 81–123.

[134] *Ibid.*, pp. 100–101.

[135] *Ibid.*, p. 101.

[136] *Ibid.*, p. 95.

[137] *Ibid.*, pp. 96–97.

[138] *Ibid.*, pp. 99–100.

[139] *Ibid.*, p. 95.

[140] *Ibid.*, p. 100.

[141] There were a variety of badges and other sorts of images on sale by this time; *ibid.*, pp. 91–95.

[142] *Ibid.*, p. 99.

[143] *Ibid.*, p. 95.

the twelfth century, because the *Gesta* of Innocent III tells us that this Pope had them removed from the doors of the Lateran kitchens, where they were accustomed to set up their benches.[144] But was there also a thriving market on the steps and in the atrium of S. Pietro in the twelfth century? We know almost nothing about this but one vital clue may have been provided for us by Nikolas of Munkathvera. Nikolas's pilgrimage, as we know, took him to S. Pietro. Here he describes what he saw, not only the basilica and 'Petrs Nal' but also the 'kauphús Petrs Postola'.[145] But what did Nikolas mean by 'kauphús', a word which in modern Icelandic has come to mean 'shop'?[146] If Nikolas had wanted to say that he had simply seen a market at S. Pietro, there were already many existing words in Old Icelandic which he could have used, like *torg* (market), *kaupstefna* (fair, market), *markaðr* (market), or *kaupangr* (market-place). That he was in fact trying to describe something the like of which he had never seen before, is suggested by his use of 'kauphús', a term which he may have coined himself.[147] It is a compound word, formed from *kaup* meaning a 'bargain' or 'agreement', ultimately a loan word from the Latin *caupo*, meaning a 'small tradesman', and *hús*, a 'building'. Geoffrey Harlow has pointed out that the word is grammatically singular and so cannot refer to a row of buildings or shops. Instead he has proposed that Nikolas may have been trying to suggest some sort of 'trade-building' or 'market-building'. We do not know if Nikolas was actually trying to describe a thriving market inside the atrium of S. Pietro but this is certainly a possibility. In any case, whatever we make of *kauphús*, it certainly seems to suggest that there was some kind of trade taking place in the vicinity of S. Pietro long before the fourteenth century.

In trying to assess how pilgrims spent their time in Rome in the twelfth century, we are hampered by the paucity of the sources. In most cases, when we find the name of a pilgrim, we are only told his destination. Usually no information is given about what he did and saw. Where details do exist, as in some of the saints' *Lives* in the *Acta Sanctorum*, they are only of a very sketchy and uninformative nature. What evidence we do have, however, seems to suggest that the way twelfth-century *Romipetae* spent their time in the apostolic city had changed little since the tenth century. Indeed, a comparison between the itineraries of Sigeric, archbishop of Canterbury, and Nikolas of Munkathvera shows considerable similarity, with both visiting a variety of the city's churches, which lay both inside and outside the walls. The major difference appears to be that the twelfth-century *Romipetae* were

---

144 *Gesta*, col. lxxx.
145 Werlauff, *Symbolae ad Geographiam Medii Aevi*, pp. 23–24.
146 I am grateful to Mr Geoffrey Harlow for giving his opinion on the meaning of this word.
147 Geoffrey Harlow has checked 'kauphús' in various Old Icelandic dictionaries, which give meanings such as 'building where one buys and sells' and 'shop'. The only occurrence of the word which these dictionaries cite, however, is the one in the text of Abbot Nikolas.

far more demanding than their tenth-century counterparts, wanting relics which they could actually see. The acquisition of new relics by the canons of S. Pietro in particular would seem to confirm this and may indicate that for many *Romipetae* a body hidden inside a tomb, even that of St Peter himself, was no longer considered a sufficient attraction in its own right.

6

Welfare Provisions for Pilgrims in Rome

The purpose of this chapter is to consider what welfare provisions were made for the *Romipetae* in the apostolic city itself. As the numbers of pilgrims travelling to Rome began to increase so facilities had to be provided for them. They needed places where they could stay, as well as other practical provisions such as baths and public conveniences. For the many pilgrims who had little money, food handouts were also essential. Consideration will be given first to the welfare provisions which were made for pilgrims prior to the twelfth century, which are relatively well documented. Secondly, an analysis will be made of the provisions for those pilgrims travelling to Rome in the twelfth and early thirteenth centuries. Lastly, this chapter will explore another neglected area – the measures taken to protect dying pilgrims and their property and the arrangements which were made in Rome for their burial.

Welfare Provisions before the Twelfth Century

Diaconiae

The deaconry, or *diaconia*, had originated as a service initiated by the monasteries of lower Egypt in the mid-fourth century and consisted of the distribution, by monks, of food to the poor.[1] Over the course of the next two centuries the *diaconia*, transposed to the west, seems to have been developed from a charitable service into a series of autonomous institutions, each owning their own property. Food hand-outs, the *annonae*, were supplemented by the distribution of furniture and even of land and special cells were also built at some *diaconiae* to provide lodgings for strangers.

---

1   A thorough investigation of the *diaconiae* has been carried out by Frances Niederer. See her dissertation, 'The Roman Diaconiae' (unpublished dissertation, New York University, 1951), and her article 'Early Medieval Charity', *Church History*, 21 (1952), pp. 285–295. This subject has also been treated by O. Bertolino, 'Per la Storia delle Diaconie Romane [ell' alto medio evo sino alla fine del secolo VIII', *ASRSP*, 70 (1947), pp. 1–145; J. Lestocquoy, 'Administration de Rome et Diaconies du VIIe au IXe Siècle', *Rivista di Archeologia Cristiana*, 7 (1930), pp. 261–298.

By the pontificate of Leo III (795–816) twenty-two *diaconiae* could be found in Rome itself[2] and most of these seem to have been involved in the distribution of food supplies to the inhabitants of the city. Nine *diaconiae*, S. Angelo, S. Giorgio, S. Lucia in Septem Vias, S. Maria Antiqua, S. Maria in Cosmedin, SS. Sergio e Bacco, S. Adriano, SS. Cosma e Damiano and S. Teodoro, were established in the commercial and civic heart of the city, between the East bank of the Tiber and the Roman Forum and seem to have been set up to facilitate access to the incoming food supplies.[3] S. Maria in Cosmedin, the earliest recorded of these *diaconiae*, was certainly in existence by the end of the sixth century and those of S. Teodoro and S. Giorgio are probably also of sixth- or early seventh-century date.[4]

Five *diaconiae*, S. Maria in Adriano, SS. Sergio e Bacco apud S. Pietro, S. Maria in Caput Portici, S. Martino and S. Silvestro, were established in the Borgo S. Pietro. It is likely, as Niederer has argued, that the primary function of these *diaconiae* was to provide food for pilgrims.[5] When they first appeared is uncertain. The evidence of the *Liber Pontificalis* suggests that the *diaconia* of SS. Sergio e Bacco had been established prior to the middle of the eighth century. In the *Vita* of Gregory III (731–741) it is recorded that this pope extended the small oratory of the *diaconia* of SS. Sergio e Bacco, which had already existed there for a long time.[6] Two other of these *diaconiae* certainly pre-date the middle of the eighth century. In the *Vita* of Stephen II (752–757) it is recorded that this pope founded two *xenodochia*[7] at S. Pietro, which he merged with the *diaconia* of S. Silvestro and with another dedicated to the Virgin, which was probably S. Maria in Caput Portici.[8] These *diaconiae* are referred to in Stephen II's *Vita* as 'venerable' and 'already existing'.[9] The *xenodochia* were perhaps added so that these *diaconiae* could not only feed pilgrims but could also provide them with a bed for the night.

The *Vita* of Hadrian I (772–795) in the *Liber Pontificalis*, however, claims that it was this pope who established three *diaconiae* in the vicinity of S. Pietro. These *diaconiae* are named as S. Maria in Adriano, S. Maria in Caput Portici and S. Silvestro.[10] At first this would seem to conflict with the evidence cited above from the *Liber Pontificalis* but then Hadrian I's biographer

---

[2] For the list of churches, monasteries and *diaconiae* which existed in Rome by the pontificate of Leo III, see *Liber Pontificalis*, vol. 2, pp. 1–34.

[3] Niederer, 'Early Medieval Charity', p. 289.

[4] *Ibid.*, p. 288.

[5] *Ibid.*, pp. 289–290.

[6] *Liber Pontificalis*, vol. 1, p. 420.

[7] On *xenodochia*, see below pp. 126–129.

[8] *Liber Pontificalis*, vol. 1, p. 440. Duchesne (*Liber Pontificalis*, vol. 1, p. 520, note 80) identifies the *diaconia* dedicated to the Virgin in this *Vita* of Stephen II as S. Maria in Caput Portici. P. Kehr (*Italia Pontificia*, vol. 1, p. 150) and Bertolino ('Per la Storia delle Diaconie Romane', pp. 44–45) follow Duchesne's identification.

[9] *Liber Pontificalis*, vol. 1, p. 440–441.

[10] *Ibid.*, vol. 1, pp. 505–506.

modifies his claims. He continues with the explanation that Hadrian had in fact discovered these *diaconiae* hidden away and no longer producing works of mercy.[11] Thus, this pope neither established nor founded the *diaconiae* referred to but actually restored them and then presented them with many gifts.[12] He also ordained that on every Thursday at these three *diaconiae* there should be a distribution of alms to the poor at the bath-house.[13] It seems likely, therefore, that the *diaconia* of S. Maria in Adriano had been established at S. Pietro long before the pontificate of Hadrian I. It is uncertain when the *diaconia* of S. Martino was established. The first reference to it occurs in the *Liber Pontificalis* in the *Vita* of Leo III, where it is recorded that this pope gave this *diaconia* a silver crown weighing 5 pounds and 4 ounces.[14]

Each *diaconia* was run by either a *dispensator*, who was a layman, or a *pater diaconiae*, who was a cleric. In either case the individual was appointed by the pope.[15] Under him were the *diaconitae*, who were monks, and below them lesser servants and slaves of both sexes. According to the *Liber Diurnus* the primary concern of the *dispensator* (or *pater diaconiae*) was with secular matters, the administration of the property of the *diaconia* and its maintenance.[16] He was also responsible for the payment of priests who said masses in the small chapels at the *diaconia* and prayers for benefactors. Up until the middle of the eighth century the ecclesiastical functions of the *diaconiae* were not as important as those of other churches within the city. This began to change, however, in the late eighth and early ninth centuries as the small chapels within the *diaconiae* gave way to large churches and their ecclesiastical importance gradually eclipsed their role as distributors of charity.

Other food handouts

As well as the food handed out by the *diaconiae*, the *Liber Pontificalis* also indicates that, at least during the eighth century, some provisions of this kind were also being made by the popes themselves. Pope Zacharias (741–752) ordered alms to be distributed amongst the poor and the pilgrims who dwelt at S. Pietro.[17] The *Vita* of Hadrian I also recounts how this pope provided for the daily feeding of 'one hundred of our brethren Christ's poor'.[18] If there were more who needed feeding, they were not to be turned away.[19] They

---

[11] *Ibid.*, vol. 1, p. 506.
[12] *Ibid.*, vol. 1, p. 506.
[13] *Ibid.*, vol. 1, p. 506. Hadrian also established two deaconries within the city walls at S. Adriano and SS. Cosma e Damiano. Here too he ordered that refreshment should be provided for pilgrims at the deaconry bath house. See *ibid.*, vol. 1, pp. 509–510. See also *Lives of the Eighth Century Popes*, p. 165, note 170.
[14] *Liber Pontificalis*, vol. 2, p. 22.
[15] Lestocquoy, 'Administration de Rome', esp. pp. 291–292.
[16] *Liber Diurnus Romanorum Pontificum*, ed. E. de Rozière (Paris, 1889); see *formula* 95.
[17] *Liber Pontificalis*, vol. 1, p. 435.
[18] *Ibid.*, vol. 1, p. 502.
[19] *Ibid.*, vol. 1, p. 502.

were to be gathered in the portico of the Lateran, where the cellarer was to distribute to each bread, wine and broth.[20] The produce with which these people were to be fed was to be supplied by the *domusculta Capracorum*, a large rural estate to the north of Rome, which seems to have been about nine kilometres wide and twenty-four kilometres long, extending from the region of the Prima Porta to that of Calcata near Nepi.[21] If any produce from this *domusculta* was sold, then the profits, together with any other revenues accrued, were to be spent only upon the sustenance of Christ's poor.[22]

Xenodochia

Whilst pilgrims could find food at the *diaconiae* and possibly also by the middle of the eighth century a bed for the night, at least at S. Silvestro and S. Maria *in Caput Portici*, other places too may have provided pilgrims with shelter. The earliest record in the *Liber Pontificalis* of the construction of accommodation in Rome is found in the *Vita* of Symmachus (498–514). Here it says that at S. Pietro, S. Paolo and S. Lorenzo fuori le mura this pope had accommodation constructed for the poor.[23] That this accommodation may also have been intended for the use of pilgrims is suggested by its location, outside the walls and close to some of the city's most important pilgrimage churches.

Pilgrims may also have been able to find a bed for the night at one of the *xenodochia* located in the city. Before discussing the founding and location of these *xenodochia*, it is first necessary to try to establish what they were. From about 800 the Greek term, *xenodochium*,[24] and the Latin term, *hospitale* or *hospitalis*,[25] are used frequently in medieval sources to mean a travellers' inn. As travellers frequently fell ill in the course of their journey, some inns often had to provide care for the sick. Whilst some of these inns developed into places devoted only to this nursing care, others remained essentially hospices, perhaps providing some casual assistance for those stricken by disease. The terms *xenodochium* and *hospitalis*, however, were used for both institutions and so it is often difficult to determine from surviving medieval sources what kind

---

[20] *Ibid.*, vol. 1, p. 502.

[21] The *domuscultae* were large rural estates located close to Rome. Pope Zacharias established four or five and Hadrian I four more. See T. F. X. Noble, *The Republic of St Peter. The Birth of the Papal State, 680–825* (Philadelphia, 1984), pp. 246–249; P. Partner, 'Notes on the Lands of the Roman Church in the Early Middle Ages', *PBSR*, n.s. 21 (1966), pp. 68–78; N. Christie, *Three South Etrurian Churches*, Archaeological Monographs of the British School at Rome, 4 (London, 1991).

[22] *Liber Pontificalis*, vol. 1, p. 502.

[23] *Ibid.*, vol. 1, p. 263.

[24] The Greek word is τό ξενοδοχεῖον, used since Classical times for an inn or hostel. See du Cange, *Glossarium*, vol. 6, p. 924.

[25] *Ibid.*, vol. 3, pp. 702–704.

of institution is being described, a simple hospice or a true hospital concerned only with the care of the sick.[26]

It is difficult to decide from surviving sources whether the *xenodochia* founded in Rome were simply hospices, true hospitals, or whether both existed here. That there may have been some true hospitals in Rome is suggested by a list which survives in the *Liber Diurnus*, drawn up probably in the late seventh and eighth centuries. Included in the *Liber Diurnus* was a list of the duties incumbent upon those in charge of a *xenodochium*.[27] They were to ensure that the beds for their guests were made ready and covered with blankets.[28] They were always to be ready to take in and to look after those who were sick or destitute and to give to them whatever they might need.[29] This *formula* in the *Liber Diurnus* also required those in charge of the *xenodochium* to distribute an annual ration of oil to the sick and poor and anything else that they might need.[30] Doctors were also to be called in to take care of the sick.[31] This evidence, however, is too scanty to say for certain whether the *xenodochia* in Rome were intended only for the sick, or whether those who were simply in need of shelter would also have been taken in by some or all of them.[32] In a city such as Rome, with a large temporary population seeking shelter, it would seem likely that many of the *xenodochia* would have taken in those needing accommodation as well as those who had fallen ill. The ambiguity of the surviving sources, however, should be borne in mind.

There were certainly a number of *xenodochia* functioning in Rome. During the pontificate of Vigilius (537–555), a *xenodochium* was built on the *Via Lata* on what is now the site of S. Maria di Trevi. The *Liber Pontificalis* attributes the foundation of this *xenodochium* to Belisarius (c.505–565), a Byzantine general, financed by spoils taken from the Vandals.[33] By the end of the sixth century this *xenodochium* seems to have been only one of five, by then well established in Rome. Three *xenodochia* are referred to in the letters of Gregory the Great (590–604), the *xenodochium Aniciorum*,[34] the *xenodochium*

---

[26] On this problem of distinguishing hospices and true hospitals, see T. S. Miller, 'The Knights of Saint John and the Hospitals of the Latin West', *Speculum*, 53 (1978), pp. 709–733, esp. pp. 709–723. I am grateful to Professor Riley-Smith for this reference.

[27] *Liber Diurnus, formula* 66, pp. 129–130.

[28] *Ibid., formula* 66, p. 129.

[29] *Ibid., formula* 66, p. 129.

[30] *Ibid., formula* 66, pp. 129–130.

[31] *Ibid., formula* 66, p. 130.

[32] Miller ('Knights of St John', pp. 710–711) cites two hospices in Merovingian Gaul which seem to have functioned as true hospitals, another in Visigothic Spain and another in Rome. He bases his information about Rome on the passage in the *Liber Diurnus*, but as we shall see there were a number of *xenodochia* functioning in Rome by the time that the *Liber Diurnus* was composed.

[33] *Liber Pontificalis*, vol. 1, p. 296.

[34] Gregory the Great, *Regestri Epistolarum*, col. 1247.

Valerii[35] and the xenodochium Viae Novae.[36] The xenodochium Valerii was probably situated on the Celian Hill close to S. Stefano Rotundo, the residence of
the Valerii in the fourth century.[37] The locations of the other two remain
uncertain. A fifth xenodochium seems to have been founded by Gregory the
Great himself, close to the steps leading up to the atrium at S. Pietro, which
would probably have been close to where the obelisk now stands in St Peter's
Square.[38]

It was perhaps in one of these xenodochia that the envoys of the Irish abbot
Cummian stayed c.633 when they travelled to Rome to try to resolve the
problem of the date of Easter. Certainly the hospitio in which they stayed was
already catering for pilgrims of a wide range of nationalities. For these Irish
envoys stayed in the same hostel as a Greek, an Egyptian, a Hebrew and a
Scythian, with whom they celebrated Easter in S. Pietro.[39]

Four xenodochia are mentioned, although not named, in the Vita of Pope
Stephen II (752–757). The author of this Vita recorded that by this time
these xenodochia were deserted and that Stephen II renewed them, conferring
gifts upon them.[40] Which four these were is unknown. Stephen II also seems
to have been responsible for the foundation of a new xenodochium, the xenodochium in Platana, situated close to S. Maria ad Martyres and intended for
one hundred of Christ's poor.[41] The Liber Pontificalis records that Stephen II
founded another two xenodochia close to S. Pietro, which he seems to have
merged permanently with two venerable diaconiae established in that area, S.
Silvestro and another dedicated to the Virgin.[42] Surviving evidence suggests
that the xenodochia were certainly still in existence by the ninth century. In
the Vita of Leo III (795–816) it was recorded that this pope gave to the
xenodochium Aniciorum a canister weighing 2 pounds 8 ounces. and a similar
canister to the xenodochium Valerii.[43] A gift of a silver canister weighing 2
pounds 7 ounces. was made to the xenodochium Firmis, whose oratory was
dedicated to the Virgin.[44] Davis has speculated that this is probably the
xenodochium founded by Belisarius.[45] A fourth xenodochium is also mentioned,
the xenodochium Tucium with an oratory dedicated to Saints Cosmas and

35 Ibid., col. 966.
36 Ibid., col. 507.
37 Kehr, Italia Pontificia, vol. 1, p. 156.
38 Gregory the Great, Regestri Epistolarum, col. 1229. On the foundation of this xenodo-
    chium, see also Peter Mallius' description of the Vatican in Codice Topografico, vol. 3,
    esp. p. 404.
39 Cummian, Epistola ad Segienum Huensem Abbatem de Contoversia Paschali, PL 87, cols.
    977–978. See also Llewellyn, Rome in the Dark Ages, p. 181.
40 Liber Pontificalis, vol. 1, p. 440.
41 Ibid., vol. 1, p. 440.
42 Ibid., vol. 1, p. 440. See above.
43 Ibid., vol. 2, p. 25.
44 Ibid., vol. 2, p. 19.
45 Lives of the Eighth-Century Popes, p. 218, note 168.

Damian.[46] This might be the *xenodochium* referred to by Gregory the Great as *xenodochium Viae Novae* but we have no way of knowing for certain. By the pontificate of Leo III the *xenodochium in Platana*, founded by Stephen II, no longer ranked as such and seems to have been absorbed by the nearby *diaconia* of S. Eustachio.[47]

The *xenodochium* founded by Gregory the Great at S. Pietro also still seems to have been in existence in the ninth century. In the *Vita* of Hadrian I, it is recorded that the *diaconia* of S. Silvestro was situated close to the *hospitale* founded by St Gregory,[48] a good example of the way in which the terms *xenodochium* and *hospitale* were frequently interchanged. The term *hospitale* was again used to describe Gregory's foundation in the *Vita* of Stephen V (855–891), who, it is recorded, presented gifts to the *hospital* 'of B. Gregory in the portico of B. Peter the Apostle'.[49]

Other accommodation

The author of the *Vita* of Leo III mentions accommodation which was either repaired or constructed by this pope. He rebuilt some 'chambers' situated close to S. Pietro.[50] These had decayed as a result of great age and were on the verge of collapse. They may have been the same 'chambers' which Gregory III (731–741)[51] and Sergius I (687–701)[52] had rebuilt and may possibly be the accommodation originally constructed by Pope Symmachus at the beginning of the sixth century.[53] The *Vita* of Sergius I also refers to his repair of 'chambers' at S. Paolo, which, as in the case of S. Pietro, might possibly be the accommodation originally constructed during the pontificate of Symmachus.[54]

The author of Leo III's *Vita* in the *Liber Pontificalis* recorded other welfare provisions made by this pope for the use of pilgrims. According to the *Liber Pontificalis*, at S. Pietro, on the right hand side of the atrium, where the Vatican palace now stands, Leo had a house built 'of wonderful size', which was then finely decorated and in which he placed dining couches.[55] Davis has no doubt that such a building project was intended to provide accommodation here for pilgrims[56] and, as the author of this *Vita* then immediately

---

46 *Liber Pontificalis*, vol. 2, p. 25.
47 This *diaconia* is referred to as *in Platana* in medieval documents. See Kehr, *Italia Pontificia*, vol. 1, p. 98 and *Liber Pontificalis*, vol. 2, p. 46 note 108.
48 *Liber Pontificalis*, vol. 1, p. 506.
49 *Ibid.*, vol. 2, p. 195.
50 *Ibid.*, vol. 2, p. 27.
51 *Ibid.*, vol. 1, p. 420. See also *Lives of the Eighth Century Popes*, p. 26.
52 *Liber Pontificalis*, vol. 1, p. 375.
53 *Ibid.*, vol. 1, p. 263.
54 *Ibid.*, vol. 1, p. 375.
55 *Ibid.*, vol. 2, p. 28.
56 *Lives of the Eighth Century Popes*, p. 221, note 176.

mentions a bath built here for the use of pilgrims,[57] it seems likely that this
was indeed the case.

In addition, the *Liber Pontificalis* records that Leo III had a 'hospital'
dedicated to St Peter constructed at a site known as *Naumachia* situated in
the area between the Vatican and the Castel S. Angelo.[58] It is also recorded
that Leo III decorated the houses there and built a church, dedicated to St
Peter, in which he deposited the relics of many martyrs.[59] In order that
pilgrims and the poor who sought shelter there might be fed, he endowed the
'hospital' with both urban and rural estates.[60] It seems probable from what
the *Liber Pontificalis* says about this foundation that this was certainly not a
true hospital but a hospice designed to provide food and shelter.

In the *Vita* of Paschal I (817–824) it is noted that this pope gave the
hospitale Sancti Peregrini, built by his predecessor Leo III close to S. Pietro at a
place known as *Naumachia*, to the monastery of SS. Agatha and Caecilia.[61] It
seems likely, however, that the 'hospital' referred to in both the *Vitae* of Leo
III and Paschal I is the same and that the reference to St Peter by the
biographer of Leo III was a mistake for St Peregrinus. Certainly in another
place in Leo III's *Vita* there is a reference to the *oratorio sancti Peregrini . . . in
hospitale dominico ad Naumachium*.[62] The dedication of the church of a pilgrim's *hospital* to St Peregrinus, the legendary first bishop of Auxerre martyred c.261, would surely be an appropriate one.[63] Evidence that this
ninth-century 'hospital' was still functioning in the mid-eleventh century is
indicated by a Bull of Leo IX dated 1053, which confirmed certain goods and
properties to the canons of S. Pietro. Included amongst these properties was
the church of S. Peregrinus together with its 'hospital'.[64]

By the ninth century pilgrims were also being cared for at the monastery of
S. Stephano Maior, situated close to S. Pietro. In the *Vita* of Paschal I it was
recorded that pilgrims travelling to Rome 'for the love of God from distant
parts' could expect to receive hospitality there.[65]

More accommodation was founded in Rome during the early years of the
eleventh century. The conversion of Hungary to Christianity occurred during the reign of King Stephen (997–1038). It was this king too who founded
a church in Rome at the monastery of S. Stefano Minore[66] near S. Pietro,

---

[57] On the provision of baths, see below.
[58] *Liber Pontificalis*, vol. 2, p. 28.
[59] *Ibid.*, vol. 2, p. 28.
[60] *Ibid.*, vol. 2, p. 28.
[61] *Ibid.*, vol. 2, p. 57.
[62] *Ibid.*, vol. 2, p. 25.
[63] *Series Episcoporum Ecclesiae Catholicae*, ed. P. B. Gams (Leipzig, 1931), p. 501; *Butler's
     Lives of the Saints*, vol. 2, p. 326.
[64] *Collectione Bullarum*, vol. 1, p. 29.
[65] *Liber Pontificalis*, vol. 2, p. 52.
[66] This monastery was founded during the pontificate of Stephen II. See Kehr, *Italia
     Pontificia*, vol. 1, p. 148.

together with a *hospitium*. Over the door of the church, before its destruction during the pontificate of Pius VI (1775–1799), was the inscription:

ECCA HOSPITALIS sti STEPHANI REGIS HVNGROR [67]

What the *hospitium* may have been like is suggested in the *Vita* of King Stephen, which recorded that he built a circular stone wall, within the confines of which he seems to have had placed *domibus* et *hospiciis*.[68] Instead of one large building, he seems to have erected a compound for the use of the Hungarians. That this may have been a sizeable compound is perhaps suggested by the settlement of twelve canons there, whose task it was presumably to look after the hostel and the needs of those staying there.[69] A Bull of Benedict X dated 1058 gave control of this *hospitium* to the monks of S. Stefano. It was also stated in this Bull that those Hungarians who travelled to the apostolic city, whether for the sake of prayer or on business, were only to be allowed to stay at this hostel built for their use by King Stephen.[70]

Scholae

While the *xenodochia* and some *diaconiae* could provide pilgrims with somewhere to stay on a short-term basis, they were probably unsuitable for those who intended to remain longer, those who had left behind their native land in order to spend the rest of their lives as pilgrims, close to the tomb of St Peter. The increasing popularity of this way of life seems to have led to the development of four *scholae* in the Borgo S. Pietro, those of the Saxons, Frisians and Franks to the south of the basilica and that of the Lombards a little to the north.[71]

There are considerable problems in trying to determine what these *scholae* were like. The evidence of the *Liber Pontificalis* suggests that the *Schola Saxonum* itself was a settlement of considerable extent. Indeed, a fire which took place there during the pontificate of Paschal I (817–824), apparently a result of the carelessness of some of the Saxons, destroyed all of their houses as well as the portico of S. Pietro.[72] Taking pity on these Saxon pilgrims, the pope gave them food, clothing and money, together with wood to rebuild

---

[67] See L. Duchesne, 'Notes sur la Topographie de Rome au Moyen Age, XII Vaticana', *MEFR*, 34 (1914), pp. 307–356, esp. p. 329.

[68] *Vita Stephani Regis Ungariae*, MGH.SS 11, p. 235.

[69] *Ibid.*, p. 235.

[70] L. Schiaperelli, 'Le Carte antiche dell'Archivio Capitolare di S. Pietro in Vaticano', *ASRSP*, 24 (1901), pp. 393–496, esp. pp. 483–484.

[71] W. J. Moore, *The Saxon Pilgrims to Rome and the Schola Saxonum* (Fribourg, 1937); W. J. D. Croke, 'The National Establishments of England in Medieval Rome', *The Dublin Review*, 123 (1898), pp. 305–317; P. van Kessel, 'Frisoni e Franchi a Roma nell' Età Carolingia', *Les Fondations Nationales dans la Rome Pontificale, Collection de l'Ecole Française de Rome*, 52 (1981), pp. 37–46.

[72] *Liber Pontificalis*, vol. 2, p. 53.

their homes.[73] The large size and extent of the *scholae* is further indicated by the recruitment of the inhabitants of the *scholae* of the Saxons, Frisians and Franks in 846 to fight Saracens who had settled in Ostia[74] and by a second fire in 847 which again destroyed not only the houses of the Saxons and the portico of S. Pietro but also buildings of the *Schola Langobardorum*.[75] The *Liber Pontificalis*, however, also recounted the work of rebuilding which took place after this fire of 847, noting that a church was built by Pope Leo IV *supra schola Saxonum*.[76] This appears contradictory to earlier evidence, suggesting that the *schola Saxonum* was in fact not a large settlement at all but rather occupied only a small space upon which a church could be built. This seems highly unlikely and the phrase *supra schola Saxonum* should probably be interpreted as meaning on part of the site of this *schola*. It is perhaps in this way that we should also interpret a Bull issued by Leo IV in 854 of which only fragments now survive.[77] Schiaperelli's reconstruction suggests that this Bull referred to the church of 'Sancti Michaelis quae vocatur schola Frisonorum', to the church of 'S. Iustini quae vocatur schola Langobardorum' and to the 'ecclesia Sanctae Dei Genetricis virginis Mariae que vocatur schola Saxonum'.[78] These, together with the church of S. Salvatore *in Terrione*, often referred to as the *schola Francorum*,[79] were probably not the actual *scholae* themselves but by the ninth century were recognised as integral parts of these pilgrim communities, which most surviving evidence suggests must have been of a considerable size.

It is impossible to date with any accuracy the origins of these *scholae*. Probably the most that can be said is that they were already well established by the end of the eighth century. This is indicated by an entry in the *Liber Pontificalis*, which records that those living in them took part in a procession to welcome Leo III (795–816) on his return from Paderborn in 799.[80] Those sources which do attempt to date the origins of the *scholae* are certainly problematic. William of Malmesbury (d.c.1143) maintained that the *Schola Saxonum* was founded by King Offa of Mercia (757–796), whilst Matthew Paris (d.1259) in his *Chronica Maiora* attributed the foundation to Ine of Wessex, who ruled over the West Saxons until 726, when he resigned his kingdom to lead the life of a pilgrim in Rome. However a sizeable settlement such as the *schola Saxonum*, rather than being deliberately 'founded', probably developed as increasing numbers of pilgrims settled there. Perhaps, therefore, what William of Malmesbury and Matthew Paris are describing is the founda-

---

73 *Ibid.*, vol. 2, p. 54.
74 *Ibid.*, vol. 2, p. 100.
75 *Ibid.*, vol. 2, pp. 110–111.
76 *Ibid.*, vol. 2, p. 128.
77 Schiaperelli, 'Le Carte antiche', p. 433.
78 *Ibid.*, p. 433.
79 Kehr, *Italia Pontificia*, vol. 1, pp. 151–152.
80 *Liber Pontificalis*, vol. 2, p. 6.

tion of a hospice of some kind, either to serve an already existing community, or for those pilgrims who did not wish to settle in Rome but wanted only temporary shelter for the duration of their pilgrimage. It has certainly been argued that it would be erroneous to date the origins of the *schola Langobardorum* to 774 when Ansa, wife of the Lombard King, Desiderius, founded a hospice in Rome,[81] and that it is more likely that this foundation was intended to meet the needs of an already established colony.[82]

That the *scholae* and the other hostels were flourishing during the ninth century is suggested by a letter of 865 written by the pope, Nicholas I, to the Byzantine Emperor, Michael III. In this letter Nicholas was able to describe the 'thousands of men' who daily sought at Rome the protection and intercession of the prince of the apostles.[83] It was also *apud eius limina*, Nicholas noted, that these pilgrims placed their *mansura*, or dwellings, where they lived until the end of their lives.[84]

Other welfare provisions: baths, fountains and public conveniences

As well as accommodation, the *Liber Pontificalis* contains a small amount of information about other welfare provisions which were made for pilgrims by the papacy. In the *Vita* of Symmachus, it was recorded that this pope gave instructions for the building of a public convenience near S. Pietro.[85] Here he had the fountain in the portico of the basilica decorated with mosaic lambs, crosses and palms.[86] Another fountain was installed outside in the open near the steps which led up to the atrium[87] and another at his newly built church of S. Andrea, situated close to S. Pietro.[88] Another fountain was set up by this pope at S. Paolo on the Ostian Way.[89] Here too, and at S. Pancrazio, he had baths built and water piped in, presumably to enable pilgrims to wash and to refresh themselves.[90] Symmachus also seems to have had water laid on at the basilica of S. Michele on the *Via Saleria*, again presumably for a bath or a fountain.[91]

The significance of the fountains found outside or in the atria of basilicas is indicated in a fifth-century inscription which was located on the base of the fountain in the atrium at S. Paolo.[92] It was in these fountains that

---

81 Moore, *Saxon Pilgrims to Rome and the Schola Saxonum*, p. 103.
82 *Ibid.*, p. 103.
83 *Epistolae Karolini Aevi*, in MGH *Epistolae*, vol. 6 (Berlin, 1925), pp. 477–478.
84 *Ibid.*, pp. 477–478.
85 *Liber Pontificalis*, vol. 1, p. 262.
86 *Ibid.*, vol. 1, p. 262.
87 *Ibid.*, vol. 1, p. 262.
88 *Ibid.*, vol. 1, p. 262.
89 *Ibid.*, vol. 1, p. 262.
90 *Ibid.*, vol. 1, p. 262.
91 *Ibid.*, vol. 1, p. 262.
92 This is quoted in E. R. Barker, *Rome of the Pilgrims and Martyrs* (London, 1913), pp. 286–287.

pilgrims were supposed to wash their hands before entering the church. Such washing obviously enabled pilgrims to cleanse themselves but the inscription suggests that this washing was also symbolic. With the water the pilgrim could wash away bodily stains but in doing this he was to remember that faith, purer than water, could cleanse his body from sin and purify his soul.

References to similar welfare provisions can be found in the *Vita* of Hadrian I (772–795). It seems that during the siege of Rome by the Lombards in 756, the Sabbatina aqueduct, originally constructed by Trajan, had been wrecked and one hundred of its arches destroyed.[93] This had important consequences for the basilica of S. Pietro, for it was this aqueduct which had been the source of the water supply for both the fountain in the atrium and for a bath which had been erected at some unknown date close to this basilica.[94] According to the *Liber Pontificalis* it was Hadrian who saw to the reconstruction of the aqueduct and to the relaying of the water pipe to the atrium of S. Pietro, from which most of the lead had been stolen.[95] In this way the water supply seems to have been restored to the atrium of S. Pietro and to the bath also located there.[96]

Further on in the same *Vita*, however, it was recorded that Hadrian had constructed another aqueduct which was fed by the Sabbatina aqueduct. He apparently did this in order to bring water to the baptistery at S. Pietro, which had to be filled from waggons. This same conduit supplied water to the atrium of the basilica and the bath, 'for the needs of pilgrims and those who serve there'.[97] Duchesne suggested that this chapter in the *Vita* was a duplication of the earlier reference to the repair of the Sabbatina aqueduct,[98] although Davis points out that the chapter refers not to the Sabbatina aqueduct itself but to a subsidiary aqueduct leading from it.[99] Whether or not this is the same building campaign as mentioned earlier in the *Vita*, or additional later work, remains uncertain.

The *Vita* of Hadrian records repair work which was carried out to other aqueducts, probably also damaged during the siege of 756. Repairs were undertaken to the Jovia aqueduct[100] and to the Claudian aqueduct, which

93 *Liber Pontificalis*, vol. 1, p. 503. That this was damage sustained during the siege of 756 is suggested by the fact that the author of this *Vita* refers to this aqueduct and to others in the city, as having been broken for a period of twenty years. The aqueducts had also been damaged in 537 during the siege led by Vitiges, but had presumably been restored before the siege in 756. See *Lives of the Eighth Century Popes*, p. 152, note 109. The standard work on Roman aqueducts is now A. Trevor Hodge, *Roman Aqueducts and Water Supply* (London, 1992).

94 *Liber Pontificalis*, vol. 1, p. 503.

95 *Ibid.*, vol. 1, pp. 503–504.

96 *Ibid.*, vol. 1, p. 504. It seems to have been repaired again by Gregory IV. See *ibid.*, vol. 2, p. 77.

97 *Ibid.*, vol. 1, p. 510.

98 *Ibid.*, vol. 1, p. 522, note 11.

99 *Lives of the Eighth Century Popes*, p. 165, note 171.

100 *Liber Pontificalis*, vol. 1, p. 504.

the *Liber Pontificalis* notes used to bring water for washing to a bath situated at the Lateran. This was repaired and the water supply to the bath restored.[101]

Another bath was constructed in Rome, at S. Pietro close to the obelisk,[102] by Hadrian I's successor, Leo III. The author of this pope's *Vita* described the bath as 'a round construction marvellously decorated'.[103] A second bath, also wondrously decorated, was erected at S. Pietro on the instructions of Leo III, close to a house[104] which he had built near the steps to the atrium. This was specifically constructed, according to the *Liber Pontificalis*, 'for the use of Christ's poor and of pilgrims'.[105]

Twelfth-Century Accommodation

Whilst much information has survived concerning welfare provisions made for pilgrims in Rome in the period up to the ninth century, there is very little information about what practical facilities were arranged for those travelling to the apostolic city after this period, particularly during the twelfth century. Although it seems certain from the research of Bertolino and Niederer that the *diaconiae* had ceased to be important distributors of charity by the end of the ninth century, what had happened to the *scholae* and did the *xenodochia* continue to function or had they long fallen into disuse? It has certainly been argued, at least in the case of the *xenodochia*, that by the end of the eleventh century these caritative services set up by the Church had disappeared.[106]

A major problem in finding out about later provisions is one of sources. The *Liber Pontificalis*, such a vital source of information for the seventh, eighth and ninth centuries, has little or nothing at all to say about most of the popes of the tenth and eleventh centuries. When contemporary papal *Vitae* were again added to the *Liber Pontificalis* towards the end of the eleventh century, their writers were more interested in political events than in welfare provisions. Nor are the accounts written by visitors to the apostolic city useful in this respect. Even the important itineraries of pilgrims like Sigeric, Abbot Nikolas and Gerald of Wales have nothing to say about where they stayed in Rome. Had the *xenodochia* and *scholae* really disappeared, or were they simply no longer mentioned in sources like the *Liber Pontificalis*?

A search of a wider range of source material, therefore, may provide some important clues. Indeed, at the very end of the anonymous *Gesta* of Innocent III, completed in 1208, there is a long list of the gifts which this pope made to

101 *Ibid.*, vol. 1, p. 504.
102 This would have been in the obelisk's old position in the Vatican Circus.
103 *Liber Pontificalis*, vol. 2, pp. 27–28.
104 On this house, see above.
105 *Liber Pontificalis*, vol. 2, p. 28.
106 R. Krautheimer, *St Peter's and Medieval Rome*, Unione Internazionale degli Istituti di Archeologia Storia e Storia dell'Arte in Rome (Rome, 1985), p. 31.

various churches in Rome itself and in the papal state. Included in this list is a record of fifty pounds made to the *hospitales* of the city.[107] This in itself may be an indication that some of the caritative services provided for pilgrims by the Church prior to the twelfth century were still operational at this time, or that new services had been instituted.

Caritative institutions founded prior to the twelfth century

Unfortunately, the scanty nature of surviving evidence does make it impossible to say with any certainty whether the majority of the foundations caring for pilgrims from the seventh to eleventh centuries were still operational in the twelfth. References can be found, for example, in the papal bulls of the twelfth and early thirteenth centuries to the church of S. Peregrinus.[108] Unfortunately there is no further mention of its 'hospital' after Leo IX's Bull of 1053 mentioned above and whether it still continued to function in the twelfth century is not clear.

A small amount of more positive evidence, however, has survived concerning some of the other hostels. In a Bull of 15 October 1205, Innocent III granted control over various churches and properties to the canons of the Vatican. Included amongst these properties was a certain *hospitale iuxta Paradisum*.[109] The term 'paradise' usually referred to the atrium of a church and was most commonly used of S. Pietro. The 'hospital' referred to in this Bull may possibly have been founded at some time between the tenth and the late twelfth centuries. Alternatively, it may indicate that one of the 'hospitals' or *xenodochia* founded near S. Pietro in the seventh, eighth or ninth centuries was still in existence. The description of the location *iuxta Paradisum*, would certainly seem to suggest that this Bull may well have been referring to the 'hospital' or *xenodochium* which Gregory the Great himself had founded at S. Pietro, which was located close to the steps leading up into the atrium.

There is also evidence that the *hospitium* founded for the use of the Hungarians by King Stephen in the early eleventh century was still operational.[110] As well as granting to the canons of the Vatican the *hospitale iuxta Paradisum* discussed above, Innocent III's Bull of 1205 also confirmed to them the monastery of S. Stephano Minore along with its *hospitium*.[111] This *hospitium* is also referred to in a Bull of Gregory IX dated 1228.[112] Also extant is a grant of an indulgence to the church of S. Stephano 'dictam de Ungariis' by

---

107 *Gesta*, col. ccxxvii.
108 See the Bulls of 1158 of Hadrian IV, 1186 of Urban III, 1206 of Innocent III and 1228 of Gregory IX. *Collectione Bullarum*, vol. 1, pp. 58, 69, 88 and 113.
109 *Ibid.*, vol. 1, p. 84.
110 See above on its foundation.
111 *Collectione Bullarum*, vol. 1, p. 84.
112 *Ibid.*, vol. 1, p. 114.

Nicholas IV in March 1290,[113] although it makes no specific mention of the *hospitium*. Whether it was still functioning by the end of the thirteenth century, therefore, is uncertain.

Ptochium *at the Lateran*

Other evidence shows that some of the popes of the twelfth century were just as concerned as their seventh-, eighth- and ninth-century counterparts to provide accommodation for pilgrims travelling to the apostolic city. In a Bull of Paschal II dated 27 December 1105, in which the borders of the land under the control of the canons of the Lateran were defined, there is mention of a church called S. Nicolo de Hospitali.[114] Later evidence suggests that this is in fact one of the first references we have to a *ptochium*,[115] situated close to the Lateran, which Paschal II himself seems to have had restored.

While there appears to be no other mention of this church of S. Nicolo or of a 'hospital' amongst the correspondence of Paschal II, futher information is contained in a Bull of Honorius II. Dated 7 May 1128, this Bull, *Iustis votis assensum*, was addressed to Sabe and Silvio, who were described as the custodians of the venerable *ptochium* sited at the Lateran palace.[116] The Bull explained that this *hospitalis* had been restored for the use of the poor during the pontificate of Pope Paschal (II).[117] That it was also intended for the use of pilgrims visiting the apostolic city in the twelfth century was made clear at the end of the Bull, which forbade anyone to commit any act of violence against the *ptochium* or its property, which was for the use of *peregrinorum ac pauperum*.[118]

The choice of the verb *restituere* to describe Paschal II's building activity at this *ptochium* certainly implies that the institution there had already existed prior to the twelfth century, when it was re-established. Evidence of its earlier history, however, can no longer be traced. Kehr notes only that its origins are uncertain,[119] whilst Pressutti refers to the work of the eighteenth-century

---

113 Nicholas IV, *Registers*, vol. 1, p. 405, no. 2888.

114 *Acta Pontifica Romanorum Inedita*, vol. 2, pp.186–187.

115 The term *ptochium*, meaning a hostel for the poor, derives from the Greek word for a beggar or poor man, ἡ πτωχός, and in our documents seems to have been used interchangeably with the terms *hospital* and *xenodochium*.

116 *Acta Pontifica Romanorum Inedita*, vol. 2, pp. 260–261. The text of this Bull can also be found in Honorius III, *Registers*, vol. 1, pp. lxiii–lxiv. Jaffé, vol. 1, 7312.

117 *Acta Pontificum Romanorum Inedita*, vol. 2, p. 260. Although the Bull refers only to Pope Paschal, it seems most likely that it refers to Paschal II, who had died only ten years before, rather than to the ninth-century Paschal I. Both Kehr (*Italia Pontificia*, vol. 1, pp. 34–35) and Pressutti (Honorius III, *Registers*, vol. 1, p. lxiii) have no doubts about identifying the pope mentioned in the Bull as Paschal II. I follow their identification.

118 *Acta Pontificum Romanorum Inedita*, vol. 2, p. 260.

119 Kehr, *Italia Pontificia*, vol. 1, p. 34.

historian of Roman churches, Terribilini, who suggested that the origins of the hospital at the Lateran lay in the eighth century.[120] If this is the case, then no trace of the 'hospital' has yet been discovered in documents of this period. While the origins of the *ptochium* remain uncertain, it does seem that a 'hospital' of some kind had existed here prior to the twelfth century and that, by the end of the eleventh century, it was in urgent need of restoration and it was Paschal II who undertook building work on it.

The Bull of Honorius II of 1128 outlined in some detail the property granted to this *ptochium*. He confirmed to it the chapel of S. Maria de Oblationario, which was to be used for the burial of dead pilgrims.[121] This chapel seems to have been located in the fields which lay between the Lateran and S. Croce[122] and was so named because it was maintained by the oblations of the faithful. It was popularly known as *de Spazolaria*, because every evening the custodian of this church would sweep up the oblations which were left every day on the steps or floor of the church.[123]

As well as this chapel the *ptochium* was granted the adjacent land with its garden and olive grove. The boundaries were outlined precisely as being 'from the stone beneath the palace to the road which leads to S. Croce, from the upper crossroads right up to the city walls'.[124] In addition the *ptochium* was granted 'the garden between the hospital and the city wall and the land on the upper side of that hospital on one side up to the long wall and on the other up to the public road'.[125] The Bull also shows that other grants of land were made. In these grants the land was measured out in *petiae*. They included one *petia* at the Latin gate, another at the gate of Metronus[126] and one *petia* of vines near the gate of St John. This land, therefore, lay within a short distance of the *ptochium* itself. Other grants included: three *petiae* of land in Monte Portatorio, along with five at Calcatori, one *petia* at Monte Cuppuli and two *petiae* of arable land at a place known as *Spanorum*.[127] It is possible that these grants were given in order that the *ptochium* could undertake some small-scale production of food with which to feed those who stayed there. Perhaps this was the reason for the donation of the arable land and of the vines? Alternatively, the intention may have been that these lands were simply to provide the *ptochium* with a source of revenue. Honorius II's Bull ended with the decree that the *ptochium* and its property were to be inviolate. It was witnessed by four cardinal bishops, twenty-one cardinal priests and eight cardinal deacons.

---

[120] Honorius III, *Registers*, vol. 1, p. lxiii.
[121] *Acta Pontifica Romanorum Inedita*, vol. 2, p. 260.
[122] Armellini, *Chiese di Roma*, vol. 2, p. 990.
[123] *Ibid.*, vol. 2, p. 990.
[124] *Acta Pontifica Romanorum Inedita*, vol. 2, p. 260.
[125] *Ibid.*, vol. 2, p. 260.
[126] This was the gate situated between the Porta Latina and the Porta Asinaria, or gate of St John.
[127] *Acta Pontifica Romanorum Inedita*, vol. 2, p. 260.

Other twelfth-century popes also took an interest in this *ptochium*. On 21 June 1138 Innocent II reissued Honorius II's Bull of 1128.[128] This later Bull was almost identical to the earlier one, except that instead of *ptochium*, the term *xenodochium* was now used. It was also addressed only to Silvio, 'custodian of the venerable *xenodochium* at the Lateran'. Whether Sabe had died by this time we do not know but by 1138 there seems to have been only one custodian. Like the original Bull of 1128 issued by Honorius II, the Bull of 1138 noted that the hostel had been restored by Pope Paschal and it reconfirmed to the *ptochium* all of the properties which had been granted by Honorius II. It was witnessed by three cardinal bishops, ten cardinal priests and nine cardinal deacons.

The *ptochium* at the Lateran is also found in a Bull of Lucius II, *Cum universis*, dated 31 January 1145.[129] This was addressed to Bernard, prior of the Lateran and to the canons of the Basilica. This granted to the canons control of the church of S. Giovanni a Porta Latina and the *hospitale* situated at the Lateran gate, together with all its property. This Bull suggests that responsibility for the hospital was being handed over to the canons because of inefficiency in the way it was being run and organised. For the Bull records that it was being handed over to the canons for 'better running and arranging'.[130] In his *Vita* of Lucius II, Cardinal Boso also records this grant and refers to the *ptochium* as S. Nicolo in Hospitali.[131]

This 'hospital' at the Lateran seems to have continued to operate throughout the rest of the twelfth century and into the thirteenth. In a Bull, *Quanto Lateranensis*, dated 19 May 1154, Anastasius IV confirmed certain properties to the canons of the Lateran. Included amongst these properties was the '*hospitale* within the gate of St John with all its belongings'.[132] This *hospital*, together with other properties, was reconfirmed to the canons of the Lateran in a Bull dated 19 April 1155 by Hadrian IV.[133] That it was still in existence in the first half of the thirteenth century is indicated by a Bull, *Vigilanti atque supereminenti*, dated 3 February 1228 of Pope Gregory IX. This confirmed certain properties to the canons of the Lateran, including 'the *hospitale*, with the church of S. Nicolo near the gate of St John, with all its belongings'.[134]

In addition to this *ptochium* which was confirmed to the Lateran, there is the possibility that the canons also had control of another 'hospital' also situated close to their basilica. In a letter of 1212, in which he settled a

---

128 *Ibid.*, vol. 2, pp. 295–296. Jaffé, vol. 1, 7903.

129 *Ibid.*, vol. 3, pp. 64–65. Jaffé, vol. 2, 8711.

130 *Ibid.*, vol. 3, p. 64.

131 *Liber Pontificalis*, vol. 2, p. 386. See Paschal II's reference to S. Nicolo de Hospitali in a Bull of 1105 referred to above.

132 *Acta Pontificum Romanorum Inedita*, vol. 3, pp. 150–151. Jaffé, vol. 2, 9906.

133 *Ibid.*, vol. 3, pp. 166–167. Jaffé, vol. 2, 10032.

134 The text of this Bull can be found in G. Pennotto, *Generalis totius Sacri Ordinis Clericorum Canonicorum Historia Triparta* (Rome, 1624); see p. 562 for the reference to the *hospital*. Potthast, vol. 1, 8121.

dispute between the Lateran and the basilica of S. Lorenzo in Palagio, Innocent III noted that the Lateran was to be left in possession of the land 'from the arch of St Daniel . . . to the *hospitale Sanctae Mariae in Spaczolaria*'.[135] This is clearly a reference to the same church that Honorius II confirmed to the *ptochium* in 1128. The problem, however, is whether by 1212 S. Maria had its own 'hospital', or whether Innocent III was simply referring to the *ptochium* to which it had been granted. Based on this letter of 1212 in the *Registers* of Innocent III, Armellini seems to have believed that this church had its own separate 'hospital' by the early thirteenth century.[136] Surviving evidence makes it almost impossible to know with any certainty whether this was in fact the case. In all our other sources the 'hospital' is referred to in conjunction with a church of S. Nicolo, not with S. Maria in Spazolaria, which had been granted to the *ptochium* specifically for the burial of dead pilgrims. Innocent III's letter is the only one to associate the 'hospital' directly with the church of S. Maria. This may simply have been an error on Innocent's part or, alternatively, may indicate that there was a 'hospital' attached to this church by 1212. In his Bull of 1228, Gregory IX confirmed to the canons of the Lateran not only the 'hospital' and the church of S. Nicolo but also the church of S. Maria de Spazzalaria. There is no mention, however, of a 'hospital' nearby. On the other hand, this Bull does grant to the canons of the Lateran, the church *cum pertinentiis suis*. Of what these consisted we do not know but there is a possibility that it may have included a 'hospital' of some kind. The surviving evidence is too scanty to decide for certain whether or not there was another 'hospital' at S. Maria de Spazolaria but it is possible.

Scholae *in the twelfth century*

Another complex problem is whether the *scholae* still existed in the twelfth century and if so, whether they had changed in any way. Did they still consist of large settlements of pilgrims? Unfortunately, information concerning the *scholae* after the ninth century is very rare. A Bull of Leo IX dated 1053, in which all four *scholae* are mentioned, indicates that they were still in existence in the middle of the eleventh century but this Bull gives little indication of what these *scholae* were like at that time.[137] Evidence concerning the survival and nature of the *scholae* in the twelfth century is also elusive. Whilst little is known about the survival or nature of the *scholae* of the Franks, Frisians and Lombards at this time, something might perhaps be learnt from surviving evidence about the *schola Saxonum*.

The *schola Saxonum* seems to have remained in existence into the twelfth century. A letter of 1162, written by Peter, cardinal deacon of San Eustachio, to Thomas Becket, archbishop of Canterbury, refers to 'the church of B. Marie, which is called *Sassonorum*, placed in Rome for the reception of the

135 Innocent III, *Registers*, PL 216, col. 673.
136 Armellini, *Chiese di Roma*, vol. 2, p. 990.
137 Leo IX, *Epistolae et Decreta Pontificia*, PL 143, esp. cols. 704–716.

English visiting the threshold of the apostles'.[138] 'In this place', wrote the cardinal, '. . . they were once received as if in their own homes.'[139] In his day, however, the cardinal explained, the poverty was such 'that only a few clerics and almost no laymen can be found to look after the pilgrims'.[140] This was also reported to be a grave cause of concern to the pope, Alexander III, who Peter indicated, was himself sending letters to England concerning the matter through an envoy, Nicholas, a canon of the church of B. Marie.[141] Unfortunately we do not know the contents of these letters written by Alexander III.

Whilst Peter's letter refers to the *schola's* severe financial difficulties, he makes no mention of a large colony of men and women at S. Pietro but appears to refer instead to what must have been a hostel of some kind attached to the church. Perhaps this is an indication, therefore, that the *schola* of the Saxons by the twelfth century consisted no longer of a substantial settlement but rather a hostel providing temporary shelter to visiting English pilgrims. If this was indeed the case, then this may also indicate that by this time, if not long before, there had been a change in the nature of pilgrimage. Pilgrims were perhaps less willing to live out their lives as exiles at the tomb of the apostle but preferred instead to stay only a short time before returning to their homes. Unfortunately there is no evidence as yet which would show whether the *scholae* of the Franks, Frisians and Lombards had also been transformed from large colonies into hostels by the twelfth century. All that can be said is that whatever Alexander III's plans were to try to resolve the difficulties of the *schola Saxonum*, they seem to have been unsuccessful, since at the beginning of the thirteenth century, Innocent III took over the site of the *schola Saxonum*, building his new hospital of Santo Spirito upon it.

Santo Spirito

Innocent's hospital foundation seems to have been a hospital in the true sense of the word, designed to look after foreign pilgrims as well as the sick and needy from the local community and specialising in particular in the care of pregnant women. This hospital was built on the site of the old *schola Saxonum* and seems to have been well under way by 1204,[142] for in this year Innocent III linked it with the new order founded by Guy of Montpellier for

---

[138] *Materials for the History of Thomas Becket*, vol. 5, pp. 64–65.

[139] *Ibid.*, vol. 5, pp. 64–65.

[140] *Ibid.*, vol. 5, pp. 64–65.

[141] *Ibid.*, vol. 5, pp. 64–65.

[142] On the building of this hospital, see *Gesta*, cols. cc–cci. See also P. de Angelis, *L'Ospedale di Santo Spirito in Saxia*, 2 vols. (Rome, 1960); Brentano, *Rome before Avignon*, pp. 19–22; M. Maccarrone, *Studi su Innocenzo III, Italia Sacra*, 17 (Padua, 1972), pp. 290–291; Bolton, ' "Hearts not Purses" ', pp. 137–139.

maintaining hospitals.[143] This order had been approved by Innocent himself in 1198[144] and was already running two other hospitals in Rome, one near S. Maria in Trastevere and another close to S. Agatha within the city walls.[145]

The anonymous author of the Gesta notes that the building of the hospital of Santo Spirito was funded at the Pope's own expense[146] and that after its construction he had endowed it with 'benefices, possessions, rents, treasure, ornaments, books and privileges'.[147] Money for the running of this hospital was also acquired from other sources. The most well-known of these benefactors was King John (1199–1216) who assigned to the hospital of Santo Spirito an expectative from the parish church of Writtle in Essex, undertaking to pay one hundred marks a year from the Exchequer until the church fell vacant.[148] The association and past history of the site of the new hospital enabled Innocent to request such a donation from the king of England. Other donations to secure the hospital's future were acquired from Montpellier, Italy, Sicily and Hungary.[149]

In 1208 Innocent III established a new liturgical station at Santo Spirito. On the first Sunday after the Octave of Epiphany, the Veronica, the cloth on which Christ's suffering face had been imprinted, was to be carried in procession by the canons of S. Pietro, from its home at the basilica to the hospital, in a reliquary of gold, silver and precious jewels.[150] At this station Innocent himself preached a sermon, taking for his text the marriage feast at Cana, in which he exhorted all to charity and good works.[151] At the end of this station, Innocent undertook his own act of charity, providing one thousand foreign pilgrims and three hundred local people with three pence each from the papal treasury – one for bread, one for meat and one for wine.[152] All who took part in this station were granted one year's remission of penance.[153] For their prominent role in the ceremony and to cover their expenses, the canons of S. Pietro were rewarded with twelve pence and a pound of candle wax.[154] According to Matthew Paris, in 1216 a terrible event took place during this station. While being carried in procession to the hospital, the Veronica was

143 Innocent III, Registers, PL 215, cols. 376–380.
144 Ibid., PL 214, cols. 83–86.
145 Ibid., PL 214, col. 85.
146 Ibid., col. cc. 'Fecit et propriis sumptibus ad opus infirmorum et pauperum hospitale Sancti Spiritus apud Sanctam Mariam in Saxia.' Writing at the end of the thirteenth century, Riccobaldo of Ferrara (Historia Pontificia Romanorum, RIS 9, col. 126) claims that Innocent built this hospital as recompense for having used church revenues to build the Torre de' Conti.
147 Gesta, col. cc.
148 Cheney, Pope Innocent III and England, pp. 237–238.
149 Innocent III, Registers, PL 215, col. 378.
150 Gesta, cols. cci–cciii.
151 For an analysis of this sermon, see Bolton, ' "Hearts not Purses" '.
152 Innocent III, Registers, PL 215, col. 1270.
153 Innocent III, Sermones, PL 217, cols. 310–690; see esp. Sermo VIII, col. 350.
154 Innocent III, Registers, PL 215, col. 270.

blown upside down in the wind.[155] Innocent, taking this as a sign of divine displeasure, composed a prayer for the image and granted ten days worth of indulgences for its recital.[156]

In his *Historia Occidentalis* Jacques de Vitry made clear the exceptional reputation which Santo Spirito had acquired. Some hospitals, he noted, were poorly run but in others there was no lack of charity, piety, decency and discipline.[157] Included in his list of well-run hospitals was that of St Samson at Constantinople and those of St Anthony and B. Marie in Navarre but at the top of his list was this hospital in Rome.[158] Unfortunately nothing of Innocent's original hospital survived. It was burnt to the ground in the fifteenth century and rebuilt between 1473 and 1478 by Sixtus IV.[159]

Private establishments

Some accommodation was also provided in Rome at private establishments. Unfortunately, very little information survives about such lodgings, particularly before the thirteenth century but that such establishments may have existed as early as the eighth century is suggested by the visit to Rome of the founder of Farfa Abbey. Whilst there he seems to have stayed in the house of a pious widow.[160] Whether this was usual by the eighth century, we do not know.

By the thirteenth century private establishments providing lodgings for visitors to the city seem to have become more common. We know, for example, that Master Gregory stayed at an inn when he was in Rome, probably in the early years of the thirteenth century.[161] That such accommodation was usual by this time is indicated by senatorial legislation. In September 1235, the senator Angelo Malabranca acted to protect *Romipetae* from harassment by innkeepers. These innkeepers were involved in kidnapping pilgrims in the streets, or even taking them from rival establishments in which they were already settled and forcing them to stay in their own hostels.[162] This edict of Malabranca, passed by the senate, decreed that pilgrims were to be allowed to stay where they wanted and those who continued to harass them were to pay a fine, half to the canons of S. Pietro, the other half for the repair of the city walls.[163]

---

[155] Matthew Paris, *Chronica Maiora*, vol. 3, p. 7.
[156] *Ibid.*, vol. 3, p. 7.
[157] Jacques de Vitry, *Historia Occidentalis*, pp. 149–150.
[158] *Ibid.*, pp. 149–150.
[159] E. D. Howe, *The Hospital of Santo Spirito and Pope Sixtus IV* (New York, 1984).
[160] See Llewellyn, *Rome in the Dark Ages*, p. 180. *Chronicon Farfense di Gregorio di Catina*, ed. U. Balzani, 2 vols. *Fonti per la Storia d'Italia*, 33 and 34 (Rome, 1903), vol. 1, p. 11.
[161] Master Gregory, *Marvels of Rome*, p. 26.
[162] *Codice Diplomatico del Senato Romano*, pp. 143–145.
[163] *Ibid.*, pp. 143–145.

Shortage of accommodation?

It seems that by the end of the twelfth century there may have been a general shortage of accommodation for those travelling to Rome, whether as pilgrims, bishops and abbots confirming their appointments, or as appellants to the papal court. This is suggested by a comment in the *Vita* of St Raymond of Piacenza (d. c.1200). Here it is stated that during his stay in Rome he slept in the portico of S. Pietro with other poor pilgrims.[164] Did he, with others, sleep in the portico because he wanted to, or because there was simply nowhere else to go? This apparent lack of accommodation is also suggested by William of Andres who visited Rome in 1208. Indeed, he noted with gratitude that he and his party had been invited by a group of English monks, from Canterbury, to share their accommodation, having been unsuccessful in finding anywhere else to stay.[165] Where this accommodation was located or of what it consisted William of Andres does not say.

The Burial of Dead Pilgrims

While the provision of accommodation and food was an essential part of the welfare provisions which were made for pilgrims, arrangements also had to be made for those who died in the city. Whilst some pilgrims may have chosen to end their days in the apostolic city, many others who died there were the victims of disease, notably malaria. Provisions had to be made, therefore, for their burial. We know nothing of these arrangements prior to the ninth century, by which time the traditional site for the burial of dead pilgrims seems to have been the church of S. Salvatore in Terrione. This is indicated in a Bull of 854 of Leo IV, which has unfortunately not survived intact but which granted possession of numerous properties to the monastery of S. Martino, situated close to S. Pietro.[166] Amongst these possessions was included the church of S. Salvatoris Domini, which was referred to as a place *ad sepeliendos omnes peregrinos*.[167] It is probable that the burial of those pilgrims who died in the city was a costly business. Winding sheets and perhaps coffins had to be paid for, as well as the expenses of the grave-diggers.[168] If the pilgrim died at some distance from S. Salvatore in Terrione, then presumably the body had to be transported to the church, unless some regulation allowed the pilgrim to buried elsewhere. An arrangement may have been made by Leo IV between the monastery of S. Martino, the church of S. Salvatore and the people of the Leonine city to cover some of these expenses.

164 *Vita S. Raymundi Palmarii*, p. 650.
165 William of Andres, *Chronicon*, p. 737.
166 Schiaperelli, 'Le Carte antiche', p. 433.
167 *Ibid.*, p. 433.
168 On burials, see Mollat, *Poor in the Middle Ages*, pp. 145–149.

In a Bull of Leo IX dated 1053, this pope confirmed an agreement made in the presence of Leo IV that in return for the monastery's and church's care of pilgrims, the property of those who died without an heir in the Leonine city, or for one mile around it, would go to the use of the brothers who served there.[169]

It may perhaps also have been the expenses incurred in burying dead pilgrims which lay behind one particular document preserved in the Vatican Archives. Dated 797 and supposedly written by Charlemagne, this document is a forgery, the main error made by the forger being to mistake this emperor and Leo IV for contemporaries.[170] A more likely date for this document, as suggested by Schiaparelli, is c.1031–1053.[171] Listed in the document were Charlemagne's supposed gifts to the church of S. Salvatore in Terrione as well as the relics buried there, such as vestments of St Stephen and two ribs from a certain John.[172] In particular the author of this document sought to show that Charlemagne had established this church as a hospice for pilgrims journeying to Rome and as a place where all those from beyond the Alps, 'whether rich or poor, noble or commoner', should be buried if they died in the apostolic city.[173] The document noted that it was the task of the *scholastici*, perhaps those who served in the *schola Francorum*, to bury any dead pilgrims.[174] A priest, it was stated also had to be present to conduct the burial.[175] As a reward for carrying out such a worthy service, the document stated that from Charlemagne's kingdoms of Francia, Aquitaine and Gallia, a yearly sum of four hundred pounds ought to be paid to S. Salvatore.[176] A possible explanation of the purpose of this forged document, therefore, may be that it was written with the intention of trying to secure a regular income to pay for the burial of those pilgrims who died in the city.

This forged document seems to have been written before 1053. This is suggested by the Bull issued in that year by Leo IX,[177] which was essentially a confirmation of the Bull of Leo IV of 854, regranting certain estates and privileges to the monastery of S. Martino. Amongst the churches which this Bull confirmed to the monks of S. Martino was S. Salvatore, together with its *possessionibus, usibus, et utilitatibus*, 'which Charlemagne gave to the church and confirmed in a privilege'.[178] Is this a reference to the forged document attributed to Charlemagne? The following sentence in Leo IX's Bull would seem to indicate this:

[169] Leo IX, *Epistolae*, col. 709.
[170] Schiaperelli, 'Le Carte antiche', pp. 426–432.
[171] *Ibid.*, p. 427.
[172] *Ibid.*, p. 428.
[173] *Ibid.*, p. 428.
[174] *Ibid.*, p. 428.
[175] *Ibid.*, p. 428.
[176] *Ibid.*, p. 430.
[177] Leo IX, *Epistolae*, cols. 704–716.
[178] *Ibid.*, col. 706.

et census quos de ultramontaneis partibus, annuatim statuerunt mitti et recipi per manus ministrorum, concedimus eidem monasterio permanendos ad utilitatem eorum qui in Christo beati Petri Deo alacri animo serviunt.[179]

Here Leo IX refers to annual payments (*census*) from beyond the Alps (*ultramontaneis*), a reference presumably to the kingdoms of Francia, Aquitaine and Gallia, which he gives to the monastery of S. Martino for the use of those who served there. We do not know if this money was ever paid, nor if it was, whether it was ever spent to cover the expenses incurred by S. Salvatore in Terrione in the burial of pilgrims.

What Leo IX's Bull of 1053 does confirm, however, is that it remained the responsibility of those who served in the S. Salvatore in Terrione to continue to take responsibility for the burial of those pilgrims who died in Rome. In this too, Leo IX's Bull seems to take its lead from the forged document rather than Leo IV's Bull of 854. This latter noted that *omnes peregrinos* were buried at S. Salvatore, whereas the forged document of the eleventh century attributed to Charlemagne claimed responsibility only for those from beyond the Alps. Leo IX laid down that all those from beyond the Alps, 'whether pilgrims or strangers, rich or poor, nobles or commoners', who died in Rome itself or anywhere between Sutri to the north of the city, or Albano to the south, were to be buried in the church of S. Salvatore, or elsewhere if necessity compelled.[180] One exception to this rule concerned pilgrims in the *schola Saxonum*. Any *Romipetae* taken ill in the *schola Saxonum* who then died there were also to buried there, in accordance with what seems to have been an agreement between the English *schola* and S. Salvatore in Terrione.[181] Any pilgrim from the *schola Saxonum*, however, who died elsewhere, was to be buried at S. Salvatore in accordance with the *proprium jus*.[182] Another exception concerned pilgrims who came from the Italian peninsula. If they died in Rome itself or up to a distance of three miles away, the Bull laid down that they were to be buried in the church of S. Iustini, in the area of the *schola Langobardorum*.[183]

By 1058 the Hungarians had established their own separate arrangements. In a Bull of that year, Benedict X confirmed that Hungarians who died in Rome were to be buried only by the *clerici* of S. Stefano, whose duty this was.[184] In addition, the *clerici* of S. Stefano were given the right to take the dead pilgrims' goods for their own use.[185] This may have been done to ensure that those who served in S. Stefano would be able to recover whatever they

179 *Ibid.*, col. 706.
180 *Ibid.*, col. 706.
181 *Ibid.*, col. 707.
182 *Ibid.*, col. 707.
183 *Ibid.*, col. 708.
184 Schiaperelli, 'Le Carte antiche', pp. 483–484.
185 *Ibid.*, pp. 483–484.

had spent on the burial. The injunction against anyone but the *clerici* of S. Stefano burying dead Hungarian pilgrims may have been intended to ensure that no one else had a claim upon their property.

Unfortunately we have very little information about the burial of pilgrims who died in Rome in the twelfth century. Presumably the arrangements as laid down in the Bull of 1053 of Leo IX continued. Honorius II's Bull of 1128 concerning the *ptochium* at the Lateran stated that the church of S. Maria de Oblationario was to be used to bury dead pilgrims,[186] presumably those who died whilst staying at the *ptochium*. Innocent II's Bull of 1138 also refers to this church as being a place for the burial of dead pilgrims.[187]

A document of March 1224 also refers to the burial of pilgrims who died in Rome. This was a privilege granted by the senator, Peter Annibaldi, to the canons of S. Pietro.[188] In this Peter referred to both the Bull of Leo IX of 1053 as well as to the document supposedly written by Charlemagne, confirming that *peregrini et Romipetae* who died in the zone bounded by Albano to the south and Sutri to the north, were to be buried in the church of S. Salvatore in Terrione, or wherever the canons ordered. It is not clear from this document, however, whether Peter was referring to the burial of all pilgrims, regardless of whence they came, or only to pilgrims from beyond the Alps, as in both the Bull of 1053 and the forged document attributed to Charlemagne. This document makes no mention of the arrangements established by the Hungarians, nor does it make any mention of the burial of pilgrims at S. Maria de Oblationario.

The dead pilgrim's property

The Bull of 1053 of Leo IX concerned itself not only with the burial of those who died on their pilgrimage in the apostolic city but also with the property of those who were dying or who had died. No one was to hide a sick person in their house, in the hope that they might die intestate.[189] Rather they were to inform one of the priests of S. Salvatore or the procurator of S. Martino immediately, while the pilgrim was still of sane mind.[190] Similarly it was decreed that no one was to hide the goods of the deceased but was to hand them over to a priest.[191] A similar stipulation was also found in the privilege granted to the canons of S. Pietro by Peter Annabaldi. No-one was to conceal the belongings of a dead pilgrim, or to retain any such items against the wishes of the canons.[192] Anyone found so doing was likely to incur a fine of thirty pounds of gold.[193]

[186] *Acta Pontificum Romanorum Inedita*, vol. 2, p. 260.
[187] *Ibid.*, vol. 2, p. 296.
[188] *Codice Diplomatico del Senato Romano*, pp. 113–115.
[189] Leo IX, *Epistolae*, col. 708.
[190] *Ibid.*, col. 708.
[191] *Ibid.*, col. 708.
[192] *Codice Diplomatico del Senato Romano*, p. 113.
[193] *Ibid.*, p. 113.

We know that a similar regulation was contained in the customs and laws which had been established by the papacy in Sutri by the early thirteenth century. This stated that if a pilgrim became so ill that he needed a priest to read him the last rites, an official known as the *gastaldus curie* was also to be present.[194] In his absence two vassals of the Roman church had to be in attendance, for it was the task of the *gastaldus curie* to hear how the pilgrim wished to dispose of his worldly goods and then to see that this was carried out. Priests were encouraged to warn pilgrims who were travelling alone that if they died intestate, the curia had the right to claim their property.[195] In the thirteenth century, Viterbo also seems to have developed similar laws to deal with the disposition of a pilgrim's goods. A statute of 1237–1238 stated that if a pilgrim or other traveller died in Viterbo without having made a will, half his goods could be claimed and used for the *emendatione equorum*,[196] while the rest could be taken rightfully by his host,[197] with the exception of his clothes, which belonged to the 'master of the house'.[198] If, however, the pilgrim was accompanied by relatives, then his goods ought to be given over to them.[199] A further law of this kind appears in the statutes of Viterbo for the years 1251–1252. This contained the same instructions as the earlier statute but also decreed that any host who failed to inform the *camerarius militum* that he had an ill pilgrim in his house, was to be fined ten pounds and to lose any claim to the property of the pilgrim if he died intestate.[200] These arrangements seem very different to those established in the eleventh century by the Hungarians. For then the *clerici* of S. Stefano seem to have had the first claim upon a pilgrim's property.

The evidence contained in the *Liber Pontificalis* indicates that the popes of the sixth and particularly the seventh, eighth and ninth centuries, were active in providing practical facilities and amenities for pilgrims in Rome itself. We are far less well informed about what happened after this period as the main source, the *Liber Pontificalis*, is so lacking in information on this subject. While other sources provide few clues as to whether the caritative services set up during this early period were still operational in the twelfth century, they do reveal that the popes of the twelfth and early thirteenth centuries were themselves actively trying to provide facilities for pilgrims. The *ptochium* at the Lateran, reconstructed by Paschal II, seems to have

---

[194] On the *gastald*, see G. Tabacco, *The Struggle for Power in Medieval Italy. Structures of Political Rule*, trans. R. B. Jensen (Cambridge, 1989), pp. 102–103.

[195] A. Theiner, *Codex Diplomaticus Domini Temporalis S. Sedis*, 2 vols. (Rome, 1861), p. 29.

[196] *Statuti della Provincia Romana, Fonti per la Storia d'Italia*, 69 (Rome, 1930), p. 47.

[197] *Ibid.*, p. 47.

[198] *Ibid.*, p. 47.

[199] *Ibid.*, p. 47.

[200] *Ibid.*, pp. 155–156.

provided shelter for *Romipetae* throughout the twelfth century and into the thirteenth, whilst by the early thirteenth century the *ordo* founded by Guy of Montpellier was also running hospitals in the city. Whilst accommodation may not always have been sufficient, pilgrims travelling to Rome in the twelfth and early thirteenth centuries would probably not have been wholly reliant upon private establishments.

7

The Popularity of Pilgrimage to Rome
in the Twelfth Century

Having considered various aspects of pilgrimage to Rome in the twelfth century, a major question remains to be addressed. Was Rome still a popular centre of pilgrimage in the twelfth century, or was it now losing out to competition from other shrines?[1] Did pilgrims continue to flock *ad limina apostolorum* in the numbers that they had done in the seventh, eighth and ninth centuries? Or, by the twelfth century, were pilgrims beginning to go elsewhere; to the Holy Land so recently recovered from Muslim forces, to the newly fashionable shrine of St James at Compostela, or to one of the many other pilgrimage centres, such as Bari, Canterbury,[2] Cologne[3] or Vézelay, which flourished in the twelfth century?

The few historians who have considered the question of Rome's popularity with pilgrims at this time have differing opinions upon the issue. Sumption suggests that pilgrimage to Rome 'underwent a serious decline' in the thirteenth century, although some of the evidence which he cites as possible reasons for this decline and some of the examples which he gives, support the view that the decline was already well under way prior to the thirteenth century.[4] Krautheimer seems to believe that there was a decline in pilgrimage

---

[1] For some earlier thoughts on this subject, see D. J. Birch, 'Selling the Saints: Competition among pilgrim centres in the twelfth century', *Medieval History*, 2 (1992), pp. 20–34.

[2] On the rapid spread of the cult of St Thomas Becket, martyred in 1170, see H. E. J. Cowdrey, 'An Early Record at Dijon of the Export of Becket's Relics', *Popes, Monks and Crusaders* (London, 1984), no. XVIII, pp. 251–253. By 1196 his cult was obviously well established in Italy, as among the relics found at S. Marie Fluminis at Ceccano was a vestment of this archbishop. See *Annales Ceccanenses, MGH.SS* 19, p. 293.

[3] Hamilton ('Prester John and the Three Kings of Cologne', pp. 177–191) argues that the cult of the Three Kings, together with belief in Prester John, may have been deliberately promoted by Rainald of Dassel as propaganda devices to aid Frederick Barbarossa in his struggle against Alexander III. He also argues that pilgrims who flocked there did not see in the Magi an exemplar of Christian kingship, as Rainald had intended, but rather saints versed in occult learning who could give them protection.

[4] Sumption, *Pilgrimage*, pp. 226–227.

to Rome prior to the twelfth century but that by 1100 pilgrims were 'flocking to St Peter's from all over the West'.[5] Benedicta Ward has argued that 'northern visitors appeared in increasing numbers until the end of the twelfth century',[6] whilst R. I. Moore has suggested that Compostela was far more important with pilgrims at this time than Rome.[7] Labande has argued that after the Carolingian and Ottonian period fewer pilgrimages were made to Rome.[8] He has also suggested that the impression gained from the surviving evidence may indicate that Rome was the predominant shrine in the tenth century, Jerusalem in the eleventh century and Compostela in the twelfth.[9] Hitherto, however, no attempt has been made to investigate what the surviving primary sources can offer in the way of an answer to this question. The purpose of this chapter, therefore, is to investigate Rome's popularity as a centre of pilgrimage in the twelfth century and to consider the evidence which may indicate that pilgrimage to Rome was in decline at this time, particularly amongst those peoples with whom, previously, it had proved extremely popular.

New Converts

Surviving evidence suggests that pilgrimage to Rome may have remained relatively popular in the twelfth century among certain groups, most notably amongst those more recently converted to Christianity. The Icelanders, for example, were one such group. Although they travelled to many of the newly popular shrines such as Compostela, Canterbury and particularly the Holy Land, for many Rome continued to be an important destination, as it had been for the older converts to Christianity in the wake of their conversion.[10]

In the *Islendingabók* (c.1122–1133), probably the most reliable source for the conversion of Iceland, Ari the Wise, stated that it was the Norwegian king, Oláf Tryggvason (995–1000), who brought Christianity to Iceland.[11]

---

5   Krautheimer, St Peter's and Medieval Rome, p. 31.
6   Ward, Miracles and the Medieval Mind, p. 117.
7   Suggested to me in discussion at the Ecclesiastical History Society's summer meeting at Chichester in July 1990.
8   Labande, 'Recherches sur les Pèlerins', pp. 164–165.
9   Ibid., p. 164.
10 See R. Boyer, La Vie Religieuse en Islande (1116–1264) d'après la Sturlunga Saga et les Sagas des Evêques (Paris, 1979), pp. 295–300.
11 The text of Ari's Islendingabók can be found in Old Icelandic with an English translation in Origines Islandicae, ed. G. Vigfusson and F. Y. Powell, 2 vols. (Oxford, 1905), vol. 1, pp. 279–306. Also on the conversion, see D. Strömback, The Conversion of Iceland. A Survey, trans. P. Foote, Viking Society for Northern Research (London, 1975); K. Hastrup, Culture and History in Medieval Iceland. An Anthropological Analysis of Structure and Change (Oxford, 1985), pp. 179–189; J. L. Byock, Medieval Iceland. Society, Sagas and Power (Berkeley, Los Angeles and London, 1988), pp. 138–143.

Oláf's initial tactic was to use missionaries. His first, a certain Stefnir, appears to have been a failure. His second, Thrangbrandr, a Flemish or German priest, already experienced in missionary work in the Faroe Islands, fared a little better, converting a substantial number of Icelanders, as well as killing, according to Ari, two or three who had rioted against him.[12] Thrangbrandr left Iceland for Norway c.999, his mission still only partly successful and the decisive move in the conversion of the island seems to have been left to King Oláf himself. Seizing a number of Icelanders who were staying in Norway, amongst them the sons of a number of prominent pagan families, the king threatened to maim or kill the captives if the people of the island refused to accept the new religion. Eventually the hostages were rescued by a Christian delegation, led by Gizurr and Hjalti, who promised that they would do what they could to ensure the conversion of all the inhabitants. Unfortunately, the island seems then to have split into two factions and civil war threatened. The Christians chose Hallr of Sioa as their law-speaker, while Thorgeirr Thorkelsson continued to speak for the heathens. Hallr was given permission to negotiate with Thorgeirr in an attempt to reach a compromise. The latter seems to have been won over to the Christian cause and declared that all the Icelanders should convert to Christianity.[13]

Links between Iceland and the Church in Rome seem to have been forged from an early date. Indeed, the early bishops of Iceland all travelled there to confirm their appointments. The first was Isleifr, bishop of Skálholt, already fifty years old when elected. Making his way to Rome, he visited the Emperor Henry III (1039–1056), to whom he is supposed to have given a polar bear that had come from Greenland.[14] Continuing his journey with a letter of safe conduct given to him by the emperor, he reached Rome and was received by Pope Leo IV (1048–1054), who then sent him to Adalbert, archbishop of Bremen (1045–1072) to receive consecration.[15] Isleifr's son, Gizur, who succeeded him in the bishopric of Skálholt and who built a church there dedicated to St Peter, was received by Pope Gregory VII (1073–1085)[16] and Jon Ögmundarson, first bishop of Hólar, by Pope Paschal II (1099–1118).[17]

Together with the ecclesiastics who journeyed to Rome, either to confirm their appointments or perhaps even to seek advice, or to transact business at

---

12 *Origines Islandicae*, vol. 1, p. 295 and Hastrup, *Culture and History*, p. 183.
13 If the *Njal's Saga* (trans. M. Magnusson and H. Pálsson (1960), chpt. 105, p. 225) is to be believed, then Thorgeirr may have been swayed by a bribe, three silver marks, given to him by Hallr. On the gradual acceptance of Christianity in Iceland, see J. Jóhannesson, *A History of the Old Icelandic Commonwealth*, trans. H. Bessason, University of Manitoba Icelandic Studies, 2 (1974), pp. 137–144.
14 *Origines Islandicae*, vol. 1, p. 428.
15 *Ibid.*, vol. 1, pp. 428–429.
16 *Ibid.*, vol. 1, p. 434 on his reception by Pope Gregory VII, and p. 435 for the building of his church at Skálholt.
17 *Ibid.*, vol. 1, p. 436. Also on this Bishop John, see S. Kuttner, 'St Jón of Hólar: Canon Law and Hagiography in Medieval Iceland', *The History of Ideas and Doctrines of Canon Law in the Middles Ages* (Variorum Reprint, London, 1980), no. VIII, pp. 367–375.

the papal court, were a large number of laymen making the same journey, mostly as pilgrims. The popularity of pilgrimage to Rome among the Icelanders may perhaps be compared with the enthusiasm displayed by the English, Frisians, Franks and Lombards, who during the eighth and ninth centuries, in the wake of their conversion, had also made the journey to Rome in large numbers. The names of some of these Icelandic pilgrims survive in the *Sagas*. At the end of the *Njal's Saga*, after a long narrative of violence and murders, the surviving leaders of the two opposing factions, Flosi Thordarson and Kari Solmundarson, both set out on pilgrimage to Rome c.1015. The former, living in exile, set out from Wales and walked all the way to the apostolic city, where he received absolution from the pope himself, which 'he paid a large sum of money for'.[18] Kari too seems to have made his pilgrimage on foot.[19] The *Laxdaela Saga* records the pilgrimage to Rome made by Gellir Thorkelsson, shortly before his death in 1073. Advanced in years, the *Saga* relates, Gellir left Iceland and went 'on pilgrimage to Rome and paid a visit to the Apostle St Peter'.[20] He spent a long time there, according to the *Saga*, and died in Denmark on his return journey.[21] According to the *Christne Saga* the son of Sigmund Thorgil died c.1118 in the course of his pilgrimage to Rome,[22] while the *Sturlunga Saga* relates that Gizur Hallsson (d.1206), who for twenty years held the office of law-speaker, 'was more highly esteemed in Rome than any other Icelander'.[23] His knowledge of the lands of the south also seems to have been so extensive that he wrote a book entitled *Flos Peregrinationis*, which unfortunately has not survived.[24]

Some of these *Sagas*, however, were written up to three hundred years after the events which they describe and thus the information which they contain cannot be wholly relied upon. It is impossible to know whether, only fifteen years after the official date given for the conversion of Iceland, Flosi and Kari really did made their way to the shrine of St Peter. What these sagas do indicate is that there was a strong tradition of pilgrimage from Iceland to Rome. It was perhaps the strength of this tradition which resulted in the comment in one of these sagas that Pope Hadrian IV (1154–1159) never had business sufficiently urgent to keep him from talking to any of the Norsemen who wished to see him.[25]

That pilgrimage to Rome was relatively popular amongst Icelanders by the twelfth century is suggested by other evidence. In the Fraternity Register of Reichnau Abbey a twelfth-century scribe included the names of thirteen

18 *Njal's Saga*, chpt. 158, pp. 352–353.
19 *Ibid.*, chpt. 159, pp. 354–355.
20 *Laxdaela Saga*, trans M. Magnusson and H. Pálsson (1969), chpt. 78, p. 239.
21 *Ibid.*, chpt. 78, p. 239.
22 *Origines Islandicae*, vol. 1, p. 406.
23 Cited by Springer, 'Mediaeval Pilgrim Routes', p. 98.
24 H. Hermannsson, *Icelandic Manuscripts*, Islandica 19 (New York, 1929), p. 28.
25 Springer, 'Mediaeval Pilgrim Routes', p. 98.

Icelanders, both men and women, apparently *Romipetae* who had taken shelter there.[26] A further indication of the relative popularity of the Rome pilgrimage amongst Icelanders at this time is provided by Nikolas of Munkathvera, who went there himself c.1150. In the account of his own pilgrimage, he frequently refers to other Icelanders making the journey, noting in particular that while most travelled via Norway and Denmark, many others preferred a route via Deventer or Utrecht, where they received 'staff and scrip and a blessing for the pilgrimage'.[27]

As well as the conversion of Iceland, during the tenth and eleventh centuries the conversion of other Scandinavian countries was undertaken. The conquest of the Danes by the Emperor Henry I in 934 had paved the way for missionary activity in Denmark and by the beginning of the eleventh century there were a number of well-established bishoprics there. As in Iceland, so also in Norway Oláf Trygvasson had secured public acceptance of Christianity and this policy of Christianization was continued by King Oláf Haraldson (1015–1030), who became the country's patron saint. The acceptance of Christianity in Sweden, however, seems to have been slower and as late as 1181 Pope Lucius III (1181–1185), in appointing Bishop Giles of Västeras, instructed him to 'root out paganism' and to 'implant Christianity'.[28] Finland seems to have been the last Scandinavian country to receive Christian missionaries. There seems to be no evidence of any Christian presence there before the middle of the twelfth century. Not only was the Christianization of Scandinavia undertaken from the late tenth century onwards but efforts were made to bring about the acceptance of the religion in Eastern Europe. By c.1050 the rulers of Poland, Hungary and Russia had all been baptized and had begun to establish an ecclesiastical hierarchy in their kingdoms. A search of the surviving annals and histories of these Scandinavian and East European countries might well show, as in the case of Iceland, that pilgrimage *ad limina Apostolorum* from these areas was relatively popular in the twelfth century. That this was probably true at least of the Hungarians is suggested by the foundation of a hostel for them in Rome by King Stephen, where pilgrims from Hungary were still cared for in the thirteenth century.[29]

Certainly the enthusiasm amongst the new converts for undertaking the pilgrimage to Rome was clearly evident by the end of the eleventh century. In 1081 Gregory VII praised the number of pilgrims, both men and women, from the *gentes noviter ad fidem conversae*, who every year undertook the journey to Rome from the ends of the earth.[30] What is also interesting about

---

[26] Jóhannesson, *History of the Old Icelandic Commonwealth*, p. 156.
[27] Magoun, 'Pilgrim-Diary', p. 349.
[28] Lucius III, *Epistolae et Privilegia*, PL 201, cols. 1085–1086.
[29] See above pp. 130–131.
[30] Gregory VII, *Registers*, PL 148, col. 603. See also M. Maccarrone, 'I Fondamenti 'Petrini' del Primato Romano in Gregorio VII', *Studi Gregoriani*, 13 (Rome, 1989), pp. 55–122, esp. pp. 72–77.

this comment is that it is found in a letter addressed to the archbishop of Rouen, in which Gregory complained that neither the archbishop nor his suffragans would travel to the apostolic city.[31] Gregory condemned what he described as their neglect of Blessed Peter and contrasted their attitude towards Rome with that of the more recent converts to Christianity.[32] A similar criticism was levelled by Gregory VII in 1081 against the archbishop of Canterbury.[33]

The question which should now be addressed is whether the 'neglect of Blessed Peter', criticised by Gregory VII, existed only amongst the ecclesiastical hierarchy, or whether this indifference was becoming more widespread within the Christian heartland of Europe. Did the English, Frisians, Franks and Lombards still travel to Rome with the same enthusiasm and in the numbers as they had done in the wake of their conversion,[34] or were they now beginning to seek their salvation at the shrines of other saints? This is, of course, a very difficult question to answer but a start might be made by considering where some individual pilgrims were choosing to go in the twelfth century.

Some Twelfth-Century Pilgrims

The names of individual twelfth-century pilgrims and the sites to which they travelled can be found scattered throughout a wide variety of sources. Most often, however, it is the names of the famous pilgrims, or those who got into trouble, or those who died in the course of their journey, which survive.

The following examples are typical of the records of individual pilgrims which have survived in chronicles, annals and histories. We know from the *Orkneyinga Saga* that Hakon, earl of Orkney (d.1123) made a pilgrimage to Rome and to the Holy Land, 'where he visited the holy places and bathed in the Jordan as is the custom of palmers'.[35] The *Deeds of the Abbots of St Trond* record the pilgrimage to Rome made by Abbot Rudolph and Alexander, archdeacon of Liège in 1126. On their outward journey they were robbed and nearly killed in an avalanche on their way home.[36] The *Annals of Ireland by the Four Masters* record that in 1134 Imar O'Hagan, founder of the monastery

31 Gregory VII, *Registers*, col. 603.
32 *Ibid.*, col. 603.
33 *Ibid.*, cols. 621–622.
34 For some early pilgrimages to Rome, see for example B. Colgrave, 'Pilgrimage to Rome in the Seventh and Eighth Centuries', *Studies in the Language, Literature and Culture of the Middle Ages*, ed. E. B. Wood and A. A. Hill (Austin, 1969), pp. 156–172; M. D. Bloomfield, 'Anglo-Saxon Pilgrims and Rome', *Medieval World* (Nov.–Dec. 1991), pp. 22–26 and (Jan.–Feb. 1992), pp. 37–42.
35 *Orkneyinga Saga. The History of the Earls of Orkney*, trans. H. Pálsson and P. Edwards (London, 1981), chpt. 52, p. 97.
36 *Gesta Abbatum Trudonensium*, p. 306.

of SS. Peter and Paul in Armagh, died in Rome 'on his pilgrimage'.[37] John of Salisbury, in his *Historia Pontificalis*, records the visit to Rome made by Henry of Blois, bishop of Winchester, in 1151[38] and his return journey via Compostela.[39] Roger of Howden recorded the murder of Patrick, earl of Salisbury, by one Guy *de Leszinna* in 1168 on his return from Compostela,[40] whilst the *Chronicle* attributed to Benedict of Peterborough noted that in September 1170 Henry II went on pilgrimage to Rocamadour after recovering from a serious illness[41] and that in 1182 Henry the Lion travelled to Compostela.[42] The same source also contains a record of the pilgrimage made by two knights, Robertus Puer and Radulf Fraser, to the shrine of St James in 1188 and records that on their return journey they were taken prisoner by the count of Toulouse.[43] The *History of the Bishops of Auxerre* records the pilgrimage made to Rome by Bishop Hugh in 1206 which ended in his death.[44] Hugh received honourable burial in the Lateran, amongst what the author of the *History* terms the 'papal pyramids', although he noted that Hugh's mausoleum was rather more humble.[45] The *Chronicle* of William of Andres recorded that the young Lothair de Segni, the future Innocent III (d.1216), made a pilgrimage to the tomb of St Thomas Becket at Canterbury whilst a student at the University of Paris.[46]

Evidence concerning the holy places to which individual pilgrims were travelling in the twelfth century can also be found in the *Acta Sanctorum*. This collection of sources, however, should be treated with caution because it is possible that the undertaking of a pilgrimage may have been a *topos* regularly attributed to holy men and women.[47] The following examples are pilgrimages which some twelfth-century holy men and women are said to have made. St Chelidonia (c.1111) is said to have set out on pilgrimage to Rome,[48] whilst sometime around the beginning of the twelfth century St Morandus is supposed to have travelled to Compostela.[49] St John the Hermit probably set out for the Holy Land prior to 1143[50] and St Helen of Skövde is also said to have been there on pilgrimage sometime before her death in 1160.[51] St Gerlac of Valkenburg in Holland is said to have set out for Rome on pilgrim-

37 *Annals of the Kingdom of Ireland by the Four Masters*, vol. 2, p. 1047.
38 John of Salisbury, *Historia Pontificalis*, pp. 78–80.
39 *Ibid.*, p. 80.
40 Roger of Howden, *Chronica*, vol. 1, pp. 273–274.
41 Benedict of Peterborough, *Chronicle*, vol. 1, p. 7.
42 *Ibid.*, vol. 1. p. 288.
43 *Ibid.*, vol. 2, p. 35.
44 *Ex Historia Episcoporum Autissiodorensium*, p. 730.
45 *Ibid.*, p. 730.
46 William of Andres, *Chronicon*, p. 738.
47 See above pp. 14–15.
48 *De S. Chelidonia*, p. 366.
49 *De Sancto Morando. Monacho Cluniacensi in Suntgovia*, AASS June I, p. 350.
50 *De B. Iohanne Eremita*, p. 261.
51 *Vita S. Helenae Viduae et Mart.*, AASS July VII, p. 332.

age after his wife's death. After seven years, he returned to Holland and lived as a hermit until his death in 1170.[52] Reginald of Durham recorded the pilgrimages which Godric of Finchale made before his death in 1170 aged 105. These seem to have included at least three pilgrimages to Rome, once at least in the company of his mother, as well as journeys to Jerusalem, Compostela and to St Gilles in Provence.[53] The *Vita* of Albert the Hermit from Sens (d.c.1181) recorded that he went to Rome where he visited the basilicas of the Apostles. He then seems to have gone to St Michael in Gargano in Apulia and thence to Venice to see the relics of St Mark. From Venice he sailed to Palestine, where he visited the Holy Sepulchre and many other famous sites, which are not enumerated. On his return he went to northern Spain, to the shrine of St James.[54] B. Hildegunde of Meer (d.1183) is said to have travelled to Rome,[55] as did St Drogo, a Fleming of noble birth, who is supposed to have made his first pilgrimage there at the age of eighteen and who is attributed with making the journey a further eight times before his death in 1189.[56]

St Raymond of Piacenza (d.c.1200) apparently made his first pilgrimage to the Holy Land in the company of his mother.[57] Later he went to Compostela, visiting other shrines on his way home, including Vézelay.[58] Eventually he travelled to Rome as well, from where he hoped to make a further visit to the Holy Land.[59] However, whilst contemplating this journey, he was informed in a vision that, pleased as God was that he had made so many pilgrimages, rather than go again to Jerusalem, he should now return to Piacenza to look after the poor.[60] The theologian St Martin of León (d.1203) also seems to have been widely travelled. From Compostela, he went to Rome, visiting many churches along the way, especially those, his biographer, Lucas, bishop of Tuy noted, 'where there rested very sacred bodies'.[61] In Rome itself along with other pilgrims, he was said to have received a special blessing from Pope Urban III (1185–1187).[62] Leaving Rome he travelled to Monte Gargano and to the shrine of St Nicholas at Bari, before setting sail for the Holy Land.[63]

---

[52] *De S. Gerlaco*, p. 307.
[53] Reginald of Durham, *Libellus de Vita et Miraculis S. Godrici*, pp. 34, 55 and 57 for his journeys to Jerusalem; p. 28 for Rome and p. 34 for Compostela.
[54] *De B. Alberto Eremita*, p. 402.
[55] *De B. Hildegunde Comitissa, Fundatrice Coenobii Marensis Ordinis Praemonstratensis*, AASS Feb. I, p. 918.
[56] *De Sancto Drogone Recluso*, AASS April II, p. 443.
[57] *Vita S. Raymundi*, pp. 646–647.
[58] *Ibid.*, p. 650.
[59] *Ibid.*, p. 650.
[60] *Ibid.*, p. 650.
[61] Lucas, Bishop of Tuy, *Vita B. Martin Legionensis*, PL 208, col. 13.
[62] *Ibid.*, col. 13. This is questionable since there is no evidence, at least from the dating clauses in his letters, that Pope Urban III ever managed to enter Rome.
[63] *Ibid.*, col. 13.

After a sojourn there and before returning to Léon, he visited the tombs of St Martin in Gaul, St Thomas at Canterbury and St Patrick in Ireland.[64] St Bona of Pisa (d. 1207) was another widely travelled saint. As a result of a vision, she made her first pilgrimage to the Holy Land where a hermit, by the name of Ubald, told her the places she ought to visit.[65] On her voyage home she was attacked by Muslims but eventually managed to return to Pisa. There she lived as a recluse except for her frequent pilgrimages, which included a number of visits to the tomb of St Peter in Rome and nine visits to the shrine of St James in Galicia.[66] During these journeys she would eat only a modicum of food and was always bound around with chains.[67]

Narrative sources, therefore, suggest that pilgrims were travelling to a wide variety of holy places in the twelfth century, of which Rome, Jerusalem and Compostela are the sites which occur most frequently. These individual pilgrims, however, are too few to enable us to make any judgement concerning the relative popularity of even the largest of these pilgrimage centres.

Cartularies

These are valuable documentary sources which may provide some useful indications about the relative popularity of the main centres of pilgrimage in the twelfth century. In the cartularies of religious houses can be found charters recording pledges and benefactions. These frequently include those of pilgrims in which the desire to set out on pilgrimage is often expressed together with the intended destination.[68] Typical phrases found in these charters include *pergens ad sanctum Jacobum*,[69] *proficiscens Jerosolimam*,[70] *volens proficisci Romam*,[71] *volens adire Jerosolimam*,[72] *cupiens adire Jerosolimam*,[73] *Jerosolimam peregrinationem proficisci volens*,[74] *volens ire ad Sanctum Jacobum*,[75]

---

64   *Ibid.*, col. 14.
65   *De S. Bona*, p. 149.
66   *Ibid.*, p. 150.
67   *Ibid.*, p. 150.
68   There are occasionally references in charters to the intention to set out on pilgrimage in which no destination is given. See for example Talmond, no. 248, Vendôme, vol. 1, no. 243, Burton, p. 38.
69   See for example, Uzerche, no. 543.
70   See for example, Pontigny, no. 200, Chateaudun, no. 67, Marmoutier pour le Vendomois, appendix no. 8.
71   See for example, Domène, no. 188
72   See for example, Barbezieux, nos. 94, 122, 355.
73   See for example, Vendôme, vol. 2, no. 360;
74   See for example, Beaujeu, appendix, no. 5.
75   See for example, Uzerche, no. 1148.

volens visitare Sepulchrum.[76] Sometimes a pious phrase is also added such as *pro anima sua,*[77] *pro remedio animae meae,*[78] or *causa orationis.*[79]

Sometimes a pledge or sale might be made in order to finance a pilgrim's journey. In 1075, before setting out on his pilgrimage to Rome, Hugh of Doubleau gave a tithe from the seigneurie of Mondoubleau to the monastery of Vendôme.[80] In return he received money and a horse for his journey.[81] Another case from the same cartulary is that of Guicher, lord of Châteaurenaud, who, in 1075, approached the monks of Vendôme for a subsidy for his journey to Rome.[82] Guicher, however, had been imposing unfair dues and was forced by the monks to recognise the injustice of his actions. This done, he offered to lift the dues but only if the monks would give him money for his pilgrimage.[83] A charter in the cartulary of Saint-Mont records that Fort Sanz, wanting to go on pilgrimage to Rome c.1085, pledged his share of the church of Gotz for five *solidi,*[84] while we know from a charter in the cartulary of Holy Trinity de Tiron, dated 1127, that Hugh of Lièvreville, his mother and his *cognatus,* Herbert Guitum, handed over their land in Lièvreville as security to the monks of Tiron, receiving in return ten pounds. If they failed to return from their pilgrimage to Jerusalem, the land was to be kept by the monks.[85]

Other benefactions recorded in the cartularies of religious houses seem to have been intended to atone for the would–be pilgrim's past misdemeanours with the hope of securing divine protection for the journey.[86] In 1107, mindful of his calumnies against the monastery of SS. Peter and Paul of Domène, Count Vuigo decided to make restitution before beginning his pilgrimage to Compostela,[87] while among the charters of Saint-Jean-en-Vallée can be found that of Hugh, son of Guinemer, who in 1110, before undertaking his pilgrimage to Jerusalem, gave to the leper hospital of Grand Beaulieu a gift of

---

[76]   See for example, Yonne, vol. 2, no. 370, Gellone, no. 326.
[77]   See for example, Corbeil, no. 42.
[78]   See for example, Nouaillé, no. 157.
[79]   See for example, Vendôme, vol. 1, no. 252, Bourbonnais, no. 7, Saint Vincent du Mans, vol. 1, nos. 1 and 29.
[80]   Vendôme, vol. 1, no. 250. On the monastery of Vendôme, see P. D. Johnson, *Prayer Patronage and Power. The Abbey of la Trinité, Vendôme, 1032–1187* (New York and London, 1981).
[81]   Vendôme, vol. 1, no. 250.
[82]   *Ibid.,* vol. 1, no. 251.
[83]   *Ibid.,* vol. 1, no. 251.
[84]   Saint Mont, no. 26.
[85]   Tiron, no. 86.
[86]   Constable ('Medieval Charters as a Source for the History of the Crusades') argues that many charters show the desire of the crusaders for protection and help from God and the saints during their journeys and that good deeds were worthless unless the crusader was at peace with men at home.
[87]   Domène, no. 33.

land which the charter claimed he and his predecessors had held unjustly.[88] Other charters record what was to happen to the property of a pilgrim in the event of his demise *en route*. Before departing for the Holy Land c.1150, William of Porta made arrangements for the distribution of his property in the event of his death. If he returned alive, the monks of Cluny were promised twenty *solidi*.[89]

Cartularies of religious houses in France have proved the most useful because they are so rich in detail. As so many of these cartularies have survived, however, it has only been possible to examine a small selection. An attempt has been made to select from a variety of geographical areas to take account of local variations. Areas were chosen on the basis of the availability of cartularies and include the area north of the Loire, Orléans, Tours, Le Mans, Angers and Blois and to the south including Poitou, Aunis, Saintonge and a few from Bordeaux. Some cartularies from the areas of Limoges, Mâcon and Autun have been utilised, as well as a few from the areas of Montpellier and Grenoble.[90] As only a small proportion of the surviving cartularies have been examined, what follows is only suggestive but may nevertheless be indicative of trends.

In the cartularies examined, there are examples of many pilgrims who, prior to the twelfth century, had chosen to make a pilgrimage to Rome. These included some very early examples such as Domnolus, bishop of Le Mans, who seems to have set out in 572[91] and Jacob, bishop of Toul who went c.762.[92] Tenth-century *Romipetae* included Bernard, abbot of St Maixent who travelled there in 918,[93] Ralph and his wife Adelaide who went together in 951,[94] Gunter, abbot of St Aubin, in 988[95] and Amelio whose pilgrimage seems to have been made at the very end of the tenth century, possibly c.996.[96] I have found even more examples of eleventh-century *Romipetae*, such as Theobald, count of Blois, who went to the apostolic city in 1004.[97] Athanulf died on the return journey from Rome in 1007.[98] Baldwin travelled there in 1020[99] and Geoffrey Martel and his wife Agnes of Poitiers in 1040.[100] Other eleventh-century *Romipetae* included William Minor who

---

88   Saint-Jean-en-Vallée de Chartres, no. 10.
89   Cluny, vol. 5, no. 4145.
90   I am grateful to Dr Marcus Bull for his advice on the selection of cartularies and on the dates of individual charters.
91   Saint Vincent du Mans, vol. 1, no. 1.
92   Saint Bénigne de Dijon, vol. 1, no. 26.
93   Bourbonnais, no. 1.
94   Uzerche, no. 120.
95   Saint Aubin d'Angers, vol. 1, no. 23. Gunter also seems to have travelled to Jerusalem on this pilgrimage.
96   Lézat, no. 189.
97   Saint Père de Chartres, vol. 1, no. 8.
98   Marseille, vol. 1, no. 486.
99   Saint Aubin d'Angers, vol. 1, no. 162.
100 Vendôme, vol. 1, no. 36.

went in 1056,[101] Guy I, duke of Poitou, in 1061,[102] Hilgod in 1062,[103] Germund and his wife Bersenta in 1063,[104] Mathias in 1070,[105] Ernald, bishop of Le Mans, in 1071,[106] Moyses in 1074,[107] Guicher, castellan of Chateaurenaud, in 1075[108] and Hugh Dubelli, castellan of Montdoubleu who also travelled there c.1075.[109] Cartulary evidence reveals the names of a few other eleventh-century *Romipetae*, such as Hugh Langesinus who went to Rome in 1078,[110] Alberic Scarbotus and Arnold *de Vuarapio* c.1080,[111] Lancellin, castellan of Beaugency, in 1081,[112] Fort Sanz c.1085,[113] Ardencus c.1090[114] and Master Kadelo c.1095.[115] It seems that William of Warenne and his wife Gundrada had also set out with the intention of going to Rome. A charter in the cartulary of Cluny dated 1080 reveals, however, that they were unable to travel as far as the apostolic city because of the war being waged between Gregory VII and Henry IV.[116] Uncertainty concerning the dating of some charters means that the pilgrimages made to Rome by Peter, son of Sendebaud,[117] and Hugh of Insula[118] can only be dated to sometime during the latter part of the eleventh century, whilst those of Achard,[119] Hubert *de Durostallo*,[120] Isembert of Thouarcé[121] and Bernard, viscount of Comborn,[122] may have been made either during the later years of the eleventh century or the very early years of the twelfth. A reference also survives to a pilgrimage made to Rome and thence to Bari during the eleventh century. The wording of the charter, however, makes it impossible to decide whether the pilgrim

---

101 Talmond, no. 3.
102 Saint Maixent, no. 118.
103 Vendôme, vol. 1, no. 162.
104 Rouen, p. 452.
105 Vendôme, vol. 1, no. 210.
106 Saint Vincent du Mans, vol. 1, no. 29.
107 Saint Aubin d'Angers, vol. 1, no. 106.
108 Vendôme, vol. 1, no. 251.
109 *Ibid.*, vol. 1, no. 250.
110 Cormery, no. 42.
111 Saint Vincent du Mans, vol. 1, no. 51; Vienne, no. 275.
112 Vendôme, vol. 2, no. 301.
113 Saint Mont, no. 26.
114 Domène, no. 188.
115 Talmond, no. 64.
116 Cluny, vol. 4, no. 3561.
117 Poitiers, no. 218.
118 *Calendar of Documents*, vol. 1, no. 1178.
119 Cluny, vol. 4, no. 3028. This charter has been dated to 1049–1109.
120 Saint Aubin d'Angers, vol. 2, no. 826. This charter has been dated by the editor to 1082–1106.
121 *Ibid.*, vol. 2, no. 826.
122 Uzerche, no. 463. This charter is dated by the editor to 1119. It refers, however, to the Abbot Gaubertus ('Ego Bernardus vicecomes pergere volens Romam, ammonitus a domno Gauberto abbate.') who died in 1108, and must therefore date from 1097–1108.

was in fact William, abbot of Tulle, or Raymond, son and successor of Viscount Boso I of Turenne, a future first crusader.[123]

These charters have also revealed the names of numerous pilgrims who, prior to the twelfth century, had chosen to travel to Jerusalem. Those travelling there in the tenth century included Gausmarus, abbot of Savigny c.960[124] and Gunter, abbot of St Aubin in 988, presumably either before, or more likely, after his pilgrimage to Rome.[125] While the names of numerous pilgrims who travelled to Rome in the eleventh century have survived, the same is true of those travelling to the Holy Land. These included Fulk III, count of Angers, in 1003,[126] William, count of Angoulême, c.1025,[127] Avesgaudus, bishop of Le Mans, in c.1036,[128] Guy I of Laval in 1039,[129] Gislerius in 1070,[130] Aimeric, count of Fezensac[131] and Aimo Bernard of Tulle,[132] both c.1088, Gerard of Cousin[133] and Peter Carbonel[134] around 1090, Boso I, viscount of Turenne, c.1091[135] and Peter of Ussel in 1095.[136] The selection of cartularies which I have looked at also contain the names of other Jerusalem pilgrims whose journeys were probably made in the eleventh century but which cannot be easily dated.[137] Also contained in these cartularies are a large number of references to journeys by individuals to Jerusalem dated to around 1096, most of whom would have been participants in the First Crusade.[138]

[123] Tulle and Rocamadour, no. 499.
[124] Savigny, vol. 1, p. 87.
[125] Saint Aubin d'Angers, vol. 1, no. 23.
[126] Ibid., vol. 1, no. 130.
[127] Saint Cybard, no. 227. See also Adémar de Chabannes, Chronique, p. 192.
[128] Chateau du Loir, no. 17. The bishop died in 1036 on his return journey from Jerusalem.
[129] Ibid., no. 10.
[130] Vendôme, vol. 1, no. 221.
[131] Auch, no. 46.
[132] Tulle and Rocamadour, no. 474.
[133] Ibid., no. 72.
[134] Chalon, nos. 106 and 107.
[135] Tulle and Rocamadour, no. 500. Boso seems to have died in Jerusalem in c.1091.
[136] Uzerche, no. 817.
[137] For example, the pilgrimages made by Bernard (Cluny 2867); William of Sadroe (Vigeois, no. 5); Berengar (Aniane, no. 261); Hardouin d'Acre (Vendôme, vol. 2, no. 306); William de Osoenus (Saint Vincent du Mans, vol. 1, no. 23); Fulcher (Grenoble, no. 108); Aimery Bislingueas (Saint-Maixent, no. 183); Peter Paleis (Talmond no. 107); Ivo Chesnel (Nogent-le-Rotrou, no. 18); Gradulfus (Marmoutier pour le Vendomois, no. 126).
[138] See for example, the charters concerning Raimbert of Chevanville (Longpont, no. 69); Milo le Grand (ibid., no. 201); Hamo of La Hune (Saint Vincent du Mans, vol. 1, no. 460); Robert, vicarius (ibid., vol. 1, no. 522); Payen of Chevré (ibid., vol. 1, no. 745); Payen of Mondoubleau (ibid., vol. 1, no. 666); Guy (ibid., vol. 1, no. 666); Raymond, viscount of Turenne (Tulle and Rocamadour, nos. 517 and 644); Raymond of Curemonte (ibid., nos. 517–644); Gerard Cabrols and his brother Rannulf (ibid., no. 121); Bernard and his brother Odo (Cluny, vol. 5, no. 3712); Aimery of Pont-roy

Some references occur in these charters to a few pilgrims who chose to travel to Compostela prior to 1100. These included Peter Raimond c.1043,[139] Albert of La Vallette in 1048,[140] Arnold c.1060,[141] Arno of Veauce in 1080,[142] Airaud of Forges in 1090[143] and Adhémar II of Limoges sometime between 1068 and 1090.[144] There are also references to journeys made to Spain by Gormund sometime between 1036 and 1061[145] and by Robert, a priest of Mortemart, between 1052 and 1060[146] but whether a visit to Compostela was involved is unknown. The journey to Spain of Hugh of Lusignan is mentioned in the cartulary of the abbey of Nouaillé, although he is said to have been going there specifically 'contra Saracenos'.[147] I have also found a reference in these cartularies to a pilgrimage made to Mont St Michel by Rudolf, viscount of Le Mans in 994.[148]

References in these charters clearly show that most of the information which we have concerns pilgrimage to the major shrines, Jerusalem, Compostela and Rome. Indeed, we should not expect to find much else, as a pilgrimage to a local shrine would have been unlikely to entail the dangers or

(Aureil, nos. 67 and 128 and also Uzerche, no. 1157); Helias of Malemort (Uzerche, no. 552); Itier of La Rivière (ibid., no. 686); Raymond Eic, clericus (Lézat, vol. 1, no. 240); Peter de Vizium (Aureil, no. 35. Probably also the same man as Peter de Vision mentioned in ibid., no. 260); Gaufredus and his brother Guy (Marseille, vol. 1, no. 143); Rainald Superbus, Burchard of Marmande, Galterius de Monte Sorello, Geoffrey and Engelelmus (Noyers, nos. 245, 246, 251 and 252); Rainulphus (Beaujeu, no. 7). References to journeys to Jerusalem in charters dated to c.1097, 1098 and 1099 were probably again mostly crusaders rather than ordinary pilgrims. See for example references to Adémar of Las Gaydias and his brother (Uzerche, no. 683); Robert Burgundus and Rainald III of Château-Gontier (Saint Nicholas d'Angers, no. 4); Autran (Apt, no. 96); William (Vigeois, no. 107); Bertrand (Vendôme, vol. 2, no. 360); Astanove II, count of Fezensac (Auch, no. 57); Milo de Monte Leterico (Longpont, no. 45); Bruno of Ré (Angély, vol. 1, no. 416); William of Forz (ibid., vol. 2, no. 448); Archard of Born (ibid., vol. 1, no. 120); John, presbyter (ibid., vol. 1, no. 212); William Miscemalum (ibid., vol. 1, no. 86); William Peter (ibid., vol. 1, no. 332); Geoffrey, seigneur of Issoudun (Aureil, no. 226); Ascelin (Yonne, vol. 2, no. 22); Robert le Bourguignon (Manceau de Marmoutier, vol. 1, no. 13). Others who were probably also first crusaders include Peter of Vic (Auch, no. 6) and Bernard of Bré (Vigeois, no. 86). Names of other travellers to Jerusalem towards the end of the eleventh century also survive. Whether or not they were crusaders is uncertain. See for example the journeys of Peter Jordan (Cormery, no. 51); Robert (Nogent-le-Rotrou, no. 56); Stephen Bonin (Mâcon, no. 537); Wigo of Mara (Tours, no. 51); Ansculfus (Cluny, vol. 5, no. 3766); Berengar (ibid., vol. 5, no. 3804); Grimald (ibid., vol. 5, no. 3765).

139 Béziers, no. 64.
140 Uzerche, no. 1148.
141 Sorde, no. 39.
142 Bourbonnais, no. 7.
143 Mauléon, no. 1.
144 Uzerche, no. 543.
145 Aniane, 261.
146 Limoges, no. 60.
147 Nouaillé, no. 157.
148 Saint Victeur au Mans, no. 1.

expense of a long distance journey. These examples would seem to suggest that in the period up to the eleventh century pilgrims were going to all three major shrines, although in the random sample of charters consulted, references to those travelling to Compostela are relatively fewer than those either to Rome or to Jerusalem. The very large number of Jerusalem pilgrims can be accounted for by the departure of the First Crusade to the Holy Land in 1096. For most crusaders funded their journey in the same way as pilgrims, often pledging their land to religious houses.[149] Yet if we consider the period before 1096, the numbers of Jerusalem pilgrims and *Romipetae* are reasonably similar.

What should now be investigated is the pattern of pilgrimage which emerges from this random selection of cartularies for the period after 1100. Were Rome and Jerusalem pilgrimages equally numerous and did Compostela still rank in third place?[150] The charters in these cartularies which date from the twelfth century show that references to journeys to Jerusalem are undoubtedly the most numerous. This again can perhaps be explained by the fact that many of them were crusaders. The numerous references to the desire to travel to Jerusalem in charters dated to around 1100 and 1101 were probably the sentiments expressed by those who set out on the third wave of the First Crusade.[151] There are also references to a large number of journeys to Jerusalem c.1147, probably those participating in the Second Crusade[152]

---

[149] See Constable, 'Medieval Charters as a source for the History of the Crusades', pp. 73–89.

[150] Other than references to Jerusalem, Rome and Compostela, I have only found mention of three other destinations. A certain Lecberga seems to have travelled to St Gilles c.1100 (Talmond, no. 174), Adhémar, viscount of Limoges, to Le Puy in 1121 (Uzerche, no. 131) and Vuilencus Longus to Vézelay in 1100 (Savigny, no. 868).

[151] See for example references to Beraldus Silvanus (Angély, no. 450); William IX, count of Poitou (*ibid.*, no. 320); Gerald of Tuda (*ibid.*, no.326); Airald Bardo (*ibid.*, no. 321): Ramnulf of Tuinac (*ibid.*, no. 319); Gausbertus and his brother William (Aureil, no. 274); Bernard Lilballus (*ibid.*, no. 182); Fulcher *de Brucia* (*ibid.*, no. 268); Peter Gausbertus (*ibid.*, no. 259); Chartard (Savigny, vol. 1, no. 867); Hugh, archbishop of Lyon (*ibid.*, vol. 1, no. 819) Milo, *miles* (Saint Bénigne de Dijon, no. 394); Odo, duke of Burgundy (*ibid.*, no. 398); Andrew Raina (Domène no. 103); Peter Rodberti (*ibid.*, no. 237); Guy Pinellus (Longpont, no. 88); Odo de Ver (*ibid.*, no. 212); Stephen of Vitri, *miles* (*ibid.*, no. 311); Bernard Veredun (Cluny, vol. 5, no. 3755); William Rufin (Nogent-le-Rotrou, no. 57); Aimery, *capellanus* of St Clement de Chasseneuil (Boixe, no. 120); Ulric Burcel (Vendôme, vol. 2, no. 402); Bernard, viscount of Béziers (Gellone, no. 299); Bertrand of Bas, *canonicus* (Chamalières-sur-Loire, no. 103); Stephen of Neublens (Cluny, vol. 5, no. 3737).

[152] See for example the charters which refer to Bernard *del Domno* and his son Fulcher (Vigeois, no. 284); Peter of Bré and his brother William (*ibid.*, no. 316); Maingot of La Mothe (Saint-Maixent, no. 329); Giraudus Ascellini (Talmond, no. 345); Peter Aimeric of Bré (Aureil, no. 245); Arnold Seschaves (Angoulême, no. 159); Itier *de Tociaco* and Norgeot of Cruz (Pontigny, no. 69); Richard *de Percheio* (Josaphat, vol. 1, no. 141); Bartholmeus of Vendôme (Manceau de Marmoutier, vol. 1, no. 5); Bernard of Bré (Uzerche, no. 1144); Siebrand Chabot (Absie, nos. 212 and 244).

and c.1188–1190 perhaps mostly participants in the Third Crusade.[153] Many other charters refer to individuals making or intending to make the journey to Jerusalem. The research has suggested that these are equally numerous for both the first[154]

[153] See for example, Chaufers and Gerald of Orgnac (Obazine, no. 705); Geoffrey of Saint-Verain (Fontmorigny, no. 109); Rainald *de Disesia* (Cluny, vol. 5, no. 4341); Clérembaud of Noyers (Pontigny, no. 55); Stephen (Yonne, vol. 2, no. 399); John *de Bolonio* (Vendôme, vol. 2, no. 611); Peter Papillon (*ibid.*, vol. 2, no. 595); Peter *de Cenvis* (Merci-Dieu, no. 238); Raymond, viscount of Turenne (Beaulieu, no. 194); Rotrou, count of Perche (Nogent-le-Rotrou, no. 99); Geoffrey *de Tellol* (Uzerche, no. 176); Guiet (Talmond no. 390); William *de Chaone* (*ibid.*, no. 388); Juhel of Mayenne (Abbayette, no. 17); Tedbaudus *de Vis* (Absie, no. 267); William *de Chantemerle* (Bas-Poitou, no. 43); Bartholomew (Vignory, appendix no. 46); Matthew Peloquin (Noyers, no. 643); Henry II, count of Troyes (Pontigny, no. 200 and Yonne, vol. 2, no. 412); Stephen (*ibid.*, no. 217); Fulgerius (Chateaudun, no. 35); Peter, count of Nevers, Avalo *de Sellenniaco*, William, count of *Joviniaci* (Yonne, vol. 2, nos. 409, 410, 507); Dreux *de Mello* (Pontigny, no. 342); Robert of Saint-Michel (Obazine, no. 751); Stephen *de Varennis* (Beaujeu, appendix, no. 5).

[154] See for example references to the journeys of Stephen c.1100–1125 (Boixe, no. 31); Arnulf c.1101–1129 (Saint Père de Chartres, vol. 1, nos. 26 and 46); Roger *de Courson* (Uzerche, no. 493); Robert Dalmatius 1106 (Cluny, vol. 5, no. 3840 and Marcigny-sur-Loire, no. 109); Josceran of Vitry c.1106–1107 (Cluny, vol. 5, no. 3850); Gauzbertus Albonius (Vigeois, no. 104); Bormaudus c.1106–1120 (Saint Aubin d'Angers, vol. 2, no. 741); Peter Berengarii c.1106–1120 (Gellone, no. 291); Lambert c.1108 (Angély, no. 330); Guy II of Bré c.1108–1113 (Uzerche, no. 361); Peter of Murat and Peter *de Tornamira* in 1109 (Tulle and Rocamadour, nos. 167 and 464); Bernard, bishop of Mâcon c.1109–1118 (Mâcon, no. 561); Gerard of Chanac, Witard of Tulle, Guy Turpin and Hugh in 1110 (Tulle and Rocamadour, nos. 85 and 558, Vendôme, vol. 2, no. 425, and Saint Jean en Vallée de Chartres, no. 10); Hugh of Matheflon in 1111 (Saint Laud d'Angers, no. 5); Peter of Noailles c.1111–1124 (Vigeois, no. 211); Briord in 1112 (Bugey, appendix, no. 5); Garderade of La Faie c.1111–1117 (Baigne, no. 26); Guy, count of Rochefort in 1114 (Tiron, no. 6); Walter of Condat c.1114–1133 (Uzerche, no. 587); William *de Buialo* and Robertus, *Major de Ver* c.1115 (Aureil, no. 153 and Saint Père de Chartres, vol. 2, no. 156); William Guerra and Haganus of Porta in 1116 (Gellone, no. 326 and Saint Père de Chartres, vol. 2, no. 115); Ansold of Bellum Videre c.1116–1129 (Saint Père de Chartres, vol. 1, no. 69); William of Chanac, Gerard *de Sinemuro* and Hugh Dalmace in 1118 (Tulle and Rocamadour, no. 56, and Marcigny, no. 161); Berlay II de Montreuil, R. Gabardus, Rainald, bishop of Angers, William Venator, Frederick of Châtillon and Peter Racberti c.1120 (Cathédrale d'Angers, no. 89; Mauléon, no. 10, St Nicholas d'Angers, no. 10, Tours, no. 67, Longpont, no. 183 and Talmond no. 242); Itier *de Villaboe* c.1120–1140 (Cellefrouin, no. 26); Pons Palatinus c.1121 (Savigny, vol. 1, no. 921); Ruspanonus in 1123 (Vendôme, vol. 2, no. 444); Forto, *claviger* of St Seurin in 1125 (Saint Seurin de Bordeaux, no. 75); Robert of Buzençais c.1125–1131 (Cathédrale d'Angers, no. 167); Matthew Giraud c.1125–1126 (*ibid.*, no. 179); Herbert Guitum and Hugh of Lièvreville c.1127 (Tiron, vol. 1, no. 86); Helias c. 1127 (Josaphat, vol. 1, no. 26): Adhémar of Boisset c. 1127–1141 (Baigne, nos. 431, 432 and 435); Geoffrey c. 1127–1149 (Saint Aubin d'Angers, no. 117); Alo of Insula in 1128 (Saint Cybard, no. 132); Peter Bersaudi and Rainald of Charrofeizère c.1130 (Talmond, nos. 283 and 284); Gerard, Abbot of Talmond c.1130–1140 (*ibid.*, no. 392); Stephen c.1131–1141 (Saint Père de Chartres, vol. 2, no. 149); Fulco *de Lers* c.1130 (Longpont, no. 154); Guy Normand c. 1131 (Marcigny-sur-Loire, no. 306): Bernard and

and second halves of the twelfth century.[155] Which of these were crusaders and which ordinary pilgrims is, however, in most cases impossible to distinguish. The number of references to journeys to Jerusalem and the Holy Land which survive in the small sample of charters examined suggests, however, that travel there was popular and continuous throughout the twelfth century.

A random search of these twelfth-century charters has also revealed a

Umbert de Marzeu c.1137 (Savigny, vol. 1, no. 937); Ivo of La Jaille, his two brothers, Haimeric and Peter, Geoffrey of Teudon and Rainald Rufus c.1138–1148 (Cathédrale d'Angers, no. 221); Stephen Vilarensis (Lyonnais, vol. 1, no. 24); Philip, Adam Lysiard, Gerald de Monte, Hugh de Sanctus Albinus, Rainald de Motha Britonis c.1140 (Solesmes, no. 52, Longpont, no. 209, Aureil, no. 41, Tiron, vol. 2, no. 254, Talmond, no. 324); Gosselin Mauvoisin c.1141 (Saint Aubin d'Angers, no. 873); William of Martret c.1142–1143 (Obazine, no. 87); Renaud le Paysan c.1142–1149 (Saint Maixent, no. 331); Gilon of Sens c.1142–1168 (Yonne, vol. 2, no. 51); Saon of Bouilly c.1143–1144 (Pontigny, no. 138); Gosbert, viscount of Dijon and Geroius de Lunviler in 1145 (Saint Etienne de Dijon, no. 11 and Tiron, vol. 2, no. 272); Burcard c.1145–1157 (Vaux de Cernay, no. 8); Erardus de Villabum and Robert in 1146 (ibid., vol. 2, nos. 288 and 289); Gerard Siebrandus c.1146–1187 (Absie, no. 320); Itier de Villebois c.1149–1159 (Boixe, no. 300).

155 Arbert Clerenbaudi, Bernard de Meiras, William of Porta, William de Castris c.1150 (Bas-Poitou, no. 8, Aureil, no. 209, Cluny, vol. 5, no. 4145, Longpont, no. 336); Fulk de Lers c.1156–1157 (Vaux de Cernay, nos, 13 and 24); Paulin c.1157–1189 (Saint Aubin d'Angers, vol. 2, no. 837); Pontius Nauta in 1158 (Chamalières-sur-Loire, no. 281); Fulk Ribole (Solesmes, no. 75); William Meschinoti c.1161 (Talmond, no. 379); Pons c.1162–1172 (Chamalières-sur-Loire, no. 178); Berlay III de Montreuil c.1162–1177 (Cathédrale d'Angers, no. 235); Renaud IV of Chateau-Goutier c.1162–1178 (Saint Nicholas d'Angers, no. 21); Boso de Mont-Primlan c.1166 (Saint Croix de Bordeaux, no. 131); Ainardus, clericus, in 1167 (Chamalières-sur-Loire, no. 89); Raymond of l'Isle c.1168 (Gimont, nos. 15, 54 and 132); William of Lignières in 1169 (Fontmorigny, nos. 31 and 45); Ebles II, viscount of Ventadour c.1169–1170 (Obazine, no. 291); Peter de Alneto c.1169–1184 (Vaux de Cernay, no. 35); Peter Arnaldi c.1170–1171 (ibid., no. 329); Peter, count of Nevers c.1171 (Cluny, vol. 5, no. 4297); Bernard de Bilsano and Peter of Logorsan in 1174 (Berdoues, no. 547 and Gimont, no. 155); Siguinus de la Porcharia in 1177 (Obazine, no. 638); Hervé de Gien c.1177–1189 (Fontmorigny, no. 107); Odo de Alona c.1179 (Saint Père de Chartres, vol. 2, no. 47); Raymond Aimeric II de Montesquiou in 1180 (Auch, no. 113); Rainald in 1183 (Artige, no. 10); Geoffrey de Arsiaco c. 1180 (Yonne, vol. 2, no. 243); Andrew de Chauviné in 1184 (Merci-Dieu, no. 91); Rainald c.1181 (Yonne, vol. 2, no. 307); Peter, viscount de Castelo c.1186 (Uzerche, no. 520); Gacius de Remelato and Guy in 1191 (Chateaudun, no. 37 and Yonne, vol. 2, no. 432)); Milo in 1187 (Yonne, vol. 2, no. 370); Payen de Soisaco in 1192 (Corbeil, no. 42); Peter of Charenton in 1193 (Fontmorigny, nos. 121, 159, 161 and 207); William of Solignac c.1198–1215 (Bonnefoy, no. 157); Simon de la Gleiserei c.1195 (Vaux de Cernay, no. 103). For some early thirteenth century pilgrims/crusaders, see Baigne, no. 542, Bas-Poitou, no. 103, Bugey, appendix, no. 29, Chateaudun, nos. 67, 69, 71 and 75, Fontaine le Comte, no. 34, Fontmorigny, no. 140, Josaphat, vol. 1, no. 313, Lyonnais, vol. 1, no. 151, Marmoutier pour le Vendomois, appendix, no. 8, Merci–Dieu, nos. 12 and 57, Notre Dame de Chartres, no. 187, Second Cartulary of Saint Vincent du Mans, no. 342, Solesmes, no. 225, Talmond, no. 402, Vaux de Cernay, no. 118, Villeloin, nos. 44 and 156.

number of Compostela pilgrims, such as Count Vuigo,[156] Richard Malus Leporarius,[157] Ansgot de Burewelle,[158] Ulgerius, bishop of Angers,[159] Arbert Theophanie,[160] Tebert,[161] Simon de Beaugency,[162] Aimo Esyngres,[163] Bernard of Meiras,[164] Louis VII,[165] Matthew, duke of Lorraine[166] and Ansold.[167] There is also a reference in a charter dated 1200 to a pilgrimage which Savary d'Anthenaise intended to make to Compostela.[168] Several references to journeys to Spain also survive in the twelfth-century charters examined. These include those of Peter Curta Brachia, Peter de Vall and Elia de Tutela in a charter dated to 1117.[169] As this charter records that they were going to fight the Muslims, it is clear that they were participants in the Saragossa crusade of 1118. Others who travelled to Spain on crusade included Amalvin Blanquefort and Gaston IV, viscount of Béarn, who went there 'contra Saracenos' c.1120[170] and Eustace de Brione who went there on crusade in 1212.[171] Other references occur to journeys to Spain such as those of Robert Judas c.1126–1129[172] and John of Guéramé probably in the early years of the thirteenth century.[173] The reasons for their journeys, however, are uncertain and whether a visit to Compostela was involved is unknown.

Perhaps the most striking difference in the charters c.1000–c.1200 is how few references there seem to be to pilgrimages to the apostolic city in the twelfth century. Apart from the pilgrimages referred to above by Achard, Hubert de Durostallo, Isembert of Thouarcé and Bernard, viscount of Comborn which may have been made in the very early years of the twelfth century, there are few other references in these charters to individuals setting out on pilgrimage to Rome at that time. Pilgrimages ad limina apostolorum were made c.1100 by Engelbaud Meschinot[174] and probably also by Arbert de

156 Domène, no. 33.
157 Calendar of Documents, no. 1233.
158 Ibid., no 1239.
159 Cathédrale d'Angers, no. 139.
160 Talmond, no. 361.
161 Longpont, no. 347.
162 Orléans, no. 5.
163 Cluny, vol. 5, no. 4149.
164 Aureil, no. 209.
165 Saint Père de Chartres, vol. 2, no. 35, p. 648. See also Toulouse, no. 4.
166 Cluny, vol. 5, no. 4217.
167 Saint Père de Chartres, vol. 2, no. 185.
168 Saint Victeur au Mans, no. 32. Other early thirteenth-century Compostela pilgrims included Eude Bourgoin, (Fontmorigny, no. 254) and Itier de Magnac (Dorat, no. 40).
169 Tulle and Rocamadour, no. 287.
170 Saint Seurin de Bordeaux, no. 40. They may have been participants in the campaign in Spain in 1120 led by William IX of Aquitaine.
171 Léoncel, no. 73.
172 Nogent-le-Rotrou, no. 45.
173 Second Cartulary of Saint Vincent du Mans, no. 220.
174 Talmond, no. 81.

Rochifort,[175] by Aimery, lord of Fagiae c.1101,[176] by a certain Roger c.1140[177] and by Gauterius de Mont-Saint-Jean c.1150.[178] There is also a reference to a pilgrimage to Rome in the early thirteenth century by John *de Roeiria*.[179] In addition we know from a charter in the cartulary of Marcigny-sur-Loire that Narjodus, bishop of Autun, travelled to Rome in the early twelfth century but there is no indication whether it was a pilgrimage or business which had taken him there.[180] A charter in the cartulary of Cluny records the journey that Henry, bishop of Winchester, made to Rome probably in 1149.[181] The main reason for his visit, however, seems to have been to seek absolution for his non-attendance at the Council of Reims in 1148.

While charters of religious houses in France dated to the twelfth century continue to produce the names of large numbers of individuals travelling to Jerusalem and to a lesser extent to Compostela, few references exist to individuals who certainly undertook pilgrimages to Rome in the twelfth century. This is all the more striking when compared with the relatively large number of names of *Romipetae* which survive in charters dated to the eleventh century. We might ask whether this decline in the number of references to Rome pilgrims in these twelfth-century charters can be explained by the fact that scribes were failing to record these journeys in the charters. If, however, this were the case, we might expect the same to be true of references to Compostela, yet in the charters which I have examined these in fact become more numerous in the twelfth century. Furthermore, if the lack of Rome references in the twelfth century is to be explained in this way, then what we might expect to find is the number of such references declining slowly, perhaps from the later eleventh century onwards. What emerges in fact is that Rome references stop very dramatically in the early years of the twelfth century and unless we believe that large numbers of scribes over a wide geographical area ceased to record such journeys at much the same time, then this explanation seems flawed. Furthermore, the few Rome references which persist in the cartularies of St Victor and St Vincent, both in Le Mans, Noyers in the diocese of Tours, Talmond in the diocese of Poitiers, Gellone in the diocese of

---

[175] Savigny, vol. 1, no. 878.

[176] Noyers, no. 297.

[177] Gellone, no. 219.

[178] Saint Victeur au Mans, no. 21.

[179] Second Cartulary of Saint Vincent du Mans, no. 223.

[180] Marcigny-sur-Loire, no. 114.

[181] Cluny, vol. 5, no. 4142. It is unclear how many visits Henry of Blois made to Rome. Chibnall (John of Salisbury, *Historia Pontificalis*, pp. 91–94) believes that he made two journeys, one in the autumn of 1148, to seek absolution from the pope, although he may not have gone to Rome itself, but to wherever the Curia was. She believes that Henry returned home via Cluny where he granted the charter early in 1149. It is likely, Chibnall argues, that Henry was also in Rome in 1149–1150, from where he returned via Compostela, probably with the ancient statues that he had bought up in Rome. See *Historia Pontificalis*, pp. 78–80.

Montpellier and Savigny in the Lyonaisse, indicate that in these places at least there is no reason to believe that Rome pilgrimages were not being recorded. The impression given by this small sample of cartulary evidence seems to be that pilgrimages to Rome may have been fewer in number in the twelfth century than in the eleventh and that Jerusalem and Compostela were more popular destinations.

Unfortunately the cartularies of English religious houses are far less helpful than their Frankish counterparts. Rarely are the reasons given for a particular gift to a religious house, although where the occasional references to pilgrimages in twelfth-century charters do occur, they have been to either Jerusalem or Compostela but not to Rome. A charter in the cartulary of Eynsham, dated to 1109, records the death of Hardingus of Oxford in Jerusalem.[182] The cartulary of Burton records the pilgrimage of Robert, earl of Ferrers, to Santiago de Compostela c.1140.[183] Before setting out for Jerusalem c.1155–1160, William Fossard I made a gift of three carucates in Hawold to the nuns of Watton.[184] We also know that Henry of Gousla set out for the Holy Land c.1152,[185] as did Henry de Lascy c.1155.[186] Geoffrey of Rouen departed for Compostela sometime before 1157[187] and Roger of Mowbray c.1175–1182,[188] John of Penigeston c.1188–1190,[189] Walter of La Nair c.1188–1191,[190] Fulk of Rofford c.1190[191] and a certain William c.1190,[192] all for the Holy Land. The cartulary of Blyth Priory records the grant made before 1210, by Robert, son of Roger of Bevercotes, to Robert, son of Ralph of Bevercotes, of a bovate of land in Bevercotes and a meadow, for his service and the journey he made on his behalf to the shrine of St James at Compostela.[193]

Another English source, the Curia Regis Rolls, also contains a number of references to pilgrims. These Rolls record disputes over land ownership and sometimes deal with the land of pilgrims who had died on their journey. Other individuals are mentioned in disputes as being unable to give evidence

---

182 Eynsham, vol. 1, no. 7.
183 Burton, p. 50. See also M. Jones, 'The Charters of Robert II De Ferrars, Earl of Nottingham, Derby and Ferrars', Nottingham Medieval Studies, 24 (1980), pp. 7–26, esp. p. 11.
184 Early Yorkshire Charters, ed. W. Farrer et al., 12 vols. (Edinburgh, 1914–1965), vol. 2, no. 1095.
185 Ibid., vol. 3, no. 1342.
186 Ibid., vol. 3, no. 1503.
187 Fountains, vol. 1, no. 38. On the date of this pilgrimage, see Early Yorkshire Families, ed. C. Clay and D. E. Greenway (1973), p. 108.
188 Early Yorkshire Charters, vol. 1, no. 547.
189 Ibid., vol. 3, no. 1787.
190 Ibid., vol. 3, no. 1409.
191 Ibid., vol. 1, no. 556
192 Ibid., vol. 3, no. 1641.
193 Blyth, vol. 2, p. 512. For other references see Abingdon, vol. 1, no. L226 and vol. 2, no. C225; Blyth, vol. 1, p. 30; Brinkburn, no. 12; Fountains, vol. 1, no. 44 and pp. 159 and 205; Gloucester, vol. 1, pp 9 and 81; Gyseburn, vol. 1, no. 565; Haughmond, no. 1067; Hospital of St John the Baptist, vol. 2, no. 626; Whitburn, vol. 1, no. 1.

because they are absent on pilgrimage. It is unfortunate that these records only begin in 1199, yet it is perhaps still worth considering the destinations which are recorded. Disputes dated to 1199 contain three references to pilgrimages to Jerusalem,[194] those of 1200 three references to Jerusalem and one to Compostela[195] and those of 1201, two to Compostela.[196] In these years there are no mentions of any *Romipetae*. In fact, in the disputes recorded up to 1216, whilst there are references to twenty-nine pilgrims travelling to Jerusalem and ten to Compostela, only one is mentioned as travelling to Rome.[197]

Twelfth-century English enthusiasm for St James is further indicated by other evidence. A study of the dedication of monastic houses before the Norman Conquest in 1066 reveals that by far the most popular dedication was to the Virgin. In second place were dedications to St Peter and in third those to St Michael.[198] A similar study for the period 1066–1100 reveals only a slight change. Still most popular were dedications to the Virgin and then to St Peter. In joint third place now were dedications to the Holy Trinity and St Nicholas.[199] A significant change, however, is noticeable in the first half of the twelfth century. Whilst dedications to the Virgin were by far the most numerous, now in second place were dedications to St James, while dedications to St Peter alone were only fourth in popularity.[200] Binns has linked the large number of church dedications to St James to the growing fame of his shrine at Santiago, while noting that an added impetus may also have been the acquisition of the hand of St James by Reading Abbey c.1125.[201] This evidence from France and England, therefore, seems to suggest that in the twelfth century pilgrimage to Rome may have been less popular than pilgrimage either to Jerusalem and Compostela.

Reasons for a Decline in Pilgrimage to Rome in the Twelfth Century

Whilst this investigation of a small sample of surviving source material, therefore, suggests that pilgrimage to Rome may have been less popular in the twelfth century than it had been in the eleventh, at least amongst the Christians of Western Europe, what should be asked now is whether the impression given by this random selection of material is likely to be correct.

---

[194] *Curia Regis Rolls of the Reigns of Richard I and John* (London, 1922), Richard I-John II, pp. 69, 97, 85.
[195] *Ibid.*, for Jerusalem pp. 133, 143, 219 and for Compostela p. 151.
[196] *Ibid.*, pp. 417 and 432.
[197] For the only Rome pilgrimage of these years see, 8–10 John, p. 284.
[198] A. Binns, *Dedications of Monastic Houses in England and Wales 1066–1216* (Woodbridge, 1989), pp. 18–19.
[199] *Ibid.*, pp. 22–26.
[200] *Ibid.*, pp. 26–30.
[201] *Ibid.*, pp. 27–28.

Are there reasons why pilgrimage to Rome might have fallen off or become less popular in the twelfth century?

We know that the journey to Rome in the twelfth century was particularly difficult, with travel through the Italian peninsula being especially dangerous.[202] In addition, for much of the twelfth century the apostolic city itself was in turmoil, rent by warring factions and papal schism. This strife reached a peak in 1143 with the establishment of the Roman Commune and again in 1167 when Frederick Barbarossa's troops sacked the city and attacked S. Pietro itself.[203]

If pilgrims were wary of the difficulties in undertaking a journey to Rome, then they may have been further deterred from travelling there by the numerous and bitter criticisms of the apostolic city and the papacy which were rife by the twelfth century.[204] In c.1145 Arnold of Brescia condemned the College of Cardinals as a 'place of business' and a 'den of thieves'.[205] John of Salisbury also recorded Arnold's attack upon Pope Eugenius III (1145–1153): 'a man of blood . . . a tormentor of churches and oppressor of the innocent, who did nothing . . . save gratify his lust and empty other men's coffers to fill his own'.[206] Arnold of Brescia was not alone in his criticisms and St Bernard himself was moved to ask of this same pope, 'who can you quote me in the city who acknowledged your position as pope without a bribe or hope of a bribe?'[207] In a letter of 1188 addressed to Geoffrey, sub-prior at Canterbury, Brother John explained the difficulties of getting cases heard at the curia. Worst of all was the cost, which led him to believe that he would be better off falling amongst thieves than to be caught by the snares of the curia.[208] Extortion, he firmly believed, was the reason why there was now so much contempt for Rome.[209] Walter Map (c.1140–c.1210) was another fierce critic. 'The name of Rome', he wrote, 'is made up of the letters R and O and M and A, and the definition, along with the word itself is *Radix Omnium Malorum Avaricia*.'[210] He also told the story of Reginald FitzJocelin, 'elected

---

[202] See above pp. 50–51.

[203] *Liber Pontificalis*, vol. 2, p. 416. His army, however, was devastated by malaria. See *ibid.*, vol. 2, p. 418.

[204] Schmugge, 'Über nationale Vorurteile im Mittelalter', pp. 452–453; J. A. Yunck, 'Economic Conservatism, Papal Finance and the Medieval Satires on Rome', *Medieval Studies*, 23 (1961), pp. 334–351.

[205] John of Salisbury, *Historia Pontificalis*, pp. 64–65. On Arnold of Brescia, see R. I. Moore, *The Origins of European Dissent* (London, 1977), pp. 115–136.

[206] John of Salisbury, *Historia Pontificalis*, p. 65.

[207] St Bernard, *De Consideratione*, PL 182, col. 774.

[208] *Epistolae Cantuarienses*, pp. 213–215.

[209] *Ibid.*, p. 214. Complaints about the curia were also voiced, for example, by Thomas Becket, archbishop of Canterbury. See *Materials for the History of Thomas Becket*, vol. 7, pp. 280 and 284.

[210] Walter Map, *De Nugis Curialum*, pp. 168–169. Walter Map also wrote poems attacking the avarice of the curia. See *Latin Poems commonly attributed to Walter Mapes*, ed. T. Wright, Camden Society, 16 (London, 1841), esp. pp. 36–39 and 217–222.

by violence' to the see of Bath in 1173.[211] Refused consecration by the archbishop of Canterbury, Map claims he was advised by his father Jocelin, bishop of Salisbury, to hurry off to the pope.[212] 'Give him a good smack with a heavy purse and he will tumble which way you like.'[213]

Also extant is the anonymous satire, entitled *Novus regnat Salomon in diebus malis*, which was a direct attack upon Pope Innocent III.[214] The satire begins with standard complaints about the evil and corruption of the times and goes on to direct attention to the main cause of this evil, which the author reckoned to be the pope himself. Perhaps one of the most virulent attacks made against Innocent in this satire is that he was a bad pastor to his flock. Innocent is blamed in particular for failing to tackle the Cathar heresy which spread through northern Italy.[215] The pope is likened to a shepherd who has abandoned his flock, leaving it to the mercy of wolves. 'Where is our pastor', the author of the satire complained, 'where our leader?'[216]

Nor was the anonymous author of this satire the only critic of the papacy at the time of Innocent III. Alexander Neckam, abbot of Cirencester, attended the Fourth Lateran Council in 1215. Afterwards he wrote what might be termed a 'farewell to Rome', in which he told of his longing for the cloister and his fear of the curia.[217] He was a lover of books, he wrote, not a lover of money and found the thought of a grassy mound far more appealing than a marble tomb.[218] Matthew Paris, a noted critic of Innocent III, later accused this pope of refusing to allow those who had attended the Fourth Lateran Council to depart until they had each handed over a large sum of money.[219]

If the biographer of the eleventh-century pope, Leo IX, could claim that this pope's reputation for sanctity had increased the popularity of pilgrimage to Rome, then perhaps the bitter criticisms of the twelfth-century papacy had the opposite effect.[220] Evidence that the city's declining reputation may really have affected attitudes towards travelling there is provided by Roger of Wen-

---

[211] Walter Map, *De Nugis Curialum*, pp. 68–69.

[212] *Ibid.*, pp. 68–69.

[213] *Ibid.*, pp. 68–69. The editors note that Reginald was duly consecrated bishop of Bath by the archbishops of Canterbury and Tarentaise on 23 June 1174 on Alexander III's orders, after Reginald had visited the papal curia.

[214] M. Th. D'Alvery, '*Novus Regnat Saloman in diebus malis*. Une satire contre Innocent III', *Festschrift Bernhard Bischoff*, ed. J. Autenreith and F. Brunhölzl (Stuttgart, 1971), pp. 372–390.

[215] *Ibid.*, pp. 384–385, stanzas xii–xiii.

[216] *Ibid.*, p. 385, stanza xiv.

[217] Alexander Neckam, *De Laudibus Divinae Sapientiae*, ed. T. Wright, RS 34 (London, 1863), p. 448.

[218] *Ibid.*, p. 391.

[219] Matthew Paris, *Chronica Majora*, vol. 4, p. 70. Innocent may have had critics, but he also had admirers. The author of the *Annales S. Iustinae Patavini* (MGH.SS 19, p. 151), for example, described him as '. . . viro magnifico et prudenti, cuius magnanimitas et constantia super alios homines excellebat'.

[220] Wibert, *Vita S. Leonis*, PL 143, col. 490.

dover. In the past rulers like Caedwalla of Wessex (d.689), Cenred of Mercia (d.c.709), Offa of Essex (d.c.709) and Ine, king of Wessex until 726, had abandoned their kingdoms to live as pilgrims at the tomb of St Peter in Rome,[221] whilst others like Offa of Mercia in 793, Sigeric of Essex in 798 and Cnut in 1027 had also travelled to the apostolic city on pilgrimage. Roger, however, recounts how in 1190 King Richard, on his way to the Holy Land, passed within a few miles of Rome and was invited by Octavian, cardinal bishop of Ostia, to visit the pope there.[222] The king refused to set foot in the city, reproaching the cardinal for the simony, greed and many other abuses rampant there.[223] Rome was no longer regarded as the holy and spiritual city that it had been hitherto. Indeed Conrad, abbot of Ursperg, expressed the opinion of many at the time, that people were drawn to Rome not for reasons of devotion but to obtain legal decisions which could be bought for a price.[224]

Criticisms of the papacy and the apostolic city in the twelfth and early thirteenth centuries, together with the difficulties of the journey, may have contributed to a decline in Rome's popularity with pilgrims at this time. Yet alone they surely cannot fully explain it, for these factors, particularly the dangers and difficulties of the journey, were not new. Perhaps, therefore, one of the most important factors was the growing competition which Rome now faced from other pilgrimage centres. Most important of these rival centres, as the cartulary evidence suggests, were firstly the Holy Land, now in Christian hands for the first time in almost 450 years, and secondly the shrine of St James at Compostela.

Jerusalem and the Holy Land

During the eleventh century pilgrimage to the Holy Land had become increasingly popular amongst both the older and the more recent converts to Christianity. Radulph Glaber noted that a major reason for this was the opening up of an overland route at the end of the tenth century following the conversion of Hungary to Christianity.[225] Taking advantage of this new route, he recorded, many men and women, of all social classes, began to undertake

---

221 See C. Stancliffe, 'Kings who opted out', *Ideal and Reality in Frankish and Anglo-Saxon Society. Studies presented to J. M. Wallace-Hadrill*, ed. P. Wormald, D. Bullough and R. Collins (Oxford, 1983), pp. 154–176.

222 Roger of Wendover, *Flores Historiarum*, ed. H. G. Hewlett, 3 vols. RS 84 (London, 1886–1889), vol. 1, p. 183.

223 *Ibid.*, vol. 1, p. 183. According to Roger, Richard cited a number of examples of the curia's greed, such as the seven hundred marks taken for the consecration of the bishop of Le Mans, the 1,500 marks taken from the bishop of Ely, and the *pecuniam infinitam* extracted from the archbishop of Bordeaux.

224 Conrad of Ursperg, *Chronicon* (1609), p. 199.

225 Radulph Glaber, *Historiarum Libri Quinque*, ed. and trans. J. France, Oxford Medieval Texts (Oxford, 1989), pp. 96–97.

the pilgrimage in very large numbers.[226] This stream of pilgrims turned into a flood during the twelfth century, as the success of the First Crusade, which resulted in the recapture of Jerusalem in 1099, stimulated further interest in Holy Land pilgrimage. John of Würzburg, in Jerusalem in 1170, was clearly astonished by the variety of people whom he found there; Greeks, Bulgarians, English, Franks, Latins, Germans, Scots, Navarrese and Bretons comprise just a small selection from his long list.[227] As the popularity of Holy Land pilgrimage steadily increased, we should not be surprised if this affected the popularity of Rome. After all, if, as scholars suggest, the apostolic city owed its rise in popularity as a pilgrimage centre during the seventh century in part to the loss of the Holy Land, then the recovery of the holy places by the crusaders may well have had the opposite effect upon Rome's popularity in the twelfth century. In Rome pilgrims would find the bodies of two of Christ's apostles but in Jerusalem they could follow in the footsteps of Christ himself and here too they 'could see and touch the places where Christ was present in the body'.[228]

Compostela

Another major pilgrimage centre which flourished in the twelfth century was the shrine of St James at Compostela.[229] The body of a man believed to be this apostle had been discovered in the north-west corner of Spain in the first half of the ninth century by Theodomir, bishop of Iria.[230] King Alfonso II (791–842) had a church built on the site but it seems to have been Alfonso III (866–910) who did most to promote the cult, perhaps as Fletcher suggests, because the king of Asturia now wanted a saint of his own in the manner of the Carolingians.[231]

---

[226] *Ibid.*, pp. 198–201.

[227] John of Wurzburg's account of his pilgrimage to the Holy Land can be found in *Jerusalem Pilgrimage*, pp. 244–273. For the different people who travelled there see esp. p. 273.

[228] Paulinus of Nola, *Epistolae*, col. 407.

[229] On Compostela, see for example: *Peregrinaciones a Santiago*; V. and H. Hell, *The Great Pilgrimage of the Middle Ages. The Road to St James of Compostela*, trans. A. Jaffa (London, 1966); H. and M. H. Davies, *Holy Days and Holidays. The Medieval Pilgrimage to Compostela* (Lewisburg, 1982); J. S. Stone, *The Cult of Santiago* (London, 1927); C. M. Storrs, 'Jacobean Pilgrims from England from the Early Twelfth to the Late Fifteenth Century', unpublished M.A. thesis (University of London, 1964); D. W. Lomax, 'The First English Pilgrims to Santiago de Compostela', *Studies in Medieval History Presented to R. H. C. Davis*, ed. H. Mayr-Harting and R. I. Moore (London and Ronceverte, 1985), pp. 165–175; R. B. Tate, *Pilgrimages to St James of Compostela from the British Isles during the Middle Ages* (Liverpool, 1990).

[230] On the discovery of the body of St James, see Fletcher, *St James's Catapult*, pp. 53–77; T. D. Kendrick, *St James in Spain* (London, 1960), pp. 13–19.

[231] Fletcher, *St James's Catapult*, pp. 68–69.

We do not know who the earliest pilgrims to the shrine of St James were. The first references to such visitors seem, not surprisingly, to date to the reign of Alfonso III,[232] while the first surviving record of a foreign pilgrim is that of Godesalc, bishop of Le Puy, who was there in 951.[233] Other distinguished visitors followed, among them the abbot of Montserrat in 959 and Hugh, bishop of Reims, in 961.[234] In the course of the following centuries pilgrimage to Compostela seems to have become increasingly popular and by 1121 the author of the *Historia Compostellana*, in describing the visit of two envoys of the Almoravid sultan of Morocco, could record their astonishment at the hugh crowds which they saw coming and going.[235] The author of the *Veneranda dies* sermon emphasised the international nature of these crowds. Franks, Scots, Normans, Lorrainers, Romans, Apulians, Frisians, Saxons, Dacians, Bithinians, Bulgarians, Capadocians and the *impii Navarri* were just a small selection of those travelling to Compostela.[236]

The popularity of pilgrimage to the shrine of St James is perhaps more difficult to explain than the popularity of travelling to the Holy Land. Pilgrimage to Compostela may have been stimulated in part by a romantic association with the *Reconquista* and St James' leading role as patron of this crusading movement.[237]

It is also likely that pilgrimage to his shrine was considered a worthy alternative either by those unwilling to face the dangers of a journey to Rome or by those disillusioned with the apostolic city. As one historian has noted, the journey to the end of the Iberian Peninsula combined many of the features of the journey to Rome: it involved a journey of similar length and the crossing of a high mountain range.[238] Furthermore, at Compostela, as at Rome, the pilgrim would also find the body of an apostle.

Another possibility is that pilgrimage to Compostela increased in popularity in the early twelfth century because of successful marketing. Diego Gelmírez, elected bishop of Compostela in 1100, ensured that the city enjoyed a high profile.[239] By 1108 he had acquired from Paschal II the right to have a number of cardinals amongst his clergy, who were distinguished from the rest by the special liturgical privileges which they enjoyed.[240] The right to

---

[232] *Ibid.*, p. 79.

[233] *Ibid.*, p. 81.

[234] Storrs, *Jacobean Pilgrims*, p. 23.

[235] *Historia Compostellana*, pp. 350–351.

[236] *Liber Sancti Jacobi*, vol. 1, p. 148.

[237] According to legend St James had made a personal appearance in 834 at the Battle of Clavijo. After this battle, he became commonly known as *Santiago Matamoros* (St James the Moor-slayer) and was attributed with the killing of sixty thousand Moors single-handed. Davies, *Holy Days and Holidays*, p. 58.

[238] Bull, *Knightly Piety*, esp. p. 232.

[239] The best work on Diego is undoubtedly Fletcher, *St James's Catapult*. See also A. G. Biggs, *Diego Gelmírez, First Archbishop of Compostela* (Washington, 1949).

[240] On these non-Roman cardinals and their liturgical privileges, see S. Kuttner, 'Cardi-

appoint cardinals was by no means common and had been granted to only a small number of sees: Magdeburg (968), Treves (975), Aix-la-Chapelle (997), Besançon (1051) and Cologne (1052).[241] As well as the right to appoint cardinals, Diego was also successful in obtaining metropolitan status for his bishopric in 1124.[242] In addition, he continued the rebuilding of the cathedral at Compostela[243] and tried to foster and encourage pilgrimage through the legislation intended to protect pilgrims and their property.[244] So successful was Diego Gelmírez in building up his own reputation and that of Compostela, that his enemies seem to have had no difficulty in convincing Pope Honorius II that Diego frequently affected the papal dress and acted as the pope when receiving the offerings of pilgrims at Compostela.[245] Honorius seems to have taken these accusations so seriously that he wrote to the other Galician bishops asking if these accusations were true. He also instructed them that pilgrims were to be questioned on this matter and he even sent an envoy to Compostela to observe Diego.[246]

The promotion of Compostela seems to have continued during the twelfth century. The sermons contained in the so-called Codex Calixtinus, dating from the middle of this century, seem to have been intent upon promoting the image of St James over his holy rivals, particularly those in Rome. For St James was portrayed not only as the protector of pilgrims, playing upon fears of the dangers of travel,[247] but also as a healer.[248] Nor was this the end of the claims. Christ, one sermon recounted, 'offered the first place among the apostles to his . . . blessed James because he triumphed first as a martyr'.[249] St James shines 'in the brilliant court of the apostles as the glittering sun amid the stars'.[250] Nor it seems was there any attempt to correct the mistaken belief that drew many pilgrims here, that Compostela possessed the body of another James, the brother of Christ himself.[251]

nalis: The History of a Canonical Concept', Traditio, 3 (1945), pp. 129–214, esp. pp. 165–170.

[241] Ibid., pp. 165–166.
[242] Fletcher, St James's Catapult, pp. 196–212.
[243] See below p. 178.
[244] See above, p. 177.
[245] Historia Compostellana, p. 489.
[246] Ibid., pp. 489–490.
[247] See for example Liber Sancti Jacobi, vol. 1, p. 176
[248] The small miracle collection has been reproduced in Liber Sancti Jacobi, vol. 1, pp. 259–287. On these miracles, see Ward, Miracles and the Medieval Mind, esp. pp. 110–117.
[249] Liber Sancti Jacobi, vol. 1, p. 39.
[250] Ibid., vol. 1, p. 209.
[251] Davies, Holy Days and Holidays, p. 52.

Welfare Provisions in Jerusalem and Compostela

The popularity of both the Holy Land and Compostela with twelfth-century pilgrims can be confirmed by other evidence, particularly the growing need to provide facilities for pilgrims, as well as the evidence of church building. At Jerusalem the influx of pilgrims was so large that practical provisions had to be undertaken on a considerable scale. Here the efforts of the Military Orders, the Templars and Hospitallers, were particularly important. The size of some of their hospices were unique in Christendom. During the construction of the hospital of St John in Jerusalem, the Patriarch, Fulcher, had complained c.1150 that 'at the very door of the Holy Resurrection', the Hospitallers were erecting buildings 'which were much more costly and lofty,' than the church itself.[252] John of Würzburg recorded his own visit to this hospital c.1170, where he says he saw two thousand people accommodated. 'The house', he writes, 'feeds so many . . . outside and within, and it gives so huge an amount of alms to poor people . . . that certainly the total of expenses can in no way be counted.'[253]

Exactly the same sorts of provisioning became necessary at Compostela at this time. Even before he had become bishop in 1100, Diego Gelmírez had already established a hospice for poor pilgrims in Compostela itself.[254] As bishop he set aside half the alms received in the basilica for the support of this institution.[255] The influx of pilgrims also vividly demonstrated the inadequacy of the city's water supply. This problem too was tackled by Diego, under whose instructions an aqueduct was built. This brought water in from outside the city, delivering it through underground channels to a fountain just outside the basilica.[256] The *Guide to Compostela* records that from the centre of this fountain a bronze column arose, surmounted by four lions, from whose mouths the water gushed.[257] The bowl of this fountain was so large that it could accommodate fifteen people all bathing at once[258] and was so well made that it was impossible to see where the water came from.[259]

[252] William of Tyre, *Chronique*, ed. R. B. C. Huygens, 2 vols. *Corpus Christianorum Continuatio Mediaevalis*, 63 (Turnholti, 1986), book 18, chpt. 3, vol. 2, pp. 812–813.
[253] *Jerusalem Pilgrimage*, pp. 266–267.
[254] *Historia Compostellana*, p. 53.
[255] *Ibid.*, p. 53.
[256] *Ibid.*, pp. 369–370.
[257] *Guide du Pèlerin*, pp. 94–95.
[258] *Ibid.*, pp. 94–95.
[259] *Ibid.*, pp. 94–95.

Church Building in Jerusalem and Compostela

At both Compostela and Jerusalem large scale church building was also undertaken. The building of a new cathedral at Compostela had been initiated by Bishop Diego Paláez, deposed in 1088, and was continued by Gelmírez after his election in 1100.[260] According to the *Guide to Compostela*, the main architects were Bernard *senex*, described as *mirabilis magister*, and Robert, who worked in conjunction with about fifty other masons.[261] Their design for the new cathedral clearly shows that they were acutely aware of the need to provide for large numbers of pilgrims, incorporating into the design an ambulatory around the high altar, with five radiating chapels, as well as four transeptal chapels. The pilgrim visitors, for whom the new church was intended to cater, even played their own part in its construction, each one carrying a piece of limestone from Triacastela, probably to Castañeda, where it was burnt for lime before being transported to Compostela.[262] It is likely that much of the east end of the new cathedral had been completed by 1088[263] and, if the *Historia Compostellana* is correct, then 'the greater part' of the church had been finished by 1124.[264]

A description of the cathedral can be found in the *Guide to Compostela*. This gives the measurements of the new church as 'in length fifty-three times a man's stature . . . in width thirty-nine times'.[265] It also lists the windows, towers and portals, of which the west, the author reckoned, was the most exquisite with its sculptured images of men, women, birds, beasts, saints, angels and flowers, together with a carving of the Lord's Transfiguration.[266] After the completion of the basilica itself, however, Diego Gelmírez seems to have initiated another building campaign c.1125. Its purpose was the erection of a cloister. This, the *Historia Compostellana* informs us, the archbishop had decided to build partly as a result of the unfavourable gibes of pilgrims, who had remarked on the lack of one![267]

In Jerusalem, too, extensive building projects were undertaken, largely stimulated by the influx of pilgrims. The most important was undoubtedly

---

[260] On the rebuilding of the Cathedral at Compostela, see K. J. Conant, *The Early Architectural History of the Cathedral of Santiago de Compostela* (Cambridge, Mass., 1926); W. M. Whitehill, *Spanish Romanesque Architecture of the Eleventh Century* (Oxford, 1941), pp. 266–284.

[261] *Guide du Pèlerin*, pp. 116–117.

[262] *Liber Sancti Jacobi*, vol. 1, p. 352.

[263] The eastern parts of the cathedral were probably in use in the early years of the twelfth century, and in 1105 the high altar received its silver frontal. See Fletcher, *St James's Catapult*, p. 176.

[264] *Historia Compostellana*, p. 473.

[265] *Guide du Pèlerin*, pp. 86–87.

[266] *Ibid.*, pp. 102–105.

[267] *Ibid.*, pp. 473–474.

the construction of the church of the Holy Sepulchre.[268] In 1009 Constantine's church had been destroyed and the tomb of Christ razed to the ground. Between 1042 and 1048, under the instructions of the Byzantine Emperor, Constantine IX Monomachos, the latter was replaced by a masonry replica while over it the rotunda was rebuilt as a circular church. After the recapture of Jerusalem in 1099, however, the steady increase in pilgrimage rendered the Byzantine building inadequate and resulted in the incorporation of the Holy Sepulchre, Calvary and St Helena's Chapel within a single Romanesque church. The church was lavishly decorated with mosaics and frescoes and was consecrated on 15 July 1149, the fiftieth anniversary of the capture of the city.

Libri Indulgentiarum

There seems to be little doubt about the popularity of Jerusalem and Compostela amongst pilgrims in the twelfth century. That both these pilgrimage centres were regarded as serious rivals to Rome is clearly suggested by other, later evidence. Libri Indulgentiarum, dating from the fourteenth and fifteenth centuries, which record the huge indulgences available at many of Rome's churches by that time, have survived in large numbers.[269] A metrical version in English, entitled Stacions of Rome, is perhaps one of the better known.[270] This informs the reader, for example, that those who travelled from overseas to see the Veronica qualified for twelve thousand years of remission.[271] The Romans themselves were granted three thousand. Every day at S. Lorenzo fuori le mura seven thousand years of remission could be obtained,[272] while at S. Prassede, an unspecified Pope Innocent is said to have granted every pilgrim a thousand years' pardon.[273]

One of the most interesting features of this text, however, is the way in which the remission to be gained at Rome is promoted above that of other pilgrimage centres. Firstly, we are told that those who go to the basilica of S. Paulo every Sunday of the year will receive as much remission as if they went on a pilgrimage to the shrine of St James.[274] Secondly, the Stacions tell us that

---

[268] C. Coüasnon, The Church of the Holy Sepulchre in Jerusalem (London, 1974), pp. 54–62; B. Hamilton, 'Rebuilding Zion: The Holy Places of Jerusalem in the Twelfth Century', SCH, 14 (1977), pp. 105–116, esp. pp. 105–107.

[269] See the article by Hulbert, 'Some Medieval Advertisements of Rome', pp. 403–424. On indulgences, see Riley-Smith, What were the Crusades?, pp. 57–62.

[270] Stacions of Rome and the Pilgrims Sea Voyage, ed. F. J. Furnivall, Early English Text Society (London, 1867).

[271] Ibid., p. 3.

[272] Ibid., p. 13.

[273] Ibid., p. 18.

[274] Ibid., p. 4.

'if man did but know the pardon to be had in Rome, he would not go to the Holy Land, for in Rome is pardon without end'.[275]

Nor is this Indulgence Book the only one which attempts to promote Rome's attractions over those of its rivals. Other versions incorporated the same theme. BL Harley 2321 is a Latin prose text, which attempts to persuade its readers that the indulgences at the church of S. Giovanni in Laterano are so numerous that it is not necessary for men to cross the sea to the Holy Sepulchre in Jerusalem.[276] Another text, listing all the indulgences that were available in Rome's principle churches, recorded that if men did but know the remission which was to be had there, it would not be necessary for them to travel to Jerusalem or to St James in Galicia.[277] It seems unlikely that the competition between Rome and its two holy rivals, Jerusalem and Compostela, originated only in the fourteenth century. Rather these texts reflect a rivalry which had begun much earlier and which research detailed above suggests probably had its origins in the twelfth century.

Promotion of Rome in the Twelfth Century?

This promotion of pilgrimage to Rome in the *Libri Indulgentiarum* of the fourteenth and fifteenth centuries is perhaps what the city most lacked in the twelfth century. The obvious person to promote pilgrimage to Rome at this time was the pope. Like many of their predecessors, some of the popes of the twelfth century tried to provide accommodation for pilgrims[278] and most were interested in building and repairing the city's churches.[279]

It is likely, however, that by the twelfth century these activities were no longer sufficient. The dangers of the journey, combined with the city's declining spiritual reputation and the competition from other important pilgrimage centres, meant that a large and continuous flow of pilgrims *ad limina apostolorum* could no longer be taken for granted. What Rome needed was popes who would vigorously promote and encourage pilgrimage to the city. Some of them seem to have tried. Calixtus II made some efforts in this direction by trying to make the journey to Rome safer. He put an end to the activities of

---

275 *Ibid.*, p. 10.
276 British Library MS Harley 2321, fol. 104.
277 Quoted by Hulbert, 'Some Medieval Advertisements of Rome', p. 405.
278 See above, pp. 135–143.
279 On church building in Rome in the twelfth century, see Krautheimer, *Rome*, pp. 161–202; M. E. Avagnina, V. Garibaldi and C. Salterini, 'Strutture murarie degli edifici religiosa di Roma nel XII secolo', *Rivista dell'Instituto Nazionale d'Archeologia e Storia dell'Arte*, n.s. (1976–1977), pp. 173–255; J. E. Barclay Lloyd, 'Masonry Techniques in Medieval Rome, c.1080–c.1300', *PBSR*, 53 (1985), pp. 225–277; D. F. Glass, *Studies on Cosmatesque Pavements*, BAR International Series, 82 (Pennsylvania, 1980); H. Toubert, 'Le Renouveau Paléochrétien à Rome au Début du XIIe Siècle', *Cahiers Archéologiques*, 20 (1970), pp. 99–154.

the bandit Burdinus who was accustomed to attack pilgrims on their way to Rome[280] and in canon 14 of the First Lateran Council of 1123 singled out *Romipetae* as deserving of special protection.[281] In addition he attempted to promote Rome's links with St Peter, renewing the high altar in the basilica, which he consecrated in 1123.[282] Alexander III also seems to have tried to promote pilgrimage to Rome especially by granting indulgences for the making of the journey. In a letter of 1181, addressed to the archbishop and bishops of Sweden, Alexander III expressed his belief that pilgrims travelling to the apostolic city should each be rewarded according to their labour.[283] All those travelling from Sweden to Rome, therefore, were to receive three years' remission of penance. Those travelling from England were to receive two years and those journeying lesser distances, just one.[284]

That there were only a few attempts to promote pilgrimage to Rome by the popes of the twelfth century, however, is perhaps not surprising. For much of the twelfth century conflict with the emperor and then with the Roman commune had meant that many of the popes were unable to maintain their positions in the city.[285] Paschal II spent long periods out of Rome, taking refuge in France in 1106–1107, as did Gelasius II in 1118, dying at Cluny in January 1119. His successor Calixtus II does not seem to have been able to enter Rome until June 1120, although Honorius II seems to have been relatively secure there, with only the winter of 1127–1128 being spent outside of the city. Innocent II, however, was driven out immediately after his election in 1130. He spent much of his exile in France and was unable to return to Rome until April 1133. Nor did he stay there long, spending most of 1134–1136 at Pisa and then travelling to southern Italy in 1137. He eventually re-entered Rome in November 1137. Celestine II's short six month pontificate seems to have been spent in Rome, as does that of Lucius II, although his position was far from secure and he died whilst trying to recapture the Capitol where the Senate was installed. Eugenius III, elected in 1145, seems to have entered the city briefly in December of that year but departed again in March 1146 and spent much of 1147 and 1148 in France. He returned briefly to Rome in December 1149, only to leave again in June 1150, returning once more in December 1152. His successor Anastasius IV seems to have been able to maintain his position in Rome, although Hadrian IV died at Anagni in September 1159. The new pope, Alexander III, was consecrated at Ninfa and entered Rome in September 1159, only to be driven out almost immediately. He seems to have spent most of 1160 and

---

[280] *Liber Pontificalis*, vol. 2, p. 323; Andreae Danduli, *Chronicon*, col. 269.

[281] *Conciliorum Oecumenicorum Decreta*, p. 193.

[282] Toynbee and Ward Perkins, *Shrine of St Peter*, pp. 223–224.

[283] Alexander III, *Epistolae et Privilegia*, col. 1316.

[284] *Ibid.*, col. 1316.

[285] See the dating clauses of papal correspondence listed in Jaffé and Potthast. On the papacy in the twelfth century, see I. S. Robinson, *The Papacy 1073–1198. Continuity and Innovation* (Cambridge, 1990).

early 1161 at Anagni, making a brief return to Rome in June 1161. He left again in the same month and travelled to France in the following year. His sojourn there lasted until 1165 and in the December of that year he was back at the Lateran. He was able to remain there during 1166 and early 1167 but had left again by the August of that year. He returned briefly in 1178 and again in 1179 but died in exile in 1181. Lucius III left Rome in March 1182, never to return, while his two successors Urban III and Gregory VIII never seem to have entered Rome at all. The papacy was returned to Rome by Clement III in 1188 but its position was still far from secure.

While these popes were engaged in such struggles, it is hardly surprising that few took time to consider the popularity of Rome amongst pilgrims at that time. Furthermore, it would probably also have been difficult to judge at first whether there was a decline in pilgrims travelling to the apostolic city. For large numbers of individuals continued to travel to Rome, especially those wanting to transact business at the papal court. Perhaps it was not until institutions such as the *Schola Saxonum* got into difficulties towards the end of the twelfth century that the issue of the city's popularity as a pilgrimage centre became a significant item on the papal agenda. It certainly seems to have been an important issue for Innocent III, whose pontificate witnessed the first sustained attempt to encourage and foster pilgrimage to Rome.[286]

In the twelfth century Rome seems to have lagged behind its holy rivals. It was not even able to offer its pilgrims a token or badge, something which the *Veneranda dies* sermon shows that both the Holy Land and Compostela were able to offer at least by the middle of the twelfth century.[287] While it is likely that pilgrimage to the apostolic city remained relatively popular amongst the Church's more recent converts, the Christians of Western Europe who had traditionally flocked to Rome now seem to have found that the Holy Land and Compostela were more attractive destinations. Thus, while the Hungarian hostel founded by King Stephen was still functioning in the thirteenth century, the English were unable or perhaps unwilling to provide the means to keep the Saxon hostel running.[288] By the twelfth century Rome had little to offer that the pilgrim could not find elsewhere and with the dangers of the journey and the city's poor spiritual reputation there can have been little incentive for the pilgrim to undertake the long and difficult road to Rome. Perhaps symbolic of Rome's declining fortunes with pilgrims in the twelfth century was the desecration perpetrated by the Viterbans in 1167, who stole the bronze doors from S. Pietro as well as the grills from the fountain in the atrium, in which so many pilgrims had washed themselves prior to approaching the tomb of St Peter.[289]

---

286 See below, pp. 187–194.
287 *Liber Sancti Jacobi*, vol. 1, pp. 153. On the significance and importance of these badges, see above, pp. 77–79.
288 See above, pp. 140–141.
289 *Gesta*, col. clxxxiii.

Why did Pilgrimage Centres Compete?

In concluding this chapter it is worth briefly considering why there was competition at all amongst pilgrimage centres. What did those who pro-moted a pilgrimage centre, great or small, hope to achieve? Pilgrimage, one of the powerful manifestations of popular religious fervour, brought a constant flow of pilgrims to the tomb of a saint or martyr, which reaffirmed the importance of the particular shrine, bringing it prestige and spiritual renown. Competition to achieve such prestige was fierce among both monasteries and towns. Geary has pointed out that in the mid-sixth century, the translation to Ravenna of relics of Saints Andrew, John the Baptist, John the Evangelist and Thomas, together with relics of four other apostles, was an attempt to increase the city's ecclesiastical importance over that of Milan, Rome and Aquileia.[290] Nor was it a coincidence that in the twelfth century, the growing popularity of Bari with pilgrims suddenly led to the Venetians' 'rediscovery' of their patron, St Mark.[291]

Yet while pride in their relics and the desire for prestige were important motives for those who sought to promote a pilgrimage centre, they might also gain the added benefit of increased revenues. Geary has argued, in relation to monasteries in particular, that the maintenance of lay patronage was essential to their survival and that competition for this patronage could not be ig-nored.[292] In the ninth century the monks at Conques found themselves in competition for patronage with the newly founded monastery of Figeac. Figeac seems to have enjoyed a rather more favourable location to that of Conques and so the monks of the latter decided that they now needed the relics of an important saint which would attract the pilgrims back again. It was for this reason, therefore, that they stole the relics of St Foy from the monks of Agen.[293] Geary shows that the monks of Figeac were not to be outdone, retaliating by acquiring for themselves the relics of St Bibanus.[294] The monastery which failed to acquire for itself relics of an important saint, which would attract endowments and oblations, might not survive.

Other evidence shows the potential importance of the profit motive. The *Deeds of the Abbots of St Trond* contains a story about an English monk who had sought hospitality at the monastery of St Trond c.1199.[295] Here he was told by the monks of the house how sometime before the miracles performed by St Trond had brought them great wealth. In return for his hospitality,

---

[290] Geary, *Furta Sacra*, p. 91.
[291] The body of St Nicholas was translated from Myra to Bari in 1087. The Venetians 'rediscovered' their patron with great ceremony in 1094. *Ibid.*, pp. 102–103.
[292] *Ibid.*, p. 58.
[293] On the theft of the relics of St Foy, *ibid.*, pp. 58–63. Two accounts of the translation of St Foy can be found in AASS Oct. III, pp. 289–299.
[294] *Ibid.*, p. 62.
[295] *Gesta Abbatum Trudonensium*, p. 391.

therefore, the English monk sought to please the abbot by 'creating' a miracle spring, through the laying of a system of underground pipes.[296] The news of this spring, reported to be a 'miracle' wrought by St Trond, soon spread and pilgrims flocked to the abbey once more, leaving much money upon the altar. The monks of St Trond, however, were unable to conceal this fraud for long and when news of it reached Pope Innocent III, he deprived the abbot of his mitre.[297]

Bari also seems to have sought to make its fortune from pilgrimage. The Norman Conquest of Bari combined with wars against Byzantium had resulted in a disruption of trade links between Bari and the East. This had led to a rise in the importance of the Venetian merchants who competed with those at Bari for the transport of grain from Apulia. Geary has shown that the translation of St Nicholas from Myra to Bari in 1087 was a response to this threat posed to Bari's economy by the Venetians.[298] If Bari was no longer able to compete with Venice in trade, then it could achieve status, prestige and money through the acquisition of a powerful patron, St Nicholas. Conant has shown that from the beginning it was intended that Bari should become an important pilgrimage centre.[299] Indeed as early as 1089 work was already well under way on the cathedral, which was carefully designed with crowds of pilgrims in mind; it was deliberately built with a large crypt with stairs placed at either side to allow easy and safe access.

The Treasurers' Rolls which survive from Canterbury may provide some indication of how much a successful shrine, like that of St Thomas Becket, martyred in 1170, might make from the oblations of pilgrims. It has been calculated that in the years 1198–1213 offerings averaged about £426 a year.[300] Offerings between 1213 and 1219 varied but in the Jubilee year of 1220, however, oblations were greatly increased, amounting to £1,142 and 5 shillings, an indication perhaps of the importance of such special events.[301] It would surely, however, be a mistake to assume that the oblations left by pilgrims were always pure profit. Although pilgrims might leave money at a particular tomb or altar, they themselves might also cost that church or holy place money. Indeed, if we consider Rome, Compostela or the Holy Land, all

---

[296] Ibid., p. 391.

[297] Ibid., p. 391.

[298] On the translation of St Nicholas, see Geary, Furta Sacra, pp. 94–103.

[299] Conant, Carolingian and Romanesque Architecture, pp. 214–216.

[300] C. E. Woodruff, 'The Financial Aspect of the Cult of St Thomas of Canterbury', Archaeologia Cantiana, 44 (1932), pp. 13–32, esp. p. 16.

[301] Ibid., pp. 17–18. An idea of the significance of these sums can be obtained by comparing them with calculations of the net annual value of the lands of the archbishopric of Canterbury. In three years of the first half of the thirteenth century, 1212, 1229 and 1232, the annual value of the archbishop's demesne was £1,409, £1,507 and £1,788. These sums are based on records in the Pipe Rolls of the reign of King John, for periods when the see was vacant. See F. R. H. Du Boulay, The Lordship of Canterbury. An essay on medieval society (London, 1966), pp. 240–246.

kinds of practical provisions had to made there for the influx of pilgrims. The building of accommodation, the laying on of a water supply, together with the construction of baths and fountains, as well as the need to provide food or to bury the dead, all cost money. That the oblations may sometimes have failed to cover the cost of such expenditure seems to be suggested by the Treasurers' Rolls from Canterbury. From these it can be shown that in 1220, the year of Jubilee when oblations reached a very high level, the allowance made to the cellarer for the entertainment of pilgrims was raised to more than £1,150, from a more normal average of about £440.[302]

Another way in which pilgrimage centres might raise money from their relics and avoid such expenditure was to carry the relics out among the people. Guibert of Nogent related the activities of the canons of Laon in 1112–1113.[303] Travelling around northern and central France and on a second trip even venturing as far as England, they carried with them their 'feretories and relics of the saints' with which 'they showed many miracles where they went'.[304] Many of these miracles involved the 'ordinary healing of sickness',[305] including the curing of a deaf and dumb man at the castle of Nesle.[306] Guibert, however, was more interested in the more unusual variety, such as the miraculous disintegration of a wedding ring, which had become stuck on the finger of a lady in Angers,[307] and the canons' safe delivery from pirates as they crossed the Channel.[308] Guibert describes the canons' activities, as 'the customary way . . . of raising money'.[309]

Those who promoted pilgrimage centres, therefore, seem to have been motivated first and foremost by the desire to achieve spiritual renown for their particular tomb or shrine. Most also undoubtedly hoped to make money from the pilgrims whom they attracted, although whether they would always have been able to do so is uncertain. In the twelfth century there were a number of shrines, like Bari, Canterbury, Cologne and above all Compostela, which were very well promoted and marketed. Rome, however, seems to have been a notable exception and as a result of the growing popularity of

---

[302] Woodruff, 'Financial Aspect', p. 18.
[303] Self and Society in Medieval France, pp. 191–197. See also J. S. P. Tatlock, 'The English Journey of the Laon Canons', Speculum, 8 (1933), pp. 454–465.
[304] Ibid., p. 191.
[305] Ibid., p. 195.
[306] Ibid., p. 194.
[307] Ibid., pp. 192–193.
[308] Ibid., pp. 194–195.
[309] Ibid., p. 191. Geary (Furta Sacra, pp. 63–65) argues that the carrying of relics around was often the way in which money was raised for church construction. This would also account for the activities of the canons of Laon, whose church seems to have been badly damaged by fire. See Self and Society in Medieval France, p. 190. See also P. Héliot and M.-L. Chastang, 'Quêtes et Voyages de Reliques au Profit des Eglises Françaises du Moyen Age', Revue d'Histoire Ecclesiastique, 59 (1964), pp. 789–822 and 60 (1965), pp. 5–32.

these newly fashionable shrines, together with the opening up of the Holy Land, pilgrimage *ad limina apostolorum* seems to have gone into decline. What Innocent III and his thirteenth-century successors managed to do to reverse this trend is examined in the following chapter.

8

The Thirteenth-Century Revival

An analysis of surviving evidence suggests that in the twelfth century popular enthusiasm for pilgrimage to Rome was waning. If Rome suffered in part because there were few attempts to encourage pilgrimage to the city by the papacy, then the situation was reversed in the thirteenth century. Symbolic perhaps of this change in fortune was Innocent III's reversal of the humiliation suffered in 1167 when the Viterbans had stolen the bronze doors and the fountain grill from S. Pietro itself.[1] Innocent's recovery of these items enabled the doors to be replaced and the fountain, in which so many *Romipetae* had washed themselves, to be restored to full working order. Innocent III's pontificate seems to have marked a turning point in papal attitudes towards pilgrimage to Rome and this chapter will consider the measures taken by this pope and some of his successors to turn a pilgrimage centre in decline into one which in 1300 attracted crowds so large that *Romipetae* were crushed to death.

Innocent III

With regard to pilgrimage Innocent III was concerned by many of the same issues which had claimed the attention of his predecessors. He attempted, for example, to reduce the dangers for those travelling to the apostolic city. His policy to return the towns of the papal state to the dominion of the Church certainly seems have eased the situation here.[2] For with control over these lands the pope could ensure some measure of protection for those who travelled through them. The *Gesta* gives some idea of just how successful Innocent was in carrying out this policy of recovery, suggesting that, in the first two years of his pontificate alone, large areas from the March of Ancona

---

[1] *Gesta*, col. clxxxiii.

[2] On Innocent III and the papal state, see B. Bolton, ' "Except the Lord keep the city": towns in the papal states at the turn of the twelfth century', *Church and City 1000–1500. Essays in Honour of C. N. L. Brooke*, ed. D. Abulafia, M. J. Franklin and M. Rubin (Cambridge, 1992), pp. 199–217. See also D. Waley, *The Papal State in the Thirteenth Century* (London, 1961); P. Partner, *The Lands of St Peter. The Papal State in the Middle Ages and the Early Renaissance* (London, 1972).

in the north-east to the Duchy of Spoleto were recovered.[3] In these areas, so recently returned to the authority of the Church, Innocent was keen to demonstrate his own personal authority. He did this, it has been recently argued, by visiting these places himself and by leaving behind tangible reminders of his presence.[4] The gift list in the *Gesta* shows just how many towns benefited from his patronage. Viterbo was the recipient of many gifts. Here the churches of S. Lorenzo, S. Angelo de Spata, S. Sisto and S. Maria Nova all received chasubles, orphreys and altar cloths and even a papal ring.[5] At Rieti, Innocent consecrated both the church of S. Elutherio and S. Giovanni and to the former he presented an altar cloth decorated with lions and to the latter one decorated with leopards.[6] To the church of S. Maria de Spoleto, where he consecrated the altar, he presented a silken altar cloth.[7] A similar gift was given to the church at Sutri.[8] The church of Salvatore de Monte Amiato near Radicofani was presented with a red chasuble and an orphrey,[9] while the cathedral at Anagni received a silver crozier.[10] These represent just a few of Innocent III's gifts to towns in the papal state.[11]

It was not only through gifts to churches that Innocent advertised the re-established authority of the church within the papal state, but also through building projects. *Romipetae* entering the papal state either from the north or the south were to be made immediately aware that they were entering a land of peace, where all was now once more under the authority of the Pope. At Città Castellana art historians have attributed a cosmatesque portico to his patronage.[12] They have also argued that its shape suggests that it was modelled on the Roman triumphal arch, a deliberate choice intended as a sign of the peace and prosperity which the papal state enjoyed under Innocent III.[13] The inscription on the arch itself stressed this:

> + Gloria in excelsis deo et in terra pax hominibus bene voluntatis (sic) laudamus te adoramus te glorificamus te gratias agimus +.

Unfortunately the inscription which ran along both sides of the portico is now almost completely illegible and only a few words can still be read.[14] An

---

3   *Gesta*, cols. xxiv–xxx.
4   Bolton, ' "Except the Lord keep the city" ', p. 212.
5   *Gesta*, col. ccxxviii.
6   *Ibid.*, col. ccx.
7   *Ibid.*, col. ccx.
8   *Ibid.*, col. ccxxviii.
9   *Ibid.*, col. ccx.
10 *Ibid.*, col. ccix.
11 For the full list of Innocent's gifts to churches, see *ibid.*, cols. cciii–ccxii and ccxxvi–ccxxviii.
12 P. C. Claussen, *Magistri Doctissimi Romani. Die Römischen Marmorkünstler des Miltelalters*, *Corpus Cosmatorum*, 1 (Stuttgart, 1987), pp. 82–91.
13 *Ibid.*, p. 88.
14 *Ibid.*, p. 86. +INTRANTES . . . ASC . . . SO . . . POTSA . . . A . . . INTRANTESSICETSALVA . . .

inscription along the top of the arch, however, proclaims that the work here was carried out by Master Jacobus and his son and includes the date 1210.[15] It also seems likely that these same artists were responsible for the cosmatesque depiction of Christ set in a lunette above the right hand doorway. The bright orange and gold tesserae which make up Christ's clothes formed a striking contrast to the dark blue background. A cruciform nimbus was placed around his head and he was depicted with his right hand raised in blessing and with a closed book in his left. Not only was there a gateway proclaiming the peace and prosperity of the papal state on the northern approaches to Rome but a similar one was set up in the south. A portico, of about the same date as that at Città Castellana, was added to the duomo at Terracina on the frontier between the papal state and the Regno.[16] The portico here was very similar to that at Città Castellana, with the central feature again being a large archway. Unfortunately the decoration on the portico here has not survived as well as that at Città Castellana. Indeed the mosaic work on the right-hand side of the portico has completely disappeared, as has most of that which appears to have formed the decoration of the arch itself. Only on the left-hand side does any of the decoration survive. This suggests that a mosaic frieze ran along both sides of the portico and around the archway itself. At each end of the frieze on the left-hand side are two dragons. In the centre is a Greek cross and on either side of this are two horses facing each other. Both have riders on their backs. One horse is white and the other dark, an attempt perhaps to represent the Templars and Hospitallers. There is also a representation of a ship on the sea, with the words 'PETRUSPBRI' in mosaic above it. Also portrayed in this frieze are pairs of animals and birds, positioned on either side of trees, buildings or drinking vessels. The decoration which survives on the left-hand side also suggests that an inscription probably ran along both sides of the portico above the frieze. Only a couple of words can now be read:

GUTFRED: EGIDII MILES   MILES

Who these men were or what the message of the inscription was cannot now be determined.

This recovery of the papal state and the extension of papal authority enabled Innocent III to provide some protection for those who travelled through these lands. This is clearly demonstrated by his ability to suppress the activities of two notorious bandits, Nicholas and Guy, both of noble

---

OP . . . E . . . CAI . . . EGEXAIDIO . . . ESK . . . INEM . . . P . . . For an alternative reading see Bolton, ' "Unless the Lord keep the city" ', p. 213, note 122 + INTRANTES . . . ASC . . . . S . . POTESA . VA . . . . . RANTESSICETSALVA .OP ECAI . . . CEXAVD . . .

[15] + MAGISTER IACOBVS CIVIS ROMANVS CVM COSMA FILIO SVO + CARISIMO FECIT HOC OPVS ANNO DNI MCCX

[16] A. Contadore, *De historia Terracina: Libri Quinque* (Rome, 1706); A. Bianchini, *Storia di Terracina* (Tivoli, 1952).

birth.[17] They operated in the area of Rispampini, probably on the bridge where the Via Cassia from Radicofani to Aquapendente crossed the River Rigo. Here the *Gesta* tells us they seized, wounded and robbed those making their way to Rome.[18] Finding such a situation intolerable, Innocent instructed his rectors, his representatives in the papal state,[19] to take action against them. The rectors were able to besiege Guy and Nicholas at Rispampini, destroying their crops and burning their trees.[20] The bandits were forced to surrender, and took oaths promising to leave the roads in peace and to cease from molesting pilgrims and other travellers on their way to the apostolic city.[21]

His control of the papal state enabled Innocent not only to make the roads safer but also to establish rights and laws in these areas. Here his concern for *Romipetae* is evident. A document dated 1208 relating to Sutri, shows that this Pope established laws to protect the property of a pilgrim there in the event of his death.[22] If a pilgrim became so ill that he needed a priest to read him the last rites, an official known as the *gastaldus curie* was also to be present.[23] In his absence two vassals of the Roman Church had to be in attendance. For it was the task of the *gastaldus curie* to hear how the pilgrim wished to dispose of his worldly goods and then to see that this was done. Priests were also encouraged to warn pilgrims who were travelling alone that if they died intestate, the curia had the right to claim their property.[24] Other towns in the patrimony developed similar laws to deal with the disposition of a pilgrim's goods.[25]

Like his predecessors Innocent III was keen to make practical provisions for pilgrims. One of his most important building projects was the foundation of the hospital of Santo Spirito on the site of the old *Schola Saxonum* for the use of pilgrims as well as those from the local community.[26] His concern to carry out charitable works both for the local poor and visiting pilgrims may also have provided some motivation for his Bull, *Gradiente Domino super aquas*, dated 2 April 1212. In this Innocent enjoined all pilgrims to leave their oblations on the main altar at S. Pietro, rather than on the many side altars.[27] They were specifically requested to pass this message on in their home-lands and to transmit it to all fellow *Romipetae* whom they met on the road. Innocent's reasons for issuing this Bull are uncertain but they may in

---

17 *Gesta*, col. xxix.
18 *Ibid.*, col. xxix.
19 On the rectors and their responsibilities, see Richards, *Consul of God*, pp. 129–137
20 *Gesta*, col. xxix.
21 *Ibid.*, col. xxix.
22 Theiner, *Codex Diplomaticus*, p. 29.
23 On the *gastald*, see Tabacco, *Struggle for Power in Medieval Italy*, pp. 102–103.
24 Theiner, *Codex Diplomaticus*, p. 29.
25 See above, p. 148.
26 *Gesta*, col. cc. See also above, pp. 141–143.
27 *Collectione Bullarum*, vol. 1, pp. 96–97.

part be explained by what was to happen to the money left on the main altar. According to the Bull, a quarter of the oblations left there was to be used to support the canons of the basilica, another quarter was to be put towards the huge maintenance costs of the fabric, another towards the costs of lighting the basilica[28] and the rest was to be used to provide for the needs of the poor and destitute. While this undoubtedly raised income for the basilica, it also provided money for looking after visitors to and residents of the city.[29] It is possible that the declaration of how money left at S. Pietro would be spent was also designed to counter the many criticisms of the papacy's avidity. If this was so, then Innocent was certainly unsuccessful, since he was as widely criticised as his twelfth-century predecessors in this respect.[30]

A Turning Point?

While Innocent III was preoccupied, therefore, with many of the issues relating to pilgrimage which had concerned his predecessors, his pontificate also marks a turning point. Now the papacy seems to have been no longer satisfied only with improving conditions for those who had decided to travel to Rome but also wanted to encourage and to foster pilgrimage *ad limina apostolorum*.

One of Innocent III's important contributions was the introduction of a pilgrim badge for Rome. In this respect Rome was certainly lagging well behind its holy rivals. Whereas the *Veneranda dies* sermon indicates that both Jerusalem and Compostela had such tokens by the middle of the twelfth century, there is no evidence of any such item associated with Rome before the very end of the twelfth century.[31] The right to produce these items was granted by Innocent III to the canons of S. Pietro in a letter dated 18 January 1199. This letter began with an apology by Innocent that he had been unable to attend services in the basilica as often as he would have liked.[32] Other pressing ecclesiastical matters like the reform of the Church, efforts to agree truces between those at war and the need to raise a subsidy for the Holy Land had taken up much of his time.[33] In this same letter Innocent went on to offer a gift to honour this basilica where he had been *nutritus*. This gift was

---

[28] On the lights in the basilica see the *Descriptio Basilicae Vaticanae* of Peter Mallius in *Codice Topografico*, vol. 3, pp. 425–427. Also H. Geertman, 'L'Illuminazione della Basilica Paleocristiana secondo il Liber Pontificalis', *Rivista di Archeologia Cristiana*, 64 (1988), pp. 135–160.

[29] Innocent III's Bull of 1212 was re-issued by two of his successors, Innocent IV in 1252 and Alexander IV in 1259. See *Collectione Bullarum*, vol. 1, pp. 130 and 139–140.

[30] See above, p. 172.

[31] *Liber Sancti Jacobi*, vol. 1, p. 153. Also see above, pp. 77–79.

[32] Innocent III, *Registers*, PL 214, cols. 490–491.

[33] *Ibid.*, col. 491.

the monopoly of the production and sale of pilgrim badges.[34] Cast either in tin or lead, they were to bear the double image of St Peter holding a key and St Paul a sword and the inscription, *Signa Apostolorum Petri et Pauli*. Whilst these items were a sign that the pilgrim had made the journey and marked him out as someone deserving of special privileges, they were of course a good advertisement for the particular shrine.

Innocent III's determination that Rome should be firmly re-established on Christendom's 'spiritual map,' was further reflected in his calling of the Fourth Lateran Council for November 1215.[35] This Council was to be such a special occasion that it was summoned on 19 April 1213, two and a half years in advance.[36] This was the first genuine universal council since Chalcedon (451) and drew to Rome well over one thousand dignitaries, the leaders of both clergy and laity from the whole of Christendom.[37]

It was perhaps to advertise Rome's links with St Peter, and the splendour and spirituality of the holy see to these leading churchmen, that a major building campaign was carried out at S. Pietro. To decorate the area of the tomb itself, a special protective bronze and Limoges enamel-work grill was made for the *confessio*.[38] Forming part of this decorative covering were a set of appliqué reliefs of Christ and the twelve apostles.[39] Only the figure of Christ and five of the apostles now survive, kept in the Vatican museums.[40] Made of copper, the enamel work which covers the figures is of blue, turquoise, green, red and white. The figure of Christ is seated and is twice the size of the apostles. He wears a crown on his head, has his right hand raised in blessing and holds a book in his left. The apostles are all standing and only one can be identified for certain, that of St Peter, who holds a key in his right hand.

---

[34] *Ibid.*, col. 491. This gift was confirmed in a Bull of Honorius III of 1222. See *Collectione Bullarum*, vol. 1, pp. 107–108.

[35] S. Kuttner and A. García y García, 'A New Eyewitness Account of the Fourth Lateran Council', *Traditio*, 20 (1964), pp. 115–178; B. Bolton, 'A Show with Meaning: Innocent III's Approach to the Fourth Lateran Council', *Medieval History*, 1 (1991), pp. 53–67; P. J. Dunning, 'Irish Representatives and Irish Ecclesiastical Affairs at the Fourth Lateran Council', *Medieval Studies Presented to Aubrey Gwynn*, ed. J. A. Watt, J. B. Morrall and F. X. Martin (Dublin, 1961), pp. 90–113.

[36] The Council was announced in the Bull *Quia Maior*. See Innocent III, *Registers*, PL 216, cols. 817–822.

[37] An estimate of the number of dignitaries who attended can be found in *Annales Ceccanenses*, p. 300. That the city was very crowded at the time of the Council is suggested by a comment in a letter of Gervase of Prémontré who noted how expensive food and accommodation were in Rome in November 1215. See *Sacrae Antiquitatis Monumenta Historica, Dogmatica, Diplomatica*, ed. C. L. Hugo (1725), pp. 96–97. Also C.R. Cheney, 'Gervase, Abbot of Prémontré. A Medieval Letter Writer', *Bulletin of the John Rylands Library*, 33 (1950–1951), pp. 25–56.

[38] M. M. Gauthier, 'La Clôture Emailleé de la Confession de Saint Pierre au Vatican, lors du Concile de Latran IV, 1215', *Synthronon* (Paris, 1968), pp. 237–246.

[39] *Ibid.*, p. 246, for an attempt to reconstruct the grill with its figures.

[40] On these figures, see *ibid.*, pp. 241–242; *Vatican Collections. The Papacy and Art* (New York, 1982), p. 33.

Perhaps even more important, however, than Innocent's attentions to the *confessio* was the repair of the mosaics. Neglect of the basilica's fabric had resulted in the decay of the facade mosaic, which was repaired under Innocent's direction.[41] He also saw to the renewal of the apse mosaic, the greater part of which seems to have been destroyed.[42] After Innocent's restoration, this mosaic claimed for S. Pietro the title of 'Mother of all Churches', hitherto reserved for the Lateran, showing the basilica dedicated to St Peter to be the spiritual head of Christendom. In addition, by placing a representation of himself in the lower register of this mosaic beneath the figure of St Paul, Innocent seems to have been emphasising the mission of the Church to all men and the dual purpose of his pontificate; the drawing of as many people within the Church as possible and the keeping of simple believers in the faith. This message was reinforced by the depiction of the Lamb of God bleeding into a chalice, a symbolic representation of the Eucharist indicating salvation for all.[43]

Whilst Innocent III, like his twelfth-century predecessor Calixtus II, was obviously keen to promote and advertise Rome's links with St Peter, his pontificate also witnessed the vigorous promotion and veneration of the *Veronica*. In 1208 he established a new liturgical station at the hospital of Santo Spirito. On the first Sunday after the Octave of Epiphany, the *Veronica* was to be carried in procession from S. Pietro to the hospital by the canons of the basilica. Participation in this liturgical station was encouraged by the granting of one year's remission of penance to all those who took part. The introduction of a procession for the *Veronica* may have been intended as a balance to the procession of the *Acheropita*, the relic kept at the Lateran.[44] This procession of the *Veronica*, however, also emphasised the importance of the basilica of S. Pietro, from whence the relic came and together with the *Acheropita* firmly associated Rome not only with St Peter but like Jerusalem, with Christ himself.[45]

---

[41] *Gesta*, col. ccv.

[42] *Ibid.*, col. ccv. A reproduction of the mosaic can be found in Krautheimer, *Rome*, p. 205. Also J. Ruysschaert, 'Le Tableau Mariotti de la Mosaïque Absidale de l'Ancien S.-Pierre', *Atti della Pontificia Accademia Romana di Archeologia, Rendiconti*, 3rd Series, 40 (1967–1968), pp. 295–317.

[43] The early thirteenth-century apse mosaic at S. Paolo also took up this theme of salvation. The renewal of this apse mosaic had also been begun by Innocent III (*Gesta*, col. ccvi), who died before its completion, and was finished by Honorius III. Strongly Byzantine in style and composition, in the lower register was placed an empty throne, a crucifix and the other instruments of the Passion. This was a striking contrast to other Roman apse mosaics, where the lower register traditionally contained twelve lambs issuing forth from Jerusalem and Bethlehem. On this mosaic, see Oakeshott, *Mosaics of Rome*, pp. 295–297; Matthiae, *Mosaici Medioevali*, vol. 1, pp. 337–340; Ladner, *I Ritratti dei Papi*, vol. 2, pp. 80–91; Wilpert, *Römischen Malereien*, vol. 2, pt 1, pp. 549–554.

[44] See above, pp. 114–116.

[45] On Innocent III's promotion of the *Acheropita* in the patrimony, see Bolton, 'Except the Lord keep the city', pp. 214–215.

Maccarrone has argued that during the second half of the thirteenth century pilgrims began travelling to Rome in large numbers, attracted there in particular by the relics kept at S. Pietro, notably the *Veronica*.[46] That knowledge of this relic spread rapidly in the thirteenth century is suggested by the inclusion of a drawing of it in Matthew Paris's *Chronica Maiora*. How or from whom he learnt of it we do not know, since Matthew himself is not known to have travelled to Rome. That this relic of Christ was extremely popular with pilgrims is indicated by the huge crowds who gathered to see it during 1300 when it was displayed every Friday and on feast days.[47] So large were the crowds who pressed forward to gain a better view of this precious relic that William of Derby, present at one such showing in 1300, had his leg crushed and did not live long enough to return home.[48] It is certainly also possible that by this date, those who wanted to take home a tangible reminder of the *Veronica* could buy a badge which had a representation of this relic upon it.[49]

Indulgences

Like Innocent III, many of his thirteenth-century successors were also keen to encourage and to promote pilgrimage to the city. This they sought to do particularly through the issuing of indulgences, which were gradually increased in number and value throughout the course of the thirteenth century.

It is likely that during the second half of the twelfth century indulgences had first been made available for the making of the actual journey to Rome. It has been argued that such indulgences were not in existence before 1100, on the basis that in 1116 Paschal II (1098–1116) granted forty days' remission of penance to all who had travelled to Rome to attend his Council.[50] This special indulgence may be an indication that grants of this kind were not generally available at that time. By the end of the twelfth century,

---

[46] Maccarrone, 'L'Indulgenza del Giubileo', p. 732.

[47] Giovanni Villani, *Historie Fiorentine*, col. 367.

[48] *Chronicle of St Mary's Abbey, York*, ed. H. H. E. Craster and M. E. Thornton, Surtees Society, 148 (Durham, 1933), pp. 30–31. Many pilgrims suffered a similar fate in Rome during the Jubilee of 1350. See Heinrich von Rebdorff, *Annales Imperatorum et paparum 1294–1362, Fontes Rerum Germanicarum*, ed. J. F. Boehmer, 4 vols. (Stuttgart, 1868), vol. 4, p. 562.

[49] Pecchai ('Banchi e Botteghe', pp. 90–95) has shown that such badges were on sale at least by the middle of the fourteenth century, while Paolo Vergerio, a fourteenth-century Florentine diplomat (*Epistolario*, ed. L. Smith, *Fonti per la Storia d'Italia* (Rome, 1934), p. 216), noted on his visit to Rome that pictures of the *Veronica* were on sale, painted on pieces of card torn out of old books.

[50] H. C. Lea, *A History of Auricular Confession and Indulgences in the Latin Church*, 3 vols. (London, 1896), vol. 3, p. 197. For the record of the grant, see Conrad of Ursperg, *Chronicon*, p. 199. On indulgences, see Riley-Smith, *What were the Crusades?*, pp. 57–62.

however, they were becoming more common-place. In a letter of 1181 addressed to the archbishop and bishops of Sweden, Alexander III expressed his belief that pilgrims travelling to the apostolic city should each be rewarded according to their labour.[51] All those travelling from Sweden to Rome, therefore, were to receive three years' remission of penance. Those travelling from England were to receive two years and those journeying lesser distances, just one.[52] Other references occur in the late twelfth and early thirteenth centuries to such indulgences. In a letter of 1198, Pope Innocent III promised to those who went to fight heretics in the Languedoc the same indulgence 'which we concede to those going to the thresholds of St Peter and St James'.[53]

By 1200 *Romipetae* could also gain indulgences when visiting the city's churches. The value of such grants, however, was very small. Gerald of Wales, in Rome on pilgrimage c.1204, tells us that between Epiphany and Easter he had managed to build up ninety-two years' worth of indulgences in visiting the city's basilicas and attending stational masses.[54] This he made up to a round one hundred by enroling himself in the Fraternity of Santo Spirito. A contemporary, William of Auxerre, was less certain about the value of indulgences which could be gained during Lent, putting their value at more than fifty years.[55] A further indication of the small size of these indulgences is provided by Peter Mallius in his description of the Vatican basilica, probably written during the pontificate of Alexander III (1159–1181). In this he lists the *maximam remissionem* which could be gained by pilgrims who visited this basilica on the feast day of its dedication.[56] As in the case of indulgences for actually making the journey, there was a tri-partite division according to the distance travelled. Those who lived in the vicinity of the apostolic city qualified for one year, those from Tuscany, Lombardy and Apulia and all others whose journey had not involved a sea-crossing, qualified for two and those from further afield for three.[57] We know too from Peter the Chanter that by the end of the twelfth century on the 'Feast Day of the Lord' small indulgences were granted to pilgrims which were worth three years for all who had had to cross the Alps and two years for all whose journey had begun in Italy.[58]

The indulgences that could be gained by visiting the city's principal pilgrimage churches were gradually increased by the popes of the thirteenth

[51] Alexander III, *Epistolae et Privilegia*, col. 1316.
[52] *Ibid.*, col. 1316.
[53] Innocent III, *Registers*, PL 214, cols. 81–83.
[54] Gerald of Wales, *De Invectionibus*, p. 137.
[55] N. Paulus, *Geschicte des Ablasses im Mittelalter vom Ursprunge bis zur Mitte des 14 Jahrhunderts*, 3 vols. (Paderborn, 1922–1923), vol. 2, p. 295, note 4.
[56] *Codice Topografico*, vol. 3, p. 385.
[57] *Ibid.*, vol. 3, p. 385.
[58] Peter the Chanter, *Summa de Sacramentis et Animae Consiliis*, ed. J. A. Dugauquier, *Analecta Mediaevalia*, 7 (1957), pp. 194–195.

century. In 1222, Honorius III (1216–1227) granted an indulgence of one year and forty days for the consecration feast of S. Maria Maggiore.[59] The most numerous grants, however, were those made to S. Pietro. In 1240, Gregory IX (1227–1241) granted to all those who were truly penitent and confessed and who visited S. Pietro between Pentecost and 6 July, the Octave of Saints Peter and Paul, a remission of three years and one hundred and forty days.[60] In 1260, Alexander IV (1254–1261) granted two years and eighty days' remission of penance to all who visited S. Pietro on 25 April, the Feast of St Mark.[61] In 1263, Urban IV (1261–1264) extended the indulgence granted by Gregory IX, from 6 July to 1 August, the Feast of S. Pietro ad Vincula.[62] In 1279, after building an altar at S. Pietro dedicated to St Nicholas, Nicholas III (1277–1280) granted one year and forty days' remission for the consecration Feast of his altar and for the Feast Day of this Saint.[63] In 1289 Nicholas IV (1288–1292) issued two Bulls which listed the indulgences available at S. Pietro, some of which seem to have been introduced by Nicholas himself.[64] Seven years and 280 days remission of penance could be gained by those who visited the basilica on Christmas Day, at Epiphany, or on 22 February, the Feast of St Peter's Chair. Smaller indulgences of one year and forty days were available at other times, for example on the Feast of the Apparition of St Michael the Archangel.[65] In 1297 Boniface VIII settled the disputes over the value of indulgences for attending stational masses. Pilgrims would receive remission of penance worth one year and forty days for attending a stational mass, as well as any indulgences attached to the stational church in its own right.[66]

The granting of such indulgences reached a peak in the Jubilee year of 1300 when Boniface VIII granted a plenary indulgence to all those pilgrims who visited Rome in that year.[67] To qualify for this indulgence the pilgrim had to be truly penitent and confessed. If he came from Rome he then had to spend thirty days visiting the basilicas of Saints Peter and Paul, or fifteen days if he came from elsewhere.[68]

[59] Lea, *History of Auricular Confession*, vol. 3, p. 198.
[60] *Collectione Bullarum*, vol. 1, pp. 123–124.
[61] *Ibid.*, vol. 1, p. 141.
[62] *Ibid.*, vol. 1, p. 143.
[63] *Ibid.*, vol. 1, pp. 262–263.
[64] *Ibid.*, vol. 1, pp. 213–215. These Bulls were issued on consecutive days, 24 and 25 February.
[65] *Ibid.*, vol. 1, pp. 213–215.
[66] *Ibid.*, vol. 3, p. 6.
[67] Boniface VIII, *Registers*, ed. G. Digard, M. Faucon, A. Thomas and R. Fawtier, 4 vols. *Bibliothèque des Ecoles Françaises d'Athènes et de Rome*, 2nd series (Paris, 1884–1939), vol. 2, pp. 922–923, no. 3875.
[68] *Ibid.*, vol. 2, pp. 922–923, no. 3875.

The Jubilee of 1300

The events surrounding the grant of this plenary indulgence by Boniface VIII in 1300 are shrouded in confusion and uncertainty.[69] Was the Jubilee pre-planned and had there been a similar event a hundred years before? It seems unlikely that the Jubilee was the result of long-term planning. Indeed, any attempt to argue that this was the case must also explain why Boniface VIII did not issue the Bull concerning the Jubilee until 22 February 1300. If the Jubilee really was pre-planned, then just like the Fourth Lateran Council, it would surely have been announced long in advance, in order that as many people as possible knew about and could take advantage of the special plenary indulgence.

If it seems unlikely, therefore, that the Jubilee was the result of long-term planning, then we should perhaps consider the account of the event written by Cardinal Stefaneschi, nephew of Boniface VIII, which suggests that the Jubilee of 1300 was the result of a popular movement.[70] Stefaneschi tells us that on Christmas Eve 1299, a large crowd had gathered at S. Pietro. They seem to have been attracted there by the belief that those who visited the tombs of the apostles in the following year would receive some kind of indulgence. The numbers of pilgrims making their way to Rome gradually increased during the first weeks of January 1300. On 17 January, during the procession of the Veronica, the pope chanced to meet an old man from Savoy, aged one hundred and seven years, being borne along in the arms of his sons.[71] Boniface asked this old man why he was undertaking a pilgrimage at such an advanced age. The old man replied that at the beginning of the previous century he had accompanied his father to the apostolic city in order to gain an indulgence, which had been worth 'one hundred days every day of the year'.[72] He had also been told by his father not to forget to attend at the beginning of the next century. His story was confirmed by other centenarians.[73] Interested in this tale, Boniface VIII sent some of the cardinals to

[69] On the Jubilee see, for example, A. Frugoni, 'Il Giubileo di Bonifacio VIII', *Bullettino dell'Istituto Storico Italiano per il Medio Evo e Archivio Muratoriano*, 62 (1950), pp. 1–121; M. Maccarrone, 'L'Indulgenza del Giubileo del 1300 e la Basilica di San Pietro', *Roma Anno 1330, Atti della IV Settimana di Studi di Storia dell'Arte Medievale dell'Università di Roma 'La Sapienza' (19–24 March 1980)* (Rome, 1983), pp. 731–752; Maccarrone, *Pellegrinaggio*, pp. 363–429; H. Thurston, *The Holy Year of Jubilee* (London, 1900); P. Brezzi, *Il Giubileo del Bonifacio e Dante* (Rome, 1984); *Roma Sancta. La Città delle Basiliche*, ed. M. Fagiolo and M. L. Madonna (Rome, 1985); T. S. R. Boase, *Boniface VIII* (London, 1933), esp. pp. 231–266. On later Jubilees, see for example 'Le Jubilé de 1350', *Journal des savants* (1963), pp. 191–195; Sumption, *Pilgrimage*, pp. 236–256.

[70] For the text of Stephaneschi's account see D. Quattrocchi, 'L'Anno Santo del 1300. Storia e Bolle Pontificie', *Bessarione*, 7 (1899–1900), pp. 291–317.

[71] *Ibid.*, p. 300.

[72] *Ibid.*, pp. 300–301.

[73] *Ibid.*, p. 301.

search the papal archives for some record of this special indulgence issued a hundred years earlier by Innocent III.[74] Although no written record of such an event could be found, Boniface was unwilling to send these pilgrims away disappointed. Thus, on 22 February, the Feast of St Peter's Chair, the pope issued a Bull, *Antiquorum habet*, which granted a plenary indulgence to all those who visited Rome in 1300, an indulgence which was described as 'not only full and copious but the most full pardon of all their sins'.[75]

If we accept that the Jubilee was the result of a popular religious movement, rather than a pre-arranged event by Boniface VIII and the cardinals, then we might ask whether there really was any truth in the tale which Stefeneschi reports of a special indulgence granted during the pontificate of Innocent III. Although this might fit neatly with other evidence of Innocent's attempts to revitalise Rome's flagging pilgrimage trade, no contemporary evidence of such a grant seems to exist. In 1300 Boniface VIII had sent his cardinals to search the papal archives for a record of such an event. The reference in the Jubilee Bull itself, however, indicates that none was found. For this refers not to any written record of such an event but rather to the 'trustworthy tradition of our ancestors'.[76] Surely if there had been such a precedent Boniface VIII would have mentioned it.

Furthermore, whereas references to the Jubilee of 1300 occur in a wide variety of sources, there seems to be no such contemporary record of any event in 1200. The only reference which we have is found in the chronicle of Alberic of Trois Fontaines. Under the year 1208 it is recorded that 'this year was celebrated as the fiftieth year or the year of Jubilee and of remission in the curia at Rome'.[77] There was, indeed, a new indulgence granted in this year, that of Innocent III for participation in the procession of the *Veronica*. This indulgence, however, was in no way special, being worth only one year's remission.[78] It was certainly not worth the 'one hundred days every day of the year' referred to by the centenarian from Savoy. A problem also exists concerning Alberic's chronicle, because it has been extensively added to by later writers. The reference to a Jubilee in 1208, therefore, may have been added at a much later date. It seems likely, however, that this entry pre-dates 1300, otherwise we should really expect to find it under 1200, evidence that a Jubilee had occurred exactly one hundred years before. It would appear that this entry in Alberic's chronicle is not evidence of a Jubilee under Innocent III but rather further evidence that the popular conception of a Jubilee year connected with Rome, was current in men's minds before 1300.[79]

While there seems to be no evidence of a precedent for Boniface VIII's

---

74 *Ibid.*, p. 301.
75 Boniface VIII, *Registers*, vol. 2, pp. 922–923, no. 3875.
76 *Ibid.*, vol. 2, pp. 922–933, no. 3875.
77 Alberic of Tre Fontaneis, p. 889.
78 See *Sermo VIII*, in Innocent III, *Sermones*, PL 217, col. 350.
79 Thurston, *Holy Year of Jubilee*, p. 16.

grant in 1300, the popular belief that special indulgences could be gained in the apostolic city at the turn of the century may be explained by Rome's increasing popularity with pilgrims. Maccarrone has argued that during the second half of the thirteenth century pilgrims began travelling to Rome in large numbers, attracted there in particular by the relics preserved at S. Pietro, notably the *Veronica*, as well as by the special papal indulgences.[80] It is likely that Rome's popularity with pilgrims was further increased at that time because of the difficulties of journeying to the Holy Land. In 1244 Jerusalem fell to Muslim forces. Caesarea was lost in 1265, Saphet in 1266 and in 1268 Antioch was destroyed. Tripoli fell in 1289 and Acre in 1291. Just as Rome had grown in popularity as a centre of pilgrimage after the loss of Jerusalem in the seventh century, so the loss of the crusader states in the thirteenth may have had a similar effect. While travel to Jerusalem and the Holy Land became more difficult, at least in Rome pilgrims knew that they would find relics not only of two of the apostles but also those of Christ Himself.

The renewed popularity of Rome with pilgrims, a result of the promotion of its relics, the granting of special papal indulgences and the increasing difficulties of pilgrimage to Jerusalem, may have produced at the turn of the century the popular belief that some special grant would be given to all who travelled to Rome in 1300. Perhaps equally significant in this context was Boniface VIII's decision to grant a plenary indulgence. This had originally been the reward of crusaders to Jerusalem and it is possible that in granting it to pilgrims travelling to Rome in 1300 Boniface VIII decided to take advantage of the situation to present Rome as the 'new Jerusalem'.[81]

Whatever the origins or precedents for the Jubilee, it is certain that it was one of the greatest achievements of Boniface VIII's pontificate. The widespread success of the Jubilee is reflected in the numerous chronicles and histories which mention this special event of 1300. These lay emphasis on the large crowds of *Romipetae* who were attracted to the apostolic city by the lure of the plenary indulgence. The *Annales Gadenses* reports that a very great crowd of pilgrims hurried to the curia.[82] Another chronicle notes that in 1300 it seemed as though the whole world was rushing to Rome.[83] Other accounts give further details about these crowds. The *Chronicle of Bury St Edmunds* reports that in this year men and women of all ages went to Rome from all parts of the Christian world.[84] Others note that the pilgrims who hurried to Rome included those of every rank and station, great lords as well

---

80 Maccarrone, 'L'Indulgenza del Giubileo', pp. 732–733.
81 *Roma Sancta*, pp. 28–31.
82 *Annales Gadenses*, MGH.SS 16, p. 546.
83 *Annales Halesbrunnenses Maiores*, MGH.SS 24, p. 46. See also *Continuatio Florianensis 1273–1309*, MGH.SS 9, p. 751; *Annales SS. Uldarici et Afrae Augustenses*, MGH.SS 17, p. 434.
84 *Chronicle of Bury St Edmunds 1212–1301*, ed. and trans. A. Gransden (London, 1964), p. 155. See also *Sifridi Presbyteri de Balnhusin, Historia Universalis et Compendium Historiarum*, MGH.SS 25, p. 715.

as humble peasants.[85] Giles of Muisis's account of his pilgrimage to Rome in 1300 records that those travelling there in that year included religious, clerics and laymen alike.[86] Those unable to walk travelled on horseback, while young men too poor to provide animals for aged parents to ride upon carried them on their own backs.[87] It was also noted that in 1300 such was the peace throughout the whole of Italy, that here everyone was able to travel in safety to the apostolic city.[88]

Cardinal Stefaneschi's account provides similar details. Pilgrims came, he wrote, from Italy, Hungary, the Empire, Spain, France, but only occasionally from England 'on account of the wars'.[89] There were young and old, rich and poor.[90] There were laymen as well as clergy and the bishops of Italy and France, he adds, were particularly numerous.[91] The crowds that flocked to the city were so large that they seemed to him like an advancing army or a swarm.[92] Some chroniclers even tried to estimate the size of these crowds. One believed that on some days as many as thirty thousand pilgrims departed from the city and that an equally large number arrived.[93] Giovanni Villani believed that two hundred thousand pilgrims had visited Rome in the course of 1300,[94] while William of Ventura put the figure at two million.[95] While such estimates are obviously untrustworthy, other evidence does suggest that very large numbers of pilgrims really did make the journey to Rome in this year. Bautier has made a study of the records of tolls which had to be paid at Bard in the Aosta Valley by those travelling on horse-back.[96] These show that in the period from 1278 to 1295, 9,735 riders from France passed through Bard and 773 from England.[97] A study of these same records for the period from April 1300 to March 1301 suggests that around 7,987 travellers from France and 684 from England passed through.[98] These figures, there-

---

85 See for example, Chronicon Parmense ab Anno MXXXVIII usque ad Annum MCCCIX autore anonymo Synchrono, RIS 9, col. 842. Also Chronica S. Petri Erfordensis Moderna, MGH.SS 30, part 1, p. 434; E Floribus Chronicorum seu Catalogo Romanorum Pontificum, Necnon e Chronico Regum Francorum Auctore Bernardo Guidone, RHGF, 21 (Paris, 1855), p. 712.
86 D'Haenens, 'Gilles li Muisis', p. 46.
87 Annales Veteres Mutinensium ab Anno MCXXXI ad Annum usque MCCCXXXVI, RIS 11, col. 75.
88 Ibid., col. 75.
89 Quattrocchi, 'L'Anno Santo', pp. 302–304.
90 Ibid., p. 302.
91 Ibid., p. 304.
92 Ibid., p. 302.
93 Annales Colmarienses Maiores, MGH.SS 17, p. 225.
94 Giovanni Villani, Historie Fiorentine, col. 367.
95 William of Ventura, Chronicon Astense, col. 192.
96 R. H. Bautier, 'Le Jubilé romain de 1300 et l'alliance franco-pontificale au temps de Philippe le Bel et de Boniface VIII', Le Moyen Age, 86 (1980), pp. 189–216, esp. pp. 190–192.
97 Ibid., p. 190.
98 Ibid., p. 190.

fore, suggest that there was a very large increase in traffic, almost certainly to be explained by the desire to take advantage of the Jubilee indulgence.

A description by one visitor to Rome in 1300 provides a vivid impression of what the city was like during the Jubilee year. William of Ventura spent fifteen days in the city, departing on Christmas Eve.[99] He provides an insight into how crowded conditions were, reporting how he had seen many men and women crushed under foot and how he himself had almost suffered the same fate on more than one occasion.[100]

In the account of his visit to Rome in the Jubilee year of 1300, William of Ventura gives information about the provisions on sale in the city. Bread, wine, meat, fish and oats were all readily available.[101] The price of hay and lodging, he complained, was very expensive. A bed for William and stabling for his horse had cost him one *gross tournois*.[102] William's account also shows that he believed that Boniface VIII had made a substantial profit from the Jubilee. He mentioned two clerics whom he claimed stood at the altar of S. Paolo day and night drawing in money with rakes.[103] Nor was William alone in this belief. One chronicler noted that the Pope had made a very large amount of money from the oblations left by the *Romipetae*,[104] while Ptolomy of Lucca claimed that the crowds flocking to Rome were so great that every day oblations amounted to one thousand pounds.[105] Giovanni Villani suggested that the Romans too made a great profit from the Jubilee.[106] It was perhaps the desire for profits among the Romans, which led, in 1350, to the production of false Jubilee bulls, designed to keep pilgrims longer in the city. In one of these it was declared that pilgrims must visit not just the basilicas of S. Pietro and S. Paulo but seven churches at least fifteen times before they could qualify for the indulgence.[107] It was undoubtedly fears for their profits that also led to reports that the Romans were 'exceedingly vexed', that the papal legate, Guy of Boulogne, was permitted, on account of the crowds, to reduce to six the number of days that pilgrims had to spend in the city.[108]

During the course of the thirteenth century the popes seem to have taken an increased interest in pilgrimage to Rome. Like his predecessors, Innocent III

99 William of Ventura, *Chronicon Astense*, col. 192.
100 *Ibid.*, col. 192.
101 *Ibid.*, col. 192. Cardinal Stephaneschi's account (Quattrocchi, 'L'Anno Santo', p. 303) shows, however, that after the first three months of coping with the large influx of pilgrims, food did grow short. A good harvest seems to have ensured that the situation had greatly improved by the time of William's visit in December 1300.
102 William of Ventura, *Chronicon Astense*, col. 192.
103 *Ibid.*, col. 192.
104 *Chronicon Fratris Francisci Pipini*, RIS 9, col. 738.
105 Ptolomy of Lucca, *Historia Ecclesiastica*, RIS 11, col. 1221.
106 Giovanni Villani, *Historie Fiorentine*, col. 367.
107 Sumption, *Pilgrimage*, p. 240.
108 *Ibid.*, p. 241.

was keen to improve conditions for those who had decided to undertake the journey to the city and to provide facilities for them there. He also tried to encourage pilgrimage to the city. He introduced pilgrim badges for *Romipetae* and sought to advertise and to promote Rome's links not only with St Peter but with Christ Himself, particularly through the veneration of the *Veronica*. Innocent III's thirteenth-century successors continued this policy of encouraging pilgrimage to the city, particularly through the granting of indulgences. Popular devotion to the *Veronica* and the indulgences which could be gained, notably at S. Pietro, combined with the increasing difficulties of journeying to the Holy Land, seem to have drawn pilgrims to Rome in growing numbers, so much so that by 1300 there was a widespread belief that a very special indulgence could be gained in that year by all who travelled *ad limina apostolorum*. Boniface VIII was astute enough to capitalise upon this popular belief. The granting of a plenary indulgence, previously the reward of crusaders to the Holy Land, presented Rome as the new Jerusalem and firmly emphasised the city's links not only with Saints Peter and Paul but with Christ Himself.

Conclusion

The sermons addressed to pilgrims by Jacques de Vitry and the *Veneranda dies* sermon emphasised the penitential nature of pilgrimage. Such journeys were a time for atonement and suffering. For just as the pilgrim sinned with all his limbs, so too must he expect to make reparation with all of them. Surviving sources suggest, however, that many pilgrims who were in a position to do so mitigated some of the labours and hardships of the journey by taking horses or mules to ride upon or to carry the baggage, and frequently took with them large sums of money. Whilst some of this money may have been used for acts of charity or left as oblations, much of it would often have been spent on food and comfortable accommodation along the way and at the destination itself. Few perhaps, except those with no choice, or the most ascetic, would willingly have chosen the hard beds recommended by Jacques de Vitry.

There were some hardships, however, that were shared by all pilgrims. Rich and poor alike fell victim to the hazards of war, natural disasters, disease and the activities of robbers and murderers. Such difficulties made the undertaking of pilgrimages, particularly those where long distance travel was involved, extremely dangerous and hazardous. It is particularly striking that even before setting out many pilgrims showed awareness of these potential dangers, clearly realising that they might perish on their journey. Whilst some pilgrims may have set out with unworthy motives, such as curiosity or improved opportunities for begging, many more must have been motivated by religious enthusiasm. They were willing to undertake long and arduous pilgrimages because they really did believe that the rewards to be gained from the undertaking of such a journey were worth even the risk of death.

Whilst little could be done to protect pilgrims from natural disasters and diseases, throughout the medieval period there were constant attempts to try to protect them from those who might attack them on the road or innkeepers who might cheat or rob them. As early as the beginning of the seventh century the *Lex Baiwariorum* stated that pilgrims had the right to safe passage. This privilege, and that of freedom from the payment of tolls and the right to hospitality, were constantly restated during the Carolingian period and then throughout the tenth, eleventh and twelfth centuries, by which time the protection of pilgrims seems to have been a recognised obligation of the papacy itself. Those entitled to these special rights were easily identified by the letters of recommendation which they carried, and by the scrip, staff and badge which they also bore. That this privileged status had little practical effect for the pilgrim and was often ignored is suggested by the frequent attacks upon them which continued to be recorded in our sources, and also by the constant need throughout the medieval period to restate their right to travel in safety.

Those who travelled to Rome in the period 1099 to 1216 faced the same varied dangers and hardships; the usual difficulties of Alpine travel, the problems caused by malaria, the activities of bandits, and the effects of warfare across the Italian peninsula and in Rome itself, which were particularly acute. Prominent amongst those who braved these dangers at this time were the Icelanders. Indeed, our most detailed and important account of a pilgrimage made to Rome in the twelfth century is that of Nikolas of Munkathvera, an inhabitant of this 'last island' who travelled *ad limina apostolorum* c.1150.

Nikolas's account not only details some of the major routes to Rome that were commonly used by *Romipetae*, but it contains a very valuable report of how he spent his time in the apostolic city, which is unique for the twelfth century. This shows that, like Sigeric, archbishop of Canterbury, who travelled to Rome c.990, Nikolas visited a variety of churches both inside and outside the city walls, including the five patriarchal basilicas, S. Pietro, S. Paolo fuori le mura, S. Lorenzo fuori le mura, S. Maria Maggiore and the Lateran. A comparison of the basilicas visited by Nikolas and Sigeric reveals few major differences. What does seem to have been different by the twelfth century, however, was the growing interest amongst pilgrims in the rich and extensive relic collection kept at the Lateran, about which both Nikolas, and later, Gerald of Wales had much to say. It seems that by this time pilgrims were demanding more than the body of a saint lying hidden inside a tomb, and that what they now wanted were relics which they could actually see. Such demands may well have been a major factor in the appearance of more visible relics at S. Pietro in the twelfth century, notably St Peter's chair.

Unfortunately, there are many things which Nikolas of Munkathvera does not tell us in his account which it would have been useful to know, notably where he stayed during his sojourn in Rome and in what type of accommodation. Whilst we know that the popes of the seventh, eighth and ninth centuries had done much to provide accommodation and other facilities for pilgrims in Rome itself, much less is known about the following centuries. A search of surviving source material, notably papal correspondence, has shown, however, that the popes of the twelfth century at least seem to have been active in trying to provide for the needs of pilgrims. Those who stayed in the city during this period would not have been wholly dependent upon private establishments.

Whilst surviving sources indicate that pilgrimage to Rome remained relatively popular in the twelfth century amongst the more recent converts to Christianity, like the Icelanders, it appears that amongst peoples such as the English and the Franks the popularity of travelling *ad limina apostolorum* may have declined. The difficulties of the journey to Rome, the city's worsening spiritual reputation, the absence of the papacy for long periods, and, above all, the competition from other pilgrimage centres which were vigorously promoted at this time, seem to have been amongst the major reasons for Rome's declining popularity as a destination for pilgrims.

Innocent III and some of his thirteenth-century successors seem to have attempted to arrest and reverse this decline through their active encouragement of pilgrimage to Rome. Innocent III promoted and advertised the city's spiritual links and associations, notably with St Peter, but also with Christ himself. His successors continued this policy of encouraging pilgrimage, particularly through the granting of more and greater indulgences.

Whilst this policy of advertising and increasing Rome's attractions seems to have led to a resurgence in the numbers of pilgrims travelling to the apostolic city, Rome's growth in popularity, especially during the later thirteenth century, may have been further affected by the loss of the crusader states, including Jerusalem in 1244. Indeed, it seems that Rome's popularity with pilgrims was closely linked to the fate of Jerusalem and the Holy Land. With the rapid advance of Muslim forces through the Near East in the seventh century pilgrimage there had become increasingly difficult. This difficulty in travelling to Jerusalem was a major factor in the subsequent growth in popularity of pilgrimage to Rome. With the opening up of an overland route to Jerusalem in the eleventh century, pilgrimage to the Holy Land began to grow in popularity again. The success of the First Crusade, which recaptured Jerusalem in 1099, again enabled pilgrims to travel there in increasingly large numbers. This re-opening of the Holy Land seems to have been marked by a decline in the popularity of pilgrimage to Rome. Once Jerusalem had been lost to the Muslims in 1244, with the rest of the crusader states following soon after, there was another resurgence in Rome's popularity as a destination for pilgrims.

Nor was Boniface VIII slow to grasp the opportunity which presented itself in 1300. Popular belief held that a special indulgence would be granted to those who travelled to Rome in that year. By granting a plenary indulgence, similar to that previously made available to crusaders to the Holy Land, Boniface VIII presented Rome as the new Jerusalem. He emphasised, as Innocent III in particular had done, that Rome was a city associated not only with Saints Peter and Paul, but also with Christ Himself.

Bibliography

Manuscripts

Bibliothèque Nationale Latin MS 17509
Bibliothèque Nationale Latin MS 3284
British Library MS Royal 14 c vii
British Library MS Harley 2321

Primary Sources

Cartularies

Abbayette	*Cartulaire de l'Abbayette (997–1421)*, ed. M. Bertrand de Broussillon, *Bulletin de la Commission Historique et Archéologique de la Mayene*, 2nd series, 9 (Laval, 1894)
Abingdon	*Two Cartularies of Abingdon Abbey*, ed. C. F. Slade and G. Lambrick, 2 vols. Oxford Historical Society, n.s. 32 and 33 (Oxford, 1990–1991)
Absie	*Cartulaire et Chartres de l'Abbaye de l'Absie*, ed. M. B. Ledain, *Archives Historiques du Poitou*, 25 (Poitiers, 1895)
Angély	*Le Cartulaire de l'Abbaye Royale de Saint-Jean d'Angély*, 2 vols. *Archives Historique de la Saintonge et de l'Aunis*, 30 and 33 (Paris–Saintes, 1901 and 1903)
Angoulême	*Cartulaire de l'Eglise d'Angoulême*, ed. I. Nanglard, *Bulletin de la Société Archéologique et Historique de la Charente* (Angoulême, 1900)
Aniane	*Cartulaire d'Aniane*, ed. l'Abbé Cassan and E. Meynial, *Société Archéologique de Montpellier* (Montpellier, 1900)
Apt	*Cartulaire de l'Eglise d'Apt (835–1130)*, ed. N. Didier, H. Dubled and J. Barruol (Paris, 1967)
Artige	*Chartularium Prioratus Artigiensis*, ed. G. de Senneville, *Bulletin de la Société Archéologique et Historique du Limousin*, 48 (1900), pp. 291–374
Auch	*Cartulaire du Chapitre de l'Eglise Métropolitaine Sainte-Marie d'Auch*, ed. C. L. La Plagne Barris (Paris and Auch, 1899)
Aureil	*Cartulaire du Prieré d'Aureil*, ed. G. de Senneville, *Bulletin de la Société Archéologique et Historique du Limousin*, 48 (1900), pp. 1–289
Baigne	*Cartulaire de l'Abbaye de Saint-Etienne de Baigne*, ed. l'Abbé Cholet (Niort, 1868)
Barbezieux	*Cartulaire du Prieuré de Notre-Dame de Barbezieux*, ed. La Martinière, *Archives Historiques de la Saintonge et de l'Aunis*, 41 (1911)

Bas-Poitou   *Cartulaires du Bas-Poitou*, ed. P. Marchegay (Les Roches-Baritaud, 1877)

Beaujeu   *Cartulaire de l'Eglise Collégiale Notre-Dame de Beaujeu*, ed. M. C. Guigue (Lyon, 1864)

Beaulieu   *Cartulaire de l'Abbaye de Beaulieu en Limousin*, ed. M. Deloche, *Collections de Documents Inédits sur l'Histoire de France* (Paris, 1859)

Berdoues   *Cartulaire de Berdoues*, ed. l'Abbé Cazauran (La Haye, 1905)

Beziers   *Cartulaire de Béziers*, ed. J. Rouquette (Paris and Montpellier, 1918)

Blyth   *Cartulary of Blyth Priory*, ed. R. T. Timson, 2 vols. *Thornton Society Record Society Series* (London, 1973)

Boixe   *Cartulaire de l'Abbaye de Saint-Amant-de-Boixe*, ed. A. Debord, *Société Archéologique et Historique de la Charente* (Poitiers, 1982)

Bonnefoy   *Cartulaire de la Chartreuse de Bonnefoy*, ed. J.-L. Lemaitre (Paris, 1990)

Bourbonnais   *Chartes de Bourbonnais 918–1522*, ed. J. Monicat and B. de Fournoux (1952)

Brinkburn   *The Chartulary of Brinkburn Priory*, ed. W. Page, Surtees Society, 90 (Durham, 1893)

Bugey   *Petit Cartulaire de Saint-Sulpice en Bugey*, ed. M. C. Guigue (Lyon, 1884)

Burton   G. Wrottesley, 'An Abstract of the Contents of the Burton Cartulary in the Possession of Marquis of Anglesey at Beaudesert', *Collections for a History of Staffordshire edited by the William Salt Archaeological Society*, vol. 5, part 1 (1884)

Cathédrale   *Cartulaire Noir de la Cathédrale d'Angers*, ed. Ch. Urseau (Paris,
Angers   Angers, 1908)

Cellefrouin   *La Cartulaire de L'Abbaye de Cellefrouin*, ed. E. Brayer, *Bulletin Philologique et Historique du Comité des Travaux Historiques et Scientifiques* (1940–1941), pp. 85–136

Chalon   *Cartulaire du Prieuré de Saint- Marcel lès Chalon*, ed. P.C. de Chizy, *Société d'Histoire et d'Archéologie de Chalon-sur-Saône* (Chalon-sur-Saône, 1894)

Chamalières-sur- *Cartulaire de Chamalières-sur-Loire*, ed. A. Chassaing (Paris, 1895)
Loire

Chateau du Loir *Cartulaire de Chateau du Loir*, ed. E. Vallée, *Archives Historiques du Maine*, 6 (Le Mans, 1905)

Chateaudun   *Archives de la Maison-Dieu de Chateaudun*, ed. A. de Belfort (Paris and Chateaudun, 1881)

Cluny   *Recueil des Chartes de l'Abbaye de Cluny*, ed. A. Bernard, rev. A. Bruel, 6 vols. *Collection de Documents inédits sur l'Histoire de France* (Paris, 1876–1903)

Corbeil   *Le Cartulaire de Saint-Spire de Corbeil au diocèse du Paris*, ed. E. Conard-Luys, *Memoires et Documents publiées par la Société Archéologique de Rambouillet*, 6 (1882)

Cormery   *Cartulaire de Cormery*, ed. J.-J. Bourasse, *Memoires de la Société archéologique de Touraine*, 12 (Tours–Paris, 1861)

Domène   *Cartulaire Monasterii Beatorum Petri et Pauli de Domina*, ed. Ch. de Monteyard (Lyon, 1859)

Dorat   *Receuil des Textes et d'Analyses concernant le Chapitre Saint-Pierre du Dorat*, ed. J. Font-Réaulx, Bulletin de la Société Archéologique et Historique du Limousin, 72 (1927), pp. 250–346

Dublin   *Cartularies of St Mary's Abbey Dublin*, ed. G. T. Gilbert, 2 vols. RS 80 (London, 1884)

Eynsham   *Eynsham Cartulary*, ed. H. E. Salter, 2 vols. Oxford Historical Society, 49 and 51 (Oxford, 1907–1908)

Fontaine le   *Recueil des Documents de l'Abbaye de Fontaine-le-Comte (XIIe–
Comte   XIIIe)*, ed. G. Pon, Archives Historiques du Poitou, 61 (Poitiers, 1982)

Fontmorigny   *Le Chartrier Ancien de Fontmorigny Abbaye de l'Ordre de Cîteaux*, ed. A. Huchet (Bourges, 1936)

Fountains   *Abstract of the Charters and Other Documents contained in the Chartulary of the Cistercian Abbey of Fountains*, ed. W. T. Lancaster, 2 vols. (Leeds, 1915)

Gellone   *Cartulaire de Gellone*, ed. P. Alaus, l'Abbé Cassan and E. Meynial, Société Archéolgique de Montpellier (Montpellier, 1898)

Gimont   *Cartulaire de l'Abbaye de Gimont*, ed. l'Abbé Clergeac, Archives Historiques de Gascogne, 2nd Series, fasc. 9 (Paris and Auch, 1905)

Gloucester   *Historia et Cartularium Monasterii Sancti Petri Gloucestriae*, ed. W. H. Hart, 3 vols. RS 33 (London, 1863–1867)

Grenoble   *Cartulaires de l'Eglise Cathédrale de Grenoble*, ed. J. Marion, Collection de Documents Inédits sur l'Histore de France (Paris, 1869)

Gyseburne   *Chartularium Prioratus de Gyseburne*, ed. W. Brown, 2 vols. Surtees Society, 86 and 89 (Durham, 1889–1894)

Haughmond   *The Cartulary of Haughmond Abbey*, ed. U. Rees (Cardiff, 1985)

Hospital of   *Cartulaire Général de l'Ordre des Hospitaliers de S. Jean de Jérusalem
St John in   (1100–1310)*, ed. J. Delaville le Roulx, 4 vols. (Paris, 1894–1905,
Jerusalem   rprt. Munich, 1980)

Hospital of   *A Cartulary of the Hospital of St John the Baptist*, ed. H. E. Salter, 3
St John the   vols. Oxford Historical Society (Oxford, 1914–1916)
Baptist

Josaphat   *Cartulaire de Notre-Dame de Josaphat*, ed. l'Abbé Ch. Métais, 2 vols. (Chartres, 1904)

Léoncel   *Cartulaire de l'Abbaye Notre-Dame de Léoncel*, ed. C. U. J. Chevalier, Collection de Cartulaires de Dauphinois, 4 (Montelimar, 1869)

Lézat   *Cartulaire de l'Abbaye de Lézat*, ed. P. Ourliac, 2 vols. (Paris, 1984–1987)

Limoges   *Sancti Stephani Lemovicensis Cartularium*, ed. J. de Font-Réaulx, Bulletin de la Société Archéologique et Historique du Limousin, 69 (Limoges, 1919)

Longpont   *Le Cartulaire du Prieuré de Notre-Dame de Longpont*, ed. A. Marion (Lyon, 1879)

Lyonnais   *Cartulaire Lyonnais*, ed. M. C. Guigne, 2 vols. (Lyon, 1885–1893)

Mâcon   *Cartulaire de Saint-Vincent de Mâcon*, ed. M. C. Ragut, Collections de Documents inédits sur l'Histoire de France (Mâcon, 1864)

Manceau de   *Cartulaire Manceau de Marmoutier*, ed. E. Laurain, 2 vols. (Laval,
Marmoutier   1911–1945)

Marcigny-sur-Loire
Le Cartulaire de Marcigny-sur-Loire (1045–1144), ed. J. Richard, *Analecta Burgundica* (Dijon, 1957)

Marmoutier pour le Vendomois
Cartulaire de Marmoutier pour le Vendomois, ed. M. de Trémault (Paris and Vendome, 1893)

Marseille
Cartulaire de l'Abbaye de Saint-Victor de Marseille, ed. M. Guérard, 2 vols, *Collection des Cartulaires de France*, 8 and 9 (Paris, 1857).

Mauléon
Documents pour servir à l'Histoire de l'Abbaye de la Trinité de Mauléon 1090–1623, ed. B. Ledain, *Archives Historiques du Poitou*, 20 (Poitiers, 1889)

Merci-Dieu
Cartulaire de l'Abbaye de Notre-Dame de la Merci-Dieu, ed. E. Clouzot, *Archives Historiques du Poitou*, 34 (Poitiers, 1905)

Montpellier
Liber Instrumentorum Memorialium. Cartulaire des Guillems de Montpellier, *La Société Archéologique de Montpellier* (Montpellier, 1884–1886)

Nogent-le-Rotrou
Saint Denis de Nogent-le-Rotrou 1031–1789. Histoire et Cartulaire, ed. Vicomte de Sovancé and l'Abbé Ch. Métais, *Archives du Diocèse de Chartres* (Vannes, 1899)

Notre Dame de Chartres
Cartulaire de Notre-Dame de Chartres, ed. E. de Lépinois and L. Merlet, *Société Archéologique d'Eure-et-Loire*, 3 vols. (Chartres, 1862–1865)

Nouaillé
Chartes de l'Abbaye de Nouaillé du Poitou de 678 à 1200, ed. P. de Monsabert, *Archives Historiques du Poitou*, 49 (Poitiers, 1936)

Noyers
Cartulaire de l'Abbaye de Noyers, ed. l'Abbé C. Chevalier, *Mémoires de la Société de Touraine*, vol. 22 (Tours, 1872), pp. 1–710

Obazine
Le Cartulaire de l'Abbaye Cistercienne d'Obazine (XIIe–XIIe) siècle, ed. B. Barrière (1989)

Orléans
Cartulaire de l'Eglise Cathédrale Sainte-Croix d'Orléans (814–1300), ed. J. Thillier and E. Jarry, *Mémoires de la Société Archéologique et Historique de l'Orléanais*, 30 (Orleans, 1906)

Poitiers
Cartulaire de l'Abbaye de Saint-Cyprien de Poitiers, *Archives Historiques du Poitou*, 3 (Poitiers, 1874)

Pontigny
Le Premier Cartulaire de l'Abbaye de Pontigny (XIIe and XIIIe siècles), ed. M. Garrigues (Paris, 1981)

Rouen
Chartularium Monasterii Sanctae Trinitatis de Monte Rothomagi, in *Cartulaire de l'Abbaye de Saint Bertin*, ed. M. Guérard (Paris, 1841)

Saint Aubin d'Angers
Cartulaire de l'Abbaye de Saint-Aubin d'Angers, ed. B. de Broussillon, 3 vols. (Paris, 1896–1903)

Saint Bénigne de Dijon
Chartes et Documents de Saint-Bénigne de Dijon. Prieurés et Dependances des Origines à 1300, ed. G. Chevrier and M. Chaume, 2 vols. *Analecta Burgundica* (Dijon, 1943–1986)

Saint Croix de Bordeaux
Cartulaire de l'Abbaye Sainte-Croix de Bordeaux, *Archives Historiques du Départment de la Gironde*, 27 (1892)

Saint Cybard
Cartulaire de l'Abbaye de Saint Cybard, ed. M. P. Lefrancq, *Société Historique et Archéologique de la Charente* (Angoulême, 1930)

Saint Etienne de Dijon
Cartulaire de l'Abbaye de Saint-Etienne de Dijon de 1140 à 1155, ed. M. Bourrier (Paris and Dijon, 1912)

Saint Jean en Vallée de Chartres
Cartulaire de Saint-Jean-en-Vallée de Chartres, ed. P. Meriet, *Collection de Cartulaires Chartrains*, 1 (Chartres, 1906)

Saint Laud d'Angers — *Cartulaire du Chapitre de Saint-Laud d'Angers. Actes du XIe et du XIIe Siècle*, ed. A. Planchenault, *Documents Historiques sur l'Anjou*, 4 (Angers, 1903)

Saint Maixent — *Chartes et Documents pour servir à l'Histoire de l'Abbaye de Saint-Maixent*, ed. M. A. Richard, *Archives Historiques du Poitou*, 16 and 18 (Poitiers, 1886)

Saint Mont — *Cartulaire du Prieuré de Saint-Mont*, ed. J. de Jaurgain, *Archives Historiques de la Gascogne* (Paris/Auch, 1904)

Saint Nicholas d'Angers — *Cartulaire d'Azé et du Genéteil de l'Abbaye Saint Nicholas d'Angers 1080–1637*, ed. M. du Brossay, *Archives Historiques du Mans*, 3 (Le Mans, 1903), pp. 49–146

Saint Père de Chartres — *Cartulaire de l'Abbaye de Saint Père de Chartres*, ed. M. Guérard, 2 vols., *Collection de Documents inédits sur l'Histoire de France* (Paris, 1840)

Saint Seurin de Bordeaux — *Cartulaire de l'Eglise Collégiale Saint-Seurin de Bordeaux*, ed. J. A. Brutails (Bordeaux, 1897)

Saint Victeur au Mans — *Cartulaire de Saint Victeur au Mans, Prieuré de l'Abbaye du Mont-Saint Michel (994–1400)*, ed. P. de Farcy (Paris, 1895)

Saint Vincent du Mans — *Cartulaire de l'Abbaye de Saint-Vincent du Mans*, ed. R. Charles and M. d'Elbenne, 2 vols. (Mamers and Le Mans, 1886–1913)

San Cugat del Vallés — *Cartulaire de Sant-Cugat des Vallés*, ed. J. Rius Serra, 3 vols. (Barcelona, 1945–1947)

Sauxillanges — *Cartulaire de Sauxillanges*, ed. H. Doniol (Paris and Clermont-Ferrand, 1864)

Savigny — *Cartulaire de l'Abbaye de Savigny suivi du Petit Cartulaire de l'Abbaye d'Ainay*, ed. A. Bernard, 2 vols. *Collection de Documents inédits sur l'Histoire de France* (Paris, 1853)

Second Cartulary of Saint Vincent du Mans — *Liber Controversarium Sancti Vincentii Cenomannensis ou Second Cartulaire de l'Abbaye de Saint-Vincent du Mans*, ed. A. Chédeville, *Institut de Recherches Historiques de Rennes* (Paris, 1969)

Solesmes — *Cartulaire des Abbayes de Saint-Pierre de la Couture et de Solesmes* (Le Mans, 1881)

Sorde — *Cartulaire de l'Abbaye de Saint Jean de Sorde*, ed. P. Raymond (Paris, 1873)

Talmond — *Cartulaires de l'Abbaye de Talmond*, ed. L. de la Boutetière, *Mémoires de la Société des Antiquaires de l'Ouest*, 36 (1872)

Tiron — *Cartulaire de l'Abbaye de la Sainte-Trinité de Tiron*, ed. M. L. Merlet, 2 vols. *Société Archéologique d'Eure-et-Loire* (Chartres, 1883)

Toulouse — *Cartulaire de Saint-Sernin de Toulouse (844–1200)*, ed. C. Douais (Paris and Toulouse, 1887)

Tours — *Chartes de Saint Julien de Tours (1002–1300)*, *Archives Historique du Maine*, 12 (Le Mans, 1912)

Tulle and Rocamadour — *Cartulaire des Abbayes de Tulle et de Roc-Amadour*, ed. J.-B. Champeval (Brive, 1903)

Uzerche — *Cartulaire de l'Abbaye d'Uzerche*, ed. J.-B. Champeval (Paris, 1901)

Vaux de Cernay — *Cartulaire de l'Abbaye de Notre Dame de Vaux de Cernay*, ed. L. Merlet and A. Moutié, 3 vols. (Paris, 1857–1858)

Vendôme   *Cartulaire de l'Abbaye Cardinale de la Trinité de Vendôme*, ed. l'Abbé Ch. Métais, 6 vols. (Paris, 1893–1904)

Vienne   *Cartulaire de l'Abbaye de Saint-André-le-Bas de Vienne*, ed. C. U. J. Chevalier, *Collection de Cartulaires de Dauphinois*, 1 (Lyon, 1869)

Vigeois   *Chartularium Monasterii Sancti Petri Vosiensis, Bulletin de la Société Archéologique et Historique du Limousin*, 39 (1890), pp. 1–303

Vignory   *Cartulaire du Prieuré de Saint Etienne de Vignory*, ed. J. D'Arbaumont (Langres, 1882)

Villeloin   *Cartulaire de l'Abbaye de Saint-Sauveur de Villeloin*, ed. L.-J. Denis, *Archives du Cogner*, Ser. H, Art. 97 (Paris/Le Mans, 1911)

Whitby   *Cartularium Abbathiae de Whitby*, ed. J. C. Atkinson, 2 vols. Surtees Society, 69 and 72 (Durham, 1879–1881)

Yonne   *Cartulaire Général de l'Yonne*, ed. M. M. Quantin, 2 vols. (Auxerre, 1854–1860)

Acta Sanctorum

Anselm the Monk, *Dedicatio Ecclesiae et Translatio S. Remigii*, AASS Oct. I, pp. 176–185

Philip, Prior of St Frideswide's, *Miracula S. Frideswidae*, AASS Oct. VIII, pp. 567–590

De S. Adelelmo sive Elesme, AASS Jan. II, pp. 1056–1060

De S. Aderaldo Archidiacono, AASS Oct. VIII, pp. 980–995

De S. Alberto Agricola, AASS May II, p. 281

De B. Alberto Eremita in Territorio Senensi, AASS Jan. I, pp. 402–404

De S. Atto seu Atthone, AASS May V, pp. 194–203

De S. Ayberto Presbytero, AASS April I, pp. 672–682

De S. Bobone seu Bovo, AASS May V, pp. 184–191

De S. Bona Virgine, AASS May VII, pp. 144–164

De S. Chelidonia Virgine apud Sublacum in Latio, AASS Oct. VI, pp. 362–377

De S. Drogone Recluso, AASS April II, pp. 441–445

De Famiano Confessore Ordinis Cisterciensis Anachoreta, AASS Aug. II, pp. 389–395

De Furseo Confessore, AASS Jan. II, pp. 35–55

De S. Gerlaco eremita in Belgio, AASS Jan. I, pp. 304–321

De S. Guilielmo Abbate, AASS June V, pp. 112–139

Vita S. Helenae Viduae et Mart., AASS July VII, pp. 329–333

De Beato Henrico Zdiko, Episcopo in Olomucensi in Moravia, AASS June V, pp. 140–143

De B. Hildegunde Comitissa, Fundatrice Coenobii Marensis Ordinis Praemonstratensis, AASS Feb. I, pp. 916–922

De S. Iohanne Eremita Presb., AASS June I, pp. 260–263

De B. Irmgarde Virgine, AASS Sept. II, pp. 270–278

De S. Ludano Peregrino, AASS Feb. II, pp. 638–639

De S. Lutgarde Virgine, AASS June III, pp. 231–263

De Sancta Maria Cleophae, AASS Apr. I, pp. 811–818

De S. Morando. Monacho Cluniacensi in Suntgovia, AASS June I, pp. 339–359

De B. Oldegario Archiepiscopo Tarraconensi et Episcopi Barcinonensi, AASS March I, pp. 481–498

De S. Petro, AASS May II, pp. 320–348

Vita S. Raymundi Palmarii, AASS July VI, pp. 638–663

De S. Stephano. Tertio Abbate Cisterciensi in Gallia, AASS April II, pp. 496–501

Other Primary Sources

Acta Pontificum Romanorum Inedita, ed. J. Pflugk-Harttung, 3 vols. (Stuttgart, 1881–1886)

Adam of Bremen, Hamburgische Kirchengeschichte, ed. B. Schmeidler, Scriptores Rerum Germanicarum in Usum Scholarum (Hanover and Leipzig, 1917)

Adémar de Chabannes, Chronique, ed. J. Chavanon (Paris, 1897)

Adrevaldus Monachus Floriacensi, Historia Translationis S. Benedicti, in Les Miracules de Saint Benoit, Société de l'Histoire de France (Paris, 1858), pp. 1–13

Alberic of Tre Fontaneis, Chronica, MGH.SS 23, pp. 631–950

Albert of Stade, Annales Stadenses, MGH.SS 16, pp. 271–379

Alcuin, Epistolae, ed. E. Duemmler, MGH Epistolae, 4 (Berlin, 1895), pp. 1–481

Alcuin, Vita Willibrordi Archiepiscopi Traiectensis, MGH Rerum Merovingicarum, 7 (1920), pp. 81–141

Alexander III, Epistolae et Privilegia, PL 200.

Alexander Neckam, De Laudibus Divinae Sapientiae, ed. T. Wright, RS 34 (London, 1863), pp. 357–503

St Ambrose, Liber de Viduis, PL 16, cols. 247–276

St Ambrose, Epistolae, PL 16, cols. 913–1342

Analecta Novissima Spicilegii Solesmensis Altera, ed. J. B. Pitra, 2 vols. (Paris, 1885–1888)

Anacletus II, Epistolae et Privilegia, PL 179, cols. 689–732

Andreae Danduli, Chronicon, RIS 12, cols. 14–523

Anglo-Saxon Missionaries in Germany, ed. C. H. Talbot (London and New York, 1954)

Anglo-Saxon Wills, ed. and trans. D. Whitelock (Cambridge, 1930)

Annales Ceccanenses, MGH.SS 19, pp. 275–302

Annales Colmarienses Maiores, MGH.SS 17, pp. 202–232

Annales Gadenses, MGH.SS 16, pp. 555–597

Annales Halesbrunnenses Maiores, MGH.SS 24, pp. 42–51

Annales Marbacenses, MGH.SS 17, pp. 146–180

Annales S. Iustinae Patavini, MGH.SS 19, pp. 148–193

Annales SS. Uldarici et Afrae Augustenses, MGH.SS 17, pp. 428–436

Annales Veteres Mutinensium ab Anno MCXXXI ad Annum usque MCCCXVI, RIS 11, cols. 53–86

Annals of the Kingdom of Ireland by the Four Masters, ed. J. O'Donovan, 7 vols. (Dublin, 1851)

St Anselm, Epistolae, PL 159, cols. 9–272

St Augustine, Confessions, PL 32, cols. 659–868

St Augustine, De Civitate Dei, trans. W. M. Green, 7 vols. Loeb Classical Library (London, 1972)

St Augustine, Sermones, PL 38

St Benedict, Regula cum Commentariis, PL 66, cols. 215–932.

Benedict of Peterborough, The Chronicle of the Reigns of Henry II and Richard I A.D. 1169–1192, ed. W. Stubbs, 2 vols. RS 49 (London, 1867)

St Bernard of Clairvaux, De Consideratione, PL 182, cols. 727–808

St Bernard of Clairvaux, *The Life and Death of Saint Malachy the Irishman*, trans. R. T. Meyer (Kalamazoo, 1978)

Bernard the Monk, *Itinerarium*, PL 121, cols. 569–574

Boniface VIII, *Registers*, ed. G. Digard, M. Faucon, A. Thomas and R. Fawtier, 4 vols. *Bibliothèque des Ecoles Françaises d'Athènes et de Rome*, 2nd series (Paris, 1884–1939)

St Boniface et Lul, *Epistolae*, MGH *Epistolae*, 3 (Berlin, 1892), pp. 215–433

Book of Pontiffs, ed. and trans. R. Davis (Liverpool, 1989)

Book of St Gilbert, ed. R. Foreville and G. Keir, Oxford Medieval Texts (Oxford, 1987)

Book of the Foundation of St Bartholomew's Church in London, ed. N. Moore, Early English Text Society (London, 1923)

Boso, *Life of Alexander III*, trans. G. M. Ellis (Oxford, 1973)

Bullaire du Pape Calixte II 1119–1124. Essai de Restitution, ed. U. Robert, 2 vols. (Paris, 1891)

Burchard of Worms, *Decreta*, PL 140, cols. 537–1058

Calendar of Documents Preserved in France A.D. 918–1206, ed. J. H. Round (London, 1899)

Capitularia Hludowici II, ed. A. Boretius and V. Krause, MGH *Legum*, Sectio 2, vol. 2 (Hanover, 1897), pp. 78–96

Casus Monasterii Petrihusensis, MGH.SS 20, pp. 621–683

Chanson de la Croisade Albigeoise, trans. E. Martin-Chabot, 3 vols. *Les Classiques de l'Histoire de France au Moyen Age* (Paris, 1931–1961)

Chronica S. Petri Erfordensis Moderna, MGH.SS 30, Part 1, pp. 335–472

Chronicle of Bury St Edmunds 1212–1301, ed. and trans. A. Gransden (London, 1964)

Chronicle of St Mary's Abbey, York, ed. H. H. E. Craster and M. E. Thornton, Surtees Society, 148 (Durham, 1933)

Chronicon Abbatiae de Evesham ad Annum 1418, ed. W. D. Macray, RS 29 (London, 1863)

Chronicon B. Iterii Armarii Monasterii S. Marcialis, ed. H. Duplès-Agier, *Société de l'Histoire de France* (Paris, 1874)

Chronicon Farfense di Gregorio di Catina, ed. U. Balzani, 2 vols. *Fonti per la Storia d'Italia*, 33 and 34 (Rome, 1903)

Chronicon Fratris Francisci Pipini, RIS 9, cols. 587–752

Chronicon Monasterii Casinensis, MGH.SS 7, pp. 551–844

Chronicon Parmense ab Anno MXXXVIII usque ad Annum MCCCIX autore anonymo Synchrono, RIS 9, cols. 759–880

Chronique d'Ernoul et de Bernard le Trésorier, ed. M. L. de Mas Latrie, *Société de l'Histoire de France*, 157 (Paris, 1871)

Codice Diplomatico Bares. Le Carte di Molfetta, ed. F. Carabellese (Bari, 1912)

Codice Diplomatico del Senato Romano dal 1147 al 1347, ed. F. Bartoloni, *Fonti per la Storia d'Italia*, 87 (Rome, 1948)

Codice Topografico della Città di Roma, ed. R. Valentini and G. Zuchetti, 4 vols. *Fonti per la Storia d'Italia* 81, 88, 90 and 91 (Rome, 1940–1953)

Collectione Bullarum Sacrosancta Basilicae Vaticana, ed. A. Albani, 3 vols. (Rome, 1747–1752)

Concilia Aevi Karolini, MGH *Legum*, Sectio 3, vol. 2, pt 1 (Hanover and Leipzig, 1906)

Conciliorum Oecumenicorum Decreta, ed. J. Alberigo *et al.*, 3rd ed. (Bologna, 1973)

Conrad of Ursperg, *Chronicon* (1609)

Continuatio Florianensis 1273–1309, MGH.SS 9, pp. 747–753

Corpus Iuris Canonici, ed. A. Friedberg, 2 vols. (1879–1881)

Coutumiers de Normandie, ed. E.-J. Tardif, 3 vols. (Rouen, 1881, reprt. Geneva, 1977)

Cummian, *Epistola ad Segienum Huensem Abbatem de Controversia Paschali*, PL 87, cols. 969–978

Curia Regis Rolls of the Reigns of Richard I and John (London, 1922)

Eadmer, *The Life of St Anselm Archbishop of Canterbury*, ed. and trans. R. W. Southern (London, 1962)

Early Christian Writings, trans. M. Staniforth, rev. A. Louth (London, 1987)

Early Travels in Palestine, ed. T. Wright (London, 1848)

Early Yorkshire Charters, ed. W. Farrer *et al.*, 12 vols. (Edinburgh, 1914–1965).

Early Yorkshire Families, ed. C. Clay and D. E. Greenway (1973)

E Floribus Chronicorum seu Catalogo Romanorum Pontificum, Necnon e Chronico Regum Francorum Auctore Bernardo Guidone, RHGF, 21 (Paris, 1855), pp. 690–734

Egeria's Travels, ed. J. Wilkinson (London, 1971)

Emonis Chronicon, MGH.SS 23, pp. 465–523

Epistolae Cantuariensis, in *Chronicles and Memorials of the Reign of Richard I*, ed. W. Stubbs, 2 vols. RS 38 (London, 1864–1865)

Epistolae Karolini Aevi, MGH Epistolae, vol. 6 (Berlin, 1925)

Epistulae Imperatorum Pontificum Aliorum Inde ab Anno CCCLXVII usque ad Annum DLIII Datae, ed. O. Guenther, *Corpus Scriptorum Ecclesiasticorum Latinorum*, 35 (Vienna, 1895)

Eunapius of Sardis, *Lives of the Philosophers and Sophists*, trans. W. C. Wright, Loeb Classical Library (London, 1952)

Eusebius, *Ecclesiastical History*, trans. K. Lake, 2 vols. Loeb Classical Library (London, 1926)

Eusebius, *Life of Constantine the Great*, in *Nicene and Post-Nicene Fathers of the Christian Church*, ed. H. Wace and P. Schaff, New Series, vol. 1 (Oxford, 1890), pp. 481–559

Ex Annalibus Aquicinctensis Monasterii, RHGF 18 (Paris, 1879), pp. 534–554

Ex Auctario Aquicinctino, RHGF 13 (Paris, 1869), pp. 278–282

Ex Gestis Trevirensium Archiepiscoporum, RHGF 18 (Paris, 1879), pp. 670–676.

Ex Historia Episcoporum Autissiodorensium, RHGF 18 (Paris, 1879), pp. 725–741

Florence of Worcester, *Chronicon*, ed. B. Thorpe, 2 vols. (London, 1848–1849)

Formulae Merowingici et Karoli Aevi, ed. K. Zeumer, MGH Legum, Sectio 5 (Hanover, 1886)

Fuero del Estella, ed. G. Holmér, *Leges Hispanicae Medii Aevi*, 10 (Karlsham, 1963)

Fulcher of Chartres, *Historia Hierosolymitana (1095–1127)*, ed. H. Hagenmeyer (Heidelberg, 1913)

Gerald of Wales, *De Invectionibus*, in *Opera*, ed. J. F. Dimmock, G. F. Warner and J. S. Brewer, 8 vols. RS 21 (London, 1861–1891), vol. 1, pp. 125–196

Gerald of Wales, *De Iure et Statu Menevensis Ecclesiae*, in *Opera*, vol. 3, pp. 101–373

Gerald of Wales, *De Rebus a se Gestis*, in *Opera*, vol. 1, pp. 3–122

Gerald of Wales, *Speculum Ecclesiae*, in *Opera*, vol. 4, pp. 3–354

Gerald of Wales, *Gemma Ecclesiastica*, ed. J. J. Hagen (Leiden, 1979)

Gervase of Tilbury, *Otia Imperialia*, ed. G. G. Leibnitz, *Scriptores Rerum Brunsuicensium* (Hanover, 1707)

Gervase the Monk, *The Chronicles of the Reigns of Stephen, Henry II and Richard I*, in

The Historical Works of Gervase of Canterbury, ed. W. Stubbs, 2 vols. RS 73 (London, 1879–1880)

Gesta Abbatum Trudonensium, MGH.SS 10, pp. 213–448

Gesta Innocentii PP III, PL, 214, cols. xvii–ccxxviii

Giovanni Villani, *Historie Fiorentine*, RIS 13, cols. 9–1002

Gregory VII, *Registers*, PL 148, cols. 283–643

Gregory of Tours, *History of the Franks*, ed. and trans. O. M. Dalton (Oxford, 1927)

Gregory of Tours, *Miraculorum Libri Duo*, PL 71, cols. 705–828

Gregory the Great, *Regestri Epistolarum*, PL 77, cols. 442–1352

Gregory the Great, *Dialogues*, PL 77, cols. 149–430

Guibert of Tournai, *Sermones ad Omnes Status de Novo correcti et emendati* (1510)

Guide du Pèlerin de Saint-Jacques de Compostelle, ed. J. Vielliard, 3rd ed. (Mâcon, 1963)

Haito, Bishop of Basle, *Capitula Ecclesiastica 807–823*, MGH Legum, Sectio 2, vol. 1 (Hanover, 1883), pp. 362–366

Heinrich von Rebdorff, *Annales Imperatorum et paparum 1294–1362*, Fontes Rerum Germanicarum, ed. J. F. Boehmer, 4 vols. (Stuttgart, 1868)

Histoire des Conciles, ed. H. Leclerq, 11 vols. (Paris, 1907–1952)

Histoire Générale de Languedoc, ed. C. Devic and J. Vaissète, and later by E. Roschach and A. Molimier *et al.* (Toulouse, 1872–1904, reprt. 1973)

Historia Compostellana, ed. E. Flórez, España Sagrada, vol. 20 (Madrid, 1765)

Historia Episcoporum Autissiodorensium, RHGF vol. 18, pp. 725–741

Honorius III, *Opera Omnia*, ed. C. A. Horoy, 2 vols. *Medii Aevi Bibliotheca Patristica* (Paris, 1879)

Honorius III, *Registers*, ed. P. Pressutti, 2 vols. (Rome, 1888–1895)

Honorius *Augustodunensis*, *Elucidarium*, PL 172, cols. 1109–1176

Hugh Farsit, *Libellus de Miraculis B. Mariae Virginis in Urbe Suessionensi*, PL 179, cols. 1777–1800

Innocent III, *De Sacro Altaris Mysterio*, PL 217, cols. 763–914

Innocent III, *Registers*, PL 214–217

Innocent III, *Sermones*, PL 217, cols. 310–690

Innocent IV, *Registers*, ed. E. Berger, 4 vols. *Bibliothèque des Ecoles Françaises d'Athènes et de Rome*, 2nd series (Paris, 1884–1921)

Instrumenta Insigniora ad Historiam Legionensem, ed M. Risco, España Sagrada, 36 (Madrid, 1787)

Itinerarium Burdigalense, ed. P. Geyer and O. Cuntz, Corpus Christianorum Series Latina, 175 (1965), pp. 1–26

Ivo of Chartres, *Decretum*, PL 161, cols. 9–1036.

Jacques de Vitry, *Historia Occidentalis*, ed. J. F. Hinnesbusch (Fribourg, 1972)

Jacques de Vitry, *Lettres*, ed. R. B. C. Huygens (Leiden, 1960)

St Jerome, *Commentariorum in Ezechielem*, PL 25, cols. 15–490.

St Jerome, *Epistolae*, PL 22, cols. 325–1192

St Jerome, *Liber Contra Vigilantium*, PL 23, cols. 353–368

Jerusalem Pilgrimage 1099–1185, ed. J. Wilkinson, J. Hill and W. F. Ryan (London, 1988)

Jocelin of Brakelond, *Chronicles concerning the Acts of Samson Abbot of the Monastery of St Edmund*, trans. H. E. Butler (London, 1949).

John of Salisbury, *Historia Pontificalis*, ed. M. Chibnall, Oxford Medieval Texts (Oxford, 1956)

Karoli Magni Capitularia, ed. A. Boretius, *MGH Legum*, Sectio 2, vol. 1 (Hanover, 1883), pp. 44–186

Karoli Magni et Pippini Filii Capitularia Italica, ed. A. Boretius, *MGH Legum*, Sectio 2, part 1 (Hanover, 1883), pp. 187–212

P. Kehr, *Italia Pontificia*, 8 vols. (Rome, 1906)

Lambert, Bishop of Arras, *Epistolae*, *RHGF* vol. 15, pp. 178–207

Lampert of Hersfeld, *Opera*, ed. O. Holder-Egger (Hanover, 1852).

Latin Poems commonly attributed to Walter Mapes, ed. T. Wright, Camden Society, 16 (London, 1841)

Laxdaela Saga, trans M. Magnusson and H. Pálsson (1969)

Leo IX, *Epistolae et Decreta Pontificia*, PL 143, cols. 591–798

Lex Baiwariorum, ed. E. L. B. de Schwind, *MGH.Legum*, Sectio 1, vol. 5 (Hanover, 1888), pp. 179–473

Liber Censuum de l'Eglise Romaine, ed. P. Fabre and L. Duchesne, 3 vols. (Paris, 1905–1910)

Liber Diurnus Romanorum Pontificum, ed. E. de Rozière (Paris, 1889)

Liber Pontificalis, ed. L. Duchesne, 2 vols., 2nd ed. *Bibliothèque des Ecoles Françaises d'Athènes et de Rome* (Paris, 1955), vol. 3 Additions et Corrections de Mgr. L. Duchesne publiées par C. Vogel (Paris, 1957)

Liber Sancti Jacobi, Codex Calixtinus, ed. M. M. Whitehill, 2 vols. (Santiago de Compostela, 1944)

F. Liebermann, *Die Gesetze der Angelsachsen*, 3 vols. (Halle, 1903–1916)

Life of St Hugh of Lincoln, ed. D. L. Douie and H. Farmer, 2 vols. (London, 1961–1962)

Lives of the Eighth Century Popes, ed. and trans. R. Davis (Liverpool, 1992)

Lives of the Ninth Century Popes, ed. and trans. R. Davies (Liverpool, 1995)

Lucas, Bishop of Tuy, *Vita B. Martin Legionensis*, PL 208, cols. 9–24

Lucius III, *Epistolae et Privilegia*, PL 201, cols. 1071–1376

Master Gregory, *The Marvels of Rome*, ed. and trans. J. Osborne (Toronto, 1987)

Materials for the History of Thomas Becket, ed. J. C. Robinson and J. B. Sheppard, 7 vols. RS 67 (London, 1875–1895)

Matthew Paris, *Chronica Maiora*, ed. H. R. Luard, 7 vols. RS 57 (London, 1872–1883)

Memorials of St Dunstan Archbishop of Canterbury, ed. W. Stubbs, RS 63 (London, 1874)

Mirabilia Urbis Romae, ed. and trans. F. M. Nichols, 2nd ed. (New York, 1986)

Miracles de Notre Dame de Chartres, ed. A. Thomas, in *Bibliothèque de l'Ecole des Chartes*, 42 (1881), pp. 505–550

Miracles de Notre Dame de Rocamadour au XIIe siècle, ed. and trans. E. Albe (Paris, 1907)

Nicholas IV, *Registers*, ed. E. Langlois, 2 vols. *Bibliothèque des Ecoles Françaises d'Athènes et de Rome* (Paris, 1886–1893)

Njal's Saga, trans. M. Magnusson and H. Pálsson (1960)

Notae Tegernseenses, MGH.SS 15, Part 2, pp. 1066–1068

Orderic Vitalis, *The Ecclesiastical History*, ed. and trans. M. Chibnall, 6 vols. (Oxford, 1969–1978)

Origines Islandicae, ed. G. Vigfusson and F. Y. Powell, 2 vols. (Oxford, 1905)

Orkneyinga Saga. The History of the Earls of Orkney, trans. H. Pálsson and P. Edwards (London, 1981)

Otto of Freising, *Gesta Friderici I Imperatoris*, ed. R. G. Waitz, *Scriptores Rerum Germanicarum in Usum Scholarum*, 3rd ed. (Hanover, 1912)

Paolo Vergerio, *Epistolario*, ed. L. Smith, *Fonti per la Storia d'Italia* (Rome, 1934)

Paulinus, *Vita Sancti Ambrosii*, PL, 14, cols. 29–50

Paulinus of Nola, *Epistolae*, PL 61, cols. 153–438

Paulinus' Churches at Nola, ed. R. Goldschimdt (Amsterdam, 1940)

G. Pennotto, *Generalis totius Sacri Ordinis Clericorum Canonicorum Historia Triparta* (Rome, 1624)

Peter the Chanter, *Summa de Sacramentis et Animae Consiliis*, ed. J. A. Dugauquier, *Analecta Mediaevalia*, 7 (1957)

Peter the Venerable, *Letters*, ed. G. Constable, 2 vols. *Harvard Historical Studies*, 78 (Massachusetts, 1967)

Peter William, *Miracula S. Aegidii*, MGH.SS 12, pp. 316–323

Pippini Capitularia, Capitularia Regum Francorum, ed. A. Boretius, MGH *Legum*, Sectio 2, vol. 1 (Hanover, 1883), pp. 31–43

Prefect and Emperor. The Relationes of Symmachus A.D. 384, ed. and trans. R. H. Barrow (Oxford, 1973)

Prudentius, *Peristephanon* in *Opera*, trans. H. J. Thomson, 2 vols. Loeb Classical Library (London, 1962–3)

Ptolomy of Lucca, *Historia Ecclesiastica*, RIS 11, cols. 753–1242

Radulph Glaber, *Historiarum Libri Quinque*, ed. and trans. J. France, Oxford Medieval Texts (Oxford, 1989)

Ralph de Diceto, *Ymagines Historiarum*, ed. W. Stubbs, 2 vols. RS 68 (London, 1876)

Regesta Pontificum Romanorum ab condita ecclesia ad annum post Christum natum MCXCVIII, ed. P. Jaffé, 2 vols. (Leipzig, 1885–1888)

Regesta Pontificum Romanorum inde ab Anno Post Christum natum MCXCVIII ad Anno MCCCIV, ed. A. Potthast, 2 vols. (Berlin, 1874, reprt Graz, 1957)

'Regesto del monastero di S. Silvestro di Capite', ed. V. Federici, ASRSP, 22 (1899), pp. 213–300

Reginald of Durham, *Libellus de Vita et Miraculis S. Godrici heremitae de Finchale*, ed. J. Stevenson, Surtees Society, 20 (1847)

Riccobaldo of Ferrara, *Historia Pontificia Romanorum*, RIS 9, cols. 103–186

Roger of Howden, *Chronica*, ed. W. Stubbs, 4 vols. RS 51 (London, 1868–1871)

Roger of Wendover, *Flores Historiarum*, ed. H. G. Hewlett, 3 vols. RS 84 (London, 1886–1889)

Sacrae Antiquitatis Monumenta Historica, Dogmatica, Diplomatica, ed. C. L. Hugo (1725)

Sacrorum Conciliorum Nova et Amplissima Collectio, ed. J. D. Mansi *et al.*, 55 vols. (Venice and Florence, 1759–1962)

Selected Letters of Pope Innocent III Concerning England (1198–1216), ed. C. R. Cheney and W. H. Semple (London, 1953).

Self and Society in Medieval France. The Memoirs of Guibert of Nogent, ed. J. F. Benton (1974)

Series Episcoporum Ecclesiae Catholicae, ed. P. B. Gams (Leipzig, 1931)

Sifridi Presbyteri de Balnhusin, Historia Universalis et Compendium Historiarum, MGH.SS 25, pp. 679–718

Stacions of Rome and the Pilgrims Sea Voyage, ed. F. J. Furnivall, Early English Text Society (London, 1867)

Statuti della Provincia Romana, Fonti per la Storia d'Italia, 69 (Rome, 1930)

Suger, *De Consecratione*, in *Abbot Suger on the Abbey Church of St Denis and its Art Treasures*, ed. and trans. E. Panofsky, 2nd ed. (Princeton, 1979).

The Miracles of Saint James: Translations of the 'Liber Sancti Jacobi', ed. T. Coffey, L. Davidson and M. Dunn (New York, 1996)

The Pilgrim's Guide to Santiago de Compostella, ed. W. Melczer (New York, 1993)

Tertullian, *Adversus Marcionem*, ed. and trans. E. Evans, 2 vols. (Oxford, 1972)

A. Theiner, *Codex Diplomaticus Domini Temporalis S. Sedis*, 2 vols. (Rome, 1861)

Theodulph of Orléans, *Carmina*, MGH *Poetae Latini*, 1 (Berlin 1881), pp. 437–581

Thesaurus Palaeohibernicus. A Collection of Old-Irish Glosses Scholia Prose and Verse, ed. W. Stokes and J. Strachan, 3 vols. (Cambridge, 1901–1910)

Thomas of Monmouth, *Life and Miracles of St William of Norwich*, ed. A. Jessopp and M. R. James (Cambridge, 1896)

Tractatus de legibus et consuetudinibus regni Anglie qui Glanvilla vocatur, ed. D. G. D. Hall (London, 1965)

Translatio Sanctorum Alexandri Papae et Iustini Presbyteri, MGH.SS 15, pp. 286–288

Udalrico, *Antiquiores Consuetudines Cluniacensis Monasterii*, PL 149, cols. 635–778

Vita Stephani Regis Ungariae, MGH.SS 11, pp. 222–242

Vitae Patrum, PL 73

Walter Map, *De Nugis Curialium*, ed. and trans. M. R. James, rev. C. N. L. Brooke and R. A. B. Mynors (Oxford, 1983)

E. C. Werlauff, *Symbolae ad Geographiam Medii Aevi ex Monumentis Islandicis* (Hauniae, 1821)

Wibert, *Vita S. Leonis*, PL 143, cols. 457–504

William of Andres, *Chronicon*, MGH.SS 24, pp. 684–773

William of Malmesbury, *De Gestis Regum Anglorum*, ed. W. Stubbs, 2 vols. RS 90 (London, 1887–1889)

William of Malmesbury, *Vita Wulfstani*, ed. R. R. Darlington, Camden Society, 40, 3rd series (London, 1928)

William of Tyre, *Chronique*, ed. R. B. C. Huygens, 2 vols., *Corpus Christianorum Continuatio Mediaevalis*, 63 (Turnholti, 1986)

William of Tyre, *Historia Rerum in Partibus Transmarinsi Gestarum*, PL 201, cols. 209–892

William of Ventura, *Chronicon Astense*, RIS 11, cols. 153–282.

William the Breton, *De Gestis Phillippi Augusti*, RHGF 17 (Paris, 1878), pp. 62–116

Secondary Sources

Angliolini, A., *La Capsella Eburnea di Pola* (Bologna, 1970)

Apollonj-Ghetti, B. M., 'La Chiesa di S. Maria di Vescovio', *Rivista di Archeologia Cristiana*, 23–24 (1947–1948), pp. 253–303

Appollonj-Ghetti, B. M., A. Ferrua, E. Josi, E. Kirschbaum, *Esplorazioni sotto la Confessione di San Pietro in Vaticano*, 2 vols. (Città del Vaticano, 1951)

Apollonj-Ghetti, B. M., *Santa Prassede* (Rome, 1961)

Apollonj-Ghetti, B. M., *I SS. Quattro Coronati* (Rome, 1964)

Apollonj-Ghetti, B. M., *S. Susanna* (Rome, 1965)

Apollonj-Ghetti, B. M., *S. Crisogono* (Rome, 1966)

Armellini, M., *Le Chiese di Roma dal Secolo IV al XIX*, 2 vols. (Rome, 1942)

Atlas of the Christian Church, ed. H. Chadwick and G. R. Evans (London, 1987)

Avagnina, M. E., V. Garibaldi and C. Salterini, 'Strutture murarie degli edifici re-ligiosa di Roma nel XII secolo', *Rivista dell'Instituto Nazionale d'Archeologia e Storia dell'Arte*, n.s. (1976–1977), pp. 173–255

Avril F., and J.-R. Gaborit, 'L'*Itinerarium Bernardi Monachi* et les Pèlerinages d'Italie du Sud Pendant le Haut-Moyen-Age', *MEFR*, 79 (1967), pp. 269–298

Barber, M., *The Two Cities. Medieval Europe 1050–1320* (London, 1992)

Barber, R., *Pilgrimages* (Woodbridge, 1991)

Barclay Lloyd, J. E. 'Masonry Techniques in Medieval Rome, c.1080–c.1300', *PBSR*, 53 (1985), pp. 225–277

Bardy, G., 'Pèlerinages à Rome vers la fin du iv Siècle', *Analecta Bollandiana*, 67 (1949), pp. 224–235

Barker, E. R., *Rome of the Pilgrims and Martyrs* (London, 1913)

Barlow, F., 'Roger of Howden', *EHR*, 65 (1950), pp. 352–360

Barnes, P., 'The Anesty Case', *Publications of the Pipe Roll Society*, n.s. vol. 36 (1960), pp. 1–23

Barrett, A., *Caligula: The Corruption of Power* (London, 1989)

Bartoccetti, V., *Santa Maria ad Martyres* (Rome, undated)

Bautier, R. H., 'Le Jubilé romain de 1300 et l'alliance franco-pontificale au temps de Philippe le Bel et de Boniface VIII', *Le Moyen Age*, 86 (1980), pp. 189–216

Benson, R. L., 'Political *Renovatio*: Two Models from Roman Antiquity', *Renaissance and Renewal in the Twelfth Century*, ed. R. L. Benson and G. Constable (Oxford, 1982), pp. 339–386

Bertolino, O., 'Per la Storia delle Diaconie Romane nell' alto medio evo sino alla fine del secolo VIII', *ASRSP*, 70 (1947), pp. 1–145

Bertonière, G., *The Cult Centre of the Martyr Hippolytus on the Via Tiburtina*, BAR International Series, 260 (1985)

Bianchini, A., *Storia di Terracina* (Tivoli, 1952)

Biggs, A. G., *Diego Gelmírez, First Archbishop of Compostela* (Washington, 1949)

Binns, A., *Dedications of Monastic Houses in England and Wales 1066–1216* (Wood-bridge, 1989)

Birch, D. J., 'Selling the Saints: Competition among pilgrim centres in the twelfth century', *Medieval History*, 2 (1992), pp. 20–34

Birch, D. J., 'Medieval Pilgrimage: with particular reference to Rome in the period from Paschal II to Innocent III' (London Ph.D. thesis, 1994)

Blessings of Pilgrimage, ed. R. Ousterhout (Urbana and Chicago, 1990)

Bloch, H., 'The New Fascination with Ancient Rome', *Renaissance and Renewal in the Twelfth Century*, ed. R. L. Benson and G. Constable (Oxford, 1982), pp. 615–636

Bloomfield, M. D., 'Anglo-Saxon Pilgrims and Rome', *Medieval World* (Nov.–Dec. 1991), pp. 22–26 and (Jan.–Feb. 1992), pp. 37–42

Blumenthal, U. R., *The Early Councils of Pope Paschal II 1100–1110* (Toronto, 1978)

Boase, T. S. R., *Boniface VIII* (London, 1933)

Bolton, B. M., *The Medieval Reformation* (London, 1983)

Bolton, B. M., 'A Show with Meaning: Innocent III's Approach to the Fourth Lateran Council', *Medieval History*, 1 (1991), pp. 53–67

Bolton, B. M., 'Philip Augustus and John: Two Sons in Innocent III's Vineyard?', *The Church and Sovereignty c.590–1918: Essays in Honour of Michael Wilks*, SCH, Subsidia 9 (Oxford, 1991), pp. 113–134

Bolton, B. M., 'Too Important to Neglect: The *Gesta Innocentii Papae III*', *Church and*

Chronicle in the Middle Ages: Essays Presented to John Taylor, ed. G. A. Loud and I. R. Wood (London, 1991), pp. 87–99

Bolton, B. M., 'Advertise the Message: Images in Rome at the turn of the Twelfth Century', SCH, 28 (1992), pp. 117–130

Bolton, B. M., ' "Except the Lord keep the city": towns in the Papal State at the turn of the twelfth century', *Church and City 1000–1500. Essays in Honour of C. N. L. Brooke*, ed. D. Abulafia, M. J. Franklin and M. Rubin (Cambridge, 1992), pp. 199–217

Bolton, B. M., ' "Hearts not Purses": Innocent III's Approach to Social Welfare', *Through the Eye of a Needle. Judaeo–Christian Roots of Social Welfare*, ed. E. A. Hanawalt and C. Lindberg (Missouri, 1994), pp. 123–145

Boyer, R., *La Vie Religieuse en Islande (1116–1264) d'après la Sturlunga Saga et les Sagas des Evêques* (Paris, 1979)

Brentano, R., *Rome Before Avignon. A Social History of Thirteenth Century Rome* (London, 1974)

Brezzi, P., *Il Giubileo del Bonifacio e Dante* (Rome, 1984)

Brooke, C., *The Twelfth Century Renaissance* (London, 1969)

Brooke, R. and C., *Popular Religion in the Middle Ages. Western Europe 1000–1300* (London, 1984)

Brown, P., *The Cult of the Saints. Its Rise and Function in Latin Christianity* (London, 1981)

Brundage, J. A., 'Cruce Signari: The Rite for taking the Cross in England', *Traditio*, 22 (1966), pp. 289–310

Brundage, J. A., *Medieval Canon Law and the Crusader* (Madison, Milwaukee and London, 1969)

Buddenseig, T., 'Le Coffret en ivorie de Pola. Saint Pierre et le Lateran', *Cahiers Archéologique*, 19 (1959), pp. 157–195

Bull, M. G., *Knightly Piety and the Lay Response to the First Crusade: The Limousin and Gascony c.970–c.1130* (Oxford, 1993)

Butler's Lives of the Saints, ed. and rev. H. Thurstan and D. Attwater, 4 vols. (London, 1956)

Byock, J. L., *Medieval Iceland. Society, Sagas and Power* (Berkeley, Los Angeles and London, 1988)

Caselli, G., *La Via Romea. Cammino di Dio* (Florence, 1990)

Celli–Fraentzel, A., 'Contemporary Reports on the Medieval Roman Climate', *Speculum*, 7 (1932), pp. 96–106

Chadwick, H., 'St Peter and St Paul in Rome: The Problem of the Memoria Apostolorum ad Catacumbas', *Journal of Theological Studies*, 8 (1957), pp. 31–52

Chélini J., and H. Branthomme, *Les Chemins de Dieu. Histoire des Pèlerinages Chrétiens des Origines à nos Jours* (Paris, 1982)

Cheney, C. R., 'Gervase, Abbot of Prémontré. A Medieval Letter Writer', *Bulletin of the John Rylands Library*, 33 (1950–1951), pp. 25–56

Cheney, C. R., *Pope Innocent III and England, Papste und Papsttum*, 9 (Stuttgart, 1976)

Christie, N., *Three South Etrurian Churches*, Archaeological Monographs of the British School at Rome, 4 (London, 1991)

Claussen, P. C., *Magistri Doctissimi Romani. Die Römischen Marmorkünstler des Miltelalters, Corpus Cosmatorum*, 1 (Stuttgart, 1987)

Cohen, E., 'In Haec Signa: Pilgrim Badge Trade in Southern France', *Journal of Medieval History*, 2 (1976), pp. 193–214

Cohen, E., 'Roads and Pilgrimage: A Study in Economic Interaction', *Studi Medievali*, 3rd Series, 21 (1980), pp. 321–341

Colgrave, B., 'Pilgrimage to Rome in the Seventh and Eighth Centuries', *Studies in the Language, Literature and Culture of the Middle Ages*, ed. E. B. Wood and A. A. Hill (Austin, 1969), pp. 156–172

Collins, R., 'Merida and Toledo: 550–585', *Visigothic Spain: New Approaches*, ed. E. James (Oxford, 1980), pp. 189–219

Collins, R., *Early Medieval Europe* (London, 1991)

Conant, K. J., *The Early Architectural History of the Cathedral of Santiago de Compostela* (Cambridge, Mass., 1926)

Conant, K. J., 'Medieval Academy Excavations at Cluny', *Speculum*, 29 (1954), pp. 1–43

Conant, K. J., 'Cluniac Building during the Abbacy of Peter the Venerable', *Petrus Venerabilis 1156–1956*, ed. G. Constable and J. Kritzeck (Rome, 1956), pp. 121–127

Conant, K. J., *Carolingian and Romanesque Architecture 800–1200* (Harmondsworth, 1959)

Constable, G., 'Monachisme et pèlerinage au Moyen Age', *Religious Life and Thought (11th–12th Centuries)* (Variorum Reprint, London, 1979), pp. 3–27

Constable, G., 'Opposition to Pilgrimage in the Middle Ages', *Religious Life and Thought (11th and 12th Centuries)* (Variorum Reprint, London, 1979), pp. 125–146

Constable, G., 'Medieval Charters as a Source for the History of the Crusades', *Monks, Hermits and Crusaders in Medieval Europe* (Variorum Reprint, London, 1988) VIII, pp. 73–89

Contadore, A., *De historia Terracina: Libri Quinque* (Rome, 1706)

Cook, M., *Muhammad* (Oxford, 1983)

Coüasnon, C., *The Church of the Holy Sepulchre in Jerusalem*, The Schweich Lectures of the British Academy (London, 1974)

Cowdrey, H. E. J., 'An Early Record at Dijon of the Export of Becket's Relics', *Popes, Monks and Crusaders* (London, 1984), no. XVIII, pp. 251–253

Croke, W. J. D., 'The National Establishments of England in Medieval Rome', *The Dublin Review*, 123 (1898), pp. 305–317

D'Alvery, M. Th., '*Novus Regnat Saloman in diebus malis*. Une satire contre Innocent III', *Festschrift Bernhard Bischoff*, ed. J. Autenreith and F. Brunhölzl (Stuttgart, 1971), pp. 372–390

Dauphin, H., *Le Bienheureux Richard Abbé de Saint-Vanne de Verdun*, *Bibliothèque de la Revue d'Histoire Ecclésiastique*, Fasc. 24 (Louvain and Paris, 1946)

Davies, H., and M. H., *Holy Days and Holidays. The Medieval Pilgrimage to Compostela* (Lewisburg, 1982)

Davis, L. F., 'A Twelfth Century Pilgrim's Guide to the Holy Land', *Yale University Literary Gazette*, 65 (1990), pp. 11–19

Davis, R., 'The Value of the Liber Pontificalis as Comparative Evidence for Territorial Estates and Church Property from the Fourth to the Sixth Century', unpublished Ph.D. thesis (University of Oxford, 1976)

de Angelis, P., *L'Ospedale di Santo Spirito in Saxia*, 2 vols. (Rome, 1960)

de Gaiffier, B., 'Pellegrinaggi e Culto dei Santi: Réflexions sur le thème du Congrès', *Pellegrinaggi e Culto dei Santi in Europa fino alla I^A Crociata*, 8–11 Oct. 1961, *Convegni del Centro di Studi sulla Spiritualità Medievale*, IV (Todi, 1963), pp. 11–35

Delahaye, H., 'Les Premiers Libelli Miraculorum', Analecta Bollandiana, 29 (1910), pp. 427–434

Delahaye, H., The Legends of the Saints, trans. D. Attwater (London, 1962)

Delisle, L. V., 'Itinéraire d'Innocent III', Bibliothèque de l'Ecole des Chartes, 18 (1857), pp. 500–534

De Magistris, R. A., 'Il Viaggio D'Innocenzo III nel Lazio e il Primo Ospedale in Anagni', Storia e Diritto, 19 (1898), pp. 365–78

Demougeot, E., 'Grégoire le Grand et la Conversion du Roi Germain au VIe Siècle', Grégoire le Grand, Colloques Internationaux du Centre de la Recherche Scientifique, Chantilly 15–19 Sept. 1982 (Paris, 1986), pp. 191–203

de Rossi, G. B., La Roma Sotterranea, 3 vols. (Rome, 1864–1877)

Devos, P., 'La Date du Voyage d'Egérie', Analecta Bollandiana, 85 (1967), pp. 165–194

D'Haenens, A., 'Gilles li Muisis, Pèlerin de la Première Année Sainte', Bulletin de l'Institut Historique Belge de Rome, 29 (1955), pp. 31–48

D'Haenens, A., 'Aller à Rome au Moyen Age', Bulletin de l'Institut Historique Belge de Rome, 50 (1980), pp. 93–129

Dillard, H., Daughters of the Renconquest. Women in Castilian Town Society, 1100–1300 (Cambridge, 1984)

D'Onfrio M., and C. M. Strinati, S. Maria in Aquiro (Rome, 1972)

Donnet, A., 'Le Grand Saint Bernard, Trésors de Mon Pays, 45 (Neufchâtel, 1950)

Donnet, A., Saint Bernard et les Origines de l'Hospice du Mont-Joux (St Maurice, 1942)

Drescher, J., 'Apa Claudius and the Thieves', Bulletin de la Société d'Archéolgie Copte, 8 (1942), pp. 63–86

Dubois, J., and L. Beaumont-Maillet, Sainte Geneviève de Paris (Paris, 1982)

Du Boulay, F. R. H., The Lordship of Canterbury. An essay on medieval society (London, 1966)

Du Cange, Glossarium Mediae et Infirmae Latinatis, 10 vols. (1883–1887)

Duchesne, L., 'Notes sur la Topographie de Rome au Moyen Age, XII Vaticana', MEFR, 34 (1914), pp. 307–356

Dudden, F. H., The Life and Times of St Ambrose, 2 vols. (Oxford, 1935)

Dunning, P. J., 'Irish Representatives and Irish Ecclesiastical Affairs at the Fourth Lateran Council', Medieval Studies Presented to Aubrey Gwynn, ed. J. A. Watt, J. B. Morrall and F. X. Martin (Dublin, 1961), pp. 90–113

Dupront, A., 'Pèlerinages et lieux sacrés', Méthodologie de l'Histoire et des Sciences Humaines, Mélanges en Honneur de Fernand Braudel (Toulouse, 1973), pp. 189–206

Ebersolt, J., Orient et Occident (Paris, 1954)

Evans, J., Life in Medieval France, 3rd ed. (New York, 1969)

Finucane, R. C., 'The Use and Abuse of Medieval Miracles', History, 60 (1975), pp. 1–10

Finucane, R. C., Miracles and Pilgrims. Popular Beliefs in Medieval England (London, 1977)

Fletcher, R. A., St James's Catapult. The Life and Times of Diego Gelmírez of Santiago de Compostela (Oxford, 1984)

Forni, A., 'Giacomo da Vitry, Predicatore e Sociologo', La Cultura. Rivista di Filosofia Letteratura e Storia, 18 (1980), pp. 34–89

Franz, A., Die kirchlichen Benediktionen des Mittelalters, 2 vols. (Graz, 1960)

Frolow, A., La Relique de la Vraie Croix. Recherches sur le Développement d'un Culte, Archives de l'Orient Chrétien, 7 (Paris, 1961)

Frugoni, A., 'Il Giubileo di Bonifacio VIII', *Bullettino dell'Istituto Storico Italiano per il Medio Evo e Archivio Muratoriano*, 62 (1950), pp. 1–121

Funk, P., *Jacob von Vitry. Leben und Werke* (Leipzig and Berlin, 1909)

Ganshof, F. L., 'L'Etranger dans la Monarchie Franque', *Recueils de la Société Jean Bodin*, 10 (Brussels, 1958), pp. 5–36

Garrisson, F., 'A Propos des Pèlerins et de leur Condition Juridique', *Etudes d'Histoire du Droit Canonique Dediées à Gabriel le Bras*, 2 (Paris, 1965), pp. 1165–1189

Gauthier, M. M., 'La Clôture Emailleé de la Confession de Saint Pierre au Vatican, lors du Concile de Latran IV, 1215', *Synthronon* (Paris, 1968), pp. 237–246

Geary, P., *Furta Sacra. Thefts of Relics in the Central Middle Ages* (Princeton, 1978, rev. ed. 1990)

Geertman, H., 'L'Illuminazione della Basilica Paleocristiana secondo il Liber Pontificalis', *Rivista di Archeologia Cristiana*, 64 (1988), pp. 135–160

Gilles, H., 'Lex Peregrinorum', *Cahiers de Fanjeaux*, 15 (1980), pp. 161–189

Glass, D. F., *Studies on Cosmatesque Pavements*, BAR International Series, 82 (Pennsylvania, 1980)

Grabois, A., 'Christian Pilgrims in the Thirteenth Century and the Latin Kingdom of Jerusalem: Burchard of Mount Sion', *Outremer. Studies in the History of the Crusading Kingdom of Jerusalem presented to Joshua Prawer* (Jerusalem, 1982), pp. 285–296

Grabois, A., 'Les Pèlerins occidentaux en Terre Sainte et Acre', *Studi Medievali*, 3rd series, 24 (1983), pp. 247–264

Grabois, A., 'Le concept du "contemptus mundi" dans les pratiques des pèlerins occidentaux en terre sainte', *Mediaevalia Christiana XIe–XIIe Siècles. Hommage à Raymond Foreville*, ed. C. E. Viola (1989), pp. 290–306

Guarducci, M., 'L'Inscrizione di Abercio a Roma', *Ancient Society*, 2 (1971), pp. 174–203

Guarducci, M., *La Capsella Eburnea di Samagher*, Atti e Memorie della Società Istriana di Archeologia e Storia Patria, n.s. vol. 26 (Trieste, 1978)

Guarducci, M., *Pietro in Vaticano* (Rome, 1984)

Guerra, A., *Notizie Storiche del Volto Santo di Lucca* (Lucca, 1881)

Hahn-Woernle, B., *Die Ebstorfer Weltkarte* (1989)

Hamilton, B., 'Rebuilding Zion: The Holy Places of Jerusalem in the Twelfth Century', *SCH*, 14 (1977), pp. 105–116

Hamilton, B., 'Prester John and the Shrine of the Three Kings of Cologne', *Studies in Medieval History Presented to R. H. C. Davis*, ed. H. Mayr-Harting and R. I. Moore (London and Ronceverte, 1985), pp. 177–191

Hamilton, B., *Religion in the Medieval West* (London, 1986)

Harding, C. D., 'Façade Mosaics of the Dugento and Trecento in Tuscany, Umbria and Lazio', unpublished Ph.D. Thesis (London, 1983)

Haskins, C. H., 'The Norman *Consuetudines et Iusticie* of William the Conqueror', *EHR*, 23 (1908), pp. 502–508

Haskins, C. H., *The Renaissance of the Twelfth Century* (London, 1927)

Hastrup, K., *Culture and History in Medieval Iceland. An Anthropological Analysis of Structure and Change* (Oxford, 1985)

Head, T., *Hagiography and the Cult of Saints. The Diocese of Orléans, 800–1200* (Cambridge, 1990)

Héliot P., and M.-L. Chastang, 'Quêtes et Voyages de Reliques au Profit des Eglises Françaises du Moyen Age, *Revue d'Histoire Ecclesiastique*, 59 (1964), pp. 789–822 and 60 (1965), pp. 5–32

Hell, V., and H., *The Great Pilgrimage of the Middle Ages. The Road to St James of Compostela*, trans. A. Jaffa (London, 1966)

Hermannsson, H., *Icelandic Manuscripts, Islandica*, 19 (New York, 1929)

Hertling L., and E. Kirschbaum, *The Roman Catacombs and their Martyrs* (London, 1960)

Hill, J., 'From Rome to Jerusalem: An Icelandic Itinerary of the mid-twelfth century', *Harvard Theological Studies*, 76 (1983), pp. 175–203

Trevor Hodge, A., *Roman Aqueducts and Water Supply* (London, 1992)

Hohler, C., 'A Note on Jacobus', *Journal of the Warburg and Courtauld Institutes*, 35 (1972), pp. 31–80

Holmes U. T., and F. R. Weedon, 'Peter of Blois as Physician', *Speculum*, 37 (1962), pp. 252–256

Horn W., and E. Born, *The Plan of St Gall*, 3 vols. (Berkeley, 1979)

Huelsen, C., *Le Chiese di Roma nel Medio Evo* (Florence, 1927)

Howe, E. D., *The Hospital of Santo Spirito and Pope Sixtus IV* (New York, 1984)

Hulbert, J. R., 'Some Medieval Advertisements of Rome', *Modern Philology*, 20 (1922–23), pp. 403–424

Hunt, E. D., *Holy Land Pilgrimage in the Later Roman Empire A.D. 312–460* (Oxford, 1982)

Hunt, N., 'Cluniac Monasticism', *Cluniac Monasticism in the Central Middle Ages*, ed. N. Hunt (London, 1971), pp. 1–10

Hyde, J. K., 'Medieval Descriptions of Cities', *Bulletin of the John Rylands Library*, 48 (1965–1966), pp. 308–340

Jenkins, C., 'Christian Pilgrimages A.D. 500 to 800', *Travel and Travellers in the Middle Ages*, ed. A. P. Newton (London, 1926) pp. 39–69

Jóhannesson, J., *A History of the Old Icelandic Commonwealth*, trans. H. Bessason, University of Manitoba Icelandic Studies, 2 (1974)

Johnson, P. D., *Prayer Patronage and Power. The Abbey of la Trinité, Vendôme, 1032–1187* (New York and London, 1981)

Jones, M., 'The Charters of Robert II De Ferrars, Earl of Nottingham, Derby and Ferrars', *Nottingham Medieval Studies*, 24 (1980), pp. 7–26

Jounel, P., *Le Culte des Saints dans les Basiliques du Lateran et du Vatican au Douzième Siècle, Collection de l'Ecole Française de Rome*, 26 (Rome, 1977)

Jusserand, J. J., *English Wayfaring Life in the Middle Ages*, trans. L. T. Smith, 4th ed. (London, 1950)

Kealey, E. J., *Medieval Medicus. A Social History of Anglo-Norman Medicine* (Baltimore, 1981)

Kendall, A., *Medieval Pilgrims* (London, 1970)

Kendrick, T. D., *St James in Spain* (London, 1960)

Kirschbaum, E., *The Tombs of St Peter and St Paul*, trans. J. Murray (London, 1959)

Kitzinger, E., 'A Virgin's Face: Antiquarianism in Twelfth Century Art', *Art Bulletin*, 62 (1980), pp. 6–19

Kötting, B. J., *Peregrinatio Religiosa. Wallfahrten in der Antike und das Pilgerwesen in der alten Kirchen* (Münster, 1950)

Krautheimer, R., S. Corbett, and W. Frankl, *Corpus Basilicarum Christianorum Romae*, 5 vols. (Città del Vaticano, 1937–1977)

Krautheimer, R., 'The Carolingian Revival of Early Christian Art', *Art Bulletin*, 24 (1942), pp. 1–38

Krautheimer, R., 'The Architecture of Sixtus III: A Fifth-Century Renascence', *De*

Artibus Opuscula XL. Essays in Honor of Erwin Panofsky, ed. M. Meiss, 2 vols. (New York 1961), vol. 1, pp. 291–302

Krautheimer, R., *Rome: Profile of a City 312–1308* (Princeton, 1980)

Krautheimer, R., *Three Christian Capitals. Topography and Politics* (London, 1983)

Krautheimer, R., *St Peter's and Medieval Rome*, Unione Internazionale degli Istituti di Archeologia Storia e Storia dell'Arte in Rome (Rome, 1985)

Kuttner, S., 'Cardinalis: The History of a Canonical Concept', *Traditio*, 3 (1945), pp. 129–214

Kuttner, S., 'St Jón of Hólar: Canon Law and Hagiography in Medieval Iceland', *The History of Ideas and Doctrines of Canon Law in the Middles Ages* (Variorum Reprint, London, 1980), no. VIII, pp. 367–375

Kuttner S., and A. García y García, 'A New Eyewitness Account of the Fourth Lateran Council', *Traditio*, 20 (1964), pp. 115–178

Labande, E. R., 'Recherches sur les Pèlerins dans l'Europe des XI et XII Siècles', *Cahiers de Civilisation Médiévale X–XII Siècles*, 1 (1958), pp. 159–169 and 339–347

Labande, E. R., 'Ad Limina: Le pèlerin médiéval au terme de sa démarche', *Mélanges offerts à René Crozet*, ed. P. Gallais and J.-Y. Riou (Poitiers, 1966), pp. 283–291

Labande, E. R., 'Pellegrini o Crociati? Mentalità e Comportamenti a Gerusalemme nel secolo XII', *Aevum*, 54 (1980), pp. 217–230

La Cathedra Lignea di S. Pietro in Vaticano, Atti della Pontificia Accademia Romana di Archeologia, Memorie, 10 (1971)

Ladner, G. B., *I Ritratti dei Papi nel Antichità e nel Medievo*, 3 vols. (Città del Vaticano, 1941)

Lawrence, C. H., *Medieval Monasticism* (London, 1984)

Lea, H. C., *A History of Auricular Confession and Indulgences in the Latin Church*, 3 vols. (London, 1896)

Lefort, L. Th., 'La Chasse aux Reliques des Martyrs en Egypte au IV Siècle', *La Nouvelle Clio*, 6 (1954), pp. 225–230

Lestocquoy, J., 'Administration de Rome et Diaconies du VIIe au IXe Siècle', *Rivista di Archeologia Cristiana*, 7 (1930), pp. 261–298

Lewis, F., 'The Veronica: Image, Legend and the Viewer', *England in the Thirteenth Century. Proceedings of the Harlaxton Conference*, ed. W. M. Ormrod (Woodbridge, 1985), pp. 100–106

Lewis, S., *The Art of Matthew Paris in the Chronica Maiora* (London, 1987)

Llewellyn, P., *Rome in the Dark Ages* (London, 1971)

Lomax, D. W., 'The First English Pilgrims to Santiago de Compostela', *Studies in Medieval History Presented to R.H.C. Davis*, ed. H. Mayr-Harting and R. I. Moore (London and Ronceverte, 1985), pp. 165–175

Lubin, H., *The Worcester Pilgrim*, Worcester Cathedral Publications, 1 (1990)

Ludwig, F., *Untersuchungen Über die Reise und Marschgesschwindigkeit im XI und XIII Jahrhundert* (Berlin, 1897)

Maccarrone, M., *Studi su Innocenzo III*, Italia Sacra, 17 (Padua, 1972)

Maccarrone, M., 'Pellegrinaggio a S. Pietro e il Giubileo del 1300', *Rivista di Storia della Chiesa in Italia*, 34 (1980), pp. 363–429

Maccarrone, M., 'L'Indulgenza del Giubileo del 1300 e la Basilica di San Pietro', *Roma Anno 1330, Atti della IV Settimana di Studi di Storia dell'Arte Medievale dell'Università di Roma 'La Sapienza' (19–24 March 1980)* (Rome, 1983), pp. 731–752

Maccarrone, M., 'La Cathedra Sancti Petri nel Medioevo: Da Simbolo a Reliquia', *Rivista di Storia della Chiesa in Italia*, 39 (1985), pp. 349–447

Maccarrone, M., 'I Fondamenti "Petrini" del Primato Romano in Gregorio VII', *Studi Gregoriani*, 13 (Rome, 1989), pp. 55–122

Maccarrone, M., *Romana Ecclesia Cathedra Petri*, 2 vols., *Italia Sacra*, vols. 47 and 48 (Rome, 1991)

MacKay, A., *Spain in the Middle Ages. From Frontier to Empire, 1000–1500* (London, 1977)

Magoun Jr, F. P., 'The Rome of Two Northern Pilgrims: Archbishop Sigeric of Canterbury and Abbot Nikolas of Munkathvera', *Harvard Theological Review*, 33 (1940), pp. 267–289

Magoun Jr, F. P., 'The Italian Itinerary of Philip II (Phillippe Auguste) in the Year 1191', *Speculum*, 17 (1942), pp. 367–376

Magoun Jr, F. P., 'The Pilgrim-Diary of Nikulas of Munkathvera: The Road to Rome', *Medieval Studies*, 6 (1944), pp. 314–354

Malaeczek, W., *Papst und Kardinalskolleg von 1191 bis 1216* (Wien, 1984)

Mancini, A., 'La Chiesa Medioevale di San Adriano nel Foro Romano', *Pontificia Accademia Romana d'Archeologia*, 40 (1967–1968), pp. 191–245

Markus, R. A., 'Gregory the Great and Missionary Strategy', SCH, 6 (1970), pp. 29–38

Matthiae, G., *Mosaici Medioevali delle Chiese di Roma*, 2 vols. (Rome, 1967)

McCulloh, J., 'From Antiquity to the Middle Ages: Continuity and Change in Papal Relic Policy from the 6th to 8th Centuries', *Pietas. Festschrift für Bernhard Kötting*, ed. E. Dassmann and S. Frank, *Jarhbuch für Antike und Christentum*, Ergänzungsband 8 (1980), pp. 313–324

Miller, T. S., 'The Knights of Saint John and the Hospitals of the Latin West', *Speculum*, 53 (1978), pp. 709–733

Mitchener, M., *Medieval Pilgrim and Secular Badges* (London, 1986)

Mollat, G., 'Le Jubilé de 1350', *Journal des savants* (1963), pp. 191–195

Mollat, M., *The Poor in the Middle Ages. An Essay in Social History*, trans. A. Goldhammer (London, 1986)

Moore, R. I., *The Origins of European Dissent* (London, 1977)

Moore, W. J., *The Saxon Pilgrims to Rome and the Schola Saxonum* (Fribourg, 1937)

Morey, A., *Bartholomew of Exeter, Bishop and Canonist. A Study in the Twelfth Century* (Cambridge, 1937)

Morini, E., 'The Orient and Rome: Pilgrimages and Pious Visits between the Ninth and the Eleventh Century', *Harvard Ukranian Studies*, 12–13 (1988–1989), pp. 849–869

Morris, C., *The Papal Monarchy. The Western Church from 1050–1250* (Oxford, 1989)

Nees, L., 'Charles the Bald and the Cathedra Petri', *Charles the Bald. Court and Kingdom*, ed. M. T. Gibson and J. L. Nelson, 2nd ed. (Aldershot, 1990), pp. 340–347

Niederer, F., 'The Roman Diaconiae' (Unpublished Dissertation, New York University, 1951)

Niederer, F., 'Early Medieval Charity', *Church History*, 21 (1952), pp. 285–295

Noble, T. F. X., *The Republic of St Peter. The Birth of the Papal State, 680–825* (Philadelphia, 1984)

Noble, T. F. X., 'A New Look at the *Liber Pontificalis*', *Archivum Historiae Pontificae*, 23 (1985), pp. 347–358

Oakeshott, W., *The Mosaics of Rome from the Third to the Fourteenth Centuries* (London, 1967)

Ohler, N., *The Medieval Traveller*, trans. C. Hillier (Woodbridge, 1989)

Orbis Latinus. Lexikon lateinischer geographischer Namen des Mittelalters und der Neuzeit, 3 vols. (1972)

Ortenberg, V., 'Archbishop Sigeric's journey to Rome in 990', *Anglo Saxon England*, 19 (1990), pp. 197–246

Osborne, J., 'The Roman Catacombs in the Middle Ages', *PBSR*, 53 (1985), pp. 278–328

Oursel, R., *Les Pèlerins du Moyen Age* (1963)

Oxford Illustrated History of Christianity, ed. J. McManners (Oxford, 1990)

Palgrave, F., *Collected Historical Works*, ed. R. H. I. Palgrave, 7 vols. (Cambridge, 1921)

Papi, M., 'Crociati, Pellegrini e Cavalieri nei Sermones di Gilberto di Tournai', *Studi Francescani*, 73 (1976), pp. 373–409

Parks, G. B., *The English Traveller to Italy. The Middle Ages (to 1525)*, Storia e Letteratura, 46 (Rome, 1954)

Partner, P., 'Notes on the Lands of the Roman Church in the Early Middle Ages', *PBSR*, n.s. 21 (1966), pp. 68–78

Partner, P., *The Lands of St Peter. The Papal State in the Middle Ages and the Early Renaissance* (London, 1972)

Paulus, N., *Geschicte des Ablasses im Mittelalter vom Ursprunge bis zur Mitte des 14 Jahrhunderts* 3 vols. (Paderborn, 1922–1923)

Pecchai, P., 'Banchi e Botteghe Dinanzi alla Basilica Vaticana nel Secoli XIV, XV e XVI', *Archivi*, 2nd series, 18 (1951), pp. 81–123

Peschi, B., 'L'Itinerario Romano di Sigerico Archievescovo di Canterbury e la Lista dei Papi da lui portata in Inghilterra', *Rivista di Archeologia Cristiana*, 13 (1936), pp. 43–60

Poole, R. L., 'The Early Correspondence of John of Salisbury', *Studies in Chronology and History*, ed. A. L. Poole (Oxford, 1934), pp. 259–286

Price, L., *The Plan of St Gall in Brief* (Berkeley, 1982)

Quattrocchi, D., 'L'Anno Santo del 1300. Storia e Bolle Pontificie', *Bessarione*, 7 (1899–1900), pp. 291–317

Richards, J., *Consul of God. The Life and Times of Gregory the Great* (London, 1980)

Riley-Smith, J. S. C., *The Knights of St John in Jerusalem and Cyprus c.1050–1310* (London, 1967)

Riley-Smith, J. S. C., *What were the Crusades?* (1977)

Riley-Smith, J. S. C., *The Crusades. A Short History* (London, 1987)

Riley-Smith, J. S. C., *The First Crusaders, 1095–1131* (Cambridge, 1997)

Riley-Smith, L., and J. S. C., *The Crusades, Ideal and Reality, 1095–1274* (1981)

Robinson, I. S., *The Papacy 1073–1198. Continuity and Innovation* (Cambridge, 1990)

Robson, C. A., *Maurice of Sully and the Medieval Vernacular Homily* (Oxford, 1952)

Roma Sancta. La Città delle Basiliche, ed. M. Fagiolo and M. L. Madonna (Rome, 1985)

Ross, J. B., 'A Study of Twelfth Century Interest in the Antiquities of Rome', *Medieval and Historiographical Essays in Honour of James Westfall Thompson*, ed. J. L. Cate and E. N. Anderson (Chicago, 1938), pp. 302–321

Rowling, M., *Everyday Life of Medieval Travellers* (New York, 1971)

Ruysschaert, J., 'Réflexions sur les Fouilles Vaticanes', *Revue d'Histoire Ecclésiastique*, 48 (1953), pp. 573–631 and 49 (1954), pp. 5–58

Ruysschaert, J., 'Le Tableau Mariotti de la Mosaïque Absidale de l'Ancien S.-Pierre', *Atti della Pontificia Accademia Romana di Archeologia, Rendiconti*, 3rd Series, 40 (1967–1968), pp. 295–317

Schiaperelli, L., 'Le Carte antiche dell'Archivio Capitolare di S. Pietro in Vaticano', *ASRSP*, 24 (1901), pp. 393–496

Schmugge, L., 'Über nationale Vorurteile im Mittelalter', *Deutsches Archiv für Erforschung des Mittelalters*, 38 (1982), pp. 439–459

Schmugge, L., 'Die Anfänge des Organisierten Pilgerverkehrs im Mittelalter', *Quelen und Forschungen aus Italienischen Archiven und Bibliotheken*, 64 (1984), pp. 1–83

Settia, A. A., 'Strade e Pellegrini nell'Oltrepo pavese: Una Via *Romea* dimenticata', *Annali di Storia Pavese*, 16–17 (1988), pp. 79–89

Shotwell J. T., and L. R. Loomis, *The See of Peter* (New York, 1927)

Sigal, P. A., *Les Marcheurs de Dieu* (Paris, 1974)

Sigal, P. A., 'Reliques, Pèlerinage et Miracles dans l'Eglise Médiévale (XIe–XIIIe Siècles)', *Revue d'Histoire de l'Eglise de France*, 76 (1990), pp. 193–211

Simon, P., *Sankt Liborius Sein Dom und Sein Bistum* (Paderborn, 1936)

Spencer, B. W., 'Medieval Pilgrim Badges', *Rotterdam Papers: A Contribution to Medieval Archaeology* (Rotterdam, 1968), pp. 137–153

Springer, O., 'Mediaeval Pilgrim Routes from Scandinavia to Rome', *Medieval Studies*, 12 (1950), pp. 92–122

Spufford, P., *Handbook of Medieval Exchange* (London, 1986)

Stancliffe, C., *St Martin and His Hagiographer. History and Miracle in Sulpicius Severus* (Oxford, 1983)

Stancliffe, C., 'Kings who opted out', *Ideal and Reality in Frankish and Anglo-Saxon Society. Studies presented to J.M. Wallace-Hadrill*, ed. P. Wormald, D. Bullough and R. Collins (Oxford, 1983), pp. 154–176

Stenton, D. M., 'Roger of Howden and Benedict', *EHR* 68 (1953), pp. 574–582

Stone, J. S., *The Cult of Santiago* (London, 1927)

Storrs, C. M., 'Jacobean Pilgrims from England from the Early Twelfth to the Late Fifteenth Century', unpublished M.A. Thesis (University of London, 1964)

Strömback, D., *The Conversion of Iceland. A Survey*, trans. P. Foote, Viking Society for Northern Research (London, 1975)

Sullivan, R. E., 'The Papacy and Missionary Activity in the Early Middle Ages', *Medieval Studies*, 17 (1955), pp. 46–106

Sumption, J., *Pilgrimage. An Image of Mediaeval Religion* (London, 1975)

Tabacco, G., *The Struggle for Power in Medieval Italy: Structures of Political Rule*, trans. R. B. Jensen (Cambridge, 1989)

Tate, R. B., *Pilgrimages to St James of Compostela from the British Isles during the Middle Ages* (Liverpool, 1990)

Tatlock, J. S. P., 'The English Journey of the Laon Canons', *Speculum*, 8 (1933), pp. 454–465

Taylor, J. E., *Christians and the Holy Places. The Myth of Jewish-Christian Origins* (Oxford, 1993)

Tellenbach, G., 'La Città di Roma dal IX al XII Secolo vista dai Contemporanei d'Oltre Frontiera', *Studi Storici in Onore di Ottorino Bertolini*, 2 vols. (Pisa, 1972) vol. 2, pp. 679–734

Testini, P., *San Saba* (Rome, 1961)

Thurston, H., *The Holy Year of Jubilee* (London, 1900)

Tosti, D. L., *Storia della Badia di Monte Cassino*, 3 vols. (Naples, 1842–1843)

Toubert, H., 'Le Renouveau Paléochrétien à Rome au Début du XIIe Siècle', *Cahiers Archéologiques*, 20 (1970), pp. 99–154

Toynbee, J. M. C., *Death and Burial in the Roman World* (London, 1971)

Toynbee J., and J. Ward-Perkins, *The Shrine of St Peter and the Vatican Excavations* (London, 1956)

Turner, V., and E., *Image and Pilgrimage in Christian Culture* (New York, 1978)

Tyler, J. E., *The Alpine Passes. The Middle Ages (962–1250)* (Oxford, 1930)

van Kessel, P., 'Frisoni e Franchi a Roma nell'Età Carolingia', *Les Fondations Nationales dans la Rome Pontificale, Collection de l'Ecole Française de Rome*, 52 (1981), pp. 37–46

Váquez de Parga, L., J. M. Lacarra and J. U. Ríu, *Las Peregrinaciones a Santiago de Compostela*, 3 vols. (Madrid, 1948–1949)

Vatican Collections. The Papacy and Art (New York, 1982)

Vogel, C., 'Le Pèlerinage Pénitential', *Pellegrinaggi e Culto dei Santi in Europa fino alla I^A Crociata*, 8–11 Oct. 1961, *Convegni del Centro di Studi sulla Spiritualità Medievale*, IV (Todi 1963), pp. 37–94

Waley, D., *The Papal State in the Thirteenth Century* (London, 1961)

Walker, P. W. L., *Holy City, Holy Places? Christian Attitudes to Jerusalem and the Holy Land in the Fourth Century* (Oxford, 1990)

Ward, B., *Miracles and the Medieval Mind. Theory, Record and Event 1000–1215* (London, 1982, rev. 1987)

Ward Perkins, B., *From Classical Antiquity to the Middle Ages. Urban Public Building in Northern and Central Italy A.D. 300–850* (Oxford, 1984)

Ward Perkins, J. B., 'The Shrine of St Peter and its Twelve Spiral Columns', *JRS*, 42 (1952), pp. 21–33

Whitehill, W. M., *Spanish Romanesque Architecture of the Eleventh Century* (Oxford, 1941)

Wilkinson, J., 'Christian Pilgrims in Jerusalem during the Byzantine Period', *Palestine Exploration Quarterly*, 108 (1976), pp. 75–101

Willis, G. G., *Essays in Early Roman Liturgy* (London, 1964)

Willis, G. G., *Further Essays in Early Roman Liturgy* (London, 1968)

Wilpert, G., 'L'Acheropita ossia L'Immagine del Salvatore nella Capella del Sancta Sanctorum', *L'Arte. Rivista di Storia dell'Arte Medioevale e Moderna e d'Arte Decorativa*, 10 (1907), pp. 161–177 and 246–262

Wilpert, J., *Die Römischen Malereien und Mosaiken der Kirchlichen Bauten vom IV bis XIII Jahrhundert*, 4 vols. (Freiburg, 1917)

Wilson, I., *Holy Faces, Secret Places. The Quest for Jesus's True Likeness* (London, 1991)

Wolbach, W. F., 'Il Christo di Sutri e la Venerazione del SS Salvatore nel Lazio', *Atti della Pontificia Accademia de Archeologia, Rendiconti*, 3rd Series, 17 (1940–1941), pp. 97–126

Woodruff, C. E., 'The Financial Aspect of the Cult of St Thomas of Canterbury', *Archaeologia Cantiana*, 44 (1932), pp. 13–32

Yunck, J. A., 'Economic Conservatism, Papal Finance and the Medieval Satires on Rome', *Medieval Studies*, 23 (1961), pp. 334–351

Zingerle, I. V., *Reiserechnungen Wolfger's von Ellenberchtskirchen, Bischofs von Passau, Patriarchen von Aquileja* (Heilbronn, 1877)

Selective Index

Other Volumes in
Studies in the History of Medieval Religion